TI
AL
ENIGMA

Facts do not cease to exist because they are ignored.

Aldous Huxley

EXTRATERRESTRIALS: SCIENCE FICTION OR
SCIENCE FACT?

THE ALIEN ENIGMA

JP Robinson

EARTHRISE

EARTHRISE BOOKS
Kingston upon Hull, England

Published by Earthrise Books 2016

A catalogue record for this book is available from the British Library

ISBN 978-153323405-6

Typeset in Book Antiqua 11pt
Chapter headings in Albertsthal Typewriter/Adler

CONTENTS

INTRODUCTION

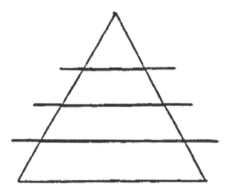

We cannot take credit for our record advancement in certain scientific fields alone. We have been helped. And we have been helped by the people of other worlds.

Dr. Hermann Oberth (the German father of rocketry)

THE ALIEN ENIGMA is a collection of deeply researched material spanning over twenty years of interest in the related topics, pieced together in an attempt to further understand the complexities of these mysteries in relation to an extraterrestrial presence here on our beloved planet.

The subject of alien beings continues to be one of mystery and misunderstanding. As we approach fifty years since the alleged first NASA moon landing, we appear to be as ignorant as we have ever been regarding our understanding of life beyond this planet. People still ask the question "do you believe in aliens?" as if they are asking whether you believe in Santa Claus or the Tooth Fairy.

The alien enigma continues to confound us all. We appear to be divided into three distinct groups here; the believers, the sceptics, and the undecided. It doesn't really matter which group any of us belong to, it doesn't change a thing. Extraterrestrials either exist or they don't. And that is precisely what this book will be addressing.

Presently, the concept of alien life existing at all appears to have been relegated to the realms of fantasy and science fiction. The western world is saturated with imagery, movies and stories of creatures from other worlds, commonly depicted as malevolent beings hell-bent on destroying Earth and its un-evolved occupants.

Any public figure brave enough to confront the media and declare themselves a believer faces ridicule from all sides, simply as the subject continues to be somewhat taboo and is very rarely considered in a serious light. So why have we become so against the idea that we are not alone in the universe? Do we feel threatened as a species that there may be others out there smarter than us or is it because it would change everything we consider to be true? There is no doubt that proof of alien life would rattle us all should it be presented as absolute fact on a global scale, and we are talking about alien beings here, not some microscopic bacteria found deep within a piece of meteoric rock.

The UFO phenomenon has increased in popularity in a social sense over the last few decades, not only are more people aware of such activity but many are beginning to accept the possibility that there is a great deal that we don't understand about our world and what may lie beyond.

The concept of alien beings travelling from other worlds to ours is a fairly recent one historically speaking, but unexplained sightings of aerial phenomena go back as far as one cares to venture. The ancient astronaut theory popularised by writers such as Erich Von Daniken advocates the existence of highly evolved races of beings from the stars in our ancient past, and researchers like Zecharia Sitchin have suggested that these advanced beings may well be much more than inquisitive space travellers.

Sitchin's translations of ancient Sumerian cuneiform stone tablets dating back over six thousand years describe how the Annunaki (the men who from heaven came) genetically altered our earliest human ancestors and created modern man as a slave race to help them mine for gold. Evidence to support these claims may not be concrete but many unexplained mysteries of the ancient world are given credence using Sitchin's hypothesis.

The wealth of information pertaining to the very real existence of biological entities from other worlds and/or dimensions is of such a voluminous amount that it demands closer inspection and consideration in order to shed more light on the true reality of human life here on Earth in both the present and in antiquity.

History is replete with tales of visitors from beyond this world to the extent that simply sweeping aside such notions as all being either pure imagination or primitive ignorance would seem somewhat premature. Deeper investigation into the extraterrestrial phenomenon reveals a plethora of information, with evidence often providing more questions than answers. The truth still remains however, that any unforeseen questions raised, as impossible as they may be to answer employing a limited mindset, will most certainly each *have* an answer. Just because we don't have the capacity to fully understand something does not negate its existence. Just because you cannot see it doesn't mean it isn't there.

It is precisely because of their allusiveness and rarity that strange phenomena like UFOs, alien encounters and cattle mutilations continue to confound and intrigue us with their mystery. In fact, many of the topics covered in this book require lateral thinking and an open mind if one is to ascertain anything of value from the words on these pages.

This book is by no means designed as a conclusive piece of writing intended to convince the sceptics out there, quite the contrary. It is an invitation to all those readers sat before these pages to question every word written, every quotation borrowed, every piece of information printed and presented as factual. It should act as a starting point or stepping stone towards a greater understanding of the topics covered within. Research and investigate everything you feel compelled to delve into and never take the word of an author as gospel, instead one should follow the scent which first materialises during the reading process.

I am a great believer in the notion that there exists only one ultimate truth to all things; a universal truth which embodies the multitude of beliefs, perceptions, dimensional realities and life-forms. Since my late teens I became fascinated with seeking the truth, trying to understand the true origins of humankind and our forbidden hidden history. The extraterrestrial hypothesis inadvertently became the central theme of the mystery and has refused to go away despite the common consensus that there is nothing to such fantastical notions.

Undeterred by popular preconceptions, my research has only expanded in depth and content over the years, and although I may lean more towards the possibility that aliens *do* exist right here on Earth and that much of the material exposed in *The Alien Enigma* seems credulous and valid, I believe it is paramount to remain grounded and open-minded.

Until one has had personal experiences with extraterrestrials, it would be presumptuous and unproductive to claim with absolute certainty that such entities are real. But without first reading the information available, any perceptions one may have regarding their true existence shall remain just that, a perception.

In order to understand more it is imperative that we improve our knowledge before choosing which side of the fence we feel compelled to belong, so enjoy your read and always bear in mind that facts really can be stranger than fiction.

1

SKY GHOSTS

I can assure you the flying saucers, given that they exist, are not constructed by any power on earth.

U.S. President Harry S. Truman (White House press conference, April 4, 1950)

THE QUESTION isn't whether or not UFOs exist, they exist. The question we should be asking is what are they? Sightings of UFOs worldwide are a real consideration and we have come too far at this point in time to deny that unknown flying objects are penetrating Earth's atmosphere and flitting around our skies. Human testimony continues to provide us with a wealth of information and personal experience regarding this widely reported phenomenon; however we now find ourselves amidst the information age which arose with the birth of the internet, enabling visual evidence to reaffirm stories that were previously only expressed orally.

Video footage of bizarre lights in the sky has become commonplace and readily available. It is reasonable to declare however, that the majority of UFOs caught on film, especially in an amateur capacity, are more often than not inconclusive to say the least. Many home videos are shaky, low quality and lacking in detail, revealing nothing more than an illegible blurred blob against a vast expanse of sky. But the basis of the UFO phenomenon is not based on such footage alone. Besides, no matter how inconclusive such video may be, they do still confirm the existence of unknown flying objects on a global scale.

The corroboration of simultaneous video recordings belonging to complete strangers who were all witnessing the same aerial activity helps to authenticate mass sightings. The recognition of the UFO phenomenon by prominent figures of officialdom has also reinforced the notion that such objects are truly real in a physical sense, and not just figments of imaginative expression.

Explanations for UFOs offered to the public in the past by military and government officials have often made a mockery of the whole affair, killing the credibility of so many eyewitnesses and believers alike with one foul swoop. They suggest that UFOs are most likely caused by hoaxers or possibly the result of mass hallucinations. Failing that, people are probably reporting misidentified aircraft, weather balloons, atmospheric phenomena, light aberrations or in specific cases they have been attributed to the rising of swamp gas into the air.

But putting the debunkers and discrediting aside, where does one start in the search to truly understand what these mysterious objects might be and who, if anyone, is responsible for their movements? What kind of advanced technology enables these elusive sky ghosts to perform seemingly impossible aerial manoeuvres? How do they affect humankind physically and mentally? And why isn't it publicly acknowledged that UFOs have been sighted throughout recorded history and beyond, and continue to make their presence known to the present day?

The association between UFOs and extraterrestrials is so intrinsic that it has become a common assumption that the two go together. Saying UFOs are real is not the same as saying spaceships are real. No amount of credible source material, whether human testimony, photographically recorded or the result of video evidence, can determine absolutely that UFOs are operated by inter-dimensional alien beings. Only the substantial collation of information from a variety of sources over a long period of time could lead the intrepid researcher to the assumptive conclusion that ETs control and manipulate UFOs. Being an unidentified flying object means precisely that – nobody has been able to identify what that object actually is and where it originated.

As nuclear physicist and UFO investigator Stanton Friedman suggested, "One of the problems with so-called UFO research by debunkers is that they ask the wrong questions. Their question is what are UFOs? Really what they're saying is, are all UFOs alien spacecraft? And the answer of course is no. The proper question is, are *any*?"[1]

Presently, to the best of this author's knowledge, there is no *solid* evidence which proves beyond doubt that the objects spotted performing incredible, gravity-denying manoeuvres above our heads are being piloted by beings from another world. That is not to say that they are not, just that no video or photograph has conclusively proven it as of yet.

Any existing evidence that does prove that 'flying saucers' are predominantly manned by extraterrestrial entities has most certainly been contained and hidden from public scrutiny by military and government authorities. Disclosure of such material, should it exist as many insiders claim that it does, is unlikely to arrive any time soon. So we must endeavour to fit the pieces of the puzzle together using the information and evidence available to us at this time, and see where it takes us.

THE MICHIGAN AFFAIR

During the month of March in 1966, spates of unusual UFO sightings over Michigan were being reported by a myriad of people from different professions. Starting on March 14, more than a hundred witnesses, one of whom was William Van Horn, a civil defense director, described watching a football-shaped object for four hours as it flitted around in the sky above the University of Michigan campus then close to a nearby airport and a local swamp.

Seven eyewitnesses reported a UFO flying over Livingston and Washtenaw counties, the reports were taken seriously as they were made by police officers and sheriff's deputies. The sightings caused such uproar that the whole region went on a wild UFO chase.

At 4:25 a.m. on March 17, Sgt. Neil Schneider and Deputy David Fitzpatrick spotted three or four red, white and green round objects glowing and oscillating near Milan; and in the northern part of Washtenaw on March 20, two more county deputies, Buford Bushroe and John Foster saw similar objects in the sky which they attempted to follow. Reports of the same objects also came in from Livingston and Monroe county residents the same day. The story of the police chasing the UFO was carried by the Detroit News the following day.

Deputy Sheriff Bushroe described the incident, "It looked like an arc. It was round. We turned and started following it through Dexter for five miles. It was headed west and we stopped. We lost it in the trees. Either the lights went off or it took off with a tremendous burst of speed. It was about 1,500 feet above the ground. It moved along at about 100 mph. We were doing 70 before losing it near Wylie Road."[2]

The following is the log of "Complaint No. 00967" signed by Cpl. Broderick and Deputy Patterson of the Washtenaw County Sheriff's Department:

8

"3:50 a.m. Received calls from Deputies Bushroe and Foster, car 19, stating that they saw some suspicious objects in the sky, disc, star-like colors, red and green, moving very fast, making sharp turns, having left to right movements, going in a Northwest direction.

4:04 a.m. Livingston County [sheriff's department] called and stated that they also saw the objects, and were sending car to the location.

4:05 a.m. Ypsilanti Police Dept. also called stated that the object was seen at the location of US-12 and I-94 [intersection of a U.S. and an Interstate highway].

4:10. a.m. Monroe County [sheriff's department] called and stated that they also saw the objects.

4:20 a.m. Car 19 stated that they just saw four more in the same location moving at a high rate of speed.

4:30 a.m. Colonel Miller [county civil defense director] was called; he stated just to keep an eye on the objects that he did not know what to do, and also check with Willow Run Airport.

4:54 a.m. Car 19 called and stated that two more were spotted coming from the Southeast, over Monroe County. Also that they were side by side.

4:56 a.m. Monroe County [sheriff's department] stated that they just spotted the object, and also that they are having calls from citizens. Called Selfridge Air Base and they stated that they also had some objects [presumably on radar] over Lake Erie and were unable to get any ID from the objects. The Air Base called Detroit Operations and were to call this Dept. back as to the disposition.

5:30 a.m. Dep. Patterson and I [Cpl. Broderick] looked out of the office and saw a bright light that appeared to be over the Ypsilanti area. It looked like a star but was moving from North to East.

6:15 a.m. As of this time we have had no confirmation from the Air Base."[3]

In a formal statement, deputies B. Bushroe and J. Foster declared; "This is the strangest thing that [we] have ever witnessed. We would have not believed this story if we hadn't seen it with our own eyes. These objects could move at fantastic speeds, and make very sharp turns, dive and climb, and hover with great manoeuvrability. We have no idea what these objects were, or where they could have come from. At 4:20 a.m. there were four of these objects flying in a line formation, in a north westerly direction, at 5:30 these objects went out of view, and were not seen again."

The sightings continued over Dexter and Hillsdale on March 22, and were reported by local residents who explained that the strange flying objects were emitting unusual sounds and lights. The next day, another sighting was reported by a teenager from Monroe. It was at this point that the U.S. Air Force intervened and sent in alleged UFO expert Dr. J. Allen Hynek to investigate the sightings.

Hynek was quick to debunk the stories and publicly claimed that the unusual objects had been misinterpreted and were simply the result of marsh gas emanating from the swamp. To backup his theory Hynek quoted Belgian astronomer Marcel Minnaert's description of marsh gases, "The lights resemble tiny flames, sometimes seen right on the ground, sometimes merely floating above it. The flames go out in one place and suddenly appear in another, giving the illusion of motion. The colors are sometimes yellow, sometimes red and blue-green."

Hillsdale resident Van Horn was furious by Hynek's assertions, claiming that he knew more about swamp gas than Hynek. Outraged by the manner in which the Air Force had treated "the Michigan affair", Van Horn charged that "a lot of good people are being ridiculed."

A TALE OF TWO REPORTS

As a result of the numerous sightings being reported in the state of Michigan during 1966, Congressman Gerald Ford (later to become the 38th American President) called for a public hearing by the Armed Services Committee. In November 2000, Ford confirmed the validity of his actions stating, "I undoubtedly wrote Chairman Mendel Rivers of the Committee on Armed Services that such an investigation be taken."

In 1966, the U.S. Air Force commissioned the University of Colorado to study UFOs further and on January 9, 1969 the project headed by noted physicist Dr. Edward Uhler Condon published a report titled "Scientific Study of Unidentified Flying Objects", which unfortunately only succeeded in debunking all UFO related phenomena. Documents released through the Freedom of Information Act in recent years have revealed that the CIA were covertly involved in the report and were responsible for the discrediting report.

Dr. Condon, a former director of the National Bureau of Standards, was a man who was all too familiar with the strategic nuances of government secrecy, having already being involved in the development of the atomic bomb and radar.

Condon's attitude towards the report was evident after only twelve weeks since the study began when he was quoted in *Look* magazine as saying, "It is my inclination right now to recommend that the government get out of this business. My attitude right now is that there is nothing to it." He then added wryly, "But I'm not supposed to reach a conclusion for another year."[4]

Nearly a year after the official release of the report, Condon was quoted in the New York Times as saying that the whole affair "was a bunch of damned nonsense" and that he was "sorry I ever got involved in such foolishness."[5] The same article stated that Dr. James McDonald, a meteorologist from the University of Arizona, had complained that the Air Force was "writing off the UFO problem, which cries for rigorous scientific study."

Condon had officially dismissed the whole UFO phenomenon in one single report, thus it was no longer deemed necessary to investigate the subject further. However, the report which was intended to quell public curiosity in the subject suffered a severe blow along with the credibility of project co-ordinator Robert Low, as a memo written on August 9, 1966, from Low to the Dean of Colorado University's graduate school was discovered. The leaked memo exposed the fraudulent nature of the project, and dictated what the conclusion would be, long before it had even begun.

The Low memo stated, "The trick would be, I think, to describe the project so that, to the public, it would appear a totally objective study but, to the scientific community, would present the image of a group of non-believers trying their best to be objective, but having an almost zero expectation of finding a saucer."

Low concluded with, "If we set up the thing right and take pains to get the proper people involved and have success in presenting the image we want to present to the scientific community, we could carry the job off to our benefit..."[6]

Representative J. Edward Roush, Democrat of Indiana and a confirmed NICAP[1] supporter, read the controversial memo and the publicity printed in *Look* magazine and urged Congress to take over the investigation which was being conducted by the Air Force because he questioned the objectivity of the study.

In 1968, one year before the phony Condon Report reached its predictable conclusion, the Committee on Sciences and Astronautics conducted a symposium in which Roush outlined to Congress serious concerns he had developed about the implications of outside influences on the Condon committee. Roush gave an interview to the Denver Post and attracted quite an array of distinguished speakers from major universities who attended the symposium. Among those who attended were such notables as Dr. Carl Sagan, Dr. J. Allen Hynek, Dr. Robert L. Hall, Dr. McDonald and two engineers, Dr. James A. Harder and Dr. Robert M. Baker.

Dr. Hall suggested that in order to gain some clarity and defuse concern over the issue, that the government should release its files on UFOs. Dr. James Harder of the University of California stated, that "On the basis of the data and ordinary rules of evidence, as would be applied in civil or criminal courts, the physical reality of UFOs has been proved beyond a reasonable doubt." He went on to tell those in attendance that it was evident that the objects were "interplanetary" in nature.

The information contained in the 'Condon Report' led to another high profile public UFO investigation, Project Blue Book, being terminated on December 17, 1969 by the new Secretary of the Air Force, Robert C. Seamans Jr. He also announced that the Air Force would no longer be involved in any UFO investigations.

Author Jim Marrs wrote, "There is no question that the Condon Committee – the most recent and last official word on UFOs – was superficial as a scientific document and inadequate as a response to a legitimate public concern. Sceptics of officialdom claimed the

---

[1] NICAP stands for National Investigations Committee on Aerial Phenomena, an organisation which was formed in 1956 under the guidance of Major Donald E. Keyhoe. Following the Condon Report, NICAP membership support began drying up and thus so did the operating funds.

air force paid for the Condon study simply to avoid any meaningful investigation by Congress."[7]

The irony is that inside the 1,485 page report lay a handful of legitimate unexplained UFO cases which unfortunately will most likely be lost to history. Although the report was produced by a panel of scientists, the summary – which was the section read by the press – was written solely by Dr. Condon. He managed to ignore the data and asserted that there was nothing to the phenomenon, as his summary confirmed, "Our general conclusion is that nothing has come from the study of UFOs in the past 21 years that has added to scientific knowledge."

The following two case reports taken straight from the pages of the Condon Report reveal that the subject matter investigated by the panel wasn't all so easily explained away:

Case 46 – McMinnville, Oregon – 14 May 1950
"This is one of the few UFO reports in which all factors investigated, geometric, psychological and physical, appear to be consistent with the assertion that an extraordinary flying object, silvery, metallic, disk-shaped, tens of meters in diameter, and evidently artificial, flew within sight of two witnesses."

Case 21 – Colorado Springs, Colorado – 13 May 1967
"This must remain as one of the most puzzling radar cases on record, and no conclusion is possible at this time."

The fact that official UFO reports appear to go to great lengths to discredit the phenomenon actually seems to have the opposite effect in hindsight. It is clearly evident that the intention of the U.S. Air Force was not to investigate the subject in depth, but rather it was setup to convince the American public that the Condon committee was using the 500,000 dollars to conduct a thorough and objective investigation.

One man who is familiar with such public curiosity pleasing tactics is Dr. Paul Tyler, former director of the Armed Forces Radiobiology Research Laboratory at Bethesda, Maryland. His long-standing connections with the military and the scientific community gave him a valuable insight into certain methods of deception.

In 1993, Dr. Tyler told author Marrs, "A classic case of having your mind made up before you start was the Condon Report. Everybody read the Executive Summary and all everyone got was that there was nothing to it [UFOs]. But you go back and look at the raw data and maybe 15 to 20 percent of the case reports say, 'Hey, there's something here. This one may be real'."[8]

John Northrop, founder of Northrop Aircraft Company and co-founder of Lockheed Corporation, shares the sentiments of so many people critical of the final report saying that he believed it to be "one of the most deliberate cover-ups ever perpetrated on the public. The 21st century will die laughing at the Condon Report."[9]

In stark contrast to the shabby investigation undertaken by Condon and his peers, another UFO report was written in 1999 by an independent group mostly consisting of former 'auditors' at the Institute of Advanced Studies for National Defence (IHEDN). The institute is a French public institution under direct responsibility of the French Prime Minister.

The COMETA group, made up of high-level French military officers and scientists, produced the most pro-UFO public document ever written by men of such professional stature. The name COMETA stands for "Committee for in-depth studies" (in English).

The COMETA report was written using data which the group received from numerous scientific agencies and much of the content originated from military and civilian pilot reports. The study was undertaken over several years and culminated in a 90-page report consisting of around 500 UFO cases from around the world, with a focus on the associated issues of national defence. The title of the report was *Les Ovni Et La Defense: A quoi doit-on se preparer?* Which translates as *UFOs and Defence: What must we be prepared for?*

The report was not solicited by the French government, however it was sent to President Jacques Chirac and Prime Minister Lionel Jospin before being finally published in French weekly news and leisure magazine *VSD* in July 1999. Since COMETA was a private, non-profit ufological study group, the COMETA report cannot technically be termed as an 'official' document even though *VSD* referred to it as such.

Unlike the fallible investigative work presented by Condon, the 1999 publication delved deeply into the UFO mystery with great aplomb, intending to identify and separate the easily resolved cases from the unexplained. Written by such influential figures as Prof. Andre Lebeau (former Chairman National Centre for Space Studies), Gen. Bernard Norlain (former Commander French Tactical Air Force) and Jean-Claude Ribes (former Director Observatory at Lyon), the study was taken seriously in an attempt to understand more about the elusive objects appearing at random in our skies. The report questioned if they are physically real, what are they, and are they are a threat to national security?

Nuclear physicist and UFO researcher Stanton Friedman commented, "It's an important report for what it says. No other report with names, with people with excellent cases...has come close to taking as a strong a stand – that some UFOs are extraterrestrial craft."

Remarkably, the controversial report has never been published outside of France, in fact only one article has ever been printed in the American press. The *Boston Sunday Globe* covered it once stating that, "UFO theorists gain support abroad, but repression at home. Study by French officials, routine unexplained sightings, U.S, military safety aspects combine to boost believers."[10]

The introduction to the report states that in order to justify the in-depth study, it is worthwhile presenting several facts and testimonies; included are three testimonies of French civilian and military pilots who encountered UFOs in flight, five major aeronautical cases around the world, three sightings from the ground and four cases of close encounters in France.

One of the pilot testimonies dating back to January 28, 1994 reveals how such strange aerial phenomena can appear under the most ordinary of circumstances. Witnessed by commercial pilot Jean-Charles Duboc, captain of Air France flight AF 3532, and his co-pilot Valerie Chauffour whilst flying from Nice to London, the UFO reported in this testimony was initially seen by the chief steward who believed he had seen a weather balloon. Very quickly however, Duboc and Chauffour realised "they were seeing something that did not resemble anything that they knew of."

Capt. Duboc estimated the unknown object to be at an altitude of 10,500m and approximately 50km away. The report read, "Taking into account its apparent diameter, they deduced that the craft was large. They were struck by the changes in the shape of the craft, which first appeared in the form of a brown bell before transforming into a chestnut brown lens shape, then disappearing almost instantaneously on the left side of the aircraft, as if it had suddenly become invisible."[11]

The Taverny Air Defence Operations Centre (CODA) was informed of the sighting and an investigation ensued which revealed that the object had been tracked by radar at a time and location which corresponded with that reported by Duboc. The phenomenon then disappeared from radar at the same time as the crew lost sight of it.

According to the report, "The investigations conducted by CODA enabled both the hypothesis of a weather balloon to be ruled out and the precise crossing distance of the two trajectories to be determined, consequently bringing the approximate length of the craft to 250 m in length."[12]

Another case investigated by the COMETA report details a 1957 UFO sighting from a military pilot flying an RB-47 bomber over the United States. The case has been cited and studied extensively for forty years, but was only seen fit to be catalogued as "unidentified" in the Condon report, showing once again the lack of commitment involved in the making of the Air Force report.

Included in the French document are four fascinating accounts of close encounters which have occurred in France. The first came from Maurice Masse from Valensole on July 1, 1965. Masse claimed that whilst working in his lavender field, a flying object landed in his field only ninety metres away from where he was stood. As he cautiously approached, he saw two small beings, one of whom took out a tube from a sort of bag hanging on his left side, and pointed it at Masse, immobilizing him on the spot. He was numb and paralysed for around fifteen minutes but was completely aware of his surroundings the whole time and managed to watch as the two figures returned to their 'vehicle' as six legs which it had been resting on retracted underneath before lifting up off the ground. "The object then ascended in a vertical direction before tilting diagonally and disappearing more rapidly than a jet", the report states.

On August 29, 1967 another incident took place in Cussac, located on the high plateaus of Central France, which involved two young boys who were out watching the family's herd. One of the boys who was thirteen years old at the time, went to retrieve a wandering cow when he spotted four children he didn't recognise on the other side of the road. As he called for his sister he noticed "an extremely bright sphere behind the unknown children."

It was then that he realised that they were not children but "small black beings whose height did not exceed 1.20 m." The boy reported seeing two of these beings stood by the sphere, another was kneeling before it and the fourth was stood with some sort of mirror in his hand which blinded the children. The boy called out to the beings but this caused them to return hurriedly to the sphere, which took off with a hissing sound, spiralling continuously at high speed into the sky.

Such an incredulous account by a couple of children does not necessarily hold much weight in terms of evidential proof, but the French scientists who chose to investigate the matter further had reason to believe that this was not just a case of two kids stretching their imaginations. They reported a strong sulphur odour emanating from the spot where the sphere had been and this smell was later confirmed by the gendarme who was at the scene shortly after the beings departed.

The children themselves actually gave off a strong smell of sulphur and suffered from physiological disorders for several days after the incident, constantly watering eyes being one of the issues. The family doctor certified these facts and later in a counter-investigation, the judge gave his opinion on the witnesses and their testimony and declared that "...despite the young age of the principal witnesses, and as extraordinary as the facts that they have related seem to be, I think that they actually observed them."[13]

The case reports and general information contained within the pages of the COMETA report certainly expose the Condon report's inadequacies and blatant bias in favour of the hidden agenda, to conceal rather than reveal. In contrast, rather than dismiss the high percentage of UFO reports and debunk the witness testimonies, the French report appears fully open to the possibility of extraterrestrial visitation.

Here are some of the conclusions reached by the COMETA group:

"These craft demonstrate the reality of UFOs, with remarkable silent flight performances, apparently operated by intelligent beings."

"...in the absence of explanations for the phenomena sighted, the hypothesis of an extraterrestrial origin can no longer be ruled out."

"These extraterrestrials are highly endowed intellectually and are technologically advanced over us to have been able to achieve what we do not yet know how to do."

It is evident by the manner in which the phenomenon as a whole was investigated, that the COMETA report was attempting to deal with the subject as reasonably and objectively as it could. As the report stated, "The UFO problem cannot be eliminated by mere caustic and offhand witticisms." Former Chief of Defence Staff, Admiral Lord Hill-Norton, who was also one of thirty other lords in a House of Lords UFO study group in the eighties, echoed the sentiments expressed by the French group when he said; "This should be the subject of vigorous scientific investigation and not the subject of rubbishing by the tabloid newspapers."

ATOMIC INTERCEPTION

Since the 1999 report, information has not been very forthcoming and the subject as a whole remains shrouded in secrecy. However, thanks to the efforts of a North Carolina doctor, Dr. Steven M. Greer, the collaborative testimonies of a variety of professionals were publicly announced in May 2001, in an attempt to raise awareness on the subject.

A press conference was held at the National Press Club, Washington D.C., and featured twenty retired Air Force, Federal Aviation Administration and intelligence officers testifying to their experiences with UFOs and/or ETs via the Disclosure Project.

Founded in 1993 by Dr. Greer, the Disclosure Project is a non-profit research project "working to fully disclose the facts about UFOs, extraterrestrial intelligence, and classified advanced energy and propulsion systems."[14]

Greer has managed to bring together over 500 military, government, and intelligence community witnesses, all willing to come forward and testify in an attempt to lift the lid of secrecy which has been almost impenetrable for so long.

1st Lt. Robert Jacobs, a Photo-Optical Inst. Officer for the USAF, came forward to disclose information regarding an extraordinary incident that took place in 1964 whilst he was in the 1369th photo squadron at Vandenberg AFB in California. The bizarre situation arose while he was in charge of photo-optical instrumentation at a tracking site in Big Sur, 124 miles away from the base.

His mission was to film an Atlas ICBM[2] rocket as it went through all three stages of powered flight. On this particular occasion, Jacobs's mission was part of a Nike-Zeus objective for the development of an anti-missile missile during the height of the cold war. Jacobs began to film from Big Sur once they heard "lift-off" over the radio from Vandenberg, and following what appeared to have been a successful mission, he took the cans of film back to base where they were to be developed that same night.

First thing next morning Jacobs was called to the office of his superior, Major Florence J. Mansmann, where a 16mm projector and screen were already setup. He sat down next to Mansmann and two other men wearing grey civilian clothes, which Jacobs found a little unusual, and Mansmann said to Jacobs, "Watch this!"

The film showed the missile launch from the previous day. As the missile entered the frame Jacobs saw the whole third stage filling the frame from about 160 miles away, along with the 'dummy' warhead which was attached to the rocket. This was a test run to see how well everything was functioning so it wasn't necessary to employ a real warhead at this stage.

As the rocket was travelling between 11,000 and 14,000 mph, suddenly a saucer shaped craft entered the frame. As Jacobs described, "It flew into the frame and shot a beam of light at the warhead – hits it – then this thing flies up – fires another beam of light – goes around – fires another beam of light – goes down –

---

[2] Intercontinental ballistic missile

fires another beam of light and then flies out the way it came in and the warhead tumbles out of space."[15]

Mansmann asked "What was that?" and Jacobs replied, "It looks to me like we got a UFO." According to Jacobs, Major Mansmann was a very good reader of film, and his instinct at the time was that it must have been extraterrestrial. They assumed that the beam of light must have been some sort of plasma beam. Following some discussion on the matter, Mansmann told Jacobs, "You are never to speak of this again. As far as you are concerned, this never happened."

Mansmann wrote about the incident years later in a letter dated November 18, 1991 claiming that two agents took the footage. He wrote, "They did not sign out for all the footage but took out the part that showed the encounter and returned the rest of the film as a "complete package."" Continuing he declared that, "The one agent stated as he handed me back the film, "That leaves you off the hook but not off any disclosure – understood?" Naturally my answer was "Yes Sir"."

Three years later on March 16, 1967 another UFO encounter took place at Malmstrom AFB in Cascade County, Montana. In the event of a nuclear war, nuclear 'minute men' missiles were to be launched as a counterattack, and one of the men responsible for their deployment was Lt. Col. Robert Salas, SAC (Strategic Air Command) Launch Controller.

Whilst on duty that day, Salas was contacted by his topside guard who was claiming that there was an unidentified object above the missile site. Minutes later he radioed Salas again saying that there was a reddish-orange, oval-shaped object hovering quietly outside the front gate. This was going on in the early hours of the morning but Salas had to wake up his commander and inform him of the two phone calls. During their conversation, all the missiles on site went into a no-go condition, one after the other. They lost in excess of ten missiles in one morning. The malfunction of one missile should not affect the others because they are individually operated and separated by miles.

Salas remarked, "Somehow this object was able to disable these missiles." Following the incident, everyone involved including Salas were forced to sign documents swearing to never disclose this information, ever.

A recently declassified preliminary report dated March 24, 1964 supports his claims that a UFO disabled all the nuclear missiles at Malmstrom AFB that day; "Between the hours 2100 and 0400 MST numerous reports were received by Malmstrom AFB agencies of UFO sightings in the Great Falls, Montana area." The document went on to say, "Reports of a UFO landing near Belt, Montana were received from several sources including deputies of Cascade County Sheriff's Office."

Another formerly classified secret Air Force telex confirmed the incident stating that, "the fact that for no apparent reason the loss of ten missiles can be readily identified is cause for grave concern to this headquarters."

As usual, matters of this kind are rarely entered into the public domain and a veil of secrecy is always quick to conceal such delicate issues exposing the nation's defensive frailties. A letter sent from Col. James H. Rix, USAF Director of Administration to Lee M. Graham reveals why the military authorities feel compelled to deny that such occurrences have ever taken place: "As regards this subject matter, mere existence or non-existence is currently and properly classified per Executive Order and exempt from mandatory disclosure under the Freedom of Information Act because it would reveal defense capability or lack thereof."[16]

In 2001, Robert Salas stated, "Unknown aerial objects have in fact been observed over many of our nuclear weapons bases and other nuclear facilities, and in some cases the appearance of these objects coincided with compromising the operational readiness of our nuclear weapons."[17]

Retired USAF Nuclear Missile Launch Officer Jerome Nelson testified to a series of events which occurred at Site 9, west of Roswell, New Mexico starting in the winter of 1963. Just like Capt. Salas, Nelson was alerted by his topside guard that a large UFO was hovering above the site, but once he contacted his commanding officer he was met with indifference and told to get on with his work. Over the years that followed that particular incident, Nelson claimed that several more sightings occurred over the same facility, reported by a number of different guards, all of whom appeared "shaken up" by what they had just witnessed.

In September 1966, Patrick McDonough, a USAF Nuclear Missile Site Geodetic Surveyor experienced a UFO encounter whilst temporarily assigned to Malmstrom AFB. There were around 150 'minute-men' missile sites in the area and he was ordered to perform geodetic surveys for the last fifty sites, his task being to calculate their precise latitude and longitude.

The first peculiar thing he noticed was that the blast hatch of the missile silo he was working on that evening was open; he found this to be very unusual as they were always closed. At around 1-1:30 a.m. a spherical UFO roughly 50ft. in diameter with pulsating lights all around it, came from the north and stopped about 300ft. above their heads. McDonough described seeing a white light appear from the centre of the object and shine directly down into the missile silo. Without wind or noise and from a complete standstill, the UFO then shot off into the night sky eastwards until it was out of sight. The Montana Highway Patrol later revealed that they had received in excess of twenty reports of UFO sightings in the area that same night.

"I worked everywhere on these guidance systems and I never saw anything in the air force infantry that could perform like this UFO did", remarked McDonough.

UFOs have been monitoring Earth's nuclear activities since the first atomic tests took place during Operation Crossroads at Bikini Island in the Pacific on July 12, 1946 when a series of photographs showing the billowing mushroom cloud rising revealed a number of UFOs fleeing the scene.

According to UFO researcher Robert Hastings who is heavily involved in the Disclosure Project, UFOs continue to intercept and tamper with nuclear missiles to the present day. In April 2003, a number of UFOs were spotted manoeuvring near the bunkers at the nuclear facility located at Nellis AFB in Nevada. The latest incident involving a UFO at a nuclear test facility took place at Malmstrom AFB in 2007, but civilian UFO sightings in Orange County, California, have been reported near a series of nuclear bunkers at the Seal Beach Naval Weapons Station as recently as March 2009.

Other incidents reported during the Disclosure Project press conference involved a UFO shaped like a "pregnant cigar" which was seen hovering silently over several launch sites in the same evening. Each time the commanding officers in charge were informed that something unusual seemed to be 'investigating' the nuclear facilities under their command; the informant was quickly told there was nothing to be concerned about and to return to their post.

Current USAF policy on UFOs states that, "No UFO reported or investigated or evaluated by the Air Force was ever an indication of threat to our national security." The fact that it is not publicly acknowledged that unexplained aerial phenomena have been reported as either directly intercepting nuclear warheads or taking more than a keen interest in them, speaks volumes. If we are not informed about something of this magnitude it is usually for reasons of national security or their innate fear that such incidents, should they become publicly known, would undermine their military expertise and expose their lack of defensive capabilities.

THE RENDLESHAM FOREST LANDING

Air Force bases have played host to a large number of UFO sightings over the years, particularly those housing atomic weaponry. The reason for such visits isn't fully understood at this juncture but one *could* speculate that whoever controls the unknown craft appears to have an avid interest in mankind's destructive capabilities.

Most military UFO reports have originated on American soil near USAF bases but one significant close encounter occurred in England near two RAF bases in Suffolk. Often referred to as 'Britain's Roswell', a term first coined by Georgina Bruni, the Rendlesham Forest incident has become an integral part of modern UFO folklore. Located at the rear of two of the most important military facilities in England, RAF Bentwaters and RAF Woodbridge (operated by the USAF), the forest was the site of an incredible UFO landing in late 1980.

However, a lesser known incident which was investigated by the Condon committee back in 1956 occurred in the same area when a UFO was tracked by radars at both RAF Lakenheath and RAF Bentwaters. That incident, which took place between the 13th and 14th August, was never explained and remains filed as such to this day.

The Condon Report stated, "This is the most puzzling and unusual case in the radar-visual files. The apparently rational, intelligent behaviour of the UFO suggests a mechanical device of unknown origin as the most probable explanation of this sighting.

However, in view of the inevitable fallibility of witnesses, more conventional explanations of this report cannot be entirely ruled out."

The 1980 incident was much more than a sighting of an unknown object; it actually landed long enough to be touched by human hand before departing. It all started at around 3 a.m. on December 27, when two USAF security police patrolmen saw unusual lights outside the back gate of RAF Woodbridge. They called for permission to investigate what they believed could have been a crashed aircraft; the on-duty flight chief responded and requested that three patrolmen should go on foot.

Airman John F. Burroughs, who had reported seeing the light, was then accompanied by Sgt. James Penniston and Amn. Edward N. Cabansag, the latter being on Security One and in charge of mobile security at Woodbridge. They headed towards Rendlesham Forest where they could see something sitting in the tree-line and Cabansag was sent back to help transmit radio communications between the other two officers, who went to investigate further with their malfunctioning radios.

Penniston explained, "It was apparent that it wasn't an aircraft crash, we knew that much. There was a craft of some sort that was sitting just inside the tree-line. The closer we got, the more the white light dissipated, but what appeared was a triangular craft."

He described the craft as about 9 ft. long and approximately 6 ft. high with light emanating from the object which would move around the whole craft. Penniston and Burroughs undertook a 45-minute ground investigation with Penniston taking notes as he walked all the way around the foreign machine. His observation notes read: "type of craft still unknown – no apparent landing gear – no sound but appears to be pulsating somehow – very warm to touch – identifying markings on left front side".

As has become a common feature of such mysterious objects, the markings on the craft described by Penniston were reminiscent of Egyptian hieroglyphs, like some form of pictographic writing. As he touched them he observed that the text was raised slightly from the metallic surface of the rest of the craft, with a different texture too.

It was noted that at the time of the incident that the animals on a nearby farm went into a frenzy as the object slowly rose from the ground where Penniston and Burroughs were stood watching in amazement, before maneuvering itself through the trees, ascending into the sky and vanishing. Apart from making another brief appearance one hour later near the back gate of the base, the UFO seemed to be gone.

The following day Lt. Col. Charles Halt, USAF Deputy Base Commander, investigated the alleged landing site and admits he was as skeptical as anyone; "I really expected to find a logical explanation"[18], Halt commented. Much to his amazement he found traces of radiation, landing imprints and abrasions on the trees that had been facing inwards in the direction of the craft, some of which had broken branches. The radiation readings were between eight to ten times higher than the average background readings of about 0.015 mR which Halt claimed "were not enough to be dangerous to somebody but significant." Plaster casts were taken of the indentations in the ground – all three of which were identical in size and depth.

An official memo dated 13 January, 1981 stated, "The next day, three depressions 1½ inches deep and 7 inches in diameter were found where the object had been sighted on the ground. Beta/Gamma readings of 0.1 milliroentgens were recorded with peak readings in the three depressions and near the centre of the triangle formed by the depression."

Whilst Halt was scanning the area for more evidence, a red sun-like object was spotted through the trees by one of his colleagues. Halt turned to look, and described what happened next; "Off through the forest was a bright glowing object, the best way I can describe it – it looked like an eye, with bright red and a dark centre. It appeared to be 'winking'. It was shedding something like molten metal, it was dripping off it. It silently moved through the trees, avoiding any contact, it bobbed up and down, and at one point it actually approached us. We tried to get closer; it receded out into the field, beyond the forest, and silently exploded into five white objects. Gone."

They then noticed three or four objects in the north which were moving around at very high speeds, "as if they were doing a grid search", recalled Halt. Then to the south they saw two more objects hovering in the sky. "One object approached us at very high speed, best guess is three to five thousand feet...stopped directly overhead and sent down a concentrated beam of light at our feet, about one foot in diameter."

Standing there awestruck, Halt wondered what was going on. Was it a warning or an attempt to communicate? Was it a weapon or just a probe? Whatever it was, it disappeared as suddenly as it had appeared. Then, about a mile and a half away they noticed the other UFOs in the north sending down beams over Woodbridge base, it was established at the time through radio communication between bases, that some if not all of the beams were falling into weapons storage areas. "There was a great deal of concern", remarked Halt.

Halt recorded all notes, observations and thoughts on the incident on a cassette throughout the experience, and was requested to write a 'cleaned up' version of events in a memorandum which explained that mysterious lights had been observed. It wasn't until a Freedom of Information request was submitted to Bentwaters several years later that the story became public.

Halt concluded, "I have no idea what we saw that night. I do know it was under intelligent control. And my personal opinion – it was either from another dimension or extraterrestrial."[19]

At the time the initial incident took place in the forest, Sgt. Jim Penniston reported what he had observed to his superiors, but failed to disclose everything that he had written down that night. It wasn't until thirty years later in October 2010, whilst filming for an episode of the History Channel's documentary *Ancient Aliens* that Penniston finally revealed to everyone on set that something even stranger had happened to him in the forest that night.

He claimed that once he had touched the triangular craft he had telepathically received mental images which he felt compelled to write down in his notebook. He had a mental image of a complex numerical sequence of ones and zeros which made no sense to him whatsoever. Recalling the incident Penniston said, "It's like someone's holding a picture up…of those zeros and ones, I could see it in my mind's eye, so I recorded those – one after another. What do they mean – I don't know."[20]

Knowing that what was happening to him was so bizarre, he knew that should he disclose it to his superiors at the time that his sanity would have been questioned and he would most likely have been asked to leave the Army. He only decided to reveal the details of the incident once he had left the Air Force and returned home to America and after been plagued by persistent dreams about that night and the mysterious message he'd received.

He entrusted some of the pages of zeros and ones to computer programmer and binary code expert Nick Ciske in 2010, who much to his own amazement, managed to decipher part of the code after putting all the numbers into his computer. A fragmented sentence emerged once Ciske typed out the first five pages of Penniston's binary notes (he wrote sixteen pages in total, but has yet to transfer them all). Below is what transpired once the seemingly random numbers Jim Penniston was impelled to record became computerized:

"EXPLORATION [of] HUMANITY 666 8100
52 09' 42.532" N
13 13' 12.69" W
CONTI [NUOUS]
FOR PLANETARY ADVAN[CE]"

The coordinates which Ciske received point to a mysterious sunken island known in Celtic legend as Hy-Brasil (located west of South-West Ireland) which is also referred to as 'the other Atlantis'. It is believed that the people living there thousands of years ago were part of a highly advanced civilization with high morals. Visitors claimed that they saw "gold-roofed towers and domes, healthy cattle, and opulent citizens."

Included on ancient maps, Hy-Brasil was above water prior to the last ice-age 11,000 years ago but forced to migrate by the rising flood waters. Author David Wilcock postulated that, "When they got to Europe they actually became the builders of the stone-circles and the standing stone-like megaliths and menhirs and so forth."[21]

Researcher Linda Moulton Howe contacted retired American astronomer Michael A. Reed and former Australian astrophysicist Horace R. Drew to perform another analysis of Penniston's alleged code. This resulted in a different set of coordinates appearing, simply because the decision to move the decimal point from 13.131269 (Hy-Brasil) to 1.3131269 changed the location to Woodbridge town centre in Suffolk. This second analysis acts as a useful reminder that such information is often open to interpretation, hence the discrepancies between the two suggested locations.

The association between a suspected alien communication and a once high civilization believed to have been Hy-Brasil would be a fascinating connection, should it prove to be the intended message. However, Howe's second location of Woodbridge also raises some interesting questions as it is the nearest town to the Rendlesham forest landing, from where the binary code was alleged to have originated in the first place.

Some of the people involved such as Jim Penniston and John Burroughs still show signs of post-traumatic stress disorder after thirty years. They claim they were not offered the proper support necessary after the events in December 1980, and some have even asserted that some of the witnesses were threatened and indecently interrogated with the use of drugs in an attempt to either reveal or conceal the truth of the situation.

Even after all these years, some witnesses are considering legal action against the USAF for their part in the maltreatment they inflicted on them, as well as calling for Congressional hearings on the matter. At the heart of the campaign is a *Facebook* group entitled *Justice for the Bentwaters 81st Security Police at Rendlesham Forest 1980*, which has in excess of 3,500 members to date.

CRASHED AT KECKSBURG

In December, 1965 a large fireball was seen by thousands of witnesses as it streaked across the night sky over at least nine American states and Canada. The object was considered by sources at the Pentagon to have been a meteorite from the constellation of Gemini – a Geminid meteor. Speaking about the likelihood of the object being as Pentagon officials had suggested, Dr. Nicholas Wagman, director of the Allegheny Observatory said, "As a rule, they are numerous but not bright. A bright one, such as the one sighted last night, is generally sporadic."

The object reportedly dropped hot metal over Michigan and northern Ontario, possibly leading to a number of grass fires over three states, and the possible cause of shock waves and sonic booms as was reported by the associated press. Wagman stated that, "there were reports of a shock wave in parts of Western Pennsylvania at the time of the sighting."[22] The unknown object was later spotted near Greensburg in Westmoreland County before it suddenly changed direction – moving past Norvell towards Kecksburg, Pennsylvania.

Eyewitness Bill Bulebush described the scene, "I looked up and I seen this bluish fireball or whatever you call it, in the sky coming from Norvell and going towards the mountains. It looked like it wanted to go over the mountain but couldn't...It seemed like it hesitated. And it finally came back and made a U-turn and went down into Kecksburg."[23]

Randy Overly was only a ten year old boy playing in an open field with a friend when he saw the strange object from a distance away, getting closer, then flying straight past them overhead before leaving the region. Overly described the object as "sort of acorn-shaped" with a raised area around the back and brownish-greyish in colour with fire coming out of the back of it. With a rounded part on the very tip of the object, he explained that it also seemed to be covered in some kind of vapour which enveloped it as it flew by. Only a mere 200ft. in the air and hissing as it passed him, Overly recalled, "It was moving no faster than a small aircraft. I know what I saw, and it definitely wasn't a meteor. I really can't explain what it was, but it certainly seemed to be a constructed thing – it had smooth edges and smooth lines."[24]

Whatever the object was that had been seen by so many people over a large distance, at around 4:46 p.m. EST it crash-landed in a patch of woods, southeast of Pittsburgh near a town called Kecksburg. Mable Mazza, bookkeeper and office manager at local station *WHJB Radio*, said that from 5pm onwards they were receiving a lot of calls from different radio and television stations concerning a crashed object at Kecksburg.

Recalling that day Mazza explained that, "...of course I thought these are just a bunch of people playing pranks, but as the evening went on I realised that something definitely did happen. They were serious and they were excited and their voices were full of emotion." Before long they were also receiving calls from the military, the Air Force and the Pentagon. A reporter for the local newspaper remembered arriving at the scene of the crash, and being unable to breach the cordoned off area setup by the large military presence, he was told to stay away as there may be radiation. The following day, the *Tribune-Review* printed the headline; "Army Ropes Off Area. 'Unidentified Flying Object' Falls Near Kecksburg."

A State Police officer informed the press that the search "uncovered absolutely nothing" and even suggested that the whole incident "may have been stirred by the imagination of two young boys", referring to the young Randy Overly and his friend. If the numerous witness testimonies are to be believed, whatever had crashed in the woods that evening was far from being a figment of childhood imagination.

The first person to reach the crashed object was Bill Bulebush who initially thought he was witnessing a couple of kids playing with sparklers in the woods. Before approaching the mysterious object, Bulebush could see blue flames between the gaps in the trees. As he got closer he could hear a sizzling noise, and shining his torch on it he could see that whatever it was resembled his trashcan – a burnt orange colour. With blue flames arcing out of it and still sizzling, Bulebush claimed, "it was embedded in the ground a little bit, where it came down and like, belly landed."

It had a ring around the backend of it with "some kind of Egyptian marking" around it which he also described as looking like "backward writing". He could see where the trees were bent in one direction, where the object had come in "like an airplane". Bulebush continued, "...it seemed like it was controlled. Seemed like it just glided in and embedded itself into the bank."

18 year old James Romansky was a member of the Latrobe Volunteer Fire Department at the time of the incident and recalled seeing a fiery object in the sky coming from the north. Shortly after, the fire whistle sounded and Romansky who answered the call was informed that a search team was needed because they believed that it was a downed aircraft. He thought, "My God, this is what I have just seen."

The team searched on foot with torches and finally found the crash site. "We didn't discover a conventional aircraft as we know it. What we did find was a very large metallic object. There was no signs of entry to it. There was no signs of windows, portholes, doors...wings...assembly...no signs of motors of one kind or another. It caught us totally by surprise"[25], explained Romansky.

Entirely made from metal, the object had no seams, cracks or rivet marks to show how it had been put together, it was perfectly smooth as if it had been cast. With no signs of a propulsion unit either, the craft was unlike anything he had ever seen before and just as Bulebush had described, Romansky also stated that the front end appeared to have "ploughed into the ground."

He also described the object as bronze coloured and shaped like an acorn with a lightly blunt backend, and he estimated it to be around 12 ft. long and 25 ft. in diameter with strange markings around the base which he also commented were reminiscent of the ancient Egyptian hieroglyphics. Zigzag lines, straight lines, circles and other shapes were all present.

Describing the object he added, "It had sort of a bumper on it, like a ribbon about 6 to 10 inches wide, and it stood out. It was elliptical the whole way around and the writing was on this bumper."[26] Not long after the fire-fighters had investigated the area, two men in white overcoats arrived and told them all to leave immediately. Minutes later the site was crawling with military personnel.

Another eyewitness, Jerry Betters, watched as an Army truck with a big white star on it drove out of the woods with a UFO on the back of it. "To me it looked copper-ish looking. Maybe it was burnt or something. It was big. It was domed and I saw the hieroglyphics on it," Betters claimed.

A truck driver going by the name of Myron was working for a large Ohio supply house when he saw the object at Wright-Patterson AFB in Dayton, Ohio, notably renowned within ufology for storing crashed flying discs. This occurred a few days after the incident had taken place, whilst he was delivering special bricks to the base. Myron's firm had ordered 6,500 double-glazed bricks which he claimed "were for building a double-walled shield around a recovered radioactive object." He claimed that they were attempting to entomb the object in a corner of the base, by using the same bricks that the whole building was made of.

He first noticed the "bell-shaped" object whilst he was unloading the bricks; he said it was resting on stilts with large parachute-like screens covering it up. The shape was silhouetted by floodlights and he managed to get a closer look through a small opening in the tent.

He said, "The spaceship looked like a large acorn around about 14 ft. to the top and about 10-12 ft. wide at the bottom. It had a collar on it; it had writing on the collar. The writing went all around the bell shape of it. The bottom of the bell shape was completely black."[27]

In the same building as the object, Myron also recalled seeing a body lying under a white sheet on a workbench 10-12 ft. long and about 32 inches wide, 36 inches off the floor. He claimed that he saw something very unusual lying there; "I seen the left hand of whatever was in there sticking out from underneath a sterile white pad and it only had three fingers – 4 ft. 5 or 4 ft. 9 tall – dark green/brownish skin just like a lizard."

As the only witness to the body, Myron's testimony cannot be validated further, but official documentation referring to the Kecksburg incident does exist according to former Army Sgt. Clifford Stone who claims that he read such material whilst still actively in the service. Speaking in 1990, Stone said, "The document talked about a recovery, in the Pennsylvania area. We recovered an object that was not Soviet. It also makes it quite clear that the object did not originate on the face of the Earth."

What makes this story even more fascinating is that aside from the Geminid meteor showers that were present during the week of the alleged crash, one Soviet satellite actually re-entered the atmosphere on the same night that the unknown object went down. The Naval Space Surveillance Center in Dahlgren, Virginia confirmed this, "By reviewing our data, we were able to identify only one satellite (COSMOS 96) that decayed on Dec 9 or 10, 1965." Further research revealed more details;

"Satellite Number: 01742
Country of Origin: USSR
Object Type: Payload
Date of Launch: Nov 23, 1965
Date of Decay: Dec 9, 1965"

Some people unwilling to accept that an interstellar craft of some kind landed in the Kecksburg woods, are more inclined to believe that the object, if it was indeed metal as so many claim that it was, must have been the Soviet satellite. However, the probability of debris from the satellite surviving re-entry and landing was nigh on impossible according to Chief Scientist for Orbital Debris at the NASA Johnson Space Center, Nicholas L. Johnson. In 2003, he told investigative journalist Leslie Kean, "I can tell you categorically; that there is no way that any debris from

Cosmos 96 could have landed in Pennsylvania anywhere around 4:45 p.m. That's an absolute. Orbital mechanics is very strict."

In 1991, the U.S. Space Command reported that the Russian probe had actually crashed in Canada at 3:18 a.m. Johnson himself couldn't confirm what time COSMOS 96 decayed but he did assert that it was definitely over Canada at the time of the 'fireball' reports.

According to an Associated Press story, just before the 40th anniversary of the Kecksburg incident, in December 2005, NASA released a statement explaining that following closer examination of metallic fragments from the object, they were now claiming it was from a re-entering "Russian satellite". Unfortunately, the spokesman also claimed that the records relating to the incident had somehow been misplaced. Well at least they have finally acknowledged that an object *did* actually land that day.

Clifford Stone claims that he was told from sources who are extremely interested in UFOs within the Russian Government that, "they were informed that COSMOS 96 had collided with an object of unknown origin that came from outer space, and caused it to veer off and plunge back to Earth."

Another theory exists that suggests that the object could have been a Nazi Wunderwaffe (wonder weapon) called Die Glocke (the Bell). Speculation as to the existence of such weaponry continues to this day, but some researchers such as American author Joseph P. Farrell assert that 'the Bell' was considered so important to the Nazis that they killed 60 scientists that worked on the project and buried them in a mass grave.[28] Furthermore, Farrell stated that the device *was* the object recovered at Kecksburg in 1965.[29] Such theories only add to the mystery of the Kecksburg crash and reinforce the notion that whatever landed in the woods was of extreme interest to the U.S. military, enough so to enforce a cover-up which would last nearly half a century and counting.

Stone concluded, "Something entered the Earth's atmosphere, something went down in Pennsylvania, something was recovered by the military, and whatever that something is – is considered by the United States intelligence committee to be so sensitive that they will even lie to members of Congress to keep that information highly classified and buried away from the public."[30]

MASS SIGHTINGS

Those sceptics not convinced by the often fantastical testimonies of unknown individuals claiming to have witnessed mysterious flying objects firsthand, would do well to remember that there have been a plethora of mass UFO sightings around the world. To have backup from a large number of other eyewitnesses is far more convincing and also much harder to discredit.

There have been many incidents occurring over the years, where large groups of people have unwittingly seen and reported strange aerial activity that defies logical explanation. This next section highlights some of the better known mass sightings that have taken place during the last fifty years, highlighting the fact that UFO reports aren't always reliant on the credibility of one individual alone. When a cross-section of society experiences the same phenomena simultaneously, it is only reasonable to accept that there must be a certain amount of validity to such an array of collaborative testimonies.

i.   Battle of Los Angeles

On February 25, 1942 less than three months after the attack on Pearl Harbour and only two days after an oil facility near Santa Barbara had been bombed by a Japanese submarine, an unknown object was spotted in the skies above Los Angeles. Five years before the Roswell incident (see next chapter), and five years before the beginning of the modern UFO era, the Battle of L.A. is one of the most dramatic mass UFO sightings on record.

A huge flying object which was initially sighted as it hovered over MGM Studios in the Culver City region triggered all of Los Angeles and most of Southern California into an immediate blackout in the wake of recent events. The city was blacked out from 2:25 to 7:21 a.m. and in effect reached from L.A. to the Mexican border and inland to the San Joaquin Valley.

Air Raid Wardens were quick to react to the suspicious craft and soon the UFO was lit up by the huge spotlights of the Army's 37th Coast Artillery Brigade. Military aircraft were called to the scene and before long a relentless barrage of shots were fired from the ground at the mysterious object. Remarkably, despite the ensuing maelstrom no airplanes were shot down and no bombs were dropped and only two people were reported as being injured by the descending fragments of antiaircraft shells. The incident occurred early in the morning and due to the firing of an estimated 1,400 antiaircraft shells the whole city was alerted to the UFOs presence. Hundreds and hundreds of rounds were fired at the glowing ship by the Coastal Defence gunners, leaving few in the city asleep that night.

"It was huge! It was just enormous! And it was practically right over my house. I had never seen anything like it in my life!" recalled female Air Raid Warden Katie. "It was just hovering there in the sky and hardly moving at all", she added. "It was a lovely pale orange and about the most beautiful thing you've ever seen. I could see it perfectly because it was very close. It was big!" Other eyewitnesses described the UFO as being like a "surreal, hanging, magic lantern", according to newspaper reports the following day.

As the daunting sound of gunfire reverberated around the city, the Artillery Brigade landed scores of direct hits with apparently no effect whatsoever. Katie remembered the incident vividly, "It was like the Fourth of July but much louder. They were firing like crazy but they couldn't touch it."

Los Angeles Times reporter Bill Henry watched the whole affair and wrote, "I was far enough away to see an object without being able to identify it...I would be willing to bet what shekels I have that there were a number of direct hits scored on the object."

Incredibly the newspapers the next day did not offer a single description of the object despite the fact that it was caught in the centre of a multitude of searchlights for over thirty minutes, and was watched by hundreds of thousands of witnesses. The only description afforded to it by the *Los Angeles Times* stated that, "The object...caught in the center of the lights like the hub of a bicycle wheel surrounded by gleaming spokes. The fire seemed to burst in rings all around the object."

A photograph of the object amidst the beams of light [see SOURCES} was printed the following day along with the explanatory text, "Scores of searchlights built a wigwam of light beams over Los Angeles early yesterday morning during the alarm. This picture taken during blackout shows nine beams converging on an "object" in sky in Culver City area." [31] Another article stated, "Taken before dawn on Feb. 25, 1942, by a Los Angeles Times photographer, this photo shows searchlights centred on a mystery target with anti-aircraft shells bursting nearby."

One statement printed in the article which dominated the *L.A. Times* newspaper in the aftermath of the event, was relayed by the Southern California sector of the Western Defense Command office in Pasadena, "The aircraft which caused the blackout in the Los Angeles area for several hours this a.m. have not been identified."

Still to this day, the object which caused such uproar and put fear into the hearts of so many nervous Californians remains unexplained. Thousands of locals used binoculars in an attempt to get a clearer view of the object which was lit up so clearly beneath the bright lights of the Coast Artillery. A stream of eyewitness reports verified the absence of any enemy planes, instead confirming the peculiar presence of a huge unidentified and indestructible object.

ii.   The Washington Flap

In 1952, a series of UFO sightings were reported over Washington D.C. from July 12 –29. The most publicized accounts took place on the two consecutive weekends of July 19 – 20 and July 26 – 29. On the 31st of July, the Air Force informed the Press that regular intelligence work had been seriously compromised by the inundation of "flying saucer" queries. Since the turn of the year, they had already received 432 written reports concerning "sightings of unidentified aerial phenomena". The period during which the sightings over D.C. took place became known as 'the Washington National Airport Sightings' or 'the Washington Flap'.

The July UFO sightings were a continuation of a multitude of other sightings reported nationwide during 1952 in what was the biggest UFO wave since 1947, and possibly the largest since. Former assistant director of NICAP and director of the Fund for UFO Research, Richard H. Hall wrote, "The summer 1952 UFO sighting wave was one of the largest of all time, and arguably the most significant of all time in terms of the credible reports and hardcore scientific data obtained."[32]

The Washington sightings involved a lot of data being reported by radar operators from both the Washington National Airport and Andrews AFB, who both recorded multiple sightings of unknown objects as blips on their radar screens. One famous photograph showing a fleet of UFOs passing above the White House has been proven to be a fake. The image actually shows reflected street lamps which appear as floating lights in the sky, when in fact they all align perfectly with the White House lights in front of the building.

NICAP investigator Francis Ridge wrote, "According to our photo researcher, Vicente-Juan Ballester Olmos, the photo is actually dated 1965 and the person who took the photo is unknown, so this is not only a non-UFO-event, the date is incorrect and all the items needed to document and properly qualify this photo are absent."[33] There is a short video clip claiming to be from July 12, 1952 showing the UFO fleet pass over the White House,[34] but any information regarding the authenticity of the footage is non-existent. Judging by the lack of eyewitness testimonies concerning that particular incident, it is fairly unlikely to be genuine but has yet to be disproven.

On Saturday, July 19 at 11:10 p.m. Washington National Airport air-traffic controller Edward Nugent spotted seven objects on his radar. Located 15 miles south-southwest of the city, the objects did not follow any established flight paths and no known aircraft were in the area at that time. Senior air-traffic controller Harry Barnes watched the strange objects on Nugent's radarscope and later wrote, "We knew immediately that a very strange situation existed . . . their movements were completely radical compared to those of ordinary aircraft."[35]

Barnes contacted the National Airport's other radar centre and was informed by Howard Cocklin, the controller on duty there, that they also had the objects on screen. Cocklin said he could actually see one of the objects by looking outside of the control tower window, saying that he saw "a bright orange light."

When the objects began appearing all over the radarscope and moving above the White House, Barnes called Andrews AFB which was ten miles away from the airport. From the base's control tower Airman William Brady reported sighting an "object which appeared to be like an orange ball of fire, trailing a tail... [it was] unlike anything I had ever seen before."[36] Before Brady had time to alert his colleagues in the tower, the object "took off at unbelievable speed" and vanished from sight. But half an hour later another object was reported back at the airport which was described as "an orange disk about 3,000 ft. altitude."

Shortly after, a Capital Airlines pilot, S.C. Pierman was waiting for permission to take off in his DC-4 when he was told that the tower radar had picked up more unknown objects closing in on his position. The objects described as six "white, tailless, fast-moving lights" came into view and Pierman was able to watch them from the cockpit for fourteen minutes. Barnes remained in radio contact with the pilot throughout and was able to confirm the presence of the UFOs being seen by Pierman. "Each sighting coincided with a pip we could see near his plane. When he reported that the light streaked off at a high speed, it disappeared on our scope," Barnes explained.

Staff Sgt. Charles Davenport also observed an orange-red light from Andrews AFB and insisted that the light "would appear to stand still, them make an abrupt change in direction and altitude...this happened several times."[37]

Harry Barnes stated, "There is no other conclusion I can reach but that for six hours on the morning of the 20th of July there were at least 10 unidentifiable objects moving above Washington .... I can safely deduce that they performed gyrations which no known aircraft could perform. By this I mean that our scope showed that they could make right angle turns and complete reversals of flight."[38]

Once the U.S. Air Force Defense Command were notified, several F-94 jets were sent to pursue the UFOs, however, any attempt to get close to one of them was futile because the UFOs disappeared every time the planes got airborne, reappearing only once the jets were back on the ground. Once they managed to sight the objects whilst in the air, any attempts to approach them were thwarted as the planes were either outrun by the UFOs or they simply vanished.

Pilot William Paterson told investigators, "I tried to make contact with the bogies below 1,000 ft. I was at my maximum speed but...I ceased chasing them because I saw no chance of overtaking them."

Newspapers reported on the events over the capital; the *Charleston Gazette* used the headline "Pilots Ordered to Shoot Down 'Saucers' in Range", along with the story that jet pilots were under orders to maintain a nationwide 24 hr. "alert" against "flying saucers" and shoot them down of necessary.[39]

The Washington Post printed the headline "'Saucer' Outran Jet, Pilot Reveals" and included an article which began with "Investigation On in Secret After Chase Over Capital".[40]And the headline from the *Cedar Rapids Gazette* in Iowa read, "Saucers Swarm Over Capital".

The publicity gathered momentum and questions were being answered from people in power to the people on the street. The supervisor of the Air Force's Project Blue Book investigation into the UFO mystery, USAF Captain Edward J. Ruppelt, was in Washington at the time of the sighting. He gave the official Air Force explanation for the sightings, claiming that the objects caught on radar were probably due to "temperature inversion", which in layman's terms relates to a weather phenomenon which gives the illusion of lights in the sky.

This explanation did not satisfy public curiosity; in fact it had the reverse affect. Dr. James McDonald from the University of Arizona believed that it was "physically impossible" that the objects tracked on the radarscopes could have been as a result of strange weather. Too many collaborative reports from in the air, on the ground and from three different radar stations seemed to disprove Ruppelt's dismissive suggestion.

The Pentagon quickly arranged a press conference in an attempt to pacify the nation and put to rest any security concerns that were beginning to surface. Gen. John A. Samford addressed the public on July 29, stating that the Air Force had managed to explain the "great bulk" of reports, "as hoaxes, as erroneously identified friendly aircraft, as meteorological or electronic phenomena or as light aberrations."

Continuing, Samford added, "However, there have been a certain percentage of this volume of reports that have been made by credible observers, of relatively incredible things. It is this group of observations that we now are attempting to resolve." He concluded by suggesting that they had found no reason to suspect any "conceivable threat to the United States" despite their current lack of understanding regarding the recent sightings.

The British Prime Minister Winston Churchill became aware of the increasing volume of UFO reports from across the Atlantic, and in August 1952 he wrote a personal minute to Lord Cherwell, Secretary of State for Air. "What does all this stuff about flying saucers amount to? What is the truth? Let me have a report at your convenience", requested Churchill. Cherwell responded by dismissing the American preoccupation with UFOs by claiming that they were simply "a product of mass psychology".[41]

The Minister of Supply, Duncan Sandys replied to Cherwell's comments, "There may, as you say, be no real evidence of the existence of flying saucer aircraft, but there is in my view ample evidence of some unfamiliar and unexplained phenomenon."[42]

The events which occurred during Washington that month sent shockwaves throughout the nation, particularly the Truman administration who were left with the responsibility of running the country despite the possibility of an outside threat from another world. President Truman however, was all too familiar with the UFO presence, and had already publicly announced his opinions on the subject two years previous. "I can assure you the flying saucers, given that they exist, are not constructed by any power on Earth"[43], he declared.

iii.   Eclipsed In Mexico

During the solar eclipse on July 11, 1991 thousands of excited citizens swarmed the streets of Mexico City to watch the magnificent event. Mayan Priests labeled this event as 'The Sixth Sun' and prophesised in 755 AD that the total eclipse of the Sun on that day would herald the beginning of 'cosmic awareness' for all humanity and bring about Earth changes.

American researcher Brit Elders wrote, "In the Codices, the tattered remnants of a once great civilisation, the Maya recorded their prophetic significance of the transition into the Sixth Sun as the harbinger of two life-altering occurrences: 'cosmic awareness through encounters with the masters of the stars and coming earth changes'." What transpired that afternoon at around 1:00 p.m. was witnessed by millions of people across the country and became one of the largest mass UFO sightings in history.

Many eyewitnesses armed with video cameras managed to capture the incident on film from many different vantage points in three different cities, including seventeen people from Mexico City alone. Each piece of footage revealed exactly the same event, a silvery UFO hovering high above Mexico City. The bright disc-shaped object had positioned itself beneath the eclipsing Sun precisely at the time when millions of people were looking to the skies. It was as if whatever was controlling it wanted to be seen.

The event which was perhaps the most significant mass UFO sighting of the last century was also the most unreported by the mainstream media, outside of Mexico.

The object hovered for almost half an hour before, during and after the eclipse was over. Attracted by the sheer volume of witnesses, teams of researchers from around Mexico, Japan and the United States flocked to the capital to investigate. One of those keen to interview eyewitnesses and collect data was Mexican UFO researcher Jaime Maussan.

Maussan went on to document the incredible incident in detail, always relating it to the ancient Mayan prophesies which foretold the coming of the 1991 solar eclipse and its global significance; "In the era of the Sixth Sun, all that was buried will be discovered. Truth shall be the seed of life and the sons of the Sixth Sun will be the ones who travel through the stars".[44]

Video footage of the UFO was simultaneously captured by Senor Arreguin, Sr. Alamilla, Sr. Meuta, Sr. Torres, Sr. Vallejo and Senora Hernandez. In one documentary film, Maussan put each individual video clip side by side to be viewed together as corroborative evidence, to prove that the mysterious object on screen was genuinely present at the time of the eclipse and was the same in each of the individually recorded videos. The 1991 incident was only the beginning, as the amount of UFO activity over Mexico has continued to increase since the occurrence of that remarkable event.

iv.   The Zimbabwe School Encounter

On 14th September, 1994 a UFO streaked across the sky over Southern Africa and two days later a private primary school in Ruwa, Zimbabwe, experienced a close encounter of the third kind. Pupils from Ariel School, located in the suburbs just twenty kilometers away from Harare, witnessed the bizarre incident near the school playground during recess.

Whilst the teachers were in a meeting, the children were playing in the school field during mid-morning break, when out of the blue they saw three silver balls in the sky. With a flash of light they were gone, only to reappear somewhere else. The mysterious orbs came in and out of sight three times before starting to descend towards the school, and then at approximately 10:15 a.m.

one came and landed (or hovered) in the rough woody area adjacent to the playing field.

The uncertainty to whether the craft landed or hovered is due to the fact that the sixty-two witnesses were only young children and some gave clearer testimonies than others because of their age and general awareness. The reports taken as a whole were very similar, and the overall consensus of opinion was that an object did land about 100 metres from the edge of the school field where the children were stood.

Once the silver object made its way into the woods, many of the children stopped what they were doing to go and see what had landed at the back of the field. Amazingly, the children all reported witnessing the appearance of two small beings, both dressed in tight-fitting shiny black clothing. One young observer remarked, "I felt scared because I've never seen such a person like that."[45] Another girl claimed, "They were kind of, just like looking at us. They were like, kind of astonished at what we were."

The small men were described as having large oval-shaped eyes and shoulder length black hair, with one of the figures stood by the side of the "ship" and the other was said to be running up and down on top of the silver craft. Once the being on the top became aware of the children's presence, they both quickly re-entered the object and quickly disappeared.

The children all ran back into the school en masse screaming, alerting the teachers to the incredible scenes that they had just witnessed. A few days after the incident, a BBC reporter visited the school to document the case, and many of the children were promptly interviewed regarding their personal experiences of the event by Harvard Professor of Psychiatry, John E. Mack and Cynthia Hind, MUFON'S coordinator for Africa, and author of the book *UFOs Over Africa*.

Following requests to draw what they saw, the children produced between 30 and 40 pictures, all of them strikingly similar in content and appearance. Most of the drawings contained a saucer type craft, some trees and small child-size men with large black eyes. Many of the eyewitnesses described receiving some form of message in their heads whilst looking at one of the creatures and the overall theme of the seemingly telepathic communications was of general environmental concern towards our planet. Others expressed the view that the 'aliens' were warning the children of some future cataclysmic event that could be avoided if the children were to take some responsibility as they matured.

Although there is a lack of physical evidence to support this mass sighting, only the testimonies of a group of children with no video or photographic proof; the sheer consistency of the individual recollections of the event along with the minor details relayed verbally to researchers through interviews along with their drawings, lends a certain amount of credibility to the encounter.

Being in Africa and of such tender ages, the media influence on the children was minimal and any preconceived knowledge of UFOs and aliens is unlikely to have been sufficient enough to have affected them. One child explained she had found traces of evidence that something had landed in the woods, saying that "where the spaceship had landed – all the insects and ants were all dead and there was a big black mark there."[46] The scorched grass and earth at the precise location of the alleged incident was also confirmed by researchers at the time.

Many of the kids suffered psychologically as a result of the strange encounter, some were given counselling and others claimed that they continued to dream about the incident for months afterwards. One girl explained how it had affected her, "After about a year I stopped dreaming about it. I dreamt that the same one I saw came into my bedroom and he took me from my bed. And then I woke up and screamed."

Having interviewed all of the child eyewitnesses, John Mack reached the conclusion that the children exhibited no signs of behavioural problems and ruled out the possibility that their descriptions were the result of a mass delusion. "They experienced very powerful encounters with these beings and they're left with the rather disturbing fact that this seems to be what it is. And it seems to have no other psychiatric explanation."[47]

v.   Phoenix Lights

As people stood outside their homes in Phoenix, Arizona and looked skywards towards the Hale-Bopp comet which was passing by, many local residents witnessed a sky borne anomalous object which would later be referred to as 'the Phoenix Lights'. This particular mass UFO sighting, one of the largest and spectacular in modern UFO history, was seen by thousands of local residents on March 13, 1997 as it moved slowly and silently across the Phoenix skyline. Described as a vast, gun-metal black triangle with huge round lights, the object which was first spotted at 8:15 p.m. continued to travel through the night sky for 106 minutes in total before finally disappearing from view.

One eyewitness Sue Watson said, "It had five big lights in front and it was the shape of a boomerang."[48] Mike Watson, another local who watched the lights in triangle formation heading straight towards him insisted that, "it was a solid craft, silent, very low to the ground." Continuing, he added, "And the thing that took me was the size. Profoundly enormous, profoundly massive, we don't even have a shopping centre this big."

Seen from different vantage points across the city, the sighting caught many people's attention and public interest in the unknown craft was bordering on hysteria over the days and weeks that followed. Excessive media coverage only served to fuel the fire, as residents were beginning to demand answers which would sufficiently explain what the mysterious lights could have been.

The previous evening, retired Lieutenant and Navajo Ranger John Dover watched the mysterious and silent lights flying over a Navajo reservation in Leupp, Northern Arizona. Dover, who paid regular visits to the Indian reservations during his time as a ranger, claimed that seeing UFOs was a regular occurrence for the residents there.

As part of an agency called the Navajo Nation Rangers, Dover had the freedom to investigate paranormal cases which were constantly being reported to the Police. Policing the Navajo reservations with his partner, Stan Milford, Dover took paranormal reports from the Navajo very seriously and together they investigated some very interesting cases and even found physical evidence in some cases which helped reinforce witness testimonies. "We finally started doing UFO cases; we had some major cases where landings and occupants were seen. Very unusual cases, very large craft", Dover stated.

Dr. Lynne Kitei has written books and made a documentary about the lights, which she also saw that night in Arizona. "Most things can be explained, only a small percentage cannot and just because we don't have the technology to definitively define what these things are doesn't mean they aren't real", she explained.

According to Dr. Kitei, "The 'Phoenix Lights' is being considered around the world as the most important and most documented mass sighting in modern history."[49]

Over the weeks that followed, more than 700 witnesses called in reports to local officials and the National UFO Reporting Center, a private organisation based in Seattle. Governor of Arizona, Fyfe Symington III was coming under increasing pressure to supply some answers to the public regarding the lights. Shortly after, he gave a press conference in which he openly denied any knowledge of the incident and even mocked those residents claiming they saw something by dressing up a colleague in an alien costume and declaring that they had caught the culprit. It wasn't until fifteen years after the sighting that Symington admitted, "I knew more about the lights over Phoenix than I let on."

The evening of March 13, the Governor was eating his evening meal at home with his family when he saw the reports on the news. Deciding to personally investigate the matter further, Symington drove out to Sumida Park to see for himself what all the fuss was about. Within a few minutes of his arrival in the park, he looked up and saw what so many others had been describing; "This great big massive craft, probably 3 or 4,000 feet, took out a whole chunk of the sky," he said. Adding, "And you could see other aircraft in the distance but the airplanes looked like little toothpicks compared to the size of this craft".[50]

The official explanation given at the time was that the Arizona National Guard had sent out flying A-10s to drop high-intensity magnesium flares between 9:30 and 10 p.m. Although it is accepted that the flares *were* actually launched that night, the video footage, photographic evidence and multiple sightings across a wide expanse of the city confirmed that the lights from the flares were a completely separate event and were *not* the cause of all the reports.

When the Air Force was questioned over the appearance of the lights they avidly denied reports suggesting that they had sent out fighter planes to investigate the phenomenon. However, an anonymous phone call from an airman at Luke Air Force Base to the National UFO Reporting Center was recorded on the morning of March 14, in which he claimed that shortly after 8:30 p.m., Luke AFB *did* indeed send up two F-15 fighter jets.

"Apparently, we got a call from Prescott Valley Airport, a small airport north of us, reporting an object that had a near miss with a small Cessna" said the airman. "The call came approximately 8:32, that they encountered something over Phoenix, Arizona, over the area of 7th Avenue and Indian School Road. They don't know what it was."

One of the F-15 pilots wrote a statement which stated that they had followed the aircraft as it travelled on a straight-line course heading towards Sky Harbor Airport, at around 18,000 ft. before descending to 10,500 ft. He also described seeing five distinct lights in a triangular pattern and when he landed back at the base, the facility was immediately closed – a total lockdown, as "all hell broke loose", according to the insider. Whilst reporting the incident the airman declared, "The command pilot of this particular flight...I've never seen this man scared, and he was scared to death. He's not sure what it was."

The debate over the origins of the Phoenix lights continues to this day, as the event may have passed over fifteen years ago but the memory of that colossal UFO remains firmly etched in the minds of all those who were looking on in awe.

ANATOMY OF A SPACECRAFT

The elusive nature of UFOs has meant that not many people can offer accurate scientific explanations as to how spacecraft actually function. Robert Scott Lazar is one man who claims to have worked at a once-secret facility known as S4 near Area 51 in Nevada; back-engineering retrieved flying discs in order to understand how the propulsion systems of such incredibly advanced machines operate.

Bob Lazar, born January 26, 1959 in Coral Gables, Florida, is a physicist with a degree in Physics and Electronics Technology. In the early part of the eighties, Lazar worked at Meson Physics Facility at Los Alamos National Laboratory, New Mexico, before being hired by the head of Atomic Energy Commission and 'father of the hydrogen bomb', Edward Teller.

It was at the S4 facility on Nellis AFB in Central Nevada, just fifteen miles south of the infamous Area 51 site at Groom Lake, where Lazar was employed as a senior staff physicist between December 1988 and April 1989. Paid by the U.S. Navy, Lazar's ID number was 46 – 1007639. But how did a man with Teller's credentials and reputation end up hiring the unknown Bob Lazar?

Whilst working at Los Alamos in 1982, Lazar had designed and built a jet car which made the front page of the local newspaper. The article in the *Los Alamos Monitor* read, "LA man joins the jet set – at 200 miles an hour."

Edward Teller was giving a speech at Los Alamos on the same day as the article was printed, and Lazar managed to meet him before he started his talk and together they discussed the science behind his jet car. Lazar sent a resume to Teller in 1988, inquiring about the possibility of finding some employment. Teller rang Lazar to inform him that a position had just been taken but instead gave him a number to call regarding another job, which he did and the rest is history.

Lazar joined a program that consisted of three projects; Project Galileo which dealt with gravity propulsion, Project Sidekick which was about beam weapons with a neutron source focused by a gravity lens and Project Looking Glass experimented with the physics of seeing back in time (see Chapter 9). Lazar's focus was working on Galileo to see if the technology used in recovered flying discs could be duplicated using Earth materials, this was done by dismantling a finished product to see how it operates, a technique referred to as back engineering.

Lazar met his immediate supervisor Dennis Mariani at McCarran airport on his first day working for EG&G and together they flew to the Nellis Test Range. Both Area 51 and Sector Four (S-4) are located in the northeast corner of Nellis. To reach the facility from the airstrip Mariani and Lazar boarded a bus with blacked-out windows which took them down an unpaved road for nearly half an hour before reaching S-4 near the Papoose Mountains, by the Papoose dry lake bed.

The S-4 installation is built into the mountain with nine huge hangars with doors angled at sixty degrees which are covered with a sand-textured coating in order to blend in with the side of the mountain and the desert floor.

As Lazar's new workplace was the test site for the most experimental aircraft such as the Stealth fighter, the SR-71 Blackbird and the Vought V-173 among others, he assumed that he had been employed to work on the propulsion system for the latest model of fighter jet. Instead, he was to be part of a twenty-two man team working within Project Galileo where he was given a high level security clearance named *Majestic*, thirty-eight levels above his previous *Q* level. His ID badge had two diagonal blue stripes in the corner, one light and one dark, and beneath his photograph was the ID number E-6722MAJ [see SOURCES].

Lazar explained that the letters MAJ were an abbreviation of Majestic, the name of the group responsible for all covert extraterrestrial activities as covered in later chapters of this book. The bottom of the ID card showed where Lazar was allowed access to – S4, D5, ETL and WX.

Lazar was advised to read over 120 documents in a briefing room, which would inform him of his real purpose at S4 and the true nature of what was taking place there. According to written information which was contained in blue folders, the spacecraft technology he was due to work on was brought here by alien beings from the Zeta Reticulae 1 and 2 star systems located in the Reticulum constellation which can only be seen from the southern hemisphere.

The papers offered a detailed insight into their world, stating that the beings were from Reticulum 4 (fourth planet from Zeta Reticulae 2, approx. 30 light years from Earth), with our Sun being referred to as SOL and Earth being the third planet from the Sun was referred to as SOL 3. One day on Reticulum 4 is apparently ninety Earth days long.

As for the extraterrestrial beings or Zeta Reticulans; they were described as between three and four feet tall, weighing about 25-30 pounds with greyish skin, large heads and almond shaped wrap-around eyes. They have no hair and only sleight mouth, nose and ear positions. The entities themselves claimed to have been visiting Earth for a very long time and even had photographic evidence which they contended was over ten thousand years old.

Interestingly, they also informed us that man was actually a product of 'externally corrected evolution' and the human race as a species had been genetically altered 65 times throughout history. Although such a notion may be hard to swallow on first hearing, there are many different sources pertaining to very similar theories on human creation and evolution, biblical scholar Zecharia Sitchin being just one such advocate. In the papers humans were referred to as 'containers'. Despite the fact that Lazar claims to have definitely read the briefing documents, he also insisted that he was not in a position to vouch for the authenticity of the information contained within.

The most remarkable aspect of Bob Lazar's testimony however, is the detailed scientific explanations he offers on how the propulsion systems used on spacecraft actually operate. With at least nine extraterrestrial craft being stored at the S4 facility, he was escorted into a hangar where he was permitted to examine a disk which Lazar later named 'the sport model' due to its sleek appearance. This particular model had already been test-flown several times before Lazar arrived on the scene and would continue to be flown on Wednesday nights during his tenure at S4. Other models varied in shape in size, from 'the top hat' to the 'jello mould', all were very different in appearance.

Initially upon first inspection, Lazar thought that the sport model was one of the latest aircraft to have been secretly manufactured by human hand but he would soon realize that the object before him had not been created using Earth technology. One brief test flight conducted inside the hangar showed Lazar how the craft could ascend vertically before hovering in almost complete silence, a feat which in itself should be impossible considering the size of the object, roughly 16 feet tall and 40 feet in diameter. Whilst not in use and not energised, the disc sits on its underside or 'belly'.

The craft was comprised of a metal exterior skin, the colour of unpolished stainless steel, with a door located on the upper half of the disc with only the bottom portion of the door wrapping around the central lip of the vehicle. The interior is divided into three levels starting with a lower level which houses three gravity amplifiers and amplifier guides which are used to increase the size of the Gravity A waves. According to Lazar, there are two types of gravity waves, the other being Gravity B which is the vast gravity of which most are familiar with. The reason for increasing the Gravity A waves is due to their minute size as they exist solely at an atomic level, barely extending beyond the perimeter of an atom. Amplification of these waves is necessary until they become large enough to distort vast amounts of space-time. The gravity amplifiers do not stay on continuously; rather they can be pulsed to achieve the desired amount of power.

On the central level directly above the amplifiers sits the reactor, along with the control consoles and two seats, both of which were far too low to the floor and too small to be functional for adult human beings. Lazar never had access to the upper portion of the disc.

Inside the craft the walls are divided into archways, one of which Lazar witnessed becoming transparent once the disc was energised, revealing the outside just like a window. Once in a transparent state for a short while, Lazar claims that a unknown form of writing began to appear on the archway, writing unlike any he had ever seen before, not belonging to our alphabet and not like any scientific or mathematical symbols used on Earth.

So how did this technological marvel actually operate? One might assume that in order to traverse vast distances through space that it would be necessary to travel at the speed of light which is around 669 mph. This is not the case. These craft which are used specifically for travelling interstellar distances do not travel in the manner we are accustomed to on this planet. Bob Lazar explained, "The truth of the matter is that travelling these distances does require a level of technology that man has not yet achieved. But it has nothing to do with flying in a linear mode near the speed of light."[51]

A reactor which serves as the power source is fuelled by Element 115 and only by converting this matter into energy, by combining matter with anti-matter, is any power generated. Lazar explains that the Element 115 can only be inserted into the reactor once it has been machined into a triangular shape; it then becomes the source of the Gravity A wave as well as the target which must be bombarded with protons in order to release the anti-matter.

When one of the flying discs travels in close proximity with another source of gravity such as Earth's, the Gravity A waves which propagates outwards from the disc is phase shifted into the Gravity B wave which emanates outwardly from the Earth, thus creating the lift required to manoeuvre the craft.

The distortion of space-time around the disc increases as the intensity of the gravitational field around the disc increases. The effect of invisibility is created once the space-time around the disc reaches maximum distortion as the space-time distortion takes place 360 degrees around the disc. If one were to look at the disc from above at this point then the space-time distortion would be in the shape of a doughnut if Lazar's testimony is accurate.

Doubts over the authenticity of Lazar's claims have often led to him being discredited along with the information he purports so adamantly to be true. Investigative television reporter George Knapp at KLAS-TV in Las Vegas was the first person to take Lazar seriously enough to air his incredible story for the first time. His story went public on Channel 8 in December 1988, after recording an interview with him at the house of Lazar's friend, John Lear, although Lazar only appeared in silhouette using the pseudonym 'Dennis'.

Struggling to gather any background information confirming Lazar's outrageous claims, Knapp constantly came up against opposition. Government officials denied ever employing Lazar at LANL; in fact they claimed they had never even heard of him. But when Knapp dug a little deeper he managed to find Lazar's name in the LANL telephone directory, forcing officials from Los Alamos to begrudgingly concede that he had in fact worked there for a short time. Even officials at the hospital where Bob was born denied the fact until Knapp managed to track down the doctor who delivered him as a baby.

Once Lazar's employment at S4 was terminated, he had his security clearance revoked along with the deletion of his entire civilian background. Government agents destroyed or concealed all evidence pertaining to any of his academic records, former employment, diplomas, enrolment records and receipts, thesis notes and even university paraphernalia. Lazar knew too much and it was deemed necessary to discredit the man as much as possible, especially once he went public with his story of working with alien technology as part of a top secret U.S. Government black project.

In order to authenticate his claims, Lazar underwent regressive hypnosis and four lie-detector tests. The hypnosis sessions showed no signs of deception and indicated that he had in fact been involved in some form of flying saucer program. The last two lie-detector tests were conducted by Terry Tavernatti; an ex-police officer who was performing such tests on a daily basis in the casino industry. Hired by KLAS-TV, Tavernatti concluded, "If he's lying he ought to be in Hollywood, because he gave absolutely no physiological indications of attempting deception."[52]

During an interview with John Lear and Gene Huff on *Coast to Coast AM Radio* in 2009, host George Knapp stated, "They allowed

Bob to spill the beans, allowed us to tell the story, and in the eyes of a lot of people discredited him entirely."[53]

Attempting to validate his extraordinary claims Lazar managed to arrange for some witnesses to watch flying saucer test flights over the S-4 facility in Nevada as they stood at the edge of the base on March 22 and 29, 1989. The objects seen by those in attendance were uniformly described as being UFOs and they appeared where Lazar claimed they would, and at precisely the time that he said they would.

Although Lazar's story may seem too implausible to many, the concept of alien visitation, crashed flying discs and reverse-engineering extends way beyond the experience and testimony of one American scientist. As highlighted by the emergence of the Disclosure Project, hundreds of high ranking officials from the military, politics and NASA to name but a few, have come forward declaring that the largest conspiracy the world has ever known exists to the present day; a conspiracy which has cloaked the extraterrestrial phenomenon in complete secrecy for over half a century.

2

FINGERPRINTS OF DECEPTION

Through official secrecy and ridicule, many citizens are led to believe that unidentified flying objects are nonsense. To hide the facts the Air Force has silenced its personnel.

Admiral Roscoe H. Hillenkoetter, First Director of the CIA (New York Times, February 28, 1960)

IF THE EXTRATERRESTRIAL SCENARIO is authentic and firmly grounded in reality and the Earth *is* actually playing host to more than one species of intelligent being, then the question of how such an astounding fact has remained concealed from public view must be raised. The concept of an alien threat towards humanity has been casually expressed through science-fiction writing for years, but considering such a situation as plausibly accurate is far from being a generally accepted notion. Regardless of their true intent, the reality of extraterrestrial life on our planet would in all likelihood be considered a threat to our existence, as it not only opens up an infinite world of possibilities but also contradicts the very foundations of structured human society and the long held belief systems to which so many adhere.

There is no question that unexplained objects exhibiting unearthly manoeuvrability have been flitting through our skies for a very long time. Ancient societies with significantly diminished access to information and knowledge must have interpreted such sightings as Godly or ethereal expressions of an unknown force, with no point of reference in which to turn to for an explanation. These days, we have the ability to peruse a vast number of information outlets in order to assist our quest for answers of the unexplained, even though arriving at a satisfactory conclusion bound in veracity may be as difficult to come by as it always was.

Some researchers may rightly contend that the authorities have been covertly aware of the UFO phenomenon since prior to World War II, and that the appearance of the "foo-fighters" reported by high ranking members of the military establishment during the war had alerted even higher authorities that there existed some unknown vehicular technology which was being controlled by unknown means. It would appear that despite a history of unexplained flying machines exploiting our airspace over the ages, such as the Vimanas described in ancient Indian texts, that until recent times, an explanation of the origin of these aerial mysteries has continued to confound us. With the foo-fighters teasing the Air Force pilots by flying alongside them and out-manoeuvring them, the heads of the chain of command must have wanted nothing more than to capture one of those allusive crafts for closer inspection in an attempt to further understand not only the science involved in their creation, but also their origin of manufacture.

Their curiosity would soon be quelled in mid-1940 when an object seen zigzagging across the state of New Mexico in the United States of America, was tracked by radar installations on Tuesday, July 1, 1947. The unidentified flying object exhibited unusual manoeuvrability and flew at unconventional speeds, and on Independence Day three days later, the mysterious object disappeared from the radar screens and was believed to have crashed somewhere in the state. The discovery of the debris of an unknown object on a ranch, thirty-five miles north of the town of Roswell, would change the authorities' understanding of the existence of extraterrestrials on Earth undeterminably.

It is from the year 1947 that a cover-up of monumental proportions appears to have been orchestrated in order to deny the public access to information deemed too dangerous for mainstream consumption. Protocols were set in place instructing the United States military to conceal and deny all information pertaining to the reality of extraterrestrial visitation, in an attempt to protect the country from this newly found threat to national security. It was during the late forties and early fifties that the U.S. government's policy towards UFOs and their occupants was formulated.

Retrospectively, the decision to keep the public in the dark could be considered as irresponsible, selfish and deceitful, and has only led to a world of confusion and misunderstanding on the subject; a world brimming with conspiratorial ramblings and unsubstantiated guesswork, where to the majority in the Western World - the term 'alien' or 'extraterrestrial' brings forth memories of popular science-fiction movies rather than a serious subject firmly planted in reality. To get to the heart of this great deception, it is imperative that one first pursues its dubious beginnings, if one is to gain some form of understanding as to the scale of the conspiracy along with the reasons for its inception.

THE UFO WAVE OF 1947

The year 1947 holds great significance in the field of UFO research and the conspiracy to withhold all information regarding matters of extraterrestrial activity from the public domain. Many significant American organisations were created in the latter part of that year; organisations that would cease control of the alien situation and put into place set protocols on how to deal with highly classified matters of this sort. Secrecy and deception would become the standard tactics employed over the following decades, and such methodologies first introduced at that critical time in history set a precedent which continues to the present day.

The Kenneth Arnold UFO sightings over the Cascade Mountains in Washington on June 24, 1947, led to the common usage of the term "flying saucer", as the Associated Press reported Arnold's story of flying objects, which in his words "flew like a saucer would if you skipped it across the water". This one incident which preceded 'the Roswell Incident' by ten days has come to be considered the birth of the modern UFO era, which as research reveals, occurred during the year that heralded one of the largest UFO waves in history.

A report written in August 1949 by the Air Material Command Intelligence Department, based at Wright-Patterson AFB in Dayton, Ohio, stated that "Within the month following Arnold's report, the number of incidents reached a peak that remained unsurpassed for any like period covered by this report."

It is worth noting that on July 16, 1945, the first ever test of a nuclear weapon took place in the Jornada del Muerto Desert basin, about thirty-five miles southeast of Socorro in New Mexico at the new White Sands Proving Ground. Code-named "Trinity", the first detonation of a nuclear device was conducted by the United States Army and acted as a precursor to the atomic bombings of the Japanese cities Hiroshima and Nagasaki in the August of 1945. Developed by the nefarious Manhattan Project, which was undertaken using the innovations of the theoretical physicist J. Robert Oppenheimer, American airmen dropped two nuclear weapons, one named "Little Boy" on Hiroshima on the 6th of August followed by "Fat Man" over Nagasaki three days later. Is it plausible to assume that the rise in UFO activity that has been documented during 1947 came as a direct response to the nuclear activity performed by the American military?

The tests which succeeded "Trinity" took place during "Operation Crossroads" on July 1 and 25, 1946, at Bikini Atoll in the Micronesian Islands of the Pacific Ocean. Captain Otto Schneider of the United States Navy, formerly a member of the S.S. in Nazi Germany, worked in a medical capacity in "Operation Crossroads" as well as laying claim to the invention of a high-speed camera which was employed during the Bikini Atoll nuclear tests. According to his son Philip Schneider, the photographs of the mushroom clouds forming which his camera captured during the explosions, revealed a number of UFOs fleeing the scene that weren't spotted in real time.

The irresponsible human behaviour exhibited during this period apparently attracted the attention of some unknown visitors to our planet, resulting in the subsequent UFO wave of 1947. Surely it is no coincidence that the state of New Mexico which became the first state in world history to host a nuclear bomb test, has become such a hotspot for UFO activity. And to add more fuel to the fire, below the town of Dulce in New Mexico lies an underground military base believed by many to be the heart of a joint alien/government clandestine scheme to manipulate and control the human species.

Former civilian employee June Crain who worked for the US Government at Wright Patterson AFB from 1942 – 1952, believes there is a definite connection between the influx of UFO sightings following the nuclear tests. Before she died she told James E. Clarkson in a recorded interview, "They think the reason that became very noticeable was when we detonated the atomic bomb, 'cause that was when it really got heavy, that was when they got hot and heavy with sightings."[54]

A retired U.S. Army Field Artillery non-commissioned officer named Jan Aldrich, began an investigation into the UFO sightings from the year 1947, and started by sifting through North American and foreign newspaper articles from that time period in search of relevant articles. Beginning in the mid-1990s, PROJECT 1947 was established as "an inquiry into the UFO wave of 1947", but over time the project expanded into a "worldwide effort to document the origins of the modern UFO phenomenon" with the help of volunteers willing to continue and further the investigation by sharing their discoveries with Aldrich so that he could process them for the published PROJECT 1947 volumes.

After screening more than 3,200 publications worldwide, Aldrich discovered over a thousand documented UFO incidents between June 24 and July 15, 1947 alone, and those were only the reports that were put into print of which he successfully located. Thousands more incidents may remain undiscovered in articles yet unearthed by researchers, according to Aldrich. More information has surfaced through the Freedom of Information Act (FOIA) and the continued support of a wealth of intrepid UFO researchers aiding Aldrich with his project, which intends to "enhance the future of UFO research by establishing a solid collection of official UFO documents, newspaper articles and personal accounts from the beginning of the modern UFO era."[55] The *UFO Research Coalition* published the first volume of material called *PROJECT 1947: A Preliminary Report*, which includes an extensive collection of 1947 UFO reports and newspaper accounts from the U.S.A. but is also supplemented by a compilation of significant sightings from other countries.

Over 850 UFO reports appeared in the U.S. media by the end of July, 1947; Kenneth Arnold's sighting being one of the first. Approximately 150 of those reports made their way into the files of Technical Intelligence, T-2, at Wright Field. The National Archives in College Park, Maryland, presently contain such files as part of the USAF Project Blue Book. The American newspapers of that year were rife with stories of unusual objects seen in the skies, some bordering on the ridiculous whilst others held enough credulity to finally end up in the FBI records along with many other reported sightings that made the press.

Included in the FBI vaults is an article which was printed in July 1947 in a Wisconsin newspaper called the *Milwaukee Sentinel*:

"Seen in 36 States – First sighted June 25 and greeted generally with scornful laughs, the objects have been reported every day since by observers in 36 states. Most of the objects were reported seen July 4. Such competent observers as airline pilots said they had seen the totally unexplained discs or saucers, larger than aircraft and flying in "loose formation" at high speed. They were described as flying with an undulating motion at heights of 10,000 feet and less. Some described them as luminous or glowing."

The frenzy of interest in flying saucers was most definitely fuelled by the media following the Kenneth Arnold sightings in the June of that year. Some reports in the FBI vaults clearly demonstrate that a minority of American citizens, inspired by the Arnold case, decided to try for some publicity themselves by building disc-like objects out of all sorts of common household materials, and making them airborne so as to attract some attention.

One report dated July 12, 1947, states that following a phone call from a Sergeant of the Maryland Police Department, a "flying disc" had been spotted by locals who had informed the Police. An examination of the object ensued and the Sergeant declared that "it had been made from a Gulf Oil sign and the top of a garbage can and had been painted with aluminium paint. It had been recently painted because the paint was still wet. Attached to it were a dry cell battery, a flashlight bulb, some wires and a buzzer."

Another recorded memorandum from the same date but which occurred at Black River Falls in Wisconsin, said that someone "had found a 17 inch disc which appeared to have been possibly made out of cardboard painted with silver airplane dope. In the center was a tube and a small motor with a propeller attached to the side."

The press released another story with the headline "Priest hears a 'Bang,' Discovers a Circular Blade With Teeth; Other Disks 'Seen'", whilst another paper printed the same story but wrote "Priest Finds 'Whirring' Disc In Yard and Holds It for FBI."

Such unnecessary hoaxing only succeeded in confusing matters more and filled the morning papers with page after page of UFO nonsense. One can only surmise that such banal stories may have been printed with a little encouragement from the higher authorities as a distraction from the more legitimate cases which were undoubtedly taking place. Alternatively, upon reading some of the FBI memos of the day, it appears that following the Arnold testimony, anything unusual witnessed in American airspace was to be considered a threat until the information was examined in more detail and the possible threat nullified.

The *Milwaukee Sentinel* mentions the Arnold case in relation to the UFO phenomenon, and a sense that some sightings are of a more serious concern was established:

"First published records of the phenomena occurred June 25. Kenneth Arnold, Boise, Idaho, businessman pilot, told of seeing nine of the discs flying in formation at 1,200 miles an hour over the Cascade Mountains. SEEN BY 200 – Arnold's account was taken lightly. Various explanations were offered – "reflections", "persistent vision", "snow blindness". Soon afterwards other individuals – in New Mexico, Missouri, California and other states – reported they had also seen the flying objects.

Then on Independence Day 200 persons in one group and 60 in another saw them in Idaho. Hundreds of others in Oregon, Washington and other western states reported seeing them. July 4 also brought first reports of the flying discs from east of the Mississippi. Since then they have been reported seen in widely separated sections of the country."

ALL ROADS LEAD TO ROSWELL

Despite the voluminous array of documented UFO sightings which emerged during 1947, that year will always be synonymous with the reported events which took place near the American town of Roswell during the July of that year. It has become the most researched and well documented UFO incident in living memory, partly due to the negative connotations of the ensuing cover-up by American authorities. The fact that the Associated Press were involved in the distribution of the contradictory and changing facts of the Roswell case as it unfolded, only succeeded in adding weight to a conspiracy which could have been kept completely under wraps if the media hadn't been alerted so quickly.

The Roswell incident first began on Tuesday, the 1st of July, 1947, when an unusual speeding object was being tracked by radar in New Mexico. The next day, an object flying above Roswell was first sighted and by Thursday, some Washington officials had flown in especially to observe the object for themselves. The object vanished from the radar screens late on the Friday night of the 4th of July, leading the observers to assume the object had crashed. Indeed an object did crash, more than one in fact, as further research has revealed. Possibly four UFO crashes occurred on the night of July 4, remarkably all within the same state.

What became known as the Roswell crash happened on the property of a ranch belonging to twin brothers named Henry S.

Foster and Jasper B. Foster. The Foster family owned a substantial amount of land in New Mexico and Texas at that time. William "Mac" Brazel was the rancher in charge of the Foster ranch and was also the first to discover the remnants of the crash.

According to Brazel, the debris field extended over a vast area, three-quarters of a mile long and several hundred feet wide, and the lay of the scattered debris was so dense that his sheep were unable to walk through it. This created a serious problem for the rancher, as the debris had landed between the flock and the water, and Brazel knew it was imperative that his sheep reach the water in order to drink.

The next to arrive at the scene was the Roswell Volunteer Fire Department. It wasn't until the Sunday that the military were notified of the incident, following the suggestion from Sheriff Wilcox to Mr. Brazel that it should be officially reported. Head of intelligence, Major Jesse A. Marcel, was sent by Colonel William Blanchard to investigate the incident, subsequently spoke with Brazel later in the day and became the first official to personally witness the mysterious fallen debris. By the time Monday arrived, the Foster ranch was teeming with military personnel.

Major Marcel described the debris as a strange metal similar to aluminium foil, but once crumpled into a ball it would straighten out completely and return to its original smooth state. Rancher William Brazel described many large pieces of the metal as being unusually lightweight and of a dull grey colour, which could not be cut or burned. Marcel followed orders to fly with the debris to Carswell AFB in Fort Worth, Texas, before returning home to his family to show them what he had obtained. Marcel's son, Jesse Jr. recalled seeing strange markings on the unusual material which consisted of "different geometric shapes, leaves and circles" not unlike hieroglyphics.

Despite having being advised to keep quiet, Major Marcel explained that what he witnessed was nothing like what he had experienced before. "It was not anything from this Earth. That I'm quite sure of," he said. "Being in Intelligence, I was familiar with all materials used in aircraft and in air travel. This was nothing like this. It could not have been."

Jack Trowbridge was a 1st Lieutenant assigned to Roswell in April, 1947, which resulted in him working in Intelligence alongside Major Marcel. He recalls handling the material from the debris field and described it thusly; "The material had some peculiar properties, for instance it looked like Hershey bar wrappings, but you squeeze it up in your hand as hard as you could – let go – and it returned originally to the original shape – instantly."[56]

In a signed affidavit from 2002, Walter G. Haut went on record confirming that he too had handled the Roswell debris whilst stationed at the Roswell AFB in 1947, serving as the base Public Information Officer. On Tuesday, July 8, whilst attending the regularly scheduled staff meeting, samples of the wreckage were passed around the table. Haut recalled "It was unlike any material I had or have ever seen in my life. Pieces which resembled metal foil, paper thin yet extremely strong, and pieces with unusual markings along their length were handled from man to man, each voicing their opinion. No one was able to identify the crash debris." This type of material has been termed 'memory metal'.

Due to the secretive nature of the Roswell case there remains much controversy concerning the details of the incidents, and like pieces of a puzzle, the whole picture has become somewhat disjointed due to certain elements of the story lacking true clarification which the passing of time has only helped to diminish. Deeper investigation reveals that there was more than one crash site near Roswell that July. One location was the much reported site at the Foster ranch, approximately thirty miles southeast of the town of Corona, whilst the other debris field is believed to have been about forty miles north of Roswell as documented by Col. Philip Corso in his book *The Day After Roswell*.

Despite the many books detailing the events that unfolded during the summer of 1947, it is unlikely that any one author has succeeded in reporting the facts with 100 per cent accuracy. The U.S. officials involved in taking over the situation accomplished what was required of them, and managed to contain much of the information whilst deceiving the public into believing that nothing out of the ordinary had taken place. The fact that even today, information concerning the Roswell incident is still marred with inconsistencies and steeped in speculation and confusion is testament to the success of the deception.

As author Jim Marrs wrote, "It is a fact that this period marked a definite turn in the military's response to UFO's. Prior to

Roswell, the military had been intensely interested in UFOs and open to the idea that they represented extraterrestrial visitation. But with the knowledge gained from the Roswell incident, the military became secretive and publicly offered every mundane explanation possible to account for UFO sightings."[57]

One reason for so much conflicting evidence arising from the Roswell incident is due to the fact that there seems to have been more than one crash. One crash site was near Shaw Mountain, south of the Plains of San Augustin in western New Mexico, reported by eyewitness Gerald Anderson as having taken place on July 4. According to researcher Chuck Wade, incidentally a friend of the Brazel family, the San Augustin crash was likely caused by a U.S. mobile high-powered radar unit originally stationed at Moriarty near the centre of New Mexico, which interfered with the UFOs electromagnetic energy field thus downing the craft. Wade suggests that several craft were intentionally sabotaged during a three year period from 1945-1948. With regards to the San Augustin crash, Wade insists that the military must have been fully aware of the incident as it unfolded, as they arrived in their droves to recover the alien vehicle within hours of impact.

The crash north of Roswell took the military by surprise since they were unaware that their radar had successfully hit another vehicle, yet alone the whereabouts of the impact site. This would explain why the military personnel stationed at the Roswell AFB dealt with the situation with no apparent knowledge of the crash in the plains of San Augustin. Information was on a strict need to know basis, and information concerning the events of July 4th on the plains of San Augustin were clearly withheld from everyone, except those giving orders higher up and the military personnel involved in the retrieval of the crashed disc and its occupants.

Another crash which apparently occurred simultaneously to the aforementioned incidents at San Augustin and north of Roswell was reported in a signed affidavit by James Ragsdale, stating that on July 4, he personally witnessed a UFO crash into the north slope of the Capitan Mountains, southeast of Roswell near the Pine Lodge. Ragsdale also described the scattered debris on the mountainside as looking like "tin foil and would go back to its original shape when crumpled in your hand."

He claimed that he and his friend had climbed down to get a good look at the crashed object saying that "When we looked into the craft, we saw four bodies of a type we had never seen before, and all were dead." He then detailed his experience with the recovered occupants of the crashed disc which he described as "all about four feet or less tall, with strange looking arms, legs and fingers." He continued, "They were dressed in a silver type uniform and wearing a tight helmet of some type. This is a positive because I tried to remove one of the helmets, but was unable to do so. Their eyes were large, oval in shape, and did not resemble anything of a human nature."

Chuck Wade has spent the past thirty years researching the UFO crashes in New Mexico between 1945 and 1948, concluding that there have been seven separate incidents.

1.   The first UFO crash took place in August 1945; at San Antonio near the 'Trinity' nuclear test site (the world's first atomic test took place in the July). The recovered craft was 25 to 30' long and "avocado shaped". Locals Remigio Baca and Jose Padilla reported this incident. Baca also recalled holding some debris which he described as a piece of thin, shiny material that "When I freed it, it unfolded all by itself. I refolded it, and it spread itself out again". They saw the UFO occupants too, saying that "Strange looking creatures were moving around inside".[58]

2.   The second UFO crash was on the plains of San Augustin, the night of July 1st or 2nd 1947. This craft was 32' in diameter. Gerald Anderson and some family members claimed to have found the crashed object in which they saw four alien bodies: one was still alive, another was wounded and two were already dead. The discovery was verified by Barney Barnett who also witnessed the same downed craft, and also archaeologist Dr. Herbert Dick, a Harvard grad student.

3.   The third crash site is believed to be southwest of Roswell and happened possibly July 4, 1947. Frank Kaufmann claims to have witnessed an oval-shaped crashed UFO, 25 feet long. This incident is still under investigation by MUFON and UFO researchers, Chuck Zukowski and Debbie Ziegelmeyer.

4.   The fourth crash was north of Roswell which was reported to the military by civilians. The incident occurred July 4, 1947. Walter Haut described the crashed object as "12-15' long, not quite as wide and 6 feet high, and more of an egg shape." Col. Philip J. Corso stated in his book *The Day after Roswell* that he had

command of the artefacts from this UFO crash whilst working in the Pentagon.

5.   Site five was found by Mac Brazel at the Corona debris field, located 75 miles northwest of Roswell and 40 miles southeast of Corona on the Foster ranch. The size of the craft is unknown but it scattered "truckloads" of debris over the site.

6.   The sixth UFO crash was reported by Jim Ragsdale. Also happened the night of July 4, 1947. The site was 53 miles west of Roswell in the foothills of the Capitan Mountains. This craft was 20' in diameter. Four dead extraterrestrials were found inside. Ragsdale departed the scene as the military arrived in numbers.

7.   The seventh incident took place in March, 1948 in Hart Canyon, 9 miles north of Aztec. This craft was 100' in diameter and was completely intact. 16 dead bodies were retrieved.

Wade's research continues to shed more light on the events surrounding the infamous Roswell crash, and the interconnection between seven possible crashes in a three year period, all of them in the same American state, does raise many questions. Many UFO researchers have focused their attention on the occurrence of one isolated incident located near Corona and about 75 miles northwest of Roswell, but it is clear from the information available that the remarkable events of 1947 lend themselves to a much wider perspective. Wade has a theory, which if proven correct would explain why so many separate incidents apparently occurred in one area, some of them on the same evening.

The Los Alamos National Laboratories (LANL) in New Mexico's capital Santa Fe was constructed during the 1940's as a facility to research and build atomic bombs. Chuck Wade's theory revolves around the three high-powered radar units which were built simultaneously to watch the skies over Los Alamos to protect them from invasion and warn them of prying eyes. One radar site was at El Vado, near the Colorado border. The second radar was built in the south near the continental divide, close to the border of Arizona, and the third was a mobile unit stationed at Moriarty in central New Mexico. Wade suggests that it could have been the mobile radar unit that shot down all seven of the UFOs that crashed and were retrieved in New Mexico between 1945 and 1948.

Following the Arnold sightings in the June of '47 and the ensuing publicity which the incident received via the National media, Wade believes that orders came from the highest authority to relocate the mobile radar unit from Moriarty to the San Augustin basin. From the bowl-like plains of San Augustin, the high-powered radar was employed to shoot down the next UFO that flew overhead. The tracking radar would have enabled the military to locate the crashed object within twelve hours of impact, and organise a retrieval team to clear the site as efficiently as possible. From there, the mobile unit could have been transported to somewhere northwest of Roswell, according to Wade.

Author Art Campbell located a brother and sister who claim that they saw three huge flashes of light, about three seconds apart, occurring on the night of July 4, 1947. Driving with their mother that night between Carlsbad and Vaughn, NM, the siblings described the flashes as so brilliant that they lit up both the desert and the distant mountains. Chuck Wade put two and two together and theorised that the flashes were caused by the high-powered radar's energy beam colliding with three electromagnetic vehicles from outer space causing three separate crashes. One crashed near Corona, reported by Mac Brazel. The second landed north of Roswell, as described by Walter Haut and Philip Corso. The third incident was witnessed by Jim Ragsdale and took place in the Capitan Mountains.

Ragsdale claims he was sat in the back of his pickup truck with a friend, looking up at the stars, when they saw a tremendous flash "as bright as a flame from a welder's arc" occurring several miles to the north. The object was soon heading towards them "trailing flames" and making an incredibly loud noise before passing through the trees, and finally colliding with the mountain just a short distance from his truck. Wade believes that the loud noise and the flames were caused by the disabled craft's electromagnetic systems shorting out. Not long after the collision, Ragsdale and his friend departed swiftly as military vehicles were fast approaching. Once again, the military's ability to locate the site so efficiently, already prepared with recovery equipment, has to be due to the tracking radar locking onto and following the craft.

It is also apparent from the overwhelming array of evidence that something very extraordinary took place in New Mexico during the first week of July in 1947, only a matter of days after the Kenneth Arnold incident in Washington. A varied selection of people recall handling some rare and peculiar material believed to be crash debris, and a host of other witnesses claim to have seen non-human entities either on site or having being recovered from the scene of the crash. It is of no surprise then, that if one or more of these events did actually take place, and the bodies found in the wreckage were indeed of an extraterrestrial origin, that the initial response of the authorities was one of panic which ultimately led to the implementation of some form of cover-up.

The Public Information Officer for Roswell Air Force Base 1st Lt. Walter G. Haut, explained in his 2002 sealed affidavit that, "One of the main concerns discussed at the meeting was whether we should go public or not with the discovery. Gen. Ramey proposed a plan, which I believe originated from his bosses at the Pentagon. Attention needed to be diverted from the more important site north of town by acknowledging the other location. Too many civilians were already involved and the press already was informed. I was not completely informed how this would be accomplished." Haut continued, "At approximately 9:30 a.m. Col. Blanchard phoned my office and dictated the press release of having in our possession a flying disc, coming from a ranch northwest of Roswell, and Marcel flying the material to higher headquarters. I was to deliver the news release to radio stations KGFL and KSWS, and newspapers the Daily Record and the Morning Dispatch. By the time the news release hit the wire services, my office was inundated with phone calls from around the world."

So Haut claims that his superiors were aware of two crashes, but were keen to divert attention from the incident north of Roswell by focusing the media's attention on the Foster ranch in the northwest. What originally came out in the press was that the Army Air Force had discovered a flying disc on the ranch. The headline in the *Roswell Daily Record* dated July 8 read "RAAF Captures Flying Saucer On Ranch In Roswell Region".

This story was soon to be dismantled, and in its place came one of the first public cover-ups of its kind. The official story coming from the military to the Associated Press was that the object recovered was not anything unusual as was first suspected; rather it was simply a weather balloon. Anyone claiming to know better was quickly dealt with, as only the military know how, told to keep their mouths shut or face the consequences.

Among those who were silenced was Major Jesse Marcel, who had the humiliation of having his picture taken with the weather balloon material which had been switched from the original debris, minutes before the newspapers arrived to photograph and report the incident. He knew he had been duped into going along with the cover story and any desire to proclaim the truth was quickly extinguished.

June Crain worked for ten years at Wright-Patterson Air Base from 1942 and remembers the Roswell incident clearly; "I'm probably the last survivor of my lab group and probably the last one still around to talk about it. I had a Q clearance; I worked with scientists and with engineers. I knew a man named Clarence Smith, he was a master sergeant. He came in one day before we started to work, very upset. Clarence told us that his plane had brought back two bodies in crates from New Mexico. When I asked which plane had crashed he said 'It wasn't a plane it was a flying saucer!' Well, they knew of three crashes that I was aware of by 1952 maybe there were more. In '52 there was a crash cover-up, Roswell was in '47. That balloon story was a damn lie then and it's still a lie."[59]

Rancher Mac Brazel knew that the debris was not from any meteorological device but was also 'advised' to keep his opinions to himself, which he did. Brazel's eagerness to invite Chuck Wade's father Jesse to the Foster ranch to see something remarkable, was later completely diminished once the military had gotten involved. Brazel would later refuse to discuss the incident and Jesse Wade knew something was wrong when Mac Brazel managed to buy a meat locker in Alamogordo, and then saw him driving a new pick-up truck, which he could not possibly have afforded to purchase himself unless he had been 'paid off'. As Jesse Wade told his son, "before the crash he never had two nickels to rub together".

Authors Tom Carey and Don Schmitt located the daughter of J.B. Foster, one of the ranch owners, and managed to interview her. Joann Purdie spoke of the suspicious circumstances surrounding the Foster ranch at that time, stating that "My Dad knew that it was a flying saucer and never changed his story. And just as the Army had warned and threatened Mac Brazel, they did the same to him."[60]

Before finally being put into print in the newspapers, the press would receive information on any given story over the wire. A brief review of the chronology of reports sent to the Associated Press on 8th July, 1947 reveals how quickly the story changed:

16:26 – The first Associated Press bulletin came over the wire - "Roswell, N.M. – The army air forces here today announced a flying disk had been found on a ranch near Roswell and is in army possession."

16:30 – The first add said that Lt. Walter Haut, public information officer of Roswell field, announced the object had been found "sometime last week". The object had been sent on "to higher headquarters."

16:55 – The second add is received. Designated as a "95", meaning it is next in importance to a bulletin or bulletin matter.

17:08 – The second add was repeated for all newspapers needing it.

17:09 – Another repeat was sent which explained that the story had been broken by a radio reporter.

17:10 – Another "95" was sent, addressed to the editors, this announcement informed the editors that the AP had begun to write up the story.

17:11 – The third add was announced – "The war department in Washington had nothing to say immediately about the reported find." This suggested that the AP was already in full flow investigating the story.

17:53 – Another bulletin was sent with a Washington deadline about a statement made by Brig. Gen. Roger Ramey stating that the "disc" had been sent to Wright Field, Ohio.

17:56, 17:59 and **18:00** – Two adds to the bulletin were sent followed by a correction to a typographical error with a continuation of the 17:59 add.

18:02 – The complete story had been processed and the AP started the first transmission which included the following statement - "Albuquerque, N.M. – The army air forces had gained possession of a flying disk, Lt. Walter Haut, public information officer at Roswell army airfield, announced today."

19:03 – The first mention that the object may have been only a meteorological device arrived, from Washington.

19:15 – A new bulletin stated that General Ramey would be speaking over the National Broadcasting company network.

19:29 – Another "95" came over the wire listed "Precede Washington. Lead all disk." This meant the story was ready.

19:30 - Immediately following that bulletin, the "95" was broken in favour of a new bulletin which said, "Fort Worth - Roswell's celebrated 'flying disk' was rudely stripped of its glamour by a Fort Worth army airfield weather officer who late today identified the object as a weather balloon."

So just three hours after the initial bulletin was sent, the whole story had swung around. The cover-up was successful. It was dealt with so quickly that the public barely had time to react, although the papers did still get the first version of events out in print before they had received the alternative version.

On July 8, 1947 the *Roswell Daily Record* wrote what they originally were informed had occurred;

"The intelligence office of the 509th Bombardment group at Roswell Army Air Field announced at noon today, that the field has come into possession of a flying saucer. According to information released by the department, over authority of Maj. J. A. Marcel, intelligence officer, the disk was recovered on a ranch in the Roswell vicinity, after an unidentified rancher had notified Sheriff Geo. Wilcox, here, that he had found the instrument on his premises. Major Marcel and a detail from his department went to the ranch and recovered the disk, it was stated. After the intelligence officer here had inspected the instrument it was flown to higher headquarters. The intelligence officer stated that no details of the saucer's construction or its appearance had been revealed."

The following day of July 9, the same paper reported the latest version of the story along with the headline, "Gen. Ramey Empties Roswell Saucer. Ramey Says Excitement is Not Justified. General Ramey Says Disk is Weather Balloon." The story read as follows;

"Fort Worth, Texas, July 9 (AP) An examination by the army revealed last night that mysterious objects found on a lonely New Mexico ranch was a harmless high-altitude weather balloon - not a grounded flying disk. Excitement was high until Brig. Gen. Roger M. Ramey, commander of the Eighth air forces with headquarters here cleared up the mystery. The bundle of tinfoil, broken wood beams and rubber remnants of a balloon were sent here yesterday by army air transport in the wake of reports that it was a flying disk...The weather balloon was found several days ago near the center of New Mexico by Rancher W. W. Brazel. He said he didn't think much about it until he went into Corona, N. M. last Saturday and heard the flying disk reports...Ramey went on the air here last night to announce the New Mexico discovery was not a flying disk."

One reason that such an extraordinary event initially necessitated deceptive tactics could simply be due to the fact that the public had gained access to information which was never meant for them. For many years, the media moguls of this world have retained a great deal of control over the content and subject matter of their material. Whether on the printed page or via radio or television, what reaches the public has already passed through some filtration process by editors, managers and chief executives. What occurred at Roswell somehow found its way into print, and the story continues to be told to this day.

As an Air Material Command report explained, "In September 1947, the Air Force was forced to take official cognizance of the "flying discs" because of increasing demand from the public for an explanation, and as a result of certain publications persisting in using a sensational approach in reporting such items."[61]

Many documents have been released in recent years which pertain to the existence of a governmental cover-up regarding matters relating to extraterrestrial visitation. Through outlets like the Freedom of Information Act (FOIA), the British Public Records Office and the National Archives & Records Administration (NARA), some classified material is slowly emerging from the shadows into the public domain. Although the process of proving the legitimacy of such documentation shall continue for many more years, the information contained within is often quite revelatory.

In a document dated July 22, 1947, an Interplanetary Phenomenon Unit (IPU) Summary report used the title "The extraordinary recovery of fallen airborne objects in the state of

New Mexico, between 4 July – 6 July 1947". The report explains that radar stations in east Texas and White Sands Proving Ground (WSPG), New Mexico, tracked two unidentified aircraft on July 3, 1947. Two crash sites were located close to the WSPG, one being at the Foster ranch near Corona known as Site LZ-1, and the other (LZ-2) was described as being twenty miles southeast of Socorro. According to the IPU, "When scientists from the Los Alamos Scientific Laboratory arrived to inspect LZ-2, it became apparent to all concerned that what had crashed in the desert was something out of this world."

The IPU summary also confirms some of Chuck Wade's radar theory by stating that some downed flying objects were successfully retrieved by the military; "It has been learned that at least six radar stations in East Texas and radar stations at Alamogordo AAF and Kirtland AAF, had also picked up these objects on the 4th as well. Using topographical maps and triangularisation, a last known position and bearing was calculated which helped search parties locate the general area. Detachment 3 of the 9393rd Technical Services Unit, assigned to Alamogordo AAF, was responsible for the locating and transporting of the large sections of the craft."

The report confirms the subsequent deception which followed the Roswell incident, and maintains that details surrounding the remarkable events that occurred in the July of '47 were vehemently denied by the authorities.

"To maintain secrecy of site LZ-2, the CO of Roswell AAF was authorized to give a brief press release to local paper(s) in which 8th AF Hdqrs. promptly denied rumors that the Army had flying saucers in their possession which effectively killed press interest. Civilians who might have seen or handled some of the wreckage, or viewed bodies were detained under the McNab law until all remaining evidence was secured in restricted bases. Witnesses were debriefed by CIC and warned of the consequences of talking to the press. So far, secrecy seems to be working."

THE SECRET PROJECTS

On July 9, 1947, just four days after the UFOs crashed near Roswell, President Truman sent a letter to Lt. Gen. Nathan F.

Twining, chief of the Air Material Command, Air Technical Intelligence Center.

Truman wrote, "You will proceed to the White Sands Proving Ground Command Center without delay for the purpose of making an appraisal of the reported unidentified objects being kept there." Naturally, Twining followed orders and on July 16, he wrote up an Air Accident Report to be sent to H.Q. in which he wrote, "As ordered by Presidential Directive, dated 9 July 1947, a preliminary investigation of a recovered "Flying Disc" and remains of a possible second disc, was conducted by the senior staff of this command."

The unusual events that occurred during early summer of 1947, led to the formation of new projects and groups which were created to tackle the situation at hand following newly set protocols. The first of these "secret" projects to surface was designed to study all incoming UFO reports and determine the details of each individual case and classify them appropriately. Lt. Gen. Twining was requested to deal with this matter in a letter dated September 23, 1947. Confirmation of this fact can be found in the 1949 AMC report which explains the origins of the newly founded project and its purpose; "Hq. AMC in a letter dated 23 September 1947, requested the Commanding General, Army Air Forces, to issue a directive assigning a priority, security classification and code name for a detailed study of flying disc reports. Hq. AMC explained that their action was based on the opinion that phenomena reported appeared to be real." So whilst publicly denying any authenticity in UFO sightings, behind closed doors the U.S. Government and the Army Air Force were forming strategies to deal with the phenomenon, which in the words of Twining himself "is something real and not visionary or fictitious".

The report declared "This directive assigned a priority of 2A to the project, a RESTRICTED classification and a code name of "SIGN"." And so Project SIGN was set up following the recommendation of General Twining in late 1947, specifically with the purpose of "collecting, collating, evaluating, and distributing to interested government agencies and contractors, all information concerning sightings and phenomena in the atmosphere which might be construed to be of concern to the national security."

However, on 16 December, 1948, Dr. Vannevar Bush, the Director of Scientific Research and Development (that led to the production of the first atomic bomb) requested that Project SIGN be changed to Project GRUDGE. According to the report, "Grudge" under the U.S. Joint Services code word index refers to the title "Detailed Study of Flying Discs"".

A low-level program was set up to satisfy the public demand to officially investigate UFO sightings which was created as a disinformation project that ultimately catalogued and explained the less authentic incidents. Originating under Grudge, Project BLUE BOOK was employed to "satisfy public curiosity" and ran for eighteen years between 1951 and 1969. It was designed to continue where Project Sign had left off, as a renewed investigation taking into account any forthcoming UFO reports which surfaced.

The problem with Blue Book however, was the fact that so many reports were considered "too risky" to be included in such a public report. A UFO sighting which was deemed to contain contradictory evidence or an eyewitness testimony which lacked clarity or common sense would be omitted from the files. Although thousands of reports were collected, analysed and filed, as was the purpose of the project, a member of the investigation team sent in his own sighting report to be filed but soon discovered that it had also been omitted. Reports that were unexplained were removed from the files of Project Blue Book in case they caused the public to panic, or such is the reason that was understood amongst fellow investigators. The more "dangerous" files were passed on to a higher authority.

Blue Book was the last publicly known UFO research project led by the Unites States Air Force or any other notable organisation, which is unfortunate as such projects if run honestly with the right intentions, could serve the public well in informing them of the facts and details involved in the highly controversial subject matter of ufology.

Researcher Michael Hall who has spent many years delving into the historical aspects of Blue Book wrote, "In the last year of its existence, Blue Book received 146 UFO reports of which only one received the unidentified classification. Virtually all of the cases that came in by that point were civilian sightings. Military personnel no longer reported UFOs—they weren't supposed to.

The Air Force claimed UFOs were no longer seen by the military simply because they are trained observers that cannot be fooled by such things. Historically, however, that was not true. For the 22 years that the Air Force investigated UFOs they received 12,750 reports of which 587 were classified as unidentified."

In the modern era of serious UFO research, both Blue Book and the Condon Report have become prime examples of selective study and blatant debunking. Whilst publicly declaring that there is no reason to continue to study the phenomenon as there does not exist anything unusual or out of the ordinary in the reports, covertly the threat is considered to be very real and is dealt with as such. The U.S. Government gave the responsibility of tackling the various issues and implications associated with interplanetary craft and their occupants visiting our planet to the military forces such as the Navy, the Army and the Air Force.

Below is a list of secret projects which followed the Air Force Projects Sign and Grudge. Much of this material originates from Milton William Cooper, who claims to have read the information in 1972 as a Petty Officer in the U.S. Navy, whilst performing his duties as a Member of the Intelligence Briefing Team of the Commander in Chief of the Pacific Fleet. Cooper swore that he underwent hypnotic regression in order to make the information as accurate as possible.

• OPERATION MAJORITY is the name of the operation responsible for every aspect, project, and consequence of alien presence on earth. MAJESTY was listed as the code word for the President of the United States for communications concerning this information. MAJIC is a security classification and clearance of all alien connected material, projects, and information. MAJIC means MAJI controlled. MAJI stands for the Majority Agency for Joint Intelligence. All information, disinformation, and intelligence is gathered and evaluated by this agency. The agency is responsible for all disinformation and operates in conjunction with the CIA, NSA, and the Defense Intelligence Agency (DIA). MAJI is a very powerful organization and all alien projects are under its control, it is only answerable to MJ-12 (MAJESTIC 12 is a covert group which formed in the United States).

- Project GRUDGE (Originally SIGN) Contains 16 volumes of documented information collected from the beginning of the United States investigation of Unidentified Flying Objects (UFOs) and Identified Alien Crafts (IAC). Cooper claims that the project was funded by CIA non-appropriated funds as well as money from the illicit drug trade. The purpose of Project GRUDGE was to collect all scientific, technological, medical and intelligence information from UFO/IAC sightings and contacts with alien life forms. This orderly file of collected information has been used to advance the United States Space Program.

- Project SIGMA (originally part of Project GLEEM) is the project which first established communications with the aliens and is still responsible for communications. It became a separate project in 1976.

- Project PLATO is the project responsible for diplomatic relations with the aliens. This project secured a formal treaty with the aliens. The terms were that the aliens would give us technology. In return we agreed to keep their presence on earth a secret, not to interfere in any way their actions, and to allow them to abduct humans and animals. The aliens agreed to furnish MJ-12 with a list of abductees on a periodic basis.

- Project AQUARIUS was created in 1959 by order of President Eisenhower. The project was in the hands of the National Security Council and MJ-12. AQUARIUS is a project which compiled the history of alien presence and their interaction with Homo sapiens upon this planet for the last 25,000 years.

- Project GARNET is the project responsible for control of all information and documents regarding this subject and accountability of the information and documents.

- Project PLUTO is a project to evaluate all UFO/IAC information pertaining to space technology.

- Project POUNCE was setup to recover all downed/crashed craft and aliens. It was originally known as Project MOONDUST. Created in late December, 1980, Project Pounce consists of an elite group of Air Force Black Berets and military scientists who rush to the scene of any UFO crashes, cordon off the area then retrieve the extraterrestrial spacecraft and any occupants. They then "sanitize" the crash site back to its pre-crash appearance, and intimidate any outside witnesses into silence. This project continues to the present day.

• Project REDLIGHT is the project to test fly recovered alien craft. It is conducted at Area 51 in the Nevada desert. The initial project was believed to have been somewhat successful in that a recovered craft was flown but it exploded in midair and the pilots were killed. The project was suspended at that time until the aliens agreed to assist.

• Project SNOWBIRD was established as a cover for Project REDLIGHT. Several flying saucer type craft were built using conventional technology. They were unveiled to the press and flown in front of the press. The purpose was to explain accidental sightings or disclosure of REDLIGHT as having been SNOWBIRD craft.

• Project JOSHUA was a project to develop a LOW frequency pulse sound generating weapon. Developed and assembled at Ling Tempco Vought in Anaheim, California, it is believed to be capable of completely destroying any man-made structure from two miles away. Tested at the White Sands Proving Grounds and developed between 1975 and 1978, it has been described as a long horn-shaped device connected to a computer and amplifiers. It is said that these weapons would be effective against the alien craft and beam weapons.

• Project GABRIEL was established to develop HIGH frequency weapons pulse sound generating weapons. The project also involves working with high frequency microwaves.

• Project EXCALIBUR is a weapon which was designed to destroy the alien underground bases and is believed to have been funded by intelligence branches connected with the U.S. Navy and SDI projects. It is a missile capable of penetrating 1000 metres of hard packed soil such as that found in New Mexico with no operational damage. Missile apogee not to exceed 30,000 feet AGL and impact must not deviate in excess of 50 meters from designated target. The device will carry a one to ten megaton nuclear warhead.

OPERATION MAJESTIC-12

The day following Independence Day of 1947, when possibly up to four UFOs crashed in the state of New Mexico all in the same evening; Vannevar Bush wrote a letter of transmittal to President Truman. Discussing the rise of recent events, Bush addressed the need to put into place some form of group which could take responsibility for all issues relating to extraterrestrial matters. "The committees have given these matters the serious attention in light of recent developments; indeed they have regarded this as an opportunity to participate in shaping the policy with reference to scientific research. They have had meetings since the events of this summer began to present more challenges..." wrote Bush. He added, "A single mechanism for implementing the recommendations of the several committees is essential."[62]

What "single mechanism" was Bush referring to? Perhaps he was talking about a select group of prominent scientists and military officers answerable (at that time) only to the president. A secret group created with the sole purpose of taking complete control over all matters extraterrestrial in nature.

Less than four months after Arnold's remarkable UFO sightings above Mount Rainier, the National Security Act of 1947 was signed into law on September 15, by President Harry S. Truman. This led to the creation of the NSC (National Security Council) along with the unification of military branches under a Department of Defense, as well as the founding of the American civilian intelligence organisation - the Central Intelligence Agency (CIA). It is apparent that colossal changes were taking place in America during this period following the Roswell incident, none as significant as the creation of the covert group known as Majestic-12.

Much of the information regarding this most secretive group has derived from a number of unauthenticated top secret documents which first surfaced in the mid-80s. The earliest of these documents to mention Operation Majestic Twelve is a TOP

SECRET/EYES ONLY memorandum addressed to the Secretary of Defense - James Forrestal, from President Truman. Dated September 24, 1947, the memo states, "As per our recent conversation on this matter, you are hereby authorised to proceed with all due speed and caution upon your undertaking. Hereafter this matter shall be referred to only as Operation Majestic Twelve. It continues to be my feeling that any future considerations relative to the ultimate disposition of this matter should rest solely with the Office of the President following appropriate discussions with yourself, Dr. Bush and the Director of Central Intelligence."

Another top secret memorandum addressed to the controller of telecommunications in Ottawa, Ontario dating back to November 20, 1950, was written by a high ranking official within the Canadian government, electronics engineer Wilburt Smith. The 'Smith Memo' which derived as a result of a meeting which Smith attended with a top government official from the Pentagon also mentions Majestic Twelve though not by name, and clearly states that a conspiracy to conceal all UFO related matters does exist.

Smith wrote, "I made discreet enquiries through the Canadian Embassy staff in Washington who were able to obtain for me the following information:

a)   The matter is the most highly classified subject in the United States Government, rating higher than the H-bomb.

b)   Flying Saucers exist.

c)   Their modus operandi is unknown but concentrated effort is being made by a small group headed by Doctor Vannevar Bush.

d)   The entire matter is considered by the United States authorities to be of tremendous significance."

The first time that suspicions surrounding this mysterious group surfaced publicly was in 1978 when a Canadian researcher called Arthur Bray unearthed the classified Canadian UFO documents. It was the information contained therein which first named Dr. Vannevar Bush as the head of a top secret and anonymous UFO investigation group working within the U.S. Research and Development Board.

Three years later Paul Bennewitz, an Albuquerque physicist greatly involved in the origins of alien and UFO conspiracies in the eighties, received a document known as the "Project Aquarius Telex". Sent from AFOSI (Air Force Office of Special Investigations) headquarters in Washington to Kirtland AFB, the document was the first to mention the elusive Majestic group. One sentence in the teletype message read; "The official policy and results of Project Aquarius is still classified TOP SECRET with no dissemination outside channels and with access restricted to 'MJ TWELVE'."

The authenticity of this telex has been in doubt for years as it was sent to Bennewitz from UFO researcher William Moore during the middle of a disinformation campaign. In 1989, Moore claimed that the documents were sent to Bennewitz as part of a hoax created by U.S. Air Force Office of Special Investigations counterintelligence officer Richard C. Doty, in an attempt to confuse Bennewitz and push his already precariously balanced sanity to the limit. The hoaxed document may also have been intended to discredit the information recently revealed by Bray in the Canadian documents.

The discovery of a brown envelope on the doorstep of UFO researcher and TV producer Jaime Shandera on December 11, 1984, revealed another top secret document pertaining to the existence of the Majestic group. Inside the envelope was a roll of 35mm Tri-X black-and-white film which once developed by Shandera and William Moore, contained photos of eight pages from a November 18, 1952, "Briefing Document" prepared for President-elect Dwight D. Eisenhower concerning "Operation Majestic 12".

The contents of the 'MJ-12 Papers', as they would later become known, were no less than revelatory. The document stamped top and bottom with TOP SECRET/MAJIC EYES ONLY was prepared by Briefing Officer Adm. Roscoe H. Hillenkoetter, also referred to as MJ-1. Adm. Hillenkoetter described Operation Majestic-12 as a "TOP SECRET Research and Development/Intelligence operation responsible directly and only to the President of the United States. Operations of the project are carried out under control of the Majestic-12 (Majic-12) Group which was established by special classified executive order of President Truman on 24 September, 1947, upon recommendation by Dr. Vannevar Bush and Secretary James Forrestal."

The document then proceeds to name the twelve men chosen for the task at hand, men with great experience in their specific fields of interest. Some sources state that the top twelve from a group of thirty-two members of a secret society called the Jason

Society were selected to become Majestic-12 and that they are designated as J-1, J-2, J-3 etc., all the way through to J-32.

Listed below are the original twelve as were printed in the 1952 briefing documents, starting with J-1 and ending with J-12:

Adm. Roscoe H. Hillenkoetter was the first director of the CIA upon its formation in 1947 and the third director of Central Intelligence (CDI). He was also the third director of the post-WWII Central Intelligence Group (CIG). He later joined the board of governors of NICAP from 1957-1962 following his retirement from the United States Navy. He had spoken publicly about UFOs, stating that they were real and that "through official secrecy and ridicule, many citizens are led to believe the unknown flying objects are nonsense."[63] In his book *Aliens from Space*, Donald E. Keyhoe wrote that Hillenkoetter wanted public disclosure on the subject.

Dr. Vannevar Bush initiated the Manhattan Project as chairman of the National Defense Research Committee (NDRC) and later as the Director of the Office of Scientific Research and Development (OSRD). In 1938, Bush was appointed to the National Advisory Committee for Aeronautics (NACA) and would later become its chairman. As an eminent American scientist he had an influence on the highest levels of government, especially during WWII when as a policymaker and intellectual he was considered to be effectually the first science advisor to the President. Incidentally, he is related to the Bush family that would later produce two of America's presidents.

Secretary James V. Forrestal* became the first American secretary of Defense in July 1947. The MJ-12 documents which were written after Forrestal's death in 1949 included a footnote stating that his position in the group was later filled by Gen. Walter Bedell Smith, a former U.S. ambassador to Moscow, Eisenhower's chief of staff and also Hillenkoetter's replacement as director of Central Intelligence.

Gen. Nathan F. Twining was the commander of the Air Material Command based at Wright-Patterson AFB. In 1947, he was requested to study UFO reports which led to his recommendation to set up a formal study group which led to the creation of Project Sign. His involvement in the Roswell incident has been well documented. He replaced Gen. Hoyt Vandenberg as Chief of Staff of the U.S.A.F. in 1953, just one year after the MJ-12 papers were allegedly written. He became the first member of the Air Force to serve as Chairman of the Joint Chiefs of Staff. The USS Forrestal, the Navy's first supercarrier, was named in his honour.

Gen. Hoyt S. Vandenberg, the second Air Force Chief of Staff and the second Director of the CIA. Vandenberg AFB in California was named after him, such was his influence. He ordered the original Project Sign report stating that UFOs were real to be destroyed.

Dr. Detlev Bronk was an American neurophysiologist and biophysicist who once was President of the National Academy of Science (1950-1962) and also President of John Hopkins University (1949-1953). He chaired the National Research Council and was a member of the medical advisory board for the Atomic Energy Commission. Along with Dr. Edward Condon, he worked for the Brookhaven National Laboratory on the Scientific Advisory Committee. The Bronk crater on the Moon is named after him.

Dr. Jerome Hunsaker was an American airman who studied aerodynamics abroad before becoming an instructor at Massachusetts Institute of Technology (M.I.T.) where he was originally educated. He became head of the Mechanical Engineering Department in 1933 where he trained graduate students to become aeronautical engineers. He constructed the first wind tunnel at MIT, and also designed the first modern airship built in America along with the C and D class Navy airships. He would later become president of Goodyear Zeppelin Company. Hunsaker was the last surviving member of the original Majestic 12 when he died on September 10th, 1984 – just three months before Jaime Shandera received the anonymous package on his doorstep.

Mr. Sidney W. Souers, a retired American rear admiral and intelligence expert who became the first director of Central Intelligence and CIG on January 23, 1946. A year later he became Executive Secretary for the National Security Council until 1950 before going on to become Special Consultant to the President on military and foreign affairs during the time of the Korean War (1950-1953).

Mr. Gordon Gray was Assistant Secretary of the Army in 1947 and two years later became Secretary of the Army. In 1950, he was named a special assistant on national security affairs to President Truman. Gray was later named director of the government's Psychological Strategy Board (PSB) which was established for the purpose of creating disinformation and psychological warfare. During this time, Henry Kissinger was Gray's chief consultant, and it is believed that a psychological strategy study on UFOs was directed by Gray and consulted by CIA director Walter B. Smith.

Dr. Donald Menzel was publicly known as a respected astronomer and a director of the Harvard College Observatory. He worked covertly as a consultant for the CIA and the NSA with a top-secret security clearance, which was only discovered after physicist Stanton Friedman had studied his unpublished autobiography and interviewed his widow. His intelligence work was verified in a letter Menzel wrote to President John F. Kennedy in which he stated, "I have been associated with this activity for almost thirty years and probably have the longest continuous record of association with them [CIA]." He wrote three books which debunked the reality of UFOs as anything extraordinary, dismissing most reports whilst offering simple explanations for them stating that "All non-explained sightings are from poor observers."

Gen. Robert M. Montague was a military man who was at the centre of both the Roswell and the Operation Paperclip controversies due to his roles as the Base Commander of Fort Bliss in Texas during 1947 and as Commanding General of the Sandia Atomic Energy Commission facility in New Mexico from 1947-1951. He also was involved with security at the White Sands Proving Ground.

Dr. Lloyd V. Berkner, an American engineer and physicist who co-invented a device which measures the ionospheres' height and electron density. His investigations into the study of the Earth's atmosphere led to the International Geophysical Year in 1950, which was the largest cooperative study of the Earth ever undertaken at that time. He was president of the Associated Universities Incorporated (AUI) which was established in 1946 in order to "acquire, plan, construct and operate laboratories and other facilities that would unite the resources of universities, other research organizations and the federal government."[64] One institution which is believed to be involved with UFOs and defence weaponry is Brookhaven National Laboratory on Long Island, which is closely connected to the AUI. During his tenure as president of the AUI, Berkner was also a member of the President's Scientific Advisory Committee in 1958. Dr. Berkner was also a member of the Robertson Panel,[3] and after his death he would also have a lunar crater and a Texan high school named in his honour.

Gen. Walter B. Smith replaced Secretary Forrestal on 1st August, 1950, following his suspicious 'suicide' at Bethesda Naval Hospital in Maryland on 22nd May, 1949. James Vincent Forrestal allegedly fell to his death from a small window on the 16th floor of the hospital. Much controversy surrounds the mysterious death of James Forrestal even though it was apparent that he had been under severe pressure from Truman which ultimately led to him being replaced as Secretary of Defense by Louis Johnson. Forrestal's last public appearance was on March 28, 1949, during a formal ceremony the day he finally left office. A day later, whilst at the home of a future Secretary of Defence, Robert Lovett, Forrestal's first words to Lovett were "Bob, they're after me."[65] Forrestal claimed he was being followed by Zionist agents.

What is apparent when perusing such an auspicious list of distinguished men is that if such a secret group does exist and actually exerts great influence on national affairs - political,

---

[3] The Robertson Panel was activated by Admiral Hillenkoetter and headed by Dr. H. P. Robertson. It was a group of specialists sponsored by the CIA which was devised to deflect public interest in the UFO phenomenon by suggesting quite conclusively that such objects did not pose a threat to the security of the nation. It was also designed to monitor civilian UFO study groups which were beginning to surface around the country.

military and social, how have they continued to operate covertly for such a sustained period? These are prominent figures with strong associations to intelligence, science and presidential decision making, they are certainly all qualified to hold such influential positions but it is remarkable that they succeeded in withholding their darker secret personae from public scrutiny.

Since all members of the original twelve died before the Eisenhower briefing document surfaced in 1984 it seems that they took their oaths of secrecy to their graves, but recent information from American microbiologist Dr. Dan Burisch, has confirmed the continued existence of the group up to the present day. Burisch has spoken out publicly about his involvement as the Working Group Leader of Project Aquarius, working in a scientific capacity with a live extraterrestrial being which was being detained at the S-4 facility near Area 51 in Nevada. He has also spoken about his previous membership of the Majestic-12 group from which he was dismissed on October 12, 2005, following twenty years of service with them. Part of his mission was to disclose certain information to the public, which he did before retiring from service in 2006.

Burisch listed a more recent Majestic 12, as of adjournment in 2005, and just like the twelve original members from the 1952 document, the names are of extremely high profile figures holding prominent positions within society:

J-1: *Vice-Admiral John 'Mike' McConnell* (former Director of NSA, former United States Director of National Intelligence)

J-2: *Richard B. Cheney* (former Vice-President of United States of America)

J-3: *Porter Goss* (former Director of the Central Intelligence Agency, former Director of Central Intelligence; succeeded George Tenant as J-3)

J-4: *Admiral Bobby Ray Inman* (former Director of Naval Intelligence, former Director of NSA, former Deputy Director of CIA, former Vice Director of DIA)

J-5: *Henry Kissinger* (former National Security Advisor, former Secretary of State)

J-6: *Zbigniew Brzezinski* (former National Security Advisor)

J-7: *General Richard B. Myers* (former Chairman of the Joint Chiefs of Staff)

J-8: *Sir Kevin Tebbit* (former British civil servant)

J-9: *Carol Ann Thatcher* (daughter of former British Prime Minister Margaret Thatcher; succeeded Dan Burisch who had succeeded Romano Prodi; former Prime Minister of Italy)

J-10: *Alan Greenspan* (Chairman of the Federal Reserve)

J-11: *Harold E. Varmus* (former Director of the National Institutes of Health)

J-12: *E. Kelly*
Alternate: *Dr. Robert Gallo* (best known for his role in the discovery of HIV and AIDS)

Some researchers have postulated that MJ-12 are also responsible for running the world's illegal drug trade, which they justified by suggesting that it was a sure way of identifying and ultimately eliminating the weak and undesirable members of society. The funds raised through the illicit trading of drugs would remain a secret kept from both Congress and the public, thus enabling Majestic to continue their involvement in the secret projects.

According to William Cooper, a retreat was built in Maryland funded by Nelson Rockefeller, which was designed as a secret meeting place for MJ-12 and the study committee (which included Henry Kissinger, David Rockefeller and Majestic member Zbigniew Brzezinski, to name but a few). Accessible only from the air, "The Country Club" as it was codenamed, is a fully sustainable facility with living quarters, eating and recreation areas and a library all under one roof.

The debate as to the authenticity of the Majestic documents shows no signs of abating, but discussions on the matter have raised some interesting concerns. Debunker Philip Klaas, a journalist renowned for his sceptical approach to UFOs and aliens, once stated that "Either [the documents] are the biggest news story of the past two millennia or one of the biggest cons ever attempted against the public."[66] Objections which Klaas raised concerning the legitimacy of the MJ-12 papers included spelling mistakes, unusual punctuation and text styles, along with the use of unpopular words of that era such as "media". He failed to grasp how men who had publicly expressed that there was nothing 'out of this world' about UFOs, could have knowledge of UFO crash retrievals and recovered alien bodies.

His understanding of the covert and deceptive inner workings of the military and the U.S. Government, borders on naivety unless Klaas himself knew more than he let on. Historically speaking, it has proven to be somewhat standard procedure for men in publicly prominent positions to lie. Words spoken publicly in this capacity can often be regarded as the complete opposite of what those speaking truly know; such is the world we live in.

Honesty has never been high on the political agenda as it more often than not exposes the frailties and inadequacies of those making the decisions. For instance, if following the events in New Mexico in 1947, the government agencies were to have addressed the nation with honesty and informed the people of precisely what events had recently unfolded, how would that appear to the common man? Admitting that unknown beings flying in unknown craft, from unknown destinations, for reasons unknown, hardly inspires confidence in the authorities charged with securing the nation's safety. It is in essence, a kind of catch-22 situation where ethically speaking, honesty should be paramount, but practically however, such an approach could have negative results.

Researcher Stanton Friedman suggested that one reason for claiming that the MJ-12 documents were authentic was the fact that the astronomer Donald Menzel was included in the twelve. His close association with fellow Majestic members Bush, Berkner and Bronk was so highly classified along with his secret connections with government intelligence, that Friedman believed that no hoaxer could possibly have been privy to such information.

Dr. Robert M. Wood, who spent forty-three years managing research and development at McDonnell Douglas, put his expertise in scientific research to good use when he became a member of an investigation team intent on either legitimatising or disproving the content of the Majestic documents. Discussing how one should determine whether a document is genuine or not, Wood wrote "The remarkableness of the content sometimes makes some people react subconsciously to reject the stories as too bizarre. The scientific method uses a systematic approach without letting emotions affect the probability of fakery vs. genuineness. Specifically, the argument that one of the documents *could be* easily faked and therefore *was* faked is illogical."[67]

The investigation team at *majesticdocuments.com* which includes author Jim Marrs and avid UFO researchers Tim Cooper, Nick Redfern and Stanton Friedman, has endeavoured to analyze all significant documents that have appeared in relation to the UFO/alien mystery. By considering various factors they have been able to offer objective responses and counter arguments to the many questions raised by skeptics in the field.

Included in his 2001 paper, *"Mounting Evidence for Authenticity of MJ-12 Documents"*, Dr. Wood listed a range of considerations that the process of authenticating many different documents may require, such as:

- Physical dating of the ink, pencil and paper
- Dating by matching the reproductive process (typewriter or printer)
- Dating by use of language of the period
- Identification of authorship using linguistics
- Comparison of handwriting
- Comparison with known events of record
- Comparison with known styles and procedures of production
- Comparison with known or expected security procedures
- Logic of content
- Records of provenance

Through such rigorous and thorough examination of the Majestic documents, Wood and his team believe they are getting closer to validating the leaked papers. Wood's conclusion was that "The greatest secret of the 20th century—crash recoveries leading to a covert official UFO program—is being gradually revealed through the leaks of classified documents held in individual files for decades. Original documents can be dated back into the 1950s and no impressive reasons have come to light that would seriously impeach the authenticity of hundreds of pages of classified material, together with thousands of pages of supportive documentation. If these crashes and recoveries occurred, such documents ought to exist."

As with the "Eisenhower Briefing" document, verifying the authenticity of any of the MJ-12 papers continues to be a problematic issue which has divided the many researchers who have endeavoured to pursue the truth trail. In one corner, the skeptical mind seems to find fault with the smallest of details, and unanswered questions and conundrums raised inevitably serve the non-believers well in their quest to disprove the improbable.

Conspiracies of any nature are always much easier to dismiss than to accept, simply due to the lack of evidence on offer in most circumstances. But as any open-minded researcher will concur, a lack of solid evidence does not constitute denial of the possible truth, it is what it is, a lack of evidence and that's all. It is quite fascinating to read how a clash of mindsets can produce such differing opinions concerning the validity of the MJ-12 papers, to see how easily each party can offer counter arguments against each other with such conviction. Whilst one argues that Area 51 didn't exist at the time the documents were printed, the other claims that publicly it may not have been known about but covertly it was already in use. The evidence for and against seems to depend on what angle the researcher chooses to come from.

Author and researcher Tim Cooper wrote "In all fairness to anti-MJ-12 arguments, some of the objections to security classification, signatures, and dating still pose problems. These arguments can be solved. What is lacking is a concerted effort to secure sworn testimony from individuals of high rank from the Executive Branch, the CIA, and the military intelligence to either refute the MJ-12 enigma or validate the existence of the United States Government's UFO Program."

However, there is certainly a consistent and linear turn of events which continues to be reiterated time and time again throughout the increasing amount of documents that are coming to light. It is these consistencies which add to the credibility of the documents and the information held therein. Dates, events and personnel are more often than not in accordance with many of the other leaked documents despite the varying sources of the material.

For example, the 1952 Eisenhower briefing document mentions the Arnold UFO sightings in June 1947, followed by the admittance that one of these unknown objects crashed into a local rancher's field in a remote region of New Mexico. Also disclosed was the discovery that on July 7, a "secret operation was begun to assure recovery of the wreckage of this object for scientific study" which led to the discovery that "four small human-like beings had apparently ejected from the craft at sometime before it exploded"[68].

Claiming it took a week to recover the dead and decomposed bodies that had fallen two miles east of the wreckage site, the document stated that a special scientific team took charge of removing the bodies whilst the wreckage of the craft was removed to several different locations. Any military or civilian witnesses were debriefed and "news reporters were given the effective cover story that the object had been a misguided weather research balloon."[69]

Analysis of the four dead occupants was undertaken by the Majestic physiologist, Dr. Detlev Bronk, whose team invented the term "Extra-terrestrial Biological Entities" or "EBEs", which became the standard term of reference for such unknown creatures. On 30th November, 1947, the group concluded that "although these creatures are human-like in appearance, the biological and evolutionary processes responsible for their development has apparently been quite different from those observed or postulated in homo-sapiens"[70].

The group informed Eisenhower that they were "virtually certain" that the craft was not of an earthly origin and that although they remained speculative as to the actual origins of these entities, Dr. Menzel considered it likely that they were dealing with beings from an entirely different solar system from our own.

The "briefing" document concluded by stressing the importance of trying to gain some understanding of the motives and intentions of the visitors for the sake of national security, which at the time of writing were completely unknown.

The papers stated that "In addition, a significant upsurge in the surveillance activity of these craft beginning in May and continuing through the autumn of this year [1952] has caused considerable concern that new developments may be imminent. It is for these reasons, as well as the obvious international and technological considerations and the ultimate need to avoid public panic at all costs, that the Majestic-12 Group remains of the unanimous opinion that imposition of the strictest security precautions should continue without interruption into the new administration. At the same time, contingency plan MJ-1949-04P/78 (Top Secret – Eyes Only) should be held in continued readiness should the need to make a public announcement present itself."

It is interesting to see that despite the need for implicating strict security measures, which involved public denial and the embellishment of lies in order to protect the fallacy, there existed a contingency plan to publicly come clean about the whole scenario. There is an element of fear in the final statement, a feeling of uncertainty and lack of control over the situation, which considering the seriousness of the implications of extraterrestrial contact, could be considered a quite natural state of affairs.

GHOST PROTOCOLS

On March 14, 1994, another MJ-12 document was posted anonymously, also on a roll of thirty-five millimeter film, this time it was received by Don Berliner, chairman of the Fund for UFO Research, a group headed by former U.S. Navy physicist Dr. Bruce Maccabee. The package had been mailed from La Crosse, Wisconsin, and when the film was developed on March 22, it contained photos of twenty-one pages from a thirty-one plus page document. Berliner, who co-authored the 1992 book *Crash at Corona* with Stanton Friedman, promptly gave a copy of the document to the General Accounting Office (GAO) since it had recently launched an investigation into claims of crashed UFOs.

Dated April 1954, the SOM 1-01 or "Majestic-12 Group Special Operations Manual" (see SOURCES) was allegedly written with secret protocols on how to deal with "Extraterrestrial Entities and Technology, Recovery and Disposal". The document claims to be TOP SECRET/MAJIC EYES ONLY with access to the material "strictly limited to personnel possessing MAJIC-12 CLEARANCE LEVEL." Any MAJIC EYES ONLY document carries a security level two points above that of Top Secret, according to the SOM 1-01.

The manual alleges to have been prepared especially for "Majestic-12 units", with the purpose of presenting all aspects of MJ-12 so that "authorized personnel will have a better understanding of the goals of the Group, be able to more expertly deal with Unidentified Flying Objects, Extraterrestrial Technology and Entities, and increase the efficiency of future operations." The papers contain information considered vital to the Group on all extraterrestrial matters such as "determination, documentation, collection, and disposition of debris, devices, craft, and occupants of such craft as defined as Extraterrestrial Technology or Extraterrestrial Biological Entities (EBEs) in Section II".

Another Majestic document which appeared on the scene in the late eighties, landing in Tim Cooper's mailbox, claims to be the "1st Annual Report" of the "Majestic Twelve Project". Undated, the report offers a brief explanation as to the purpose of the recently formed specialist group, stating that "The aforementioned panel under the direct presidential directive signed on 26 September 1947, has been tasked with responsibility of providing answers to a most troublesome and disturbing phenomenon, that of other-world visitation and what it portends for the whole human family. It is in this vein that the panel has addressed the problem and is providing possible answers."

Doubts remain as to the authenticity of the "annual report" as this particular document is littered with inconsistencies such as the date referred to as the formation of the group states it was the 26th September, when all other documents claim it was the 24th. For example, the SOM 1-01 clearly states "Operation Majestic-12 was established by special classified presidential order on 24 September 1947 at the recommendation of Secretary of Defense James V. Forrestal and Dr. Vannevar Bush, Chairman of the Joint Research and Development Board."

However, genuine or not, these documents can still offer us an insight into the secret world of government conspiracy, as the contents, even should they prove to be fraudulently produced, have a strong factual basis. Following his own thorough research on the Majestic documents, Timothy Good stated that "some information contained therein, at least, is essentially factual."[71] It may then be reasonable to suggest that if the papers *are* the result of a hoax, that the person[s] responsible have an inside knowledge of such matters, and are in all likelihood part of a plan to misinform and hoodwink meddlesome researchers who could pose a potential threat by exposing what some are trying so desperately to conceal. Author Jim Marrs arrived at a similar conclusion when he wrote, "So if the MJ-12 documents were fabrications, many researchers reasoned it signaled a sophisticated "disinformation" campaign on the part of someone within the U.S. military."[72]

Stanton Friedman included large segments of the "Special Operations Manual" in his 1996 book *Top Secret/MAJIC*, which although he was convinced enough to quote a fair amount of the information, remained of the opinion that solid proof of the paper's legitimacy was still problematic. Friedman wrote, "A detailed proposal to validate this document by investigating internal references, the appropriateness of the procedures enumerated, the relationship to other MJ-12 documents, and the occurrences of any possible anachronisms has been made by myself, Dr. Wood, Dr. Bruce Maccabee, and another researcher, and it awaits funding. Based upon past experience, authentication will be no easy task..."

The "Fund For UFO Research" group which includes Don Berliner, Jan Aldrich and Richard Hall among its members, released a joint statement on March 23, regarding the SOM 1-01 Manual. They jointly concluded that "The only way SOM 1-01 and other alleged "documentary proof" of MJ-12 could conceivably be authenticated would be by locating a documentary paper trail of certifiably original documents in government archives, or in private papers of important people. Even then, allegedly authentic documents would need to be subjected to forensic examination to determine such things as the age of the paper. And document experts would need to examine them for internal accuracy and style. Given the track record of fake documents and shoddy scholarship, rigorous peer review is essential."[73]

Denying the authenticity of *all* the leaked documents and dismissing their contents as pure fabrication could prove to be slightly non-productive, as much of the information contained within the documents appears to reflect reality in some way. The manner in which the authorities insist on dealing with the public; with regards to matters of national security, specifically involving extraterrestrials and UFOs, appears extremely credible. Listed below are excerpts taken from alleged Majestic documents which clearly demonstrate secret protocols that were established to deal with the UFO/ET problem:

1. "Any encounter with entities known to be of extraterrestrial origin is to be considered to be a matter of national security and therefore classified TOP SECRET. Under no circumstance is the general public or public press to learn of the existence of these entities. The official government policy is that such creatures do not exist, and that no agency of the federal government is now engaged in any study of extraterrestrials or their artefacts. Any deviation from this stated policy is strictly forbidden." [74]

2. "a. *Official Denial.* The most desirable response would be that nothing unusual has occurred. By stating that the government has no knowledge of the event, further investigation by the public press may be forestalled." [75]

3. "b. *Discredit Witness.* If at all possible, witnesses will be held incommunicado until the extent of their knowledge and involvement can be determined. Witnesses will be discouraged from talking about what they have seen, and intimidation may be necessary to ensure their cooperation. If witnesses have already contacted the press, it will be necessary to discredit their stories. This can best be done by the assertion that they have either misinterpreted natural events, are the victims of hysteria or hallucinations, or are the perpetrators of hoaxes." [76]

4. "c. *Deceptive Statements.* It may become necessary to issue false statements to preserve the security of the [crash] site. Meteors, downed satellites, weather balloons, and military aircraft are all acceptable alternatives…" [77]

5. "The officer in charge will act quickly to select the cover story that best fits the situation. It should be remembered when selecting a cover story that official policy regarding UFOBs is that they do not exist." [78]

6. "M. <u>Domestic and Constitutional Issues</u>

In dealing with clear violations of civic law and guarantees as defined under the Constitution, it has been discussed among members of MAJESTIC TWELVE that such protection of individual rights are out-weighed by the nature of the threat."[79]

7. "P. <u>Government Policy of Control and</u> Denial

One of the most difficult aspects of controlling the perception in the public's mind of government attempts of denial and ignorance – is actual control of the press. Until a clear intent is established with diplomatic relations firmly in hand, it is the recommendation of the President's Special Panel with concurrence from MAJESTIC TWELVE, that a policy of strict denial of the events surfacing from Roswell, N.M., and any other incident of such caliber [misspelt], be enforced. A[n] inter-active program of controlled releases to the media, in such fashion to discredit any civilian investigation, be instituted in accordance with the provisions of the 1947 National Security Act."

Although debunkers continue to highlight discrepancies and inconsistencies such as spelling mistakes and incorrect classification among other things, no one has been able to definitely disprove all of the MJ-12 documents. In fact, there are many aspects of the documentation which provides evidence to indicate their authenticity. One example that reinforces the validation process comes from the discovery made by Dr. Robert Wood, that the style and typeface used in U.S. government printing presses during the 1950's, matched that used in the "SOM 1-01 manual".

Dr. Wood claims that Ed Doty, the uncle of Rick Doty (retired special agent for AFOSI, Air Force Office of Special Investigation), informed him that he had once attended a UFO Crash Retrieval course at Los Alamos in 1954. Is it possible that the SOM 1-01 was their Tech Order for crash retrievals as Wood believes? The manual does include a Tech Order number of TO 12D1-3-11-1 on the front cover and just so happens to be dated April 1954.

Details of the current situation at the time of writing were included in the manual, which although yet to be vehemently validated with any certainty, still offers the reader food for thought when considering the phenomenon as a whole. Whether written for the purpose of informing or misinforming, the writer seems to be much more 'in the know' than any ordinary civilian could have been in the early fifties when the document is purported to have been created. Hoaxing such a document before the advent of personal computers and the internet seems as implausible as some of the subject matter contained within its pages, if not more so. Surely only an actual government insider or a fiction writer with a colourful imagination could have written the following in 1952;

"It is considered as far as the current situation is concerned, that there are few indications that these objects and their builders pose a direct threat to the security of the United States, despite the uncertainty as to their ultimate motives in coming here. Certainly the technology possessed by these beings far surpasses anything known to modern science, yet their presence here seems to be benign, and they seem to be avoiding contact with our species, at least for the present. Several dead entities have been recovered along with a substantial amount of wreckage and devices from downed craft, all of which are now under study at various locations. No attempt has been made by extraterrestrial entities either to contact authorities or recover their dead counterparts or the downed craft, even though one of the crashes was the result of direct military action. The greatest threat at this time arises from the acquisition and study of such advance technology by foreign powers unfriendly to the United States. It is for this reason that the recovery and study of this type of material by the United States has been given such a high priority."[80]

Although the authenticity of the Majestic documents continues to confound all who attempt to unravel its mysteries, much of the information contained therein, regardless of the writer's intent, appears grounded in reality. The entire extraterrestrial topic covered in this book will remain mysterious and inconclusive as long as those withholding the historical facts continue to deceive the rest of the population. If one endeavours to research and investigate the subject in more depth, then slowly more and more evidence of deception and secrecy begins to emerge from the murky waters of hidden truths. Even the greatest of lies can be uncovered if one digs deep enough, as ultimately, the truth has a knack of floating to the surface eventually.

Jim Marrs wrote, "whether bogus or not, the MJ-12 and Project Aquarius documents and others would seem to establish beyond doubt that certain persons within the government were concealing their intense interest in UFOs. If they are genuine – a determination that does not appear to be within easy reach anytime soon – they would explain much in regard to continued government secrecy."[81]

Often, secretive behaviour denotes that one has something to hide and rouses suspicion without the need for specifics. If the Roswell incident was nothing more than just a weather balloon then why the furore which ensued? If there is nothing of significance to the numerous UFO reports which flooded in during the forties and fifties, why formulate strategies to deal with them and spend government funding on devising UFO study groups and reports?

Many aspects of this subject will remain cloudy and unclear for years to come, but one thing that we can be sure of is that *something* is going on that we are not meant to know. And in order for that *something* to continue behind closed doors and away from public scrutiny, the many government agencies involved in the great deception have had to go underground.

3

OUT OF SIGHT, OUT OF MIND

The Black Budget currently consumes $1.25 trillion per year. At least this amount is used in black programs, like those concerned with deep underground military bases. Presently, there are 129 deep underground military bases in the United States.

Philip Schneider, 1995

IN ORDER TO MAINTAIN THE HIGHEST possible levels of secrecy deemed necessary by the ruling factions of this world to keep the knowledge of any extraterrestrial activity out of the public domain, those responsible for the deceit have had to go underground. Many former employees of varying occupations have come forward giving incredible accounts of what they have personally experienced regarding secret underground and underwater bases and tunnels.

Known as DUMBs or deep underground military bases, it is said that a network of these facilities have been constructed globally, with a large number having being built beneath the surface of the United States. Images of the tunnel boring machines (TBMs) used to excavate and tunnel such vast areas of land are available on the internet, and a history of some of the more well-renowned bases such as Area 51 in Nevada desert, has already been thoroughly researched and put into print.

Details of some of the activities allegedly taking place beneath our feet have been revealed by different sources; some working as security guards on site, others employed in a scientific capacity at a higher level of secrecy, some deeply involved with the construction of the bases and tunnels and others being everyday people claiming to have been abducted by aliens and transported to these underground laboratories for genetic and other nefarious scientific experimentation.

In this chapter we shall be delving deeper into the unseen world beneath the surface and attempt to ascertain some level of understanding of the truth of this complex and highly secretive subject matter. We shall be focusing our attention on one of the most secretive and disturbing of all underground facilities, located near the town of Dulce, New Mexico.

As it would take countless hours to investigate all of the DUMBs of the world, it is of more value here to concentrate our efforts on one prime example in hope of catching a glimpse into this murky world of clandestine and macabre activities. As with most material of this nature we will be relying upon the testimonies of certain individuals to illuminate us with the details which remain hidden in the shadows, and hoping that they are as genuine and honest as they appear and that their words hold enough validity to be considered valuable in the context of this research.

If there is any truth to the alien enigma that continues to confound us, then the very existence of secret underground bases and tunnels could prove to be vital evidence and offer a reason as to why we do not see these beings walking in our streets and flying overhead as commonplace as passenger planes.

There is a theory that the ETs are involved in highly covert and clandestine activities alongside humans and are trying to keep their presence concealed from the public for reasons unbeknownst to us. With all the satellite technology available today in the public arena such as Google Earth, it would seem extremely likely that in order to continue the deception, building underground would be the most viable option for all involved. What better way to keep their secret activities from the prying eyes of the rest of the world, out of sight - out of mind.

SECRET FUNDING

As written in a report for the Jason Group entitled *'Characterisation of Underground Facilities'* which was published in April 1999 by the Mitre Corporation, "Underground facilities not only protect critical activities but also conceal them. Once built, it may be very difficult to determine the nature of the facility."[82] This report comes straight from the United States industrial-military complex right at the heart of this conspiracy.

The Jason Group is a sub-group of the IDA (Institute for Defense Analysis) which was set up as an independent research and consulting organisation which works on the basis of contracts with the Pentagon dealing specifically with military research problems. The decision to create a group consisting of America's leading scientists followed the departure of many of the atomic bomb and radar research specialists at the end of WWII. In an attempt to hold on to the valuable talent which was generally heading back to University campuses around the country, the military and in particular the Defense Department sought to re-establish ongoing consultations with their best academic scientists.

Because the IDA was set up as a private non-profit organisation, the private funding meant they could afford to determine their own salary scales and attract the finest young scientists available with the promise of a free reign on their chosen subject along with the financial backing to support such projects. It was always of the upmost importance to establish the enterprise as an elite group of the highest prestige, open only to a select few of worthy ability.

Details of the Jason group are shrouded in mystery but it is understood that it was founded by members of the Manhattan Project which led to the creation of the atomic bomb. Author Annie Jacobson wrote, "To understand how black projects began, and how they continue to function today, one must start with the creation of the atomic bomb. The men who ran the Manhattan Project wrote the rules about black operations. The atomic bomb was the mother of all black projects and it is the parent from which all black operations have sprung."[83]

The Jason group is believed to consist of mainly theoretical physicists who are considered to be the absolute elite of scientific minds in the country and as of 1987 the membership even included four Nobel Prize winners. Today the government continues to receive scientific help from the Jason Group which they cannot find anywhere else as they are probably the one group of scientists in the United States that remains truly up to date with what high technology really exists outside of the public domain. The veil of secrecy surrounding the Jason Group is so tight that no leaks have ever surfaced from within this civilian group. Part of the success of this secrecy is down to the Mitre Corporation dealing with all Jason's administration. Any government contracts which are allotted to Mitre are really being diverted straight to a Jason scientist, but all paperwork and documentation will show the Mitre Corporation in print, allowing the Jason group to remain incognito.

This covert think-tank is a prime example of where important scientific projects are born and along with the vast amounts of funding secretly exchanging hands, any project regardless of scale and cost becomes feasible and more often than not becomes a reality.

Dr. Richard Sauder PhD has written extensively on the subject of secret underground and underwater bases and tunnels, often pulling resources and information from the public record to expose the U.S. Government's clandestine operations regarding this largely misunderstood area of research. Sauder discovered that billions of dollars continue to be reported as going missing and unaccounted for in different areas, to the point that the reality of financing such large scale construction projects as building underground and underwater bases has been proven to be completely viable.

The size of the Black Budget is believed to be astronomical. In the year 2000, auditors went through the accounts of HUD, the U.S. Department of Housing and Urban Development and were perplexed to discover that $59 billion was missing from their records. In another article, printed in *USA Today*, it revealed segments of a report written by the General Accounting Office (GAO) which stated that "NASA failed to account for billions of dollars spent on the space shuttle and International Space Station."

Then there is the Native American Trust Fund which was set up to try and compensate the Native American tribes for the loss of their land which had been sold as real estate. The idea was that a percentage of all funds that were raised from the sales of the petroleum that was drilled from Native American soil, or the fur from the animals, or the timber that was felled or the fish that were caught, would be put into the trust fund for the benefit of the Native Americans. The money was to be dispersed amongst all the different tribes but that didn't happen, consequently the Indians have been trying to find out what is happening to their money for years as it seems that it is being looted.

An article in the Washington Post used the headline "Unknown BILLIONS missing from Native American Trust Fund", which went on to detail decades of massive theft, missing records and shredded documents. Where does all this money go and who is taking it and for what? Well one can only speculate on the specifics of these matters but evidence suggests that there exists a secret fund which siphons off various other funds in order to accumulate enough to finance large scale secret projects. The fact of the matter is that all this missing money has to have gone somewhere; how can you hide hundreds of billions of dollars without spending it on something huge?

Back in the sixties, the Stanford Research Institute printed a document which dealt with the practical and costing issues of constructing underwater bases. The report stated that "The construction of 30 manned in-bottom bases within the ocean floors is technically and economically feasible...The cost of such a base program would be about $2.7 billion..."[84]

So, over fifty years ago it was being discussed as a real possibility and with all the secret funding accumulating behind closed doors many, many more secret bases could be built. According to the research of Bill Cooper, the Rand Corporation hosted a Deep Underground Construction Symposium in 1959. Cooper wrote "In the Symposium report, machines are pictured, and described which could bore a tunnel 45 feet in diameter at the rate of 5 feet per hour. It also displays pictures of huge tunnels and underground vaults containing what appear to be complex facilities and possibly even cities. It appears that the previous 5 years of all out underground construction had made significant progress by that time."[85]

Construction of these bases was slow to progress until large amounts of funding became available in 1957, ironically the same year that another symposium was held which was alleged to have been attended by some of the greatest scientific minds of that time.

Studies were setup by secret Executive Order of President Eisenhower to make recommendations called "Alternatives 1, 2, and 3" which were intended to explore ways of preserving humanity, should the world face some type of cataclysmic event or simply destroy itself through negligent human activity.

Alternative 1 dealt with environmental protection and the use of nuclear devices to blast holes in the stratosphere in which all pollution might escape whilst simultaneously allowing excess Ultraviolet light to reach the Earth's surface, killing millions with skin cancer.

Alternative 3 was to employ both alien and conventional technology to establish colonies on both the Moon (codenamed 'Adam') and Mars (codenamed 'Eve') in order for a select few to escape the Earth and survive in outer space.

Alternative 2 was another survival tactic which involved the construction of a vast network of underground cities and tunnels for a select representation of cultures, races and occupations to continue the human race leaving the surface dwellers to fend for themselves in an unprotected solar environment. *Alternative 1* was dismissed as unlikely to succeed but work on *Alternatives* 2 and 3 were simultaneously ordered to commence according to Cooper.

Cooper revealed that the Military Office of the White House has organised and kept a multi-million dollar secret fund which was used to build many DUMBs beneath American soil. Any inquisitive Presidents wondering what they were building were informed that the fund was to be used to build deep underground shelters to protect them in any war scenario. In reality only a few were actually built with the President's safety in mind, whilst the rest of the money was channelled through the Military Office to the MJ-12 group and finally to the private contractors who were hired to build top-secret underground bases.

In 1957, another secret fund was allegedly created obtaining funds from Congress under the name White House Underground Construction fund. Set up by President Eisenhower, the fund was said to have been for "construction and maintenance of secret sites where the President could be taken in case of military attack: Presidential Emergency Sites".[86] These sites are more like deep holes in the ground which contain high-end communication systems and were built to withstand possible nuclear attack. Bill Cooper believes that the funds were used to build more than 75 sites across the country with the Atomic Energy Commission building an additional 22 sites. All information concerning these sites is considered top- secret, especially the location of the facilities.

In order to confuse and bewilder, the money trail which continues to be controlled by the Military Office follows a circuitous path that no accountant, spy or discerning researcher can trace. Only those at the beginning and end of the trail know what the cash is to be used for. In 1980, according to Cooper, the Representative George Mahon of Texas, the chairman of the House Appropriations Committee and also the Defense Subcommittee, was at the beginning along with Representative Robert Sikes of Florida, chairman of the House Appropriations Military Construction Subcommittee. The cash trail would ultimately lead to those at the end of the line which included a commander at the Washington Navy Yard, the director of the Military Office, MJ-12 and the President. The fund was shrouded in secrecy to the extent that almost all traces of its existence could be made to disappear by the very few people who were in control of it, and there has never been an audit of this secret money and most likely never will be.

On October 20, 1991 California researcher and founder of the '20/20 Group' Michael Lindemann, gave a lecture concerning the Black Budget and the underground empire stating that "...every year the Congress dutifully passes this bloated budget that has some $300,000,000,000 or more with HUGE chunks of cash labelled like that: 'Special Projects', 'Unusual Stuff' - Ten billion dollars. O.K., well where does the 'unusual stuff' money go? Well, it DOES go to 'unusual stuff', that's for sure, and one of the places it goes is that it goes into the underground bases."

The key to successfully hiding such vast amounts of money lies in the very carefully considered and systematic approach to shifting the funds around, without those involved having access to any information on the purpose and final destination of the funds. The Department of Defense was allocated the money which had been authorised by the Appropriation Committee, as a top-secret item to be used in the Army Construction Program. However, the Army had no idea what it was for and weren't allowed to spend it anyway. In reality, the Navy had been authorised to spend the money which had been channelled to the Chesapeake Division of the Navy Engineers, although they didn't know what it was to be used for either.

As Bill Cooper wrote, "Not even the Commanding Officer, who was an Admiral, knew what the fund was to be used for. Only one man, a Navy Commander, who was assigned to the Chesapeake Division but in reality was responsible only to the Military Office of the White House knew of the actual purpose, amount, and ultimate destination of the top-secret fund."[87]

It isn't difficult to understand how money can be distributed without the details of its origin or ultimate purpose being disclosed, even to those whose fingers the money briefly slips through. In order to build secret DUMBs without the taxpayer's knowledge and keep such massive projects from the public, secret funding and the covert movement of such funds is absolutely essential.

The whereabouts of some of these bases has come to light over the years. Some are less secret than others and were built for military purposes alone. Any connection to the alien scenario is mainly reserved for the less publicly known sites such as those below Dulce Base, Area 51 and Los Alamos; although a number of Air Force bases have also seen their fair share of the action -

namely Kirtland AFB, Holloman AFB, Nellis AFB, Wright-Patterson AFB, Norton AFB and Edwards AFB. Some are said to house alien craft in underground hangars whilst others have experienced UFO sightings and alleged meetings between U.S. Government officials and the UFO occupants. It is protocol to take all alien craft retrievals to the nearest AFB and wait for further instructions. Listed below are just a handful of some of the DUMBs that are presently in use:

Cheyenne Mountain Complex, Colorado – Central command post of NORAD, under Air Force Space Command at Peterson AFB

Mount Weather Emergency Operations Centre (MWEOC), Virginia – Civilian command centre, centre of operations for the Federal Emergency Management Agency (FEMA)

Raven Rock Mountain Complex, Site R, between Maryland and Pennsylvania

Fort Meade, Maryland – National Security Agency (NSA) headquarters

Camp David, Maryland – Presidential retreat said to be built above a massive underground facility stretching for miles

Washington D.C. – Deep underground facility with multiple levels beneath White House

Los Alamos National Laboratory (LANL), New Mexico – Genetics Research and bio-technology

Pine Gap, Alice Springs, Australia - Massive multi-levelled facility believed to be run by the Club of Rome, apparently equipped with levels of computer terminals connected globally to the major computer mainframes

Mount Shasta, California - Said to consist of a multi-levelled complex over 5 miles deep and at least 20 miles in circumference

Denver International Airport – Underground multi-level city beneath airport

Oklahoma City - Multi-level underground base with underground shuttle system link between Area 51, Nevada and Dulce, New Mexico

Some of the large companies and contractors involved in the construction of these massive projects are as follows: Morrison Knudsen Corporation, Parsons Brinckerhoff, Kiewit, Black & Veatch, US Army Corps of Engineers, US Navy Sea Bees (underground and undersea construction), Bechtel, Robbins, Jacobs Engineering and the Rand Corporation. In fact, it is a former employee of some of these companies who eventually chose to come forward and share his story in the hope of exposing the dark secrets which have remained hidden from public view. If anyone is qualified to discuss the subject of underground construction, it is the American Philip Schneider and in the section which follows we shall be focusing on his incredible testimony.

THE PHIL SCHNEIDER STORY

According to *The Oregonian* newspaper obituary dated January 29, 1996, Philip Schneider (April 23, 1947 – Jan 17, 1996) was said to have died of a stroke on January 17. His death certificate officially claims that he "strangled self with surgical tubing", suggesting that he had in fact committed suicide by wrapping a rubber catheter hose around his neck three times and tying it in a half-knot at the front before collapsing head first into his wheelchair. Those close to Phil have no doubts that he was actually murdered.

He was in the process of leaking vital information to the public of which he was privy to and felt a huge sense of purpose regarding this task despite the several physical illnesses of which he was suffering at the time that included osteoporosis, multiple sclerosis and cancer. His previous lecture tour in 1995 was sponsored by Al Bielik (a crewmember onboard the U.S.S. Eldridge during the infamous Philadelphia Experiment[4]) who knew Phil's father and had become good friends with Phil during the tours. Philip was scheduled to commence another tour in 1996 but would not survive long enough to see it through as it would seem that somebody wanted him to stop talking.

---

[4] The Philadelphia Experiment was intended to use Einstein's unified field theory to attempt to render US Navy ships invisible to radar by using large electrical generators and magnetic fields to bend the light around the ships. On July 22, 1943, one test successfully managed to 'cloak' the U.S.S. Eldridge in apparent invisibility but at some cost to the crew members onboard. When the ship reappeared, it is claimed by those involved, that some went insane whilst others were found physically embedded in the metal structure of the ship itself.

There are several reasons why so many people believe that he was murdered including the fact that there was no suicide note and that he always told everyone that if he ever "committed suicide" then you would know that he had actually been murdered. He had already had thirteen attempts made on his life, which he had openly discussed in public previous to his mysterious death. He had been shot at, driven off the road, and on one occasion the wheel nuts on his car had been loosened before he was due to return to his vehicle. During one of his lectures Schneider declared, "I love my country more than I love my life. Two weeks ago I was shot in the shoulder." He received a round of applause from the audience for his patriotism and bravery whilst revealing the gunshot wound to those present.[88] Back at home he had in his possession a 9mm gun which he had borrowed to protect both himself and his family due to the death threats and the attempts to kill him. So why was Phil Schneider a target and who exactly was trying to silence him?

For the last two years of his life, Schneider toured the United States giving over thirty lectures concerning information of a conspiratorial nature regarding many issues of governmental deception and involvement in highly classified clandestine activities. His work as a structural engineer on government black projects and the construction of deep underground facilities in the United States, coupled with top secret information he was to discover following the death of his father Captain Otto Oscar Schneider, led him to finally go public and forego his oath of secrecy in the hope that exposing the truth might just encourage the nation to wake-up to the deceit and empower themselves.

Phil Schneider was being heavily monitored because of the secretive nature of his work and also because of his father's involvement in black projects. Shortly before his death Philip had completed a manuscript ready for publishing which listed all of the DUMBs, complete with longitude and latitudes, along with details of other U.S. Government deceptions including information on the alien agenda and plans for a New World Order. This led to an attempt to kidnap his daughter Marie by an agent from the Defense Intelligence Agency (DIA).

In 1947, Phil was born in a US Naval Hospital in Bethesda, Montgomery County in Maryland. His father Oscar was a Captain in the United States Navy who worked in nuclear medicine and also helped to design the Nautilus, the first US nuclear submarine. During one of his 1995 lectures, Phil stated that his father was actually a captured Nazi U-boat commander who became repatriated into the US Naval Intelligence which ultimately led to his involvement with the controversial Philadelphia Experiment during the early 1940's. Oscar laid the groundwork along with other theoreticians for the Philadelphia Experiment as well other experiments. Phil didn't condone some of his father's actions since he fought on both sides of the war, as he was a German U-boat captain before having being brought to America, but he did believe that he was very brave to join the Americans against his former allies. Phil claimed that "there was a one million dollars reward, payable in gold, to anyone who killed him."

Whilst working for the Department of the Navy Bureau of Medicine and Surgery, Oscar Schneider travelled with his son Phillip to London in the 1950's where he was to produce autopsy reports on crewmembers of the U.S.S. Eldridge who had perished during the experiment to render the ship invisible. These reports were amongst the many documents and photographs which Phil discovered in his father's basement after his death in 1993 which proved Oscar's involvement in both the Philadelphia Experiment and Operation Crossroads.

He found letters written in the 1940's and 1950's showing that Oscar had helped to quarantine the crewmembers of the Eldridge and that he later autopsied them after their death. Phil took some of these reports on the lecture circuit with him as proof of their existence along with other artefacts such as metal from a crash retrieval near Roswell which was given to him at the age of fourteen, and crystalline metals which withstand up to 10,000 degrees Fahrenheit – grown in the confines of outer space and given to us by the large Greys.

In one of the reports dated 6 March, 1955 Capt. Schneider wrote, "Conducted autopsy on #9 crew member on DE-173 with some abnormal conclusions as to foreign material (perhaps implants) found in #9's cerebellum part 14-3." He went on to report that "four long gold tipped fibre" devices 11/8 inch in length with "unknown 'script' or 'writing'" on each one, were removed from the body of the crew member as the "nasal cavity also showed implantation". Discovering small one inch objects with gold and tiny unknown writing etched onto them raised more questions than it answered.

So, even back in the fifties, Phil Schneider's father was involved with alien artefacts and top-secret research, which as it transpired, led to Phil becoming heavily involved in similar covert studies. Captain Schneider was also involved in Operation Crossroads which involved nuclear weapon testing at the Bikini Atoll lagoon in the Pacific, where he was mainly employed in a medical capacity performing examinations on the humans and animals that had been exposed to radiation after the A-bomb had been dropped. Oscar was also said to have invented a high-speed camera which was used during Operation Crossroads and inadvertently managed to photograph a number of UFOs fleeing the test site through mushroom clouds during the first atomic tests at Bikini Island on July 12, 1946.

Phil Schneider said that "Bikini Island at the time was infested with them, especially under the water, and the natives had problems with their animals being mutilated. At that time, General MacArthur felt that the next war would be with aliens from other worlds." Phil was in possession of these images and also the official documents written by his father referring to the mysterious objects which appeared in the photos. As highlighted in an earlier chapter, UFOs and nuclear tests have been synonymous since the advent of the nuclear age.

We have seen how Oscar Schneider was involved in many facets of top-secret military operations but how did his son become involved in such highly classified projects? Phil Schneider started off by going to an engineering school and built up a reputation for being a gifted geological engineer and also a structural engineer with both aerospace and military applications. He was also an expert on explosives and particularly on the effect of explosives on geological structures.

Initially, his employment was with Morrison-Knudsen Corporation building underground mountain bases whilst also working for the US Army Corps of Engineers and the US Navy. According to his ex-wife Cynthia Drayer, Phil worked using two social security numbers. Drayer commented, "I was able to prove that he had two social security numbers through the social security office when I applied for his daughter's death benefits."[89]

111

Throughout the majority of his career he worked using the wrong social security number and it was only after he was granted Social Security Income in 1981 that his 'real' number came into use. The reason for using two numbers was due to the fact that he claimed to have had one of the highest security clearances in the world called 'Rhyolite 38 - level 38'. During one of his presentations Schneider told the audience "I carried a level 1 security clearance, Rhyolite 38 Factor. There are very few of us. There's nobody except myself to my knowledge, talking like this. I'm breaking federal law coming out and talking about this to a group of people."

His decision to go public followed the murder of his friend Ron Rummell (also officially declared as suicide) whose body was found in a park in Portland in September 1993. Phil believed that 11 of his best friends had been murdered over the last 22 years, eight of which had been officially declared as suicides, and although he had experienced such loss on many previous occasions, he decided this was the last straw that it was time to spill the beans and get the information out in the open.

He ripped up his security clearance card and became an average American citizen once more, albeit one with a story to tell and a price on his head for his troubles. Rummell was evidently also a marked man, most likely due to the controversial publications entitled *The Alien Digest* which he authored under the pseudonym "Creston". Along with Phil and five other people, the magazine was starting to gain a fairly wide circulation as part of The Cosmic Voyage publications of the Aquarian Church of Universal Service. Four twenty-five page issues of *The Alien Digest* were published during the early 1990s before the publications ended abruptly due to Rummell's unexpected death. Here is a rare excerpt from one of the publications to give us some idea of what type of information might be deemed enough of a threat to national security by those behind the scenes to actually necessitate murder.

"There are several large, Deep, Underwater Mountain Bases (DUMB-2) in the world. They have been there for a very long time, with all kinds of ships, submarines and planes disappearing in their triangles from all bases in the world. These underwater bases are very old and the aliens who inhabit them are not usually networked with others, but have their own personal agenda for

112

power and survival. They have major cities to keep stocked with food, gold, raw materials, refined plutonium and slaves to do the grunt work or short life-span work. All the bases are aware of each other's base and have their own territories, seldom going into other triangles. Some of these areas are known to be owned by very nasty aliens."[90] - Creston aka Ron Rummell.

His work may appear somewhat speculative and could come across to the average reader as a work of science-fiction, but regardless of the veracity of his information which cannot be proved either way, something about his publications seems to have touched a raw nerve with someone at a very high level because he lost his life in very suspicious circumstances shortly after releasing *The Alien Digest*. He was clearly privy to some highly classified information, being such a close friend of Philip Schneider's, and he was quite proactive within his field of interest as can be seen in some home-video footage of Rummell with Schneider near Area 51 in Nevada as they filmed some UFOs at night and shared their views with each-other in front of the lens. Rummell's death had a profound effect on Schneider who decided one day to cut up his high level clearance security card and go public with his knowledge of DUMBs, the alien agenda and Black Budget operations.

Rummel was not the first UFO whistleblower to mysteriously die after having divulged detailed information concerning alien activity. In 1959, author Morris K. Jessop was found asphyxiated by the exhaust of his car shortly after his book *The Case for the UFO* had been sent to the Chief of the Naval Research in Washington. Comments had been handwritten into the book along with underlined passages, although the hand responsible for such actions was not clarified. Included in the text was a passage which read, "They have bases on the ocean floor as well as in outer space, and it is an insult to call them visitors, as they have been here longer than we have. Fortunately for us, they feel more at ease in Earth's environment on the ocean floor than at ground level."

According to Schneider, the Black Budget garners $1.023 trillion every two years, which amounts to roughly 500 billion dollars every year, about a quarter of the U.S. gross national budget. The Black Budget is an independent taxing body which is not monitored by Congress. It is believed to be mainly financed by CIA drug operations, the NSA (National Security Agency), the

DEA (Drug Enforcement Administration) and possibly the FBI. In January of 1995, an FBI agent attempted to go public with information on this matter and according to Schneider was subsequently murdered.

As of 1995, there were 131 active deep underground military bases in the United States alone, with 1,477 being built worldwide. These figures will have risen dramatically since his lectures were recorded. Each base has an average cost of between 17 and 19 billion dollars to construct, and they are being built using extremely sophisticated methods at the rate of around two bases per year. Schneider was involved working in government black projects for 17 years as a geologist and structural engineer. He was also a self taught metallurgist and, like his father, he also lays claim to an invention. He co-invented specific methods used in shaped charge explosives research which helped to facilitate the building of DUMBs as well as submarine bases. His expertise in these areas is the main reason he was given such a high level security clearance, his services were required and so highly sought after in order to proceed with the construction of such monumental and large-scale installations.

He worked on bases at Area 51 and the S-4 facility at Groom Lake in the Nevada desert and also at Los Alamos in New Mexico. He describes the bases as "basically large cities underground" which are connected to each other by high-speed magneto-leviton trains and reach speeds of up to Mach 2. Unlike the trains we are familiar with, these don't actually run on the rails, rather they are raised three quarters of an inch off the rail. We currently have no such technology on the surface at this point.

Another whistleblower, whose testimony regarding the Dulce facility, the most secret of all underground bases, is former Dulce Base security officer Thomas Edwin Castello. He has revealed some truly fascinating information much of which backs up Schneider's story, stating that "there are shuttle tubes that 'shoot' the trains at incredible speeds using a maglev and vacuum method. They travel at a speed that excels the speed of sound". He also believes there to be a vast subterranean highway called the "Sub-Global System", which criss-crosses the world like an underground freeway which has check-points at each country border.

Schneider insists that nine underground military bases have been built at Area 51, with each base measuring at about 4 and a quarter cubic miles. Idaho alone is home to another eleven bases. In general, underground bases have an average depth of just over a mile and are between 2.66 and 4.25 cubic miles in size. Researcher Michael Lindemann was informed by a colleague of his, who also worked on underground projects, that some of these bases could be between 30 and 35 stories deep.

These 'ground-scrapers' are not simply mine shafts but in Lindemann's words are "...huge, giant facilities, many city blocks in circumference, able to house tens of thousands of people. One of them, the YANO Facility we're told (by the county Fire Dept. Director, the county Fire Dept. Chief who had to go in there to look at a minor fire infraction) there's a 400-car parking lot on the 1st level of the YANO Facility, but cars never come in and out, those are the cars that they use INSIDE."[91]

The machines used to excavate such vast areas of earth are known as TBMs or tunnel boring machines, but rather than simply drilling through the ground to create a large tunnel, these machines are much more advanced and don't really bore a hole as much as they vitrify, melt and deflagrate the rock, leaving no detritus as the rock is essentially vaporised and the residue from the molten ash forms a smooth interior tunnel wall of an almost glassy consistency. The Krupp Works in Germany are allegedly responsible for the development of this technology. The machines are said to tunnel around seven miles long in a single day.

According to Schneider they have been building unceasingly night and day since the 1940's and have managed to maintain the secrecy for so long by continually forwarding the construction progress behind closed doors. "The Black Projects sidestep the authority of congress, which as we know is illegal. Right now the New World Order is depending on these bases. If I had known at the time I was working on them that the NWO was involved, I would not have done it. I was lied to extensively" asserts Schneider, who initially believed that the underground bases were top secret mainly due to legitimate reasons concerning national security.

Military secret technology is believed to increase and progress at a rate of 44.5 years per calendar year of 'conventional' technology, largely influenced by the involvement of non-human high-technology which has either been amicably shared with us via some formal treaty system or retrieved fortuitously by us and reverse-engineered. As Schneider told his audiences in reference to the Philadelphia Experiment, "This is why it is easy to understand that back in 1943 they were able to create, through the use of vacuum tube technology, a ship that could literally disappear from one place and appear in another. Right now military technology is about 1200 years more advanced than public state technology."[92]

DELVING DEEPER INTO DULCE

Philip Schneider is a well known figure within the UFO community because of his involvement with an underground base located at the Jicarilla Apache Indian Reservation in Northern New Mexico north-west of the town of Dulce, a sleepy little town perched upon the Archuleta Mesa just south of the Colorado border. Reports by a number of tourists claim that upon entering the town of Dulce they have been followed by black vehicles with heavily tinted windows until they are finally outside the city limits.

Researcher John Anderson reportedly visited Dulce, investigating numerous UFO sightings. On the day of his arrival he was fortunate to witness and photograph six UFOs descending rapidly over a compound where his investigation had led him after following a McDonnell Douglas mini-lab in a van. He later showed a shopkeeper the photo he had taken only to become engrossed in a conversation about how the store owner had experienced cattle mutilations during his tenure as a cattle rancher in Dulce. A phone call to the store interrupted their chat and John was subsequently told to leave. Immediately after, the store was closed, then a mysterious van drove up to the store and a man got out and went straight inside the closed shop. Sensing something was amiss, John left swiftly but was followed by two men in a car as he left town.[93] Cattle mutilations, UFO sightings and strange black vehicles have all been reported in this unremarkable area of New Mexico, is there more to this town than can be seen from the surface?

It is alleged that the Dulce facility is one of only two bases in the United States that was purpose built for the joint use of the alien nation and the U.S. Government where an exchange of technology could take place. The Dulce base is supposed to have been built on top of already existent ancient caverns and tunnels comparable in size to the Carlsbad Caverns (the largest and deepest in the world), which have been allegedly used by reptilian-type humanoids for centuries. The Rand Corporation which employed Schneider's services at some point repeatedly enlarged the caverns for their own purposes. Thomas Castello recalls hearing that Dulce was initially started by the Army Engineers in 1937-38 with the most recent work of connecting tunnels to the Page Arizona Base (one of the older underground facilities) being completed in 1965-66. In recent times, researchers have endeavoured to prove the existence of underground caverns beneath the surface of the Archuleta Mesa by using equipment to take sound recordings under the ground. The preliminary and computer analysis of these findings indicated that there were indeed deep cavities under the Mesa which extended to a depth of over 4,000 feet.

The other jointly occupied base is believed to be at the S-4 facility located approximately seven miles south of the western border of Area 51 in Nevada which is joined to the Dulce facility via the tube-shuttle system. Other alien bases are said to have been constructed beneath Indian reservations in the 'four corners' region of Utah, New Mexico, Arizona and Colorado. Entrances to these bases are frequently camouflaged as mining operations or sand quarries whilst other portals are located on military base territory.

Thomas Castello claims that "New Mexico and Arizona have the largest amounts of entrances followed by California, Montana, Idaho, Colorado, Pennsylvania, Kansas, Arkansas and Missouri. Of all the states, Florida and North Dakota have the least amount of entrances. Wyoming has a road that opens directly into the subterranean freeway. That road is no longer in use, but could be reactivated if they decide to do so, with minimal cost. It's located near Brooks Lake." This underground freeway system is known as the Trans-American Underground Sub-Shuttle System (T.A.U.S.S.).

As a former member of the Intelligence Briefing Team of the Commander in Chief of the Pacific Fleet, William Milton Cooper saw and read TOP SECRET/MAJIC material between the years

1970 and 1973 which revealed the alien presence on Earth to him as a definite reality. Cooper believes that "all alien bases are under complete control of the Department of Naval Intelligence and all personnel who work in these complexes receive their cheques from the Navy." In the highly classified material of which Cooper had access to in the early seventies, he learnt that the Dulce base was built in joint agreement between the CIA and extraterrestrial races back in 1969 using the Navajo river to supply water and electricity to the base.

In 1961, the 'first peaceful nuclear blast' occurred twenty-five miles from Carlsbad Caverns in New Mexico as part of a series of projects called the 'Plowshares Program' undertaken by the Atomic Energy Commission (AEC). The explosion was expected to produce steam for generating electricity by supplying a vast underground salt cavern but the blast occurred prematurely, knocking off the top of the underground chamber, releasing clouds of radioactive waste into the atmosphere and ruining the 'kettle' effect intended to produce the steam.

Project Gasbuggy was an umbrella project of Project Plowshare which also took place in New Mexico as collaboration between the AEC and the El Paso Natural Gas Company which involved a 26 kiloton blast 4,200 feet below the surface. Gassbuggy produced 214 million cubic feet of gas in 15 months but contained radioactive krypton and tritium, which was then pumped into the homes of unsuspecting gas company customers.[94] It has been suggested that this subsurface nuclear blast was actually used to hollow out a kind of large chimney as part of the development of a substation for a top-secret tunnel system leading out of an underground black project base i.e. Dulce.[95]

It is here at the Dulce underground facility, which has been described as a government-alien biogenetic laboratory, that a multitude of experiments are said to be taking place out of sight of the public, including genetic experimentation on kidnapped men, women and children alongside alien abductees. According to statistics provided by the FBI, Defence Intelligence Agency (DIA) and the CIA, 100,000 children and one million adults disappear every year which are totally unaccounted for and are not reported as kidnappings, rapes or suicides. Where do all these people disappear to? Is it possible that such macabre experiments taking place beneath our feet could hold some answers as to their whereabouts?

Other specialised science projects allegedly being performed at the Dulce base include cloning, animal/human crossbreeding, human/alien crossbreeding, human aura studies and atomic manipulation. The base has been described as being probably the deepest of all the bases, reaching 2.5 miles deep and having seven levels, starting with level one nearest the surface with one central elevator installed in the wall construction leading down to the lower levels. The elevators and lighting system are all run electromagnetically. Cooper wrote that "The U.S. government occupies the upper levels of the underground base, while the aliens control the lower levels."

A former Dulce employee told researchers that most signs on the doors and hallways within the complex are written in both an alien symbol language and a universal symbol system which is understood by humans and extraterrestrials.

Specialist teams called the Delta Group were trained by the Army via a super secret organisation to secure all alien tasked projects. Based at Fort Carson in Colorado, the organisation became the National Reconnaissance Organization (NRO). There are a number of ways to enter the underground facility; the most common was to access it using the shuttle system as there are connections to many of the major cities in the United States. Apparently you would simply drive to the designated building in the city as if going to a normal job, then once inside and out of view you would discreetly descend until you reached a shuttle access point before boarding the shuttle which would take you directly to the base incognito.

Also, many of the farms in the area are said to have been modified to allow access to the base, after many of the farmers have been paid off and sections of the farm taken over by government personnel. The farms continue to run as working farms to avoid suspicion and any visitors wishing to access the base are personally escorted there or requested to meet base commanders at specific locations nearby where they are picked up using battered up 4x4 trucks for discretion.

A state of the art system which uses large hexagonal circuits containing magnets and coils to generate energy from thin air was created by German scientists after the Second World War. So, as one source stresses "People looking for doors in the side of mountains and grills in the ground spewing out steam are going to be sadly disappointed." It is worth noting that Dulce employees are contractually bound to spend large periods of time at the base, living there between shifts in order to minimise the traffic to and from the base before and after work.

THE DULCE & GROOM WARS

Phil Schneider claims to have been involved in an alien/human war which took place at the Dulce and Los Alamos complexes in the August of 1979 where he claims that sixty-six government agents were killed, he being one of only three human survivors. Most of the sixty-six people that died were from the Delta Group security forces. The battle, as Schneider recalls, started purely by accident during a routine task whilst building an addition to the underground base at Dulce, which involved the drilling of four distinct holes in the desert before linking them together and finally blowing out large sections at a time.

According to an anonymous source, Phil worked at the base between 1977 and 1979 on the construction of the extension of levels 1-3 as a geological advisor. He helped to create the four caverns that were linked together. Schneider's job was to recommend the explosives required for the specific rock there by going down one of the four holes and checking the rock samples. Following the drilling, plumes of black smoke spurted out of the holes and a terrible stench filled the air. Schneider was then placed into a basket and pulley system and slowly lowered into one of the foul smelling holes armed solely with a small 9mm pistol and his own wits.

Describing his experience that day Schneider explained, "As I was headed down there, we found ourselves amidst a large cavern that was full of outer-space aliens, otherwise known as large Greys. I shot two of them. At that time, there were 30 people down there. About 40 more came down after this started, and all of them got killed. We had surprised a whole underground base of existing aliens. Later, we found out that they had been living on our planet for a long time, perhaps a million years. This could explain a lot of what is behind the theory of ancient astronauts. Anyway, I got shot in the chest with one of their weapons, which was a box on

120

their body that blew a hole in me and gave me a nasty dose of cobalt radiation. I have had cancer because of that." He very nearly died that day, losing some of his fingers on his left hand and receiving severe burns from the unusual weapon used against him. As unlikely a story as it may appear, Schneider's wounds remain consistent with his testimony. He often showed audiences during his lecture tour the marks on his chest and also his missing fingers which are also clearly visible in photographs of him.

Although the cause of the injuries that he sustained cannot be verified, evidence of his injuries was confirmed in his autopsy report in 1996 [see SOURCES] – "The chest and abdomen are remarkable for numerous scars including a midline scar extending from the sterna notch to the epigastria, measuring approx. 20 inches in length. There appear to be burn-type scars present in the upper chest area."

The physical description in his autopsy report matches the story described by Schneider in which he spoke of the incident stating that "...this blue beam hit me and literally opened me up like a fish, and burnt my fingers right off of me and it was some sort of electrical force because it was kind of like being hit by a lightning bolt... burnt all my toenails off of me."

Schneider claims that ever since the Dulce incident in '79 took place problems between the non-human factions and the human workers have been growing steadily over the years and still remain unresolved. In his words, "Our United States Government lied, did not tell us anything about the alien threat. There's a war underneath there, and I'm talking dead serious, that's been going on since that time. Since late August of 1979, our military, the Russian military, basically the militaries of the world have been in constant conflict with the outer-space alien...the small grey, the large grey, the reptilian, the whole thing."

Philip Schneider's beliefs are echoed by the thoughts of Michael Lindemann whose research also led him to arrive at a similar conclusion; as he said publicly in 1991 "...there is this government that has known about the alien presence for a long time, a government that has been playing an 'end game'. A government that has an agenda of concealment and control that is operated by terror."

Details of other altercations between humans and ETs are somewhat sketchy but there are a number of sources relaying similar information regarding the 'Dulce Wars' dating around 1979 (one version of which was in Schneider's testimony) and the 'Groom Wars' of 1975. It appears that following a possible revision of the 1954 Greada Treaty, (which has been suggested as an updated version of a secret Bavarian Illuminati treaty with the Greys in 1933), that the sanctioned abduction of humans by the aliens, in which a list of all abductees was to be presented to the government, was breached, as thousands of people were being abducted that weren't on the list. Because of this deception it is said that in 1978-79, an altercation took place between humans and the aliens in which 44 of our top scientists were killed along with a number of Delta Force who were attempting to free them. It is unclear whether this occurred below Dulce or below Groom Lake in Nevada but the dates involved would imply the former. John Lear released a statement in 1987 which mentioned the incident, stating that "In 1979 there was an altercation of sorts at the Dulce laboratory. A special armed forces unit was called in to try and free a number of our people trapped in the facility, who had become aware of what was really going on. According to one source, 66 of the soldiers were killed and our people were not freed."

Former Area 51 scientist Robert Lazar stated that there was an intense fire-fight between the Greys and the U.S. Military personnel in the underground facility below Groom Lake after human security officers disobeyed the orders of an alien dictate when requested to not enter a particular alien-controlled area with their loaded weapons. It is believed that on May 1, 1975 two Zeta-Reticulan Greys were in the process of demonstrating an anti-matter reactor within an underground chamber to two top-level security scientists when one of the Greys demanded that before they went any further with the experiment, all rifles and especially their bullets must be removed from the room. The elite military guards refused to surrender their weapons and as a result of this, chaos ensued leaving one alien, two scientists and forty-one military personnel dead. The one witness who survived to tell the story claimed that the Greys seemed to have used their minds as weapons as no physical weapons were seen, but whatever advanced technology was employed that day, it resulted in a lot of unnecessary deaths.

122

This incident has been labelled 'the Groom War of 1975' and has been described as more of a massacre than a war. This incident was very significant as it exposed the aliens' true colours for the first time and highlighted the fact that these non-human entities had their own agenda which was entirely separate to that of the American government. An example was made of those humans who questioned the authority of the ETs that day, and several dozen security personnel and scientists were slaughtered by a number of Greys, of which only one is said to have died. Some sources have implied that this was only the initial incident in the 'Groom Wars' and that more deaths and disappearances of other scientists, military personnel and workers, and even other ETs have come about as the result of other incidents that followed.

Four years later in 1979, according to the claims made by former Dulce security officer Thomas Castello, another terrible battle occurred within the Dulce facility which differs in description to the 'accidental incident' described by Phil Schneider during the same year. Castello maintains that following the horrific discovery made by several scientists, that thousands of human abductees were being held "in cold storage or imprisoned in cage-like enclosures" in the lower levels beneath Dulce and that they themselves were subsequently captured by the aliens. After the alien 'takeover' of Dulce which followed more killing of scientists and security staff, the base was apparently shut down for a brief period until the government were able to renegotiate terms with them which would suit both parties as after all, losing access to the high technology which the ETs offered would be a devastatingly regressive move.

Bill Cooper confirmed this scenario stating that "...a confrontation broke out between the human scientists and the aliens at the Dulce underground lab. The aliens took many of our scientists hostage. Delta Forces were sent in to free them but they were no match for the alien weapons. Sixty-six people were killed during this action. As a result we withdrew from all joint projects for at least two years..."

It appears that the Dulce Wars came about as the result of a number of overlapping factors and situations which arose around a similar period of time. The number of deaths is still unconfirmed and different accounts offer different figures, which makes it very difficult to gain any clarity of these events, however it is clear there existed a growing animosity and distrust towards the alien factions involved at that time and also that a conflict of interest between the humans and their non-human counterparts was causing severe problems within the complex.

Different security forces appear to have been involved, such as the Delta Force, Secret Service and FBI Division Five, CIA Storm troopers, Air Force Blue Berets, Black Berets and also Dulce Base security guards. Various key factors which seem to have led to the fighting include revenge for the slaughter of several scientists and security personnel below Area 51 in 1975, accidental encounters between construction workers and tall greys (Schneider's account), Castello's account of an ET attack on the human 'resistance' following the discovery of the 'Big Lie'.

It was this battle at Dulce which allegedly left the government bereft of many of their best facilities and scientists, and forced the Americans to create a counterforce which could protect them from any further humiliation. One such scheme was the Strategic Defense Initiative (SDI) which was devised as a means to shoot down any incoming UFOs that may be considered a security threat.

Researcher and experienced pilot John Lear explains why simply arming ourselves against incoming targets was not a sufficient security measure; "The mistake was that we thought they were coming inbound, in fact, they're already here. They're in underground bases all over the place. It seems that the aliens had constructed many such bases without our knowledge, where they conduct heinous genetic experiments on animals, human beings, and 'improvised' creatures of their own devising."

CASTELLO & THE DULCE PAPERS

The name Thomas Edwin Castello is synonymous with the Dulce enigma, and any research into this mysterious place will inevitably bring up this man's name. He claims to have worked at Dulce as a high level security officer starting in 1977 following a transfer to Santa Fe in New Mexico from California, where he had worked as a Security Technician for RAND Corporation since 1971. A decade previous in 1961, he had been a young sergeant stationed at Nellis Air Force Base near Las Vegas, Nevada, where he was employed as a military photographer with a top secret clearance. After being transferred to West Virginia, he trained in advanced intelligence photography and his clearance was upgraded to TS-IV due to his new assignment being in an undisclosed underground installation. RAND Corporation upgraded his clearance once more to ULTRA-3 in 1971 and a year later he married a woman named Cathy and had a son called Eric.

Once in New Mexico, Castello began work as a photo security specialist in the Dulce installation where he secured a significant pay increase along with another security upgrade to ULTRA-7, allowing him access to all seven known levels. His employment at Dulce was specifically to maintain the video monitoring equipment throughout the complex, aligning and calibrating the cameras and also escorting visitors to their destinations. Proof of his employment at this time is nearly impossible to attain due to the high level of secrecy involved, however, some evidence to authenticate his existence did arise and so must be considered worthy of consideration. In February 2012, a researcher trying to trace Castello discovered this address after years of being missing presumed dead: "Thomas E & Marilyn Castello, 614 N. Missouri Ave, Roswell, NM, (575) 623-5837, Listing Details, Age: 65+"

Of course this could well be false information but for the sake of this investigation it is worth a brief mention. Of more value to prove Castello's existence is an obituary of his sister which was found in local newspaper the *Kentwood News Ledger* on Wednesday, May 21, 2003, which in its entirety read;

"Katie Ethel Castello died at 7:42 p.m. on Saturday, May 10, 2003 at North Oaks Medical Center in Hammond. She was 82, a native of Ethel and a resident of Kentwood. She was a homemaker. Religious services were held at Spring Creek Baptist Church, Spring Creek, conducted by Rev. Danny Smith and Rev. Eric Latham, interment in the church cemetery. She is survived by a sister, Babe Ruth Warren, El Paso, TX; *a brother, Thomas E. Castello, Roswell, NM*; numerous other relatives and friends. She was preceded in death by her mother, Elivah Wall Castello; a sister, Annie I. Beck and her Grandparents, Marcus and Dolly Wall."

This could be something or nothing, but given the scarcity of background information on Mr. Castello, any possible link to the man is most certainly noteworthy. What is of the upmost importance is the revelatory testimony of Thomas Castello which comes from his alleged direct experience within the Dulce base that started with himself and several other new employees attending a mandatory meeting on arrival at the facility. Aware of the fact that these new workers would be given access to different areas of the complex, it was inevitable that they would become aware of some of the goings-on around them so a fabricated version of the basic scenario, which would become apparent over the forthcoming years, was told to Thomas and the others.

Castello says that he was informed by his superiors that "...the subjects being used for genetic experiments were hopelessly insane and the research is for medical and humane purposes." This would turn out to be a big lie. They were all issued with severe threats of punishment if anyone was witnessed conversing with any of the 'insane' or even discussing any subject with co-workers other than that of the task at hand. It was forbidden to venture beyond the boundaries of one's own work area without legitimate reasons and any discussion of the existence of the base to any outsiders was obviously strictly forbidden and could lead to the severest of punishments as one would expect.

Whilst Castello was venturing into different areas and levels of the facility as his work dictated, he began noticing some extremely shocking things; in fact he soon encountered extraterrestrial beings for the first time which he claims he found to be most exhilarating in the beginning. However, it wasn't long before he realized that something was seriously wrong as he began to sense an underlying tension around the place.

Occasionally, whilst Thomas was working on one of the lower levels, he was able to observe some of the horrific genetic experiments that were taking place in the more isolated sections of the base. It was whilst working on level 7 that he encountered humans in cages for the first time and it soon became apparent to him that the genetic experimentation which he had witnessed didn't have any connection with mental illness or medical research, as his superiors had suggested. Castello reportedly said "I frequently encountered humans in cages, usually dazed or drugged, but sometimes they cried and begged for help. We were told they were hopelessly insane, and involved in high-risk drug tests to cure insanity. We were told never to speak to them at all.

126

At the beginning we believed the story. Finally in 1978 a small group of workers discovered the truth. That began the Dulce Wars."

The more he saw, the less he understood and the less he wanted to discover, as it was all becoming far too overwhelming to accept. However, his decision to continue his search for the truth was led by his humanitarian instincts regardless of the horror which was repelling him. As Castello's curiosity grew he found himself being approached by a co-worker who quietly took him aside in the corridor where they were joined by two more employees. These men clearly knew more than they should have and were desperate to share this information with someone else with a conscience and a sense of justice, as Castello turned out to have.

His colleagues told Thomas that the men, women and children that were alleged to be 'mentally insane' and were being held captive and experimented on, were in reality, average people who had been abducted from the outside world and heavily sedated. The men were right to trust Thomas whom they had observed as being 'uncomfortable' with what was going on down there because instead of turning them in to his superiors, as was protocol for entering such discussions, he instead chose to investigate further, starting with speaking with one of the people who had been held captive in a caged area in what has become known as 'Nightmare Hall'. He asked them their name and their home town and was successful in receiving a reply even though it was murmured through a drug induced state. Much to his amazement, Castello's investigations over the weekends outside of the facility led him to discover that the person with whom he had been talking deep down inside Dulce had actually been reported as having disappeared suddenly and was now declared missing in his home town, leaving behind distraught family members who had been desperately sending out flyers with his face on, all to no avail. He would soon discover that many of the thousands of men, women and children that are reported missing each year were actually listed as unexplained disappearances.

After much intense deliberation, Castello decided that all he could do was keep his mouth shut and desert the facility when the time was right, without rousing too much suspicion. He knew that once he was on the outside never to return he must make himself invisible before those leading the deception found his whereabouts and forced him to disappear for good. In late 1979 following the Dulce wars on level-3, Castello along with a group of his new found friends managed to escape and once he had established some distance between himself and the wretched place where he had worked, he began to share what he knew about Dulce and show drawings and descriptions of the layout of the facility that he had so come to fear.

Some sources claim that one of those who also escaped was a CIA agent who managed to gather some physical evidence in the form of notes, photos and video footage of the complex interior which would later be passed on and copied, whilst others assert that it was Thomas Castello himself who fled the base with these items. Researcher William Hamilton was led to conclude that it was in fact Castello who succeeded in capturing over thirty photographs inside Dulce, and managed to remove a security video tape from the control centre that showed a variety of views of the labs, hallways, U.S. government personnel and also some of the ETs there.

In one of the 100 exits to the surface he managed to shut off the alarm and camera system and left the facility with the photos, video and documents which would later become known as the 'Dulce Papers'. The originals were hidden away whilst five sets of copies were made and placed in the hands of five individuals (only the recipients and Castello know who they are) and were each told by Thomas that he would visit each of them every six months. If however, he failed to show for three consecutive 6 month periods, they had permission to release the information or chose what they wished to do with it themselves. One of these individuals who came to Santa Fe in 1979 to visit Bill Hamilton and co-writer 'TAL' LaVesque, made drawings from the photos, video tape and documents which would later be circulated in the UFO research community as the 'Dulce Papers'.

Before Thomas could go into hiding he went to pick up his wife and child but found government agents waiting for him with a van. The agents had already kidnapped them before he arrived because, as he would later discover, he had been betrayed by a fellow worker named K. Lomas. The agents wanted to make an exchange with Castello, his family for the items he had taken from the base. Hamilton wrote "When it became apparent to him they would be used in biological experiments and were not going to be returned unharmed, he decided to get lost."[96]

In December 1987, a description of the Dulce Papers was finally leaked, most likely from one of the caretakers of the papers, and many researchers received the information for the first time since it originated in 1979. The Dulce Papers were said to have been comprised of the following:

o 25 black and white photos
o 6 minute video tape of Dulce facility with no dialogue
o set of technical papers pertaining to the facility of which the contents included at least the following:
o discussion of copper & molybdenum
o discussion of magnesium & potassium (electrolytes??)
o lots of medical terminology
o discussion of ultraviolet light & gamma rays
o discussion of true purpose of the EBE's
o discussion of usage of cow blood
o discussion of DNA manipulation
o discussion of "almost human beings"
o discussion of "creation of non gender being"
o discussion of DNA manipulation
o sketches of the photos[97]

One important sketch which has surfaced reveals the substructure of the Dulce complex, describing the purpose of each floor level. Drawn by Castello and passed on to a friend, the sketch only became public for the first time during a lecture by John Rhodes in Las Vegas on August 13, 1993. Level 1 is located nearest the surface and using the magnetic elevator system to descend through the various sub-levels, each floor gets progressively more macabre the further one descends. Castello's ULTRA-7 security clearance gave him access to the seven known floors, as an UMBRA or higher clearance was required to use 'off-limits' elevators to unknown areas of the facility. Here is a list of the levels with their purposes;

Level 1 – Security and Communications – As the first level of the facility, it is used as a garage for all vehicles on site. Strict security measures are in place and no one can drive in or out without verifying their security card and access number. All roads leading into level 1 are equipped with magnetic sensors.

Level 2 – Human Staff Housing – Primarily used as staff quarters but includes garages for the maglev shuttle trains and also tunnel boring machines. Also used as a maintenance area for alien craft. Trains using the tunnel systems leading to other underground facilities depart from this level. Destinations include facilities in New Mexico like Datil, Taos, Carlsbad, Los Alamos and Sandia. Also the Arizona facility at Page, Area 51and Area 19 in Nevada, Edwards AFB, Plant 42, Colorado Springs and many more secret locations can be reached directly from here.

Level 3 – Executive Offices and Laboratories – This is the hub of the complex, Dulce base is controlled from here as it is where the majority of the computers are located. This level is also said to hold additional housing for employees and test subjects.

Level 4 – Mind Control Experiments – Studies that take place on Level 4 include telepathy, telekinesis, human-aura research, dreams and hypnosis. Castello reported that they have the knowledge to remove the soul or 'life-force' from the human and replace it with the energy of an 'alien entity'. This process is achieved by separating the 'bioplasmic' body from the physical body.

Level 5 – Alien Housing – The living quarters of extraterrestrial species such as the Zeta Reticulans (Greys) are located deep down at Level 5. Castello estimated that approximately 18,000 Greys populate the entire complex.

Level 6 – Genetic Experiments – Privately referred to as 'Nightmare Hall' and the 'Zoo', Level 6 holds the genetic laboratories where a variety of creatures such as seals, fish, mice and birds are genetically altered from their original forms to create hybrid creatures. Humans have also been tampered with and some with multiple limbs have been seen on this floor. Cloning of 'Greys' has also been reported her, as reproduction for their species has become unfeasible due to the deterioration of their sexual organs. Castello maintains that in the manuals it was called

"The Vivarium" and describes Dulce Base as a "secured facility for tending bio-forms of all types." In another official report the base was also described as "a private subterranean bio-terminal park, with accommodations for animals, fish, fowl, reptile, and mankind."

Level 7 – Cryogenics – Cold Storage Vats – Described as the worst floor in the entire Dulce facility, Level 7 is where Thomas Castello reported seeing and speaking with imprisoned humans in cages. Thousands of humans are alleged to be kept here, row after row, along with the cold storage of human mixture remains and human embryos in various stages of development. These storage vats are said to also contain the remains of human children too. The Dulce Papers describe scenes from Level 7 in more detail, stating that what looks like glass tubes five feet tall containing womb-like grey sacs filled with amber coloured liquid, are holding genderless dark-grey creatures with white pale eyes, two toes and three fingers. The initial discovery of the atrocities taking place on this level are the main reason for the civil unrest amongst the human employees, which ultimately led to the fighting against the alien factions in the Dulce Wars.

The horrific and sinister scenarios described as occurring on Level 7 seem far too incredible and unlikely to warrant serious consideration, however, this information has not arisen from one isolated source alone. The circumstantial evidence regarding the macabre experimentation on this floor of the Dulce facility has come not only from Thomas Castello but has also been described by abductees claiming to have been taken to the base, intelligence personnel (NSA, CIA etc.) and former employees who worked in the laboratories and others who were involved with the construction of the complex. One report from a worker (CR-24/ZM 52-Files VII) who claims to have witnessed very bizarre experimentation is as follows: "I have seen multi-legged humans that look half-human, half-octopus. Also reptilian-humans, and furry creatures that have hands like humans and cry like a baby, it mimics human words, and also huge mixture of lizards (and) humans in cages."

The Dulce Papers also offer explanations as to why such experiments are taking place at Dulce, and links with cattle mutilations and the extraction of blood and body parts are also suggested. The aliens are said to use blood for nourishment by placing their hands in it and absorbing it like a sponge, but aside from using it as food, it is the DNA in cattle and humans which appears to be of greatest value to them.

This DNA is used for the purpose of genetic alteration, manipulation and cloning. Taken from information given to him by Thomas Castello, researcher William F. Hamilton explains in his book *Cosmic Top Secret* (p.109) "...According to Thomas, the alien androgynal breeder is capable of parthenogenesis. At Dulce, the common form of reproduction is polyembryony. Each embryo can, and does divide into 6 to 9 individual 'cunne' [pronounced cooney, i.e. siblings]. The needed nutriment for the developing cunne is supplied by the 'formula,' which usually consists of [human/animal blood] plasma, deoxyhemoglobin, albumin, lysozyme, cation, amniotic fluid and more."

Some of the information offered here by Castello and in the Dulce Papers was confirmed by a completely non-associated source in abductee Christa Tilton. According to Tilton's testimony, she was abducted and taken to an underground base in July 1987, where they used her to breed a human-like child which she claims was taken from her and is being held captive in the base. She described what she saw during an abduction experience, claiming that there were "...strange vats filled with eerie liquid...where aliens are being grown." During regressive hypnosis she also described seeing "dozens of creatures in each womb. Can't count tanks, maybe scores or hundreds...womb submerged in sort of yellow liquid. Looks thicker than water. Creatures float in amber colored water. Womb is greyish..."

Her description matches exactly what was described in the documents which surfaced from within the Dulce facility, where the breeding of non-human embryonic creatures with bluish-grey skin, three fingers and two toes were held in large glass tubes. She also mentioned that she saw what seemed to be human body parts floating in the "fluid".

During an interview with Christa in 1996, she talked a bit more of her experience at an underground facility which she now believes to be Dulce after choosing to research the subject in depth herself. She went on to say "The type of tanks I saw were used for breeding and cultivation of small alien beings. The only thing that

I can describe it as is of being (like) a fake womb. ...these types of breeding tanks that you're talking about were used to cultivate the fetuses that they extract from the individuals that they abduct and take there. They extract the fetus like they have done to me MANY times, and I believe they place it in this type of tank, a glass (looking) breeding tank."[98]

Tilton mentioned things which Castello had described as having being protocol for anyone entering the facility, for example she explained "I was told to step onto some type of scale-like device that faced a computer screen. I saw lights flashing and numbers computing and then a card was issued with holes punched into it. I would later realize it was used as identification inside a computer." Thomas Castello had already declared that after the second level, everyone is weighed before the weight of that person is put on a computer I.D. card each day. Any discrepancy in weight and security are summoned then a physical examination and X-ray are required if any change in weight over three pounds is detected. Castello reported that "In front of all sensitive areas are scales built into the floor by doorways and the door control panels. An individual places his computer I.D. card into the door slot then presses a numerical code and buttons. The person's card must match with the weight and code or the door will not open."

On May 7, 1980 another woman named Myrna Hansen from New Mexico, contacted Paul Bennewitz and APRO claiming to have been abducted by aliens. She also talked about having been taken to an underground base where she had seen "body parts", and claims to have been implanted with a device which controlled her thinking. These alleged experiences are just a couple that have been officially reported, thousands of other abduction stories speak of implants, mind control and foetus removal. But as hard as such tales are to prove, the fact that people with no prior knowledge of Dulce or other underground activities can come forward with testimonies that correlate with details of such places surely bears some significance. Whether all the information gathered here proves to hold some validity or not, the very existence of such material appearing from an array of different sources would suggest that there may be an element of truth amongst it all or at the very least that something is amiss and not everything is as it seems, otherwise it wouldn't be possible to accumulate such correlating evidence.

What follows is an excerpt from a synopsis of the Dulce Papers written by Val Valerian of 'Leading Edge Research' based in Washington State. He has researched the alien enigma more extensively than most and has collaborated with many leading researchers in this field to produce the book series *Matrix I-IV*. The extract below is quite lengthy but explains in detail how the genetic manipulation breeding program allegedly taking place below Dulce actually works, and also offers an explanation as to why innocent citizens like Christa Tilton are being taken from their homes and being subjected to inhumane experimentation:

"The 'Type One' creature is a lab animal. They know how to change the atoms to create a temporary 'almost human being'. It is made with animal tissue and depends on a computer to simulate memory, a memory the computer has withdrawn from another human. The 'almost human being' is slow and clumsy. Real humans are used for training, to experiment with and to breed with these 'almost humans'. Some humans are kidnapped and used completely. Some are kept in large tubes, and are kept alive in an amber liquid. Some humans are brainwashed and used to distort the truth. Certain male humans have a high sperm count and are kept alive. Their sperm is used to alter the DNA and create a non-gender being called 'Type Two'. That sperm is grown in some way and altered again, put in wombs. They resemble 'ugly humans' when growing but look normal when fully grown, which only takes a few months from fetus-size. They have a short life span, less than a year. Some female humans are used for breeding. Countless women have had a sudden miscarriage after about three months' pregnancy. Some never know they were pregnant, others remember contact some way. The fetus is used to mix the DNA in types one and two. The atomic makeup in that fetus is half human, half 'almost human', and would not survive in the mother's womb. It is taken at three months and grown elsewhere."

To consider such horrific tales as possible realities is tough to accept, but make no qualms about it; these descriptive stories which appear to belong in the realms of fantasy do indeed have their roots based firmly in reality. Those few brave enough to have come forward with their version of events are not psychologically impaired in any way, rather they have risked their lives and often also the lives of those closest to them to share what they consider to be of the upmost importance for the whole of humankind.

Phil Schneider died talking about what he knew, along with his friend Ron Rummell. Thomas Edwin Castello was forced to disappear completely to avoid losing his life, and if his testimony is accurate, he lost his wife and son to the dreaded confines of the Dulce nightmare. Even those claiming to have been abducted have clearly gone through some seriously mentally and physically emotional situations which, no matter how legitimate their stories prove to be, have definitely affected their lives and that of their families in the most profound way.

It would be nice to believe that we live in a world where regardless of how crazy someone's version of events may be, that they at least can rest assured that their voice will be heard and all judgment reserved until such a time they are proved to be speaking untruthfully or mistakenly. Unfortunately, this is not the case whatsoever; in fact it is quite the opposite. Anyone who talks about things which do not conform to a wider sense of reality is automatically considered to be talking nonsense by the vast majority, as any other conclusion would involve a paradigm shift and a completely fresh perception on the possibilities of life.

The existence of deep underground bases whether for military purposes or not, appears to hold some validity. The question one must continue to ask is for what purpose have these facilities been constructed and to what extent have they been built? Is there really a subterranean train shuttle system crisscrossing the globe? Are these large complexes really linked together around the United States so that work can continue to progress out of view of the rest of the world? As is always the case with such mysterious subject matter, there are more questions than answers, but it would be naïve to suggest that it is all simply nonsense because one is unable to solve the mystery independently.

It is clear that the U.S. Government is hiding something, it is well established that billions of dollars are vanishing into thin air without a trace, and it is a fact that we have the technology and the funding to build vast underground spaces for whatever purpose is deemed necessary by those in the positions of power. All around the world, vast cavern systems and tunnels predating modern man have already been discovered, all which were apparently built long before the technological advancements of the modern era, but still we struggle to explain their existence beneath our feet. One day, it is most likely that all will come to light and the alien presence which presently eludes us and continues to confound our sense of reason will step out of the shadows and make itself known to humankind. Let us hope that when that day arrives, things turn out a lot better than the extraordinary events allegedly unfolding within the walls of the Dulce complex would lead us to expect.

4

INTRUDERS

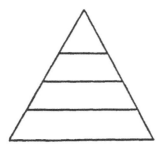

It is difficult to find a culture on Earth that does not have an ancient tradition of little people that fly through the sky and abduct humans.

Dr. Jacques Vallee – Dimensions: A Casebook of Alien Contact (1988)

HUMAN ABDUCTION by non-terrestrial entities is a vastly misunderstood phenomenon which continues to bewilder those who choose to delve into this taboo and complex subject. The concept of being taken by alien beings from another world is often met with great derision and scorn, as it quite extensively stretches the boundaries between reality and imagination. Most people may find themselves being either mildly amused by such a notion or alternatively quite intrigued. Either way, the alien abduction mystery is far from being resolved *or* taken seriously, publicly at least, partly due to a lack of understanding surrounding the topic along with a scarcity of insightful information.

Similar to stories of personal extraterrestrial contact from self-claimed 'contactees', evidence regarding alien abduction relies heavily on human testimony which will always prove to be problematic due to issues such as character type, background and incentive. Such subjective experiences are nigh on impossible to authenticate as there is predominantly a lack of hard physical evidence to reinforce the abductees' descriptions of the alleged events.

However, recent developments have finally revealed physical evidence for the first time which offers an insightful glimpse into a world of possibilities, adding weight to the reality of these bizarre and often terrifying experiences. Foreign objects implanted into the human subject during alleged abduction encounters have become a common denominator for this type of experience, but information regarding these unusual implants has been somewhat scarce and inconclusive until recent times.

The complexity of the alien abduction scenario lies in the fact that so little is fully understood. The information age which heralded the birth of the internet has allowed previously impossible communications to materialise, bringing abductees from far and wide along with their personal testimonies within reach of one another for the first time. The subject has now come to the attention of a minority of academic scholars, allowing the different experiences and stories of strange intruders entering the private lives of a myriad of people across the globe, to be collected, collated and assessed.

Most people approach this topic with the sceptical view that reports of alien abduction cannot have a basis in physical reality, but such a general hypothesis may prove inaccurate as "well respected researchers have shown that the core of the UFO-abduction phenomena cannot be explained psychologically, as hallucinations or mass delusions".[99]

So how does one best describe a typical alien abduction? Inevitably, details vary from person to person, but there remains a general theme in which most cases correlate. Firstly, it seems that no one is exempt from such an experience and that according to many researchers in this field of expertise, it is trans-generational. It is not uncommon that three to four generations of family have all had alien abduction experiences. Usually abductees claim they were taken from their beds at night, surrounded by very bright light, often described as being blue. Some have been taken from other rooms in the house and others from their immobilised cars whilst on the road. The intruders often enter through walls or closed windows before levitating the subject out of the house in a state of paralysis and lifting them up through the bottom of a craft until they are inside.

Some reports start with the awareness of a presence in the room followed by physical paralysis and the realisation that strange beings are stood by the foot of the bed. UFO sightings in the area usually coincide with abduction experiences; these are often witnessed and reported by locals unaware of the unfolding drama.

Once inside the craft (or underground facility – as is often the case), many abductees share similar experiences of medical procedures, either laid down on a table or sat in a 'dentist's chair'. The removal of sperm and ova is a key feature which has led some researchers to suggest that some form of genetic manipulation and/or cross-breeding program may be taking place. Other evidence befits this possible scenario. Implants have been placed under the skin, often behind the eye, in the nasal cavity or by the base of the brain or spine. Most abductees have similar shaped scars, cuts and bruises the following day. Common physical imprints include a three-pronged mark; puncture marks referred to as snake bites, claw marks, triangular rashes and a triangle of puncture marks. Photographic evidence of these unusual markings has been documented.

Dr. John E. Mack, a former professor of psychiatry at Harvard Medical School, published a book in April 1994 which caused uproar within the walls of Harvard due to the highly controversial subject matter which he covered in great depth. *Abduction: Human Encounters with Aliens* dealt with a controversial topic that was considered to be almost 'out of bounds' by the majority of scholars within the scientific community. In fact, such was the impact of Mack's involvement in the abduction phenomenon because of his Harvard connections, that the Dean initiated a three man panel to oversee his actions following publicity from his book. At the time Mack described the ongoing investigation which ensued as "Kaftaesque"; claiming that the nature of the complaints against his practice was constantly changing. As Angela Hind wrote in a BBC article, "It was the first time in Harvard's history that a tenured professor was subjected to such an investigation." Many of his colleagues considered Mack to have committed "professional suicide", and only after fourteen months of close monitoring and investigation did the Dean decide to allow Mack to continue with his work.

Before starting on his journey into the abduction phenomenon, Mack described himself as "an intense sceptic" but since then he has studied hundreds of abduction cases, often using hypnosis or relaxation methods to coerce some of the more hidden memories out of his subject. Describing a typical abduction case scenario Mack said "The person is in the car or sleeping, there's a light, these entities come into the room: they feel themselves paralysed. They're moved, they're taken to a ship, something happens there. Telepathic communication with aliens, there's some probing, there's a whole complicated set of events that takes place which is consistent from one person to another. But there's a basic story here which after several hundred cases in this country and many other countries, it all begins to hold together as something that has a very robust kind of truth to it and if this is real then what does that mean?"[100]

To the majority who have never experienced anything of the sort it is easy to dismiss the whole concept as pure fantasy, but the numbers of people claiming to have been abducted is exceptionally high. Alien abduction specialists, Budd Hopkins, Dr.

David Jacobs and sociologist Dr. Ron Westrum commissioned a Roper Poll in 1991 in an attempt to determine the number of Americans affected by the abduction scenario. 119 out of nearly 6,000 responded in a way which was interpreted as sufficiently related to the ET hypothesis connected with the abduction phenomenon. Based on this figure, the researchers estimated that approximately four million Americans may have been abducted by non-terrestrial entities.

The nature of statistics and the methods employed to arrive at such figures is always questionable and rarely portrays an accurate summation but they can offer a valuable estimate and approximation which reveals that such occurrences are not as rare as one might have initially presumed. According to the International Community for Alien Research (ICAR), they have published empirical and replicable research confirming that globally, approximately one billion people have been reportedly abducted by "a hyper-dimensional civilisation consisting of amphibian reptilian hybrids and grey cybernetic clones".

As highly unlikely as it may sound, there are consistent reports of interaction with a plethora of different non-terrestrial beings. Many have been described as reptilian looking, with scaly skin and slanted pupils, and a great number of abductees have had experiences with the most familiar of alien types – the greys. Although a variety of entities have been reported as involved in the abductions, the greys are almost always present.

Other entities which have been described as present during the abduction process veer away from the extraterrestrial thesis into another category altogether, but such reports are common and reveal how complex this issue really is. Elves and hairy troll-like figures with big ears have been witnessed, along with beings in the guise of dead relatives, celebrities and religious figures. Such descriptions may suggest that some of these experiences could be nothing more than lucid dreams, a valid assumption given the details on offer. However, there is more to the story.

Dr. Karla Turner, an abductee herself, has interviewed hundreds of people claiming to also have been visited. During one session an elderly woman recalled that she was forced to drink a thick liquid which had been handed to her by an alien who had appeared in her bedroom one night. Shortly after consuming the substance which seemed to make her young again, a reptilian-like being attempted to have intercourse with her but she resisted. The creature then brought her dead husband into the room, and he began to make sexual advances towards her. They engaged in sexual intercourse together before she realised much to her dismay that it wasn't her husband at all, but the strange looking reptilian figure. [101]

This highly unlikely scenario has surprisingly been described by many people, albeit with different figures in place of the dead husband. This kind of morphing from one person into something else before the abductees' eyes is not as rare as one might believe. As Dr. Turner explains in her book *Taken*, "Investigators who have not had personal experiences with the phenomenon can listen to abduction accounts and then ponder the possibilities. Was the person lying? Was it a real event, or did it occur on a mental level? What parts of the recollection are real, and which are illusionary? But the abductee understands that it may very well be both possibilities at once, both real and mental, real and illusionary. The aliens, whether by intellectual, psychic, or technological means, are able to create any perception, and therefore any illusion, for the person in their hands." [102]

Some researchers have suggested that by becoming someone familiar to the subject, the entities are much more successful at getting what they want out of the person, by keeping them in a state of calm. The reasons for such behaviour remain a mystery but sexual activity and the alien abduction phenomenon appear to be intrinsically linked. Sex with non-human beings, sex with other abductees and sex with beautiful humanoids have all been reported by those unfortunate enough to have experienced such bizarre happenings.

THE SEDUCTION OF ANTONIO VILLAS BOAS

On October 15, 1957 a Brazilian farmer experienced a most unusual encounter which became the first recorded incident of an alien abduction in modern times. The account of twenty-three year old Antonio Villas Boas has gone down in the UFO annals as an unprecedented case worthy of evaluation because of the well documented physical examinations which followed the Boas incident.

Although initially reluctant to tell his story, Boas wrote two letters to well renowned Brazilian journalist Joas Martins, who had placed an advertisement in the newspaper asking for people to come forward with any UFO experiences to supplement the articles which he'd previously written on the subject. Martins found the young man's story so intriguing that he showed the correspondence to a Rio de Janeiro doctor, Dr. Olavo T. Fontes, a Professor of Medicine at the National School of Medicine of Brazil and also an APRO[5] representative at the time. Together, Martins and Fontes decided that the Boas story was worthy of deeper investigation so they chose to pay for the several hundred mile trip from Sao Francisco de Sales to Rio, to enable Dr. Fontes to examine him in detail.

On February 22nd of the following year, Dr. Fontes subjected Antonio Villas Boas to a battery of physical and psychological tests which concluded that he was mentally stable but did exhibit signs of unusual physical symptoms which he claimed were proof of the reality of his abduction. Boas informed Fontes that along with a feeling of general lethargy, he had been suffering with nausea and bad headaches and reappearing skin lesions since the incident nearly four months earlier. Initial examinations revealed that Boas did in fact have a mild case of radiation sickness, enough to rouse Fontes' curiosity.

Other symptoms that Boas showed included 'pains throughout the body, loss of appetite, ceaselessly burning sensations in the eyes, coetaneous lesions at the slightest of light bruising...which went on appearing for months like small reddish nodules, harder than the skin around them and protuberant, painful when touched, each with a small central orifice yielding a yellowish thin watery discharge'.[103]

The whole story of the Villas Boas abduction didn't reach the public until December 1st, 1964, when the international (Spanish) edition of a prestigious Brazilian publication *O Cruzeiro* printed an article written by Joas Martins which went on sale in Buenos Aires.

---

[5] The Aerial Phenomena Research Organization was a UFO research group started in 1952 by Jim and Coral Lorenzen which remained active until 1988.

Ten days previous to his alleged abduction on the night of the 15th, Boas recalled opening a window to let in some fresh air at around 11pm and spotting a bright white light in the sky. Later that night, after having slept for a while he awoke to find that the same light was still there, and as he watched it he realised it was heading straight towards him. Full of fear, he closed the shutters forcefully and awoke his brother who watched as the bright light penetrated the shutters for awhile before disappearing.

Living on the family farm near Minas Gerais, Boas and his family often cultivated their several plantations and fields at night to avoid the excessive daytime heat. Between 9 and 10 pm on the night of the 14th, whilst tilling the fields with his brother, they both saw another extremely bright light in the sky above them, this time they claimed the object was less than three hundred feet above their heads. Intrigued by the strange light, Boas left his brother working to take a closer look. As soon as he approached, the light "suddenly darted away at tremendous speed to the opposite end of the field" so he approached it once more and again it shot off to the other side where it had just come from. This manoeuvre was repeated "no less than twenty times" before Boas decided to return to his brother.

Boas explained that "The light kept still for a few moments longer in the distance. Now and again it seemed to throw forth rays in all directions, the same as the setting sun, sparkling. Then it suddenly disappeared, as if it had been turned off."

The following night he worked in the fields alone. At 1 am, standing in the exact same spot where he and his brother first saw the unusual light the previous evening, Boas noticed a reddish light in the sky which all of a sudden flew towards him at an incredible speed. The light zoomed "so quickly that it was on top of me before I could make up my mind what to do about it", Boas recalled. It stopped abruptly once it reached about 160 feet above his head.

Describing the object as looking like "a large elongated egg", with three extendable legs which appeared from beneath it as it settled to land, Boas fled in terror and headed for his tractor. Upon reaching the tractor, the lights failed and the entire vehicle ceased to function so he attempted to escape towards the house on foot. Just then a "small figure in strange clothes" who only reached to his shoulder, grabbed his arm before he shoved him away forcefully. He was grabbed once more by three more figures that had surrounded him before lifting him clean off the ground by his arms.

Continuing to resist his attackers, Boas was dragged up a flexible metallic rolling ladder through a hatchway which closed behind them "so neatly that no seam was visible to the naked eye." He found himself in a small, bare and brightly lit square room. Square lights in the smooth metallic walls lit the room "the same as broad daylight" when an opening in the seamless wall suddenly appeared as the beings led Boas through to another room. At one side of the room stood an "oddly shaped table" which was surrounded by several backless swivel chairs that were all made of the same white metal. Both the table and the stools were one-legged, "narrowing toward the floor where they were either fixed to it (such as the table) or linked to a moveable ring held fast by three hinges jutting out on each side and riveted to that floor (such as the stools, so that those sitting on them could turn in every direction)".

Boas claimed he was held in place by his abductors whilst communicating to each other using sounds similar to those used by animals, grunting noises of which had "no resemblance whatever to human speech". He continued, "I can think of no attempt to describe those sounds, so different were they from anything I have ever heard before...Those sounds still make me shiver when I think of them! It isn't even possible for me to reproduce them...my vocal chords are not made for it." Describing the strange noises made by the beings, Boas told journalist Martins that some of the grunts were longer whilst "others shorter, sometimes containing several different sounds at the same time, at other times ending in a tremor."

Despite his constant resistance, the creatures began to undress him until he was completely naked. Boas recalled that "They obviously couldn't understand me, but they stopped and stared at me as if trying to make me understand that they were being polite. Besides, though they had to employ force, they never at any time hurt me badly, and they did not even tear my clothes, with the exception of my shirt perhaps." Once stripped of his garments, they covered him from head to toe in a thick odourless liquid before leading him alone into yet another room which he described as having red inscriptions above the door, "like scribbles of a kind entirely unknown to us".

Joined by two of the strange figures, blood was taken from his chin by apparatuses which they were carrying, and although this procedure only caused him minimal discomfort, it did leave small scars which were still present during Doctor Fonte's physical examination months later.

When describing the creatures, Villas Boas went into great detail saying that all of them wore the same grey, unevenly striped, tight-fitting suits which "reached right up to their necks where it was joined to a kind of helmet made of a grey material that looked stiffer and was strengthened back at nose level". Their eyes, which seemed to be much smaller than ours, were protected by two round glasses and appeared light in colour, possibly blue. He explained that each helmet was tall; double the size of a normal head, and from the top of their heads sprouted three "round silvery tubes which were a little narrower than a common garden hose". The central tube led down towards the backbone, whilst the other two "fitted under the shoulders at about four inches from the armpits — nearly at the sides, where the back begins." All three tubes seemed to fit directly into their clothes although it wasn't clear where or how they were attached as there was no "box or contrivance hidden under their clothes".

He surmised that the overalls must have been some kind of uniform, as every crew member wore the same red badge "the size of a pineapple slice" on their chests. A strip of silvery material, possibly even flattened metal, joined the central badge to their tight-fitting clasp-less belts. The suits were so tight that there were no wrinkles or creases, with no buttons or pockets and no visible hem between the trousers and the shoes as they were apparently a continuation of the same garment. Each being was about 1.64 metres tall except the one who originally caught him in the field, that one didn't even reach Boas' chin. "All seemed strong but not so strong that had I fought with one of them one at a time I should have been afraid of losing. I believe that in a free-for-all fight I could face any single one of them on an equal base" he explained.

Boas was left alone for around an hour in the middle of the room, where he made himself comfortable on a large featureless grey foam bed or couch. Puffs of grey smoke shot out from holes in the wall at head height causing Boas to feel nauseated enough to have to vomit in the corner of the room. Once he was breathing a little easier a short while later, a door opened and in walked a naked woman. Although Boas speculated that the thick liquid he was covered in could have been some form of aphrodisiac, others have suggested that it was possibly a type of germicide. As the naked female was the only entity there without a helmet, it is reasonable to consider that the smoke could have been used to enable her to breathe properly.

Remembering the encounter, Mr. Boas gave an in-depth account of the woman figure that was about to seduce him: "She came in slowly, unhurriedly, perhaps a little amused at the amazement she saw written on my face. I stared; open-mouthed...she was beautiful though of a different type of beauty compared with that of the women I have known. Her hair was blonde, nearly white (like hair dyed in peroxide) it was smooth, not very thick, with a part in the centre and she had big blue eyes, rather longer than round, for they slanted outward, like those pencil-drawn girls made to look like Arabian princesses, that look as if they were slit ... except that they were natural; there was no makeup. Her nose was straight, not pointed, not turned-up, nor too big. The contour of her face was different, though, because she had very high, prominent cheekbones that made her face narrowed to a peak, so that all of a sudden it ended in a pointed chin, which gave the lower part of her face a very pointed look. Her lips were very thin, nearly invisible in fact. Her ears, which I only saw later, were small and did not seem different from ordinary ears. Her high cheekbones gave one the impression that there was a broken bone somewhere underneath, but as I discovered later, they were soft and fleshy to the touch, so they did not seem to be made of bone. Her body was much more beautiful than any I had ever seen before. It was slim, and her breasts stood up high and well-separated. Her waistline was thin, her belly flat, her hips well-developed, and her thighs were large. Her feet were small, her hands long and narrow. Her fingers and nails were normal. She was much shorter than I am, her head only reached my shoulder ... Her skin was white (as that of our fair woman here) and she was full of freckles on her arms. I didn't notice any perfume...except for a natural female odour...And another thing I noticed was the hair in her armpits was bright red, nearly the colour of blood."

Whilst relaying his story with a touch of embarrassment to Dr. Fontes and Mr. Martins, he also mentioned that her pubic hair was also bright red. This detail was omitted from the original publication most likely due to the sexual mores of that era.

The woman approached Boas in silence "looking at me all the while as if she wanted something from me" then pressing her body against his it became evident what her intentions were. All fear and uncertainty dissipated as he began to get excited, "I ended up forgetting everything and held the woman close to me, corresponding to her favours with greater ones of my own" he recalled. An hour later following two encounters and a variety of sexual acts together, the woman backed away. Boas said that he had enjoyed the encounter even though they never kissed; the woman preferred to bite his chin while making "animal grunts".

Not once did the woman speak to him. Once the ordeal was over one of the other beings returned and called to the woman, "but before leaving, she pointed to her belly, and smilingly (as well as she could smile) pointed to the sky, southward I would say. Then she went away. I interpreted the signs as meaning to say that she intended to return and take me with her to wherever it was she lived" said Boas concernedly. He took her message very seriously according to Martins and the thought of leaving his family to be with this stranger from another world filled the young man with anxiety.

Once his clothes were returned to him he sat amongst the crew feeling calm "for I knew no harm would come to me" as he felt they'd got what they came for, as in his opinion "all they wanted was a good stallion to improve their stock". Following a brief walk back through the ship which Boas was adamant was a metal craft after closer inspection of his surroundings; he was directed to descend the same retractable ladder from which he had boarded the craft earlier.

Once back on the ground he watched as the craft "darted off suddenly like a bullet southward, holding itself slightly askew, at such a heady speed that it disappeared from sight in a few seconds". Four hours and fifteen minutes had passed since he had been taken, it was now 5:30 in the morning and he was finally back at his tractor which he claimed had been sabotaged by his abductors as the battery wires had been attached.

For months afterwards he suffered from minor ailments as well as excessive lethargy, and although he withdrew from public life following the publication of his story, he remained resolute in his convictions. Researcher Bruce Rux stated that "the most conservative of UFOlogists accept his abduction as an actual occurrence."

The Antonio Villas Boas abduction is fascinating because it was one of the first accounts of its kind to gain public attention and also because it was a one-off event. It is much more common for adults to have experienced repeated abductions from childhood, whilst having sexual encounters with the perpetrators, on the other hand, appears all too often throughout the array of abduction accounts on record.

Dr. John Mack interviewed a man named Peter who was living on the British Virgin Islands with his wife in the mid-nineties when he started having strange encounters with alien beings. Under hypnosis Peter explained that an extraterrestrial female had seduced him with the purpose of them breeding hybrid children together. His experiences occurred on several occasions and it got to the point where he felt like they belonged together; he told Mack during a regression session that "it feels like she's my real wife, on a soul level" and that he had a "deep, deep heartfelt connection with this being on another plane".[104]

He hadn't always felt as emotionally attached during earlier encounters when he was more traumatised by the experiences, stating under hypnosis that "they're taking my semen" and "they're happy now they've got what they wanted." Peter told John Mack that he felt like he had a dual identity, living his normal life at home with his wife Jamy and then "going home" to 'them'. His feelings for the extraterrestrial woman were putting a strain on his marriage as his wife understandably struggled to come to terms with the bizarre situation in which they had found themselves. And although he loved his wife dearly and would never be disloyal to her, the sexual experiences he was having with the female during the abductions were causing problems back home on Earth.

Karin from California, who was also interviewed by John Mack in the nineties, has had to deal with a lifetime of abductions. Like so many others, she claims to have had sexual intercourse with extraterrestrials during some of her harrowing experiences. The consequences of such activities aren't always clear, but Karin explained that on one occasion she was shown what she believed to be her hybrid offspring.

Recalling the experience she said, "A couple of years into my experience, when I was sitting in a room somewhere – I don't know if it was a ship – I don't know if it was another place in another point in time. It was very quiet, the lighting was very dim and an elder being brought in either three or four of these little beings and they looked sort of bluish in colour. They walked over to me and stood in front of me...they were quite young still. And I looked to the being who had brought them in with a question on my face and the being communicated that they were mine. [Crying] It's sad to be separated from them, and yet there's nothing I can do, I'm just here. If I could go visit them I would."[105]

To all of the abductees or 'experiencers', as some call themselves, these profound experiences are very real and affect their daily lives immeasurably. Try as they might to ignore what is happening to them and get on with living a normal life, getting away from something that will always find you is no mean feat. In Karin's words, "I stuffed all the experiences away so I could be normal, so I could fit in. But I had only put a band-aid over the wound. This is real. I can't walk away from it. I can't ignore it because every day there is still the voice inside of me that says this happened." As Karin expressed so simply, "not only are we not alone, we are really not alone".

The subjectivity involved in these bizarre happenings creates confusion and clouds the water somewhat when trying to garner some sense of reason behind such unusual activities. Brazilian psychologist Gilda Moura studied many individual cases attempting to further understand what is actually occurring to these people, like whether or not they are simply tricks of the mind or delusions creating such incredible scenarios or they are in fact very real and physical events taking place. Speaking on the subject Moura stated, "We don't know what makes it happen, but it's happening. These people can become crazy from the experience but they are not creating the experience because they are crazy. This is very clear to me now." And although she believes that the abductees are telling the truth about their experiences, Moura remains uncertain as to what is behind their ordeals, "we don't know really what they are or what reality this is happening".

THE POPULARISATION OF ALIEN ABDUCTION

These days the concept of alien abduction is one that although far from being understood or accepted by the general public, is at the very least acknowledged by many people. The reasons for the popularisation of the subject over the past few decades can be attributed to a number of factors. The mainstream film industry has certainly played a prominent role in raising public awareness about the existence of extraterrestrials but has done so in a way which has most likely undermined the possibility of alien abduction as a serious affair worthy of further study. Films such as *E.T, Close Encounters of the Third Kind, They Live, Fire in the Sky* and *Communion* among others, have allowed thoughts on alien life to enter the consciousness of many unsuspecting film-goers. But what came first, the movie representation or the abductees' testimony?

As part of Spielberg's intensive research before filming *Close Encounters*, he interviewed numerous UFO witnesses and alien abductees for accurate descriptions of the experiences to assist with the production process. The Villas Boas case predates any significant Hollywood output on the topic and going back even further into the previous century, there were already a handful of reports on the subject.

In 1897, Colonel H.G. Shaw told his story to the Stockton, California Daily Mail, following a 'mystery airship' wave in the same year. Shaw claimed that he and a friend had encountered three tall and slender humanoids covered with a fine, downy hair, who endeavoured to 'harass' himself and his companion. Only after a prolonged struggle did the men succeed in fighting off the strange abductors. As incomplete and vague as this story may be, it still pertains to the existence of a phenomenon which predates the movie industry and its inevitable influence.

Dr. David M. Jacobs, an American author, professor and historian, wrote "contactee stories were deeply rooted in a science fiction model of alien behaviour [whereas] abductee stories have a profoundly alien quality to them that are strikingly devoid of cultural programmatic content."

151

Former Pentagon official Col. Philip J. Corso believes that the notion that individuals simply fabricate stories of alien abduction based on media articles or movies played in cinemas is an oversimplification of a strange phenomenon. Corso has stated that reports of alien abduction and cattle mutilation were being investigated by the military as early as the 1950s, a decade before such events began to appear in the media.

Writing in 1997, Corso explained that "...there were the suspected cattle mutilations and reported abductions, perhaps the most direct form of intervention in our culture short of a direct attack upon our installations. While debates broke out among debunkers who said these were a combination of hoaxes, attacks by everyday predators on cattle, psychological flashback memories of episodes of childhood abuse in the cases of reported abductees, and out-and-out fabrications of the media – field investigators found they could not explain away some of the cattle mutilations, especially where laser surgery seemed to be used, and psychologists found alarming similarities in the descriptions of abductees who had no knowledge of one another's stories. The military intelligence community regarded these stories of mutilations and abductions very seriously."

Out of the hundreds of thousands of reported abduction cases, only a select few have caught the public's imagination and received global recognition since the late 1950's when the amazing story told by Antonio Villas Boas was first published. The next account to become popularised came from American couple Betty and Barney Hill in 1961, then years later in 1973 came the Pascagoula Incident involving Charles Hickson and Calvin Parker followed two years later by the abduction of Travis Walton. Along with such books as Whitley Strieber's *Communion* and Budd Hopkins' *Missing Time*, the subject of alien abduction slowly entered public consciousness through the fascinating testimonies of these self confessed abductees.

i)   Betty and Barney Hill

Mr and Mrs Hill, an interracial couple from Portsmouth, New Hampshire in the United States, had an extraordinary experience on US Route 3 whilst heading home following a short vacation in Montreal. The events which unfolded on the night of September 19, 1961 would later receive international recognition and over time would become one of the most researched and publicised abduction cases in modern history.

Barney was a 39 year old African American working for the US Postal Service whilst his 41 year old wife Betty was a supervisor for the child welfare department who owned a Master's Degree. Three miles south of the city of Lancaster between 10:30 and 11 pm, Betty noticed an unusually bright star in the sky which she thought could possibly be a planet until it began to move erratically, and once she'd pointed the object out to Barney, they both began to keep track of the strange light.

Intrigued by the object which they were beginning to think was most likely just a plane; they decided to pull over for a better look. "So we stopped the car to get out and that's when it changed direction and started coming in towards us" Betty recalled, "and then it followed us for about thirty miles."

She continued, "Barney had been in World War II, he knew planes, and he was trying to identify this, and it was flying in a very erratic manner which was very puzzling to us. We had no idea what a flying saucer looked like but we had no fear, just curiosity, we were trying to identify this craft." [106]

Excited by the possibilities, Betty started waving at the unknown object hoping to coerce it into coming closer so they might have a better view of it. She said "I'm trying to attract the attention of this craft; I'm telling it 'come on in – hi', I'm yelling at it, I've got the window down - 'hey who are you?' And at that point it left the top of the mountain, came out over the highway and stopped in midair directly in front of us, maybe about fifty feet in the sky. So Barney got out with the binoculars in an attempt to identify the craft, and when he looked up he saw a circular window with a bright light behind it and he saw these men standing behind the window looking down at him." Barney saw that the figures were dressed in black, shiny uniforms and appeared to be "somehow not human"[107]. It was at that point as the craft began to descend that he became frightened, so he ran back to the car with the feeling that whoever they were, they were trying to get them both when he told Betty "They're going to capture us!"[108]

They sped off down the highway hoping to avoid any further interaction, and could no longer see the craft anywhere. As they drove home, the Hills described hearing a series of rhythmic buzzing or beeping sounds which appeared to be vibrating off the boot of the car which sent tingling sensations and vibrations through their bodies. It was at this point that they recalled experiencing a dulling of their consciousness and only after a second series of 'code-like' beeping sounds did the couple return to full consciousness once more. Realising that they seemed to have travelled thirty-five miles in the blink of an eye, it became apparent that there was a period of unaccounted for time of which they had no memory. They vaguely recalled making a U-turn off the main road, encountering a roadblock of some sort and witnessing an orb of bright light in the middle of the road. They went straight home in silence with the feeling that something wasn't quite right and once home they both slept until the afternoon.

An array of unexplained issues were noted the following day; they both felt strange sensations and impulses which they couldn't explain and Barney felt compelled to examine his genitalia in the bathroom, though he found nothing out of the ordinary. Their watches had stopped completely and never worked again, the toes of Barney's best dress shoes had been scuffed and the leather strap of the binoculars was inexplicably torn. Betty discovered that her dress was torn at the hem, zip and lining to the extent that she decided to throw it away before changing her mind and hanging it back in the closet.

Since the event, the dress has been through chemical and forensic analyses from five different laboratories. In 1977, Leonard Stringfield, the director of public relations at Dubois Chemicals in Cincinnati, Ohio, offered to have an elemental analysis of her dress done by the chemistry department at the university. Betty received a letter dated August 30, 1977 regarding the analysis results of the garment, of which the spectroscopic emission tests discovered large amounts of sodium, aluminium, iron, magnesium, calcium, manganese and silicon on the fabric. Stringfield wrote, "The powder substance is strange in relation to its inorganic elemental content. It appears to be high in undetermined organic hydrocarbons"[109]

Whilst checking the car for further clues they noticed that there were shiny, concentric circles on the boot which made the needle of a compass spin quickly when held a few inches away. Up to this point Betty and Barney had no recollection of having being abducted but Betty began having bizarre nightmares of them both being taken onto a strange craft against their will. Betty told her sister what had happened and she advised her to at least report the UFO sighting to the nearby Pease Air Force Base, despite Barney's wish to keep quiet on the matter. She reported the incident to Major Paul W. Henderson on September 21st who informed Betty that "the UFO was also confirmed by our radar".

Days later Betty borrowed a UFO book from the local library which had been written by Major Donald Keyhoe, the head of the civilian UFO research group NICAP. She wrote Keyhoe a letter on September 26th, explaining the sighting in full including details about the humanoid figures which Barney had spotted through his binoculars. She wrote that they were considering undergoing hypnosis to help recall the 'missing time' and to maybe make sense of the lucid dreams she was experiencing daily even during waking hours. Her letter was passed on to another NICAP member Walter N. Webb.

Following some research on psychiatrists, the Hills chose to contact Dr. Benjamin Simon, a well respected doctor, neurologist and psychiatrist from Boston whom they met for the first time on December 14, 1963. Dr. Simon started hypnosis sessions with the pair on January 4, 1964, where he hypnotised them separately several times each, finishing each session by reinstating their amnesia. The sessions finished on June 6th of the same year.

Only under hypnosis was the full extent of their ordeal that night back in 1961 finally realised. Going back to the events of that evening, Barney recalled that once they'd set off on the road again after having seen the figures through the binoculars, they drove for about another thirty miles before being compelled to pull off Route 3 onto a side road where they found themselves blocked off by a group of men standing on the road before them. According to Barney, these were the same men he had seen stood lined up in the hovering craft.

Remembering the details of the incident, Betty explained what happened next; "The car motor stalled, they came up on each side – took us out of the car to a pass in the woods where the craft was on the ground – took us on board – said they wanted to find out how we were 'like them' or 'different from them'. And they were going to do some testing, and as soon as the testing was over with they'd take us back to the car and we'd be able to go home."

The Hills were then walked up a ramp into the craft but not without a little resistance from Betty who punched one of them, leading to a scuffle which resulted in her dress being badly torn. "They took us into separate rooms and they gave each of us a full-on physical examination. And there was one who spoke English, there was a total of eleven altogether", Betty said. The couple gave them names for easy reference; the leader, the examiner and the nine others who stayed in the corridor they called the crew members.

Describing the figures, Betty explained that they appeared to have been a form of human being but with larger eyes, smaller mouths and no protruding ears or hair, stating that the entities looked like "...bald-headed alien beings, about five foot tall, with greyish skin, pear-shaped heads and slanting cat-like eyes." Dr. Simon chose to finish one of Betty's hypnosis sessions early as she was exhibiting signs of emotional distress as she recalled being taken and examined by her captors. She seemed to be in considerable pain as she cried excessively during the session.

During the examinations, they took skin, hair and nail samples. Betty was informed that they were performing a pregnancy test when they inserted a long needle into her navel whilst Barney recalled a cup-like device being placed over his genitals in order for a sperm sample to be taken, even though he did not experience an orgasm. Barney was led to a room by three of the beings where he was made to lie on a small rectangular table where skin was scraped from him, and he was also given an oral and ear examination. Although the details of his experience remained fragmented even under hypnosis and his eyes were closed throughout most of the ordeal, Barney still managed to recall some detailed information. He told Dr. Simon that he remembered someone feeling and counting the vertebrae in his spine and at some point a tube or cylindrical device was inserted up his rectum.

Barney explained, "I felt my shoes being removed and my pants being opened. And, I could hear a humming-like sound that they seemed to be making. They pulled my pants all the way down to where my legs were. I could feel them turning me over and putting something in my rectum. It was like a tube. It was not painful. I thought it was just a little larger than a pencil. I felt it go in very easily and then it was withdrawn. They looked at my back and I could feel them touching my skin right down my back as if they were counting my spinal column. I felt something touch right at the base of my spine, like a finger pushing…a single finger. I could only hear this mum…mum…mum, mum, mum, mum, mum, mum, mum…mum [rapid humming] like sound and then I was turned over again. And, my mouth was opened and I could feel two fingers pulling it back."[110] The abductors were surprised to discover that Barney's full set of teeth could be removed all at once, clearly unfamiliar with the use of dentures.

Barney explained that the beings spoke a 'mumbling' language which he did not understand and that could be heard without seeing their narrow lips moving, and of the few times that they communicated with him directly, they seemed to be using telepathy or "thought transference" as he described it as he was unfamiliar with the proper terminology.

Betty's experience inside the craft was much more lucid and she insisted that 'the leader' spoke English to her throughout a number of extended conversations in which she was able to ask questions. When she asked where they came from she was shown a three-dimensional or holographic "star map" which Betty endeavoured to draw as accurately as she could under hypnosis. Amateur astronomer Marjorie Fish attempted to decipher Betty's version of the map, hoping to understand where exactly the visitors had originated from, and although much debate continues as to the accuracy of Fish's interpretation, the binary system of Zeta Reticuli 1 and 2 appeared to be the most prominent of the stars included. The infamous 'Greys' are purportedly Zeta Reticulans.

Once the examinations were complete, the Hills were returned to their vehicle and the last thing they recalled seeing was an orange glow disappearing into the night sky. After Dr. Simon had finished the sessions, the couple went back to their normal lives and did not seek further publicity; however, the *Boston Traveler* printed a front page story on October 25, 1965. Written by reporter John H. Lutrell, the article with the heading "UFO Chiller: Did THEY Seize Couple?" was picked up by the United Press International the next day which soon earned the Hills international recognition whether they wanted it or not. John G. Fuller wrote a book about their case called *The Interrupted Journey* in 1966 which also included a copy of Betty's sketch of the star map and in 2007 Stanton Friedman and Kathleen Marden authored *Captured! The Betty and Barney Hill UFO Experience.*

ii) The Pascagoula Incident

On October 10, 1973 a large, silver UFO was spotted flying slowly over a housing project in St. Tammany Parish, New Orleans, Louisiana. Fifteen different people reported the sighting, including two policemen. The following day at around 9:00 pm, two men from Gautier, Mississippi, were night fishing on the Pascagoula River when they suddenly heard an unusual sort of buzzing sound coming from behind them.

Calvin Parker (19) and Charles Hickson (42) turned around to see what was making the noise when they saw an egg-shaped craft hovering a few feet above the ground, it was glowing and had bluish lighting emanating from the front. The unknown object hovered ominously roughly thirty feet from the river's edge before a door suddenly opened allowing three peculiar looking beings to exit the craft. Hickson and Parker watched in disbelief as the strange figures floated across the water straight towards them.

Describing the unfolding events during a recorded interview less than three hours after the ordeal, Hickson recalled "And two of 'em just floated around me and lifted me off the ground... by my arms...with their pincher things. They must've done something...I just raised off the ground. No force...they didn't hurt me...I didn't feel nothin'."[111]

Young Calvin Parker passed out and didn't remember much after the initial sighting of the craft followed by the occupants floating across the surface of the water. Hickson however, remembered everything very clearly and on Thursday evening at approximately 11:00pm, the two men decided to report the incident officially to the local Sheriff's Department where an interview was conducted and recorded on cassette by Sheriff Fred Diamond and Captain Glen Ryder.

Hickson explained what happened next, "And they glided me into that thing. You know how you just guide somebody. All of us moved like we were floatin' through thin air. When I got in there they had me, you know, they just kind of had me there. There were no seats, no chain, they just moved me around. I couldn't resist them. I just floated – felt no sensation, no pain."

Both of the men described the visitors as "about five feet tall, had bullet-shaped heads without necks, slits for mouths, and where their noses or ears would be they had thin, conical objects sticking out like carrots from a snowman's head." Hickson explained that they could have had eyes but he didn't see any as he was so frightened at the time that certain details weren't very clear to him.

Inside the craft Hickson recalled being examined by a strange instrument which he described as looking "like a big eye" which had some kind of attachment to it. "It moved. And it went all over my body, up and down. And then they left me. Left me right by myself and the position they had me in – I couldn't move. Just my eyes could move", he explained to the Sheriff. Hickson was left alone for around twenty to thirty minutes where he assumed they went into another room to examine Calvin. Then they were 'floated' back out of the craft and left by the shore where they had been taken less than an hour earlier.

Once back on familiar ground Hickson found his companion in a terrible state, "The only thing I remember is that kid Calvin just standing there. I've never seen that sort of fear on a man's face before as I saw on Calvin's. It took me a while to get him back to his senses, and the first thing I told him was, son, ain't nobody gonna believe this. Let's just keep this whole thing to ourselves. Well, the more I thought about it, the more I thought I had to let some officials know." Young Calvin Parker had a nervous breakdown in the months that followed the incident and spent a short time in a hospital being treated.

After being questioned separately by Sheriff Diamond, the men were left alone in a room together and unbeknownst to them, they were being recorded in an attempt to catch them out and discover whether or not it was a hoax as the officials had initially suspected. If it was a hoax then they certainly hid it well, for as the recording testifies, both men were in a very real state of panic:

Parker – "I sure as hell almost had a heart attack. God I ain't [inaudible] you. I came one damn inch from dying."

Hickson – "I know, it scared me to death too, son. Jesus Christ – have mercy."Parker – "What's so bad about it – nobody believes us."

Hickson – "I thought I'd been through enough hell on this earth and now I had to go through this!"

159

Once the local press released the story, news of the Pascagoula incident soon spread nationwide, gaining a great deal of publicity along the way. Dr. James Harder from the University of California was sent by the Aerial Phenomena Research Organization (APRO) to investigate the case. Within a few days, Dr. Harder setup a hypnosis session for the two alleged abductees, which he performed in front of Dr. J. Allen Hynek (representing the USAF), Dr. Boskow and Dr. Richards. Harder and Hynek interviewed Parker and Hickson together, and under hypnosis Hickson became so frightened that the session was aborted. Both men were encouraged to take a lie-detector test which they passed with ease.

As remarkable as their story was, it was clear to everyone who met them that something had happened which had scared the life out of them. They were honest men, lying didn't appear to be very plausible. Hynek and Harder believed their story to be genuine and Hynek later stated that "there was definitely something here that wasn't terrestrial."Dr. Harder expressed his views on the matter, "I think particularly telling is his recalling that he was levitated as he was taken aboard the craft. I don't think Charlie at the time was sufficiently sophisticated to know that that happens fairly frequently. It wouldn't be something [I should think] that he would've made up."[112]

Up until October 21, 2001 Charles Hickson and Calvin Parker had been the only witnesses to the strange events that occurred that night by the river, despite a number of other UFO sightings the previous evening. But in 2001, Natalie Chambers of the Associated Press reported that a new witness had surfaced named Mike Cataldo, a retired Navy Chief Petty Officer. When Kenny Young discovered that Mr. Cataldo had contacted Chambers at a Mississippi newspaper a month earlier, he conducted a *Yahoo People Search* for that name and managed to track Cataldo down and gave him a call. Cataldo answered the phone personally and confirmed that he had contacted the press recently about a UFO sighting that he and two friends witnessed back in 1973.

"The story is very true", Cataldo informed Young when questioned about the Hickson/Parker incident. He, Ted Peralta and Mack Hanna were travelling west towards Buloxi, Mississippi, when they first saw something that looked like a shooting star, moving from right to left before descending to a marshy, tree-lined area and hovering there. "It was spinning and had blinking lights on the top of it all around the edge, all the way around it in a circle. These were blinking lights arranged on it just like you would tape lights to the side of a cake pan", Cataldo explained.

"We never knew of the Hickson/Parker abduction until days later. It happened on Thursday and it was not until the following Sunday that I saw the headline in the morning paper about two men taken aboard a Flying Saucer, I'm telling you I about died", he recalled. Continuing with the story Cataldo said, "I've never seen a UFO since then, not at all. Not even before then. Was it real? You're damn right it was real. I can't say anything about what they did or were involved in. I don't even know if what I saw matches what they saw, but I know what I saw and where I was at. But where we saw the thing going across the sky through our windshield is basically the area where Hickson and Parker said they were taken aboard."

iii) Travis Walton Goes Missing

In 1993, the $15.5 million Hollywood movie *Fire in the Sky* was released, telling the true account of the abduction of Travis Walton from the Apache-Sitgreaves National Forest where he had been working with his fellow loggers back in 1975. The movie followed on from his popular autobiographical book, *The Walton Experience*, which was published in 1978.

APRO investigator Dr. James Harder was once again involved, as he had been two years earlier with the Pascagoula case but on this occasion he was the first to obtain Walton's account under hypnosis. The highly successful film which played its part in raising the awareness of alien abduction as a genuine phenomenon deviated slightly from the truth, dramatizing the actual events beyond necessary means for the sake of entertainment. Harder commented, "The thing that's disturbing about the movie is that they would take such liberties and still call it a true story. I don't think he'd [Travis] willingly be a party to the distortions."[113] The real drama which unfolded on November 5, 1975 needed no embellishment.

Travis Walton was on his way home to Snowflake, Arizona, in a large truck with six other co-workers after a long day of felling trees with noisy chainsaws. The time was about a quarter past six in the evening and the sun had only recently receded out of sight for the day. Walton was sat in the front with Kenneth Peterson and his best friend and boss Mike Rogers, when a hundred yards ahead of them he noticed a light coming through the trees on the right. "What the hell was that?" he asked.

"We rolled past the intervening evergreen thicket to where we could have an unobstructed view of the source of the strange radiance. Suddenly we were electrified by the most awesome, incredible sight we had seen in our entire lives", Walton explains in his book. The truck skidded to a halt and Walton flung the passenger door wide open hoping for a clearer view as Allen Dalis yelled from the back seat, "Oh my God! It's a flying saucer!"

To their amazement, they saw a bizarre golden disc hovering silently about twenty feet above the ground and less than thirty yards from the truck. The metallic craft hung motionless in the air. The object was estimated to have had an overall diameter of between fifteen and twenty feet and around ten feet thick, resembling "two gigantic pie-pans placed lip to lip, with a small round bowl turned upside down on the top."

Afraid that he would miss the opportunity of a lifetime to see a real spaceship up close, Walton leapt out of the truck and approached the hovering craft much to the dismay of the rest of the crew. Moving quietly and cautiously nearer to the machine, he managed to get within six feet from being directly beneath it. "I stared up at the unbelievably smooth, unblemished surface of the curving hull. I was filled with a tremendous sense of awe and curiosity as I pondered the incomprehensible mysteries possible within it." He began to become aware of a barely audible sound emanating from the ship, a blend of mechanical sounds both low and high pitched. Rogers screamed at him, "Travis! Get away from there!"

Suddenly the volume of the vibrations began to intensify like a multitude of generators starting up simultaneously, and the disc started wobbling erratically on its axis. As Travis crouched down in response to the motion and increasing noise coming from above him, an immense bright, blue-green ray of light shot out from beneath the craft.

Walton wrote, "I saw and heard nothing. All I felt was the numbing force of a blow that felt like a high-voltage electrocution. The intense bolt made a sharp cracking, or popping, sound. The stunning concussion of the foot-wide beam struck me full in the head and chest. My mind sank quickly into unfeeling blackness. I didn't even see what hit me; but from the instant I felt that paralyzing blow, I did not see, hear, or feel anything more."[114]

The rest of the crew watched in horror and disbelief as they saw Travis being lifted off the ground with his body arched backward and his arms and legs outstretched. He was then hurled backwards with great force, ten feet through the air, landing limply on the hard rocky ground – right shoulder first. As he lay there spread-eagled and motionless on the forest floor, the men in the truck fled the scene with great haste. After driving about a quarter of a mile, they all saw a streak of light flash upwards through the sky, and believing that the UFO had left, they decided to go back and find Walton. He was nowhere to be found.

The workers relayed their extraordinary experience to Navajo county sheriff Marlin Gillespie when they arrived in Heber, Arizona. Despite the sheriff's skepticism and suspicions of a planned homicide, several searches for Walton were conducted over the coming days and on November 10, a lie detector test was administered by C. E. Gilson of the Arizona Department of Public Safety. Allen Dalis aside, whose test was "inconclusive", the results of the other five witnesses suggested that they were being truthful. Gilson concluded, "These polygraph examinations proved that these five men did see some object that they believe to be a UFO and that Travis Walton was not injured or murdered by any of these men…If an actual UFO did not exist and the UFO is a man-made hoax, five of these men had no prior knowledge of a hoax."

Walton was missing for five days. Despite the men passing the lie detector tests, suspicions as to his whereabouts were growing and many locals doubted the authenticity of the men's testimonies. But at five minutes past midnight on the morning of November 11, the phone rang at his sister's house and much to the relief of his family it was Travis calling from a public phone box near Heber. Finally, the truth about Walton's disappearance could be told, and no-one would have predicted the tale which he was about to reveal.

On the night he went missing Walton roused to find himself feeling weak, thirsty and disorientated, laid on a hard flat surface which he deduced must have been a raised table of some description. He straightened up, feeling as if he'd been hit with a baseball bat then suddenly the memory of what had happened in the woods before he had blacked out came flooding back. His first thoughts were that he was in hospital in an emergency room but he did wonder why he was still fully dressed in his work clothes.

He looked up and blurrily saw what he believed to be a group of doctors wearing unusual orange surgical gowns, but as his vision cleared he couldn't believe his eyes. "The sudden horror of what I saw rocked me as I realized I was definitely not in a hospital. I was looking square into the face of a horrible creature . . . with huge, luminous brown eyes the size of quarters! I looked frantically around me. There were three of them! Hysteria overcame me instantly."

He instinctively took up an aggressive stance and armed himself with one of the instruments lying on the waist-high table, preparing to defend himself from an imminent attack which never came. As he stood there screaming "Keep back, damn you!" the three figures turned and fled as his intent was clear. Not knowing what to do next, he followed his captors out of the door and walking in the opposite direction, he turned into a curved hallway which was about three feet wide. "I broke into a frightened run down the narrow corridor. The cramped hallway turned continuously in a tight curve to the right. I dashed past an open doorway on my left without looking in, only ten feet down the hall from the door I had just exited. I caught a glimpse of a room but was afraid to stop", he recalled.

He ran until he entered a round room with a domed ceiling, sixteen feet across and about ten feet high, the room was empty except for a single high-backed chair which was facing away from him. After sitting in the small chair for a while and fidgeting with various green buttons and levers, he decided that he should stop tampering with the console as strange things were beginning to happen.

The stars began moving downward in unison as he pulled on one lever as if he were actually controlling the whole direction and speed of the craft, so knowing that his actions could lead to disaster he stepped out of the chair. Hearing a faint sound, Walton turned around to find a human being standing by the door. The man was about six feet two inches tall, extremely muscular and evenly proportioned, unlike the shorter beings with large heads and eyes that he had just encountered. The man wore a helmet, a tight-fitting bright blue velour-like suit, with black boots and a black band or belt around his waist. Desperately trying to communicate with the tall stranger, Walton ranted questions at him but at no point did he hear even one word from the humanoid figure throughout his ordeal. Instead, the man gently grabbed Walton by the arm and led him out of the door into a large hangar-like room where he saw two or three oval-shaped saucers at one end of the large room.

He was escorted across the open floor through another door which opened quickly and silently from the middle outwards, where he was led down a long corridor into a white room fifteen feet square. To his amazement, aside from a table and chair, he saw three other humans, two men and a woman standing around the table. They all wore the same velvety blue uniforms as the first man but they weren't wearing helmets.

Describing the humanoid figures Walton said, "They were smooth-skinned and blemish-less. No moles, freckles, wrinkles, or scars marked their skin. The striking good looks of the man I had first met became more obvious on seeing them all together. They shared a family-like resemblance, although they were not identical."

Walton implored "Would somebody *please* tell me where I am? What in hell is going on? What is this place?" They didn't reply, instead they just looked at him before one man and the woman approached him and silently took him by the arms and led him towards the table. As he was eased back into a lying position, the woman brought a soft plastic type of oxygen mask seemingly out of thin air and proceeded to press the mask over his mouth and nose. Becoming weak, everything turned grey, then black...and the next thing he knew, he was lying on his stomach with his head on his right forearm, on the cold pavement west of Heber. Exhausted and in a state of shock, he still clearly remembered his ordeal as he lay there fully dressed but eleven pounds lighter.

Looking up, he watched as the huge craft hovered over the highway before shooting off into the night sky. "The most striking thing about its departure was its quietness. It seemed impossible that something so large, moving through the atmosphere at such speed, would not have shrieked through the air, or even broken the sound barrier with a sonic boom. Yet it had been totally silent!"

Safely back on familiar territory he walked to the nearest phone box at the nearby Exxon petrol station and dialled the operator before being put through to his sister's house as she was the only nearby relative with a telephone. His brother-in-law Grant answered; it was 12:05 A.M.

Walton's brother Duane was contacted and shortly after he drove into Heber to pick Travis up. "Everyone has been worried sick about you," Duane told him. Walton replied, "If it's already after midnight, I must have been unconscious for a couple of hours, because I only remember about an hour or an hour and a half inside that thing." Looking at him strangely, Duane told Travis to feel his face. "Good hell, I just shaved this morning and it feels like a week's growth!" Travis exclaimed, clearly still not understanding. "Travis", his brother said softly, "you've been missing for *five* days!"

The Walton case soon became big news, spreading nationwide then globally as more and more articles, news reports and documentaries began to surface over the years that followed. He was interviewed by APRO, news reporters, psychiatrists and doctors, each wanting to prove or disprove the legitimacy of his testimony. One of the psychiatrists who examined Walton was Dr. Jean Rosenbaum who told ABC News, "Our conclusion, which is absolute, is that this young man is not lying, that there is no collusion involved, and no attempt to hoax."[115] But not everybody was as easily satisfied.

UFO debunker Philip Klaas wasn't convinced, and went out of his way to disprove Walton's extravagant story, even offering ten thousand dollars to one of Walton's colleagues Steve Pierce, if he would publicly confess to hoaxing the whole affair. Pierce, to his credit never took the money even though he was struggling to feed his family at that time, and he even turned Klaas down a second time following a recent UFO conference.

Every one of the aforementioned cases stuck to their stories throughout their lives and not once deviated from their original testimonies. Interestingly, all three separate incidents which struck a chord with the public have all been one-off incidents; a case of people simply minding their own business when a sudden change of events befell them and changed their lives irrevocably. More intensive research reveals that it is much more common for abductees to experience such events on more than one occasion. But it is the sheer incidental aspect of these three cases which seems to have caught people's imagination, the fact that it could have happened to any of us.

PROOF OF PHYSICAL CONTACT

The lack of physical evidence to support the claims made by alleged abductees has always been problematic. If there is no way of showing that some form of physical contact has occurred then the whole phenomenon may as well be relegated to the realms of the supernatural, and the concept of alien beings taking humans from their beds could be perceived as just as 'real' as seeing a ghost in the room. However, this does not seem to be the case. Aside from physical scars, scratches and strange marks appearing overnight, other anomalous aspects are often present which may confirm the existence of a very physical encounter based in reality. It is not uncommon to find injection marks on the skin as well as blood on clothes and bedding.

A fireman from Bakersfield, California, was becoming increasingly frustrated at the numerous abduction experiences which he had to cope with, and the fact that very few people, if any, actually believed his stories. So one day he decided to try and find some evidence to help prove to himself and others that what was happening to him wasn't just in his head. He set up a hidden camera in the bedroom, inside a digital clock, and waited for the intruders to return. The test was unsuccessful so he invested in some specialist video equipment which captures different light among other things; the resulting images were intriguing but inconclusive. One image revealed the unusual features of a face that he believed to be one of 'them', and although he could've been right, he needed something clearer and more obvious.

Next he setup a foil laminate which he placed on the floor beneath a towel out of sight, next to a wall in his bedroom where he had watched the ETs float through as if nothing was there. One morning he was astonished to discover that they had left a solitary footprint on the foil. Although this occurred on only one occasion, on the same towel on another day he did find an unusual small and black nail or claw-like object with three black hairs growing out of it. He sent the sample to Ted Papenfuss, a research specialist at the Museum of Vertebrate Zoology who concluded, "We could not identify what species the claw came from." The sample had an exterior covering consisting of vegetable material with a second layer being comprised of carotene, like that found in human nails. DNA analysis confirmed that the object did not belong to any Earth creature.

Dr. John Mack, whose introduction into the phenomenon stemmed from studying the work of Budd Hopkins, became intrigued by the subject when he realized that certain consistencies and physical evidence appeared throughout most abduction claims.

"In virtually every case there are one or more concrete physical findings that accompany or follow the abduction experience, such as UFO sightings in the community, burned earth where UFOs are said to have landed, and independent corroboration that the abductee's whereabouts are unknown at the time of the reported abduction event," he stated. "Seemingly unexplained or missing pregnancies, a variety of minor physical lesions, odd nosebleeds, and the recovery of tiny objects from the bodies of experiencers are also widely seen."[116]

Dr. Roger K. Leir, author of *The Aliens and the Scalpel* and *Casebook Alien Implants* has spent many years researching physical evidence for proof of the reality of alien abduction. He and his surgical team have performed numerous surgeries on patients claiming to have been abducted by aliens, with the sole intent of recovering implants left in various parts of their anatomy and presenting them for biological and metallurgical research. The retrieved objects [see SOURCES] have been scientifically investigated by many prestigious laboratories including Los Alamos National Laboratory, New Mexico Tech, the University of Toronto, Southwest Labs, Seal Laboratories, York University and the University of California at San Diego. The results have been astounding.

On removal of the implants which he described as small metallic rods with strange grey biological membrane surrounding them, initial metallurgic tests drew comparisons with meteorite samples. The laboratories are never informed beforehand of the origin of the objects as this would only compromise and devalue the investigation. One such sample which was extracted from the back of a subject's wrist bone was described as 'seed-like' in appearance as it was only five by two millimetres in size. Dr. Leir commented that "this piece has similar metallurgy as to the earlier specimens and contains high amounts of iron and nickel and has isotopic ratios that are not of this Earth."

Patient John Smith asked Leir to remove a foreign object from his big toe following an abduction experience. Before the operation took place, other signs of physical evidence were discovered in Smith's backyard and master bedroom. Recounting that the alien's craft was seen hovering in the backyard above a patch of turf, soil samples were sent off to be analysed and the results concluded that there was a strange high bromine content present.

Two small four-fingered handprints were visualised under UV light on the interior of the master bedroom wall at the same area as a magnetic anomaly below the window. A biotechnologist has taken DNA from the handprints and the tests are ongoing.

Minor elements found in the toe sample were rare on Earth and *never* found in the human body. The scientific analysis revealed the presence of ruthenium, iridium, palladium, rhodium, osmium, hafnium, yttrium, rhenium, niobium, cerium, neodymium, samarium, gadolinium, dysprosium, praseodymium, europium, rubidium, thorium and uranium.

The conclusion of the analysis confirmed the object to be non-terrestrial in origin as some of the elements show non-terrestrial isotopic ratios. The iron in the sample appeared to be meteoric in origin. There were also numerous inclusions in the metal portion of the object such as biological tissue growing out of the metal and surrounding it, sodium chloride orthorhombic nano-crystals of varying size plus carbon nanostructures like nano-fibres and nano-tubes. Leir explained that carbon nano-tubes can be used in a medical capacity by injecting them into the body where they eat up cholesterol.

By comparing the isotopic ratios found in the implant to known isotopic ratios of elements in our solar system, Leir discovered that they were not the same. Sub-atomic structures in the implants are also non-terrestrial. With the origin of the material still unknown, Leir concluded that the results clearly indicated that the material is not from this planet and perhaps not even from our solar system.[117]

Leir said, "We have to draw certain conclusions that these are being manufactured by some kind of intelligence, which is certainly not within the realm of our academic science."[118] Discussing the purpose of the bizarre objects Leir speculated, "I think that these are genetic monitoring devices and I believe that there is a signal that is both going in and out. I also believe that the human race is now, and has been undergoing for some years, a genetic manipulation."

The fact that people are waking up in the morning with these unusual items implanted deep under the skin is cause for concern. Leir's research, although still in its early stages, is extremely revealing and suggestive of something greater than our understanding coming into contact with our species and physically affecting it.

The question of whether or not extraterrestrial beings are responsible for implanting the metallic devices remains inconclusive, but something physical is definitely occurring, even though it remains unclear where the responsibility lies.

DIFFERING DEPICTIONS

Whilst researching the alien abduction phenomenon it became apparent that the depictions of extraterrestrial or alien beings entering the lives of everyday people seem to be fairly recent. Is there a reason for this one may wonder? UFOs have been described in various guises throughout history along with spacemen, people from the heavens or stars, often called gods, angels or spirits. But accounts of star people coming down and taking humans from their homes and performing experiments on them, is not a commonly reported theme in the annals of recorded history. However, there are parallels to the many events described during alien abductions which exist within folklore, religion and anthropology.

Correlations between the abduction experience and shamanic experiences (including the implantation of foreign objects into the body and surgery-like procedures) or even stories of contact with fairies, suggest that modern accounts of alien abduction should be considered as part of a greater history of strange encounters.

As author Dr. Gregory L. Little wrote "there is a process that has been ongoing - probably for all of humanity's history - that manifests itself through the appearance of archetypal creatures and beings. John Keel was one of the first to recognize this. Others, including Vallee, Clark, and many British ufologists have long pointed out the resemblance between modern UFO reports and the ancient traditions. It doesn't really matter what we call the process underlying UFOs, abductions, and all of the related phenomena, but it is important to see that they all tie together."[119]

A 1960s report published by the U.S. Air Force Office of Scientific Research called *UFOs and Related Subjects: An Annotated Bibliography*, revealed the following; "Many of the UFO reports now being published in the popular press recount alleged incidents that are strikingly similar to demonic possession and psychic phenomena which has long been known to theologians and parapsychologists."

Even astronomer Carl Sagan theorised that tales of contact with demons which are common throughout history share remarkable similarities with the alien abduction experience. He wrote "...most of the central elements of the alien abduction account are present, including sexually obsessive non-humans who live in the sky, walk through walls, communicate telepathically, and perform breeding experiments on the human species."

In the past it was said that demons could assume any physical form in order to seduce their victims more successfully. Ulrich Molitor's 1489 book *De Laniis et Phitonicis Mulieribus*, included one of the first illustrations of a demon appearing physically to make love to a witch. His book contained many illustrations of demons assuming different shapes and forms for sexual purposes and was the first known publication to show engravings of demons having sexual relations with humans of whom they had abducted.

Similarities with modern abduction stories include the fact that most victims of the demonic figures were taken unwillingly from their bedrooms at night and many of them described the presence of several different types of demon at the time of their abduction, some of whom simply stood by and watched. Some alien abductees who have experienced sexual encounters with their abductors have described the sexual organ of the intruder as being cold as ice – in particular the insect-like creatures. The writer Vignate chronicled the trials of Artois in 1468, in which he wrote of Satan forcing sex on a victim; for the first time Satan's sexual organ was described as being ice-cold. St. Augustine believed that people were actually being abducted by demons and forced to engage in sexual acts with them; "(Demons) have often injured women, desiring and acting carnally with them."

Linda Moulton Howe, known for her extensive research into cattle mutilations, told a story at the 1992 Ozark UFO Convention about a man who claimed to have been visited each night by the same female alien entity, forcing herself sexually upon him. He became so frustrated at the situation that he began to masturbate every night before sleeping in an attempt to create difficulties gaining an erection and putting off the enforced sexual act which would inevitably occur during the abduction. He explained that the female alien and her "mantis-like keepers" became so disturbed by his actions that it was decided that some kind of agreement should be made with the man which would cause less aggravation and discourage him from deploying such evasive tactics in future.

In the past, demons or goblins which were often referred to as an incubus (seeks sexual intercourse with women) or a succubus (seeks males) were not considered as a figment of people's imagination, rather they were very much accepted as real entities. As Martin Del Rio wrote in his 1599 book *Disqusitionum Magicarum*, "...to disagree [with their existence] is only obstinacy and foolhardiness; for it is the universal opinion of the fathers, theologians, and writers on philosophy, the truth of which is generally acknowledges by all ages and peoples." Ten years earlier in 1589, Peter Binsfield wrote *De Confessione Maleficarum*, in which he stated "[the incubus] is an indisputable truth which is not only proved certain by experience, but also confirmed by history."

The concept of crossbreeding and genetic manipulation, which many researchers have suggested is the main purpose behind the modern abduction phenomenon, had already reared its ugly head in centuries gone by. According to ancient texts, the act of collecting sperm from abducted males and impregnating female victims with the semen taken was precisely what an incubus or succubus would do in order to create hybrid offspring. The movie *Rosemary's Baby* dealt with this exact scenario, as a demon impregnated Rosemary with the seed which would later be born as the spawn of Satan.

Much attention was given to the phenomenon of contact with demons during the 12th and 13th Centuries because of the sheer volume of reports emanating from within church walls. Medieval writing from this period mentions such demonic acts: "Devils do indeed collect human semen...therefore devils can transfer the semen which they have collected and inject it into the bodies of others" and "Devils in the form of women yield to males and receive their semen; by cunning skill, the demons preserve its potency, and afterwards,...they become incubi and pour it into female repositories."[120]

'The Devil's Mark' (also referred to as 'fairy bruising' or 'the witch's teat') features in medieval reports and describes the physical mark left upon the devil's victims for identification. These permanent scars were believed to have been caused by the demon's claws scratching the flesh or by the red hot kiss of the devil 'licking' the victim. The mark of the Devil "is imprinted on the most secret parts of the body".[121] Parallels can be drawn with the scars left following an alleged alien abduction, as in both instances the marks have appeared the next day after a nocturnal encounter with an intruder.

The marks left on alien abductees in modern accounts resemble those described in the past as the 'Devil's Mark', "cuts or scoops on the back of the legs, arms, neck, purplish circular spots around the abdomen and genitals, and in patterns consistent with those from medieval times ascribed to witches, incubi and fairies."[122] A sign of either favour or disfavour according to fairy lore is the phenomenon known as "fairy bruising" where a circular cluster of small bruises, often found around the genitals, is left by the fairies as their mark.

Ancient examples of 'fairy abductions' also share striking similarities with modern tales of alien interference. As explained in *An Encyclopaedia of Fairies* (Briggs, 1976), those who were taken by the fairies were almost always given a special drink described as a thick liquid previous to any sexual encounter. The victims (most commonly women) were then paralysed before they were carried (levitated or flown) away into "fairyland" which is always located nearby although it cannot be perceived under 'normal' conditions. The paralysis plays a central role in fairy lore as without it the abducted humans cannot enter fairyland. The word "stroke" which we associate with conditions of paralysis originated from the ancient terms "fairy-stroke" and "elf-stroke".

Another interesting connection with fairies are the tales of will-o-the-wisps, which under modern guises could be called 'orbs'. It was believed that fairies travelled in these circular globes of light before or after abductions took place; these days any witnesses to such phenomena would most likely refer to a moving ball of light as a UFO.

Interestingly, the will-o-the-wisp phenomenon has different interpretations around the world. In Argentine and Uruguayan folklore it is feared and known as Luz Mala or evil light and is mostly reported over rural areas as an extremely shiny ball of light which floats a few inches above the ground.

Myths from India and Pakistan refer to the wisp as the ghost-light (Chir Batti or Aleya) and fisherman used the term to explain unexplained strange light phenomena occurring over the marshes. Local villagers described seeing the ghost-lights as either hovering or flying balls of light since time immemorial.

In eastern Australia, the name given to an unusual formation of lights is Min Min Light and the aborigines included stories about the lights long before settlers from the west came to the country. The lights are said to sometimes follow or approach people before disappearing if fired at, then reappearing later on. Similar descriptions of balls of light, flames or energy are present in Japanese folklore too including Hitodama ('Human Soul' as a ball of energy) and Hi no Tama (Ball of Flame).

'The Naga fireballs' are an unknown phenomenon often seen in Laos and in Thailand's Mekong River, where reddish glowing balls have been witnessed rising high into the air out of the water. Reasons for such phenomena remain inconclusive.

It could just be possible that whatever is being described nowadays as extraterrestrial encounters of some sort could well have been depicted in different ways throughout the ages, depending on cultural understandings of what could be responsible for such unusual activity. Just as we today may consider the concept of fairies and demons to belong in the realms of religious superstition and folklore, future humans may well look back on our explanations of alien visitors with similar derision.

What is of importance here however is to recognise that no matter how the phenomenon is explained, perceived or understood, that something has affected humankind enough throughout history to become part of the grand tapestry of life, whether through myth, religion, legend or folklore. The consistency of the tales from ancient times to the modern era would suggest that *something* must have taken place in order to have affected so many people.

As research continues to delve into the abduction situation, many questions remain unanswered. Are we looking at a misunderstood natural phenomenon, the human imagination, psychological issues or a very real and physical problem?

John E. Mack's studies into the subject led him to conclude that "psychiatric examinations and numerous psychological tests have failed to reveal forms of mental illness that could, conceivably, explain the abduction phenomenon." He believes that from a psychiatric viewpoint, the majority of abductees have shown no signs of mental illness but are consistently shown to be very ordinary individuals. He wrote, "The intensity of affect and expressed bodily feeling that occurs during the regression sessions of abduction experiencers is so powerful that even the most determined sceptic would be hard-pressed to conclude that something quite extraordinary and reality-shattering did not occur."

Self-confessed abductee and abduction researcher Karla Turner told audiences around America what she considered to be the only "facts" that could be taken from the evidence available regarding the alien abduction scenario:

- Some of the aliens lie
- They can implant false memories and create virtual reality scenarios that appear real to the abductees
- Abductees report only what the abductors want them to report
- They control human perceptions during the encounter
- They manipulate people physically, sexually and spiritually from childhood
- They show a keen interest in human souls and also thought processes
- The alien agenda has physical procedures and aims that are not related to reproduction
- There is some element of human involvement in the UFO phenomenon

- There is a clear link between UFO abductions, the military and mind control

Researchers like Jacques Vallee and Martin Cannon have unearthed strange connections concerning the military's involvement in the abduction phenomenon especially with regards to the use of mind control and mind programming. The common occurrence of abductees reporting missing time, of not knowing how they arrived at a specific location following an incident, and memory loss and the lack of detailed information which only becomes retrievable through hypnosis; all draws parallels with the effects of mind control.

Cannon hypothesises that it is possible that alien abductions are not in reality connected with extraterrestrial beings but rather they are being used as a cover story for the military's clandestine activities and experimentation. Many abductees report the presence of military personnel in the room alongside other beings during their abduction.

Karla Turner's book *Taken: Inside the Alien-Human Agenda* includes a prologue which tells how three of the women who contacted Turner regarding their experiences told her of some involvement from army officials during their ordeals.

One woman called Pat told Turner about an incident in 1954 where she described both aliens and military men coming into her house and setting up equipment in the living room. She said, "The Army men wanted to talk to me the most. Me, an eleven-year-old girl with secrets in my head. But the aliens told me I couldn't tell because 'there will be those who will tamper with your mind.' And here they were, the tamperers, the Army men." She then said to the men "You're in my mom's room where the White, glowing ones were. You don't belong here, but they do."

Amy talked about an incident which took place in Texas in 1992 where she said that "The masked alien explained that her race had been doing things to humans that they should not be doing." Continuing, Amy explained, "She and several groups of her race, and others, wanted to stop the 'abuse' of the humans by her race. They were working with certain people on Earth to stop the process. The other humans in the room were ex-pilots, military officials, and other professionals. They were all working together to stop the alien intrusions."

It is the correlation of accounts like these which widens the parameters of the phenomenon of alien abduction and highlights the fact that there is much more to the subject than has been previously considered. The mystery has only deepened and without further investigation the likelihood of arriving at any feasible conclusions anytime soon remains greatly diminished.

As David Jacobs warns, "we must realize that the abduction phenomenon is too important to dismiss as the ravings of prevaricators or psychologically disturbed people. I hope the extraordinary lack of scientific concern to date does not in the long run prove to be a mistake with undreamed-of consequences."

The complexity of the subject and the difficulties which arise when attempting to decipher the fragmented pieces of evidence which are beginning to surface, only allows the discerning researcher to continue to hypothesise on the true nature of the phenomenon at hand. It would be decidedly foolish to draw solid conclusions at this early stage and such an approach would only prove to be detrimental to the search for clarity on the subject. The first step to understanding this topic is to remain objective, open-minded and willing to listen to new ideas and theories which may over time increase our knowledge.

The next chapter deals with a closely related subject, another unexplained area of interest which many have also attributed to physical beings from another world, the bizarre and mysterious unseen world of animal mutilation.

5

SURGEONS FROM THE STARS

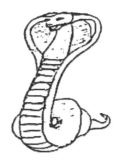

Either we've got a UFO situation or we've got a massive, massive conspiracy which is enormously well funded.

Senator Harrison Schmitt, Former Apollo 17 astronaut.

EGINNING IN THE EARLY 1970s, reports of mutilated livestock from bemused and distressed ranchers began to spread across rural America, predominantly in the Midwestern states. The cattle mutilations presented a new and mysterious phenomenon which baffled law enforcement officers who were called to the scene of the crime by the owners of the animals demanding justice. Many cattle die from natural causes and interference from hungry predators such as coyotes and wolves, but the way in which the mutilated cases were discovered defied such logical explanations.

The mutilations or 'mutes' as they are often referred to, are characterized by the removal of specific parts of the animal's anatomy along with highly unusual cuts described by most witnesses as being surgically precise. The term "mutilation" was explained by one writer as being "inappropriate to describe the extremely precise and delicate surgery performed on these animals."[123]

In 1975, it was reported by the CBI (Colorado Bureau of Investigation) that in virtually all cases reported since 1973, that the left ear, left eye, rectum, sexual organs, tongue and often the udders had all been cut away with all blood drained from the carcasses and with no traces of blood left on the ground. In some cases, the entire blood supply of the animal had been drained, yet remarkably without cardio-vascular collapse.

Some researchers who have examined mutilated cattle insist that the wounds are not caused by cuts but rather they are laser-like incisions done at estimated temperatures of close to 400 degrees Fahrenheit and the absence of footprints or any tracks whatsoever near the mutilated animals only deepens the mystery.

Investigators were confounded to discover that other strange anomalies were reported; the fact that many carcasses are found with broken legs, bruises and clamp marks led to the theory that these animals were being airlifted to another location where the mutilation could take place, before being returned to their original spot. Such suggestions were supported by some bizarre cases like

180

one report of a steer which was found in a tree five foot above the ground, another cow was found dead beneath a tree which had snapped blood-stained branches beside the carcass, and in another case the cow's horns were stuck in the ground as if the animal had been dropped from a significant height.

Some have speculated that whoever is responsible for the unprovoked attacks must have their own airpower, as many cases have reportedly taken place at the 10,000-foot level of New Mexico, where flying can be extremely difficult in the snow-covered mountains. The mutilations found in the snow have also lacked tracks of any sort; even professional trackers have been unable to trace any signs of activity.

Between eight and ten thousand cattle had been mysteriously mutilated by 1979, according to some estimates, with a large percentage of cases occurring in New Mexico and the surrounding states, although the phenomenon began to spread nationwide over the decades which followed and still continues to the present day. There has never been any question over the authenticity of the mutilation cases, the real mystery has always been trying to determine who or what could be responsible for such heinous crimes and why.

Often mutilation accounts are accompanied by sightings of either unmarked helicopters or strange lights in the sky – UFOs – and in many cases, both have been witnessed. This along with other circumstantial evidence has linked the bizarre killings to UFO activity, and by implication, alien abduction. The presence of the helicopters points to possible secretive black operations by government agencies. Another theory which arose from the outset of the attacks over four decades ago was that satanic cults of some description were using the animals as sacrifices as part of their ceremonial activities.

An increase in mute incidents in 1975, led to one of the first and most significant official inquiries on the subject which was conducted by the CBI. After examining over 200 reports, the CBI concluded that the mutilations were simply caused by predators and scavengers that feed on dead animal carcasses and the organs found within. The Bureau asserted that the evidence of knife cuts were most likely the result of "copycats"; people attempting to fuel the hysteria over the phenomenon. Regardless of the conclusions reached during the investigation, question marks still hung in the air as Carl Whiteside, the CBI official in charge of the inquiry, confirmed when he remarked that "everybody who has gotten involved with the mutilations has come away more confused than they were when they went in, including us."

Although the animal mutilation phenomenon seems to have appeared during the late sixties and early seventies, further research reveals that such cases had been reported worldwide, and some of those date back to the 1700s. In Great Britain and Australia, accounts of sheep mutilations were recorded during the 1800s, with some apparently being linked to UFO activity.

One edition of the *Farmer's Advocate*, a Kansas magazine from the Yates Center published on April 23, 1897 linked one cow mutilation to a UFO sighting. Yates Center farmer Alexander Hamilton said in a sworn statement that he awoke to the sound of disturbed cattle at around 10:30 p.m. on April 19. As he left home to investigate, Hamilton said that he saw "an airship slowly descending upon my cow lot about 40 rods from the house."[124] The craft was cigar-shaped, with a transparent and brilliantly lit undercarriage, and Hamilton estimated its size as around three hundred feet long. He claimed that the ship shone a beam of light down at him and inside the object there stood "six of the strangest beings he ever saw." Along with his son and a tenant, Hamilton watched as the ship rose to a height of about three hundred feet, where it began to make a buzzing sound before a thick red "cable" descended, pulling a two-year-old heifer aboard the craft before flying off, as they "stood in amazement to see the ship, cow and all rise slowly and sail off."[125]

The next day, much to Hamilton's dismay, a neighbouring farmer informed him that he had found the head, legs and hide of the missing heifer. Hamilton told his story and an affidavit confirming the validity of his statements was signed by a group of locals that included the local sheriff and his deputy, a banker, an attorney, justice of the peace, registrar of deeds, postmaster and the druggist.

As a former member of the U.S. House of Representatives, Hamilton was a respected member of his community, and in his statement he explained, "I don't know whether they are devils of angels, or what, but we all saw them, and my whole family saw the ship, and I don't want any more to do with them." This report could well be the first documented account of cattle mutilation on

182

record but questions surrounding its authenticity have been raised by author Jerome Clark, who debunked the story in 1982 claiming that Hamilton had concocted the tale in an attempt to win a Liar's Club competition.

Whether or not this particular incident occurred, similar accounts of bizarrely slaughtered livestock arose during that period, some of which dated back to the 1800's from places all over the world such as Australia, Europe, Central and South America, Canada and Mexico.

According to the research of Charles Fort, mysterious cases of animal mutilations were randomly occurring in England as far back as 1905. Fort wrote, "...there may be occult things, beings and events, and that also there may be something of the nature of an occult police force, which operates to divert human suspicions, and to supply explanations that are good enough for whatever, somewhat of the nature of minds, human beings have – or that, if there be occult mischief-makers and occult ravagers, they may be of a world also of other beings that are acting to check them, and to explain them, not benevolently, but to divert suspicion from themselves, because they, too, may be exploiting life upon this earth, but in ways more subtle, and in orderly, or organized fashion."[126]

SO MUCH FOR LADY LUCK

The modern era of cattle mutilations can be traced back to an incident which took place at a ranch near Alamosa, Colorado in September 1967. The story about the mysterious death of a three-year-old Appaloosa mare named Lady which was found lying in chico bush, by rancher Harry King near his home on September 9, was first published by American daily newspaper *The Pueblo Chieftain*. The story speculated that extraterrestrials and UFOs were connected to the strange mutilation of the horse and on October 5 the feature was picked up by the associated press and spread nationwide. One newspaper used the headline, "Dead Horse Riddle Sparks UFO Buffs."

The media mistakenly called the horse "Snippy", which was actually the name of Lady's mother who was corralled near the King ranch, but the word association was too good an opportunity to miss as Lady was found dead with her head and part of her neck stripped clean of flesh. The bones were bleached white and clean as if they had been exposed to strong sunlight for days but she had been alive and well less than 48 hours earlier. The rest of the body was completely untouched and there were no tracks or signs of blood around the corpse. King reported a strong medicinal odour in the air which lingered for a couple of days. Lady's owner Nellie Lewis also recalled the unusual smell, stating that it had reminded her of incense.

Explaining the precise and unnatural cut around Lady's neck Harry King said, "That neck was cut so smooth it couldn't have been done even with a sharp hunting knife." His sentiments were shared by Lewis who saw her dead horse for the first time on September 10, "It wasn't hacked off – but it was very neat and that was what was so odd." The same day Mrs. Lewis and her husband Berle found a lump of horse skin and flesh which burned her hand when she touched it, whilst a greenish fluid oozed out of the meat.

Lady's body was examined two weeks after it had been found, by Dr. John Henry Altshuler, who at that time was employed as a pathologist at Rose Medical Center in Denver. He soon discovered strange anomalous aspects present on the carcass. He found a cut from the neck down to the base of the chest by what he described as a "vertical, clean incision" which upon closer inspection appeared to have been cauterised as if by laser beam, as the edge of the cut was a darker colour and firmer to the touch. However, as Dr. Altshuler noted, "There was no surgical laser technology like that in 1967", at least not within public knowledge.

Further examination revealed that a number of Lady's internal organs were missing, including the thyroid, lungs and the heart. But what most amazed Dr. Altshuler was the lack of blood. Years later he recalled, "I have done hundreds of autopsies. You can't cut into a body without getting some blood. But there was no blood on the skin or on the ground. No blood anywhere. That impressed me the most."

Ranger Duane Martin of the United States Forest Service was contacted by Mrs. Lewis, and part of his investigation included checking the area for increased radioactivity which he duly found up to two city blocks from the scene of the crime. Martin stressed that "The death of this saddle pony is one of the most mysterious sights I've ever witnessed...I've seen stock killed by lightning, but it was never like this."[127]

As if the case wasn't strange enough, several people reported seeing a UFO in the locality prior to the mutilation being discovered. Duane Martin was amongst those who claimed to have seen a number of small "jets" zipping around at great speeds but at a low altitude in the same area where Lady's body lay. Eighty-seven-year-old Agnes King told son Harry that that she had witnessed a "large object" passing over the ranch the evening of the mare's death, but as her eyesight wasn't the best, she was unable to identify the object. With the involvement of the civilian research group NICAP, speculation about UFO connections with the mutilation began to gather momentum.

Alternative explanations for the unusual mutilation case began to appear, such as Veterinarian Dr. Robert O. Adams' belief that someone had simply cut the horse's throat knowing that she had a severe infection. Or the theory postulated by Dr. Wallace Leary who claimed that he found two bullet holes in the mare's hindquarters and assumed the horse had been put down. Another suggestion was that she was the victim of a lightning strike as there had been a spate of thunderstorms in that vicinity at the time of the mysterious incident.

But as filmmaker and animal mutilation researcher Linda Moulton Howe asserted, "None of these persons, except Dr. Altshuler, examined the horse at the time of death. This is just an attempt to reconstruct history."[128]

The tragic and bewildering death of "Snippy" the horse is widely regarded as the first documented case of animal mutilation by unknown means, although further investigation into the annals of the printed media has brought other mysterious incidents to light. One such case was dubbed "the sheep-slaying mystery of Badminton" in an edition of the *London Daily Mail*, back in November, 1905. The story at that time was that a number of sheep had been found killed in the Badminton region on the border between Gloucestershire and Wiltshire, the latter county having played host to the majority of crop circle formations in Europe in recent times.

Sergeant Carter of the Gloucestershire Police went on record stating, "I have seen two of the carcasses myself, and can say definitely that it is impossible for it to be the work of a dog. Dogs are not vampires, and do not suck the blood of sheep, and leave the flesh almost untouched."

During that period of history the idea of extraterrestrial involvement in such bizarre killings would not have been a realistic consideration, and although the 1967 incident does not represent what most would consider being a "classic" mutilation, it was the first to achieve such widespread public attention and also introduced the notion of possible alien/UFO interaction.

BRING IN THE FBI

As more reports of mutilated livestock began to surface in Colorado and other Midwestern states, the problem was beginning to be taken more seriously, as scared and angry ranchers across America demanded answers. Who was responsible for these bizarre events and how could they be stopped? Several Colorado agencies in the early seventies offered a reward of $25,000 to anyone with information that might lead to the arrest and conviction of those responsible.

The escalation of the phenomenon was devoured by the national press, quick as ever to sniff out extreme stories and sensationalise them as only the media know how. However accurate the details included in the press reports may have been, the newspapers as usual played their part in contributing to the hype surrounding the UFO connection.

An article printed in Nebraska's *Daily Tribune*, dated August 29, 1974 read:

"Are UFO Sightings and Mutilations Related?
Mutilated livestock, unauthorised helicopters and unidentified flying objects have residents wondering and worrying in some areas of Nebraska."

The story told how ten people that were gathered on a farm near Clearwater on August 21, all said they saw a strange light in the sky. One witness told reporters, "Two of the boys were out in the field to move equipment. They spotted a light and it came right down at them. It scared the devil out of them." Once back at the house, they all watched the light for about four hours.

Harold Kester was in town and described a light which a group of locals gathered together all watched. Kester explained that the object "looked as if it had little bluish-green light on each side with a glow surrounding it. It was behind a tree and moved from one side of the tree to the other." The same evening at around midnight, Mike Kruger reported seeing another light, "I walked outside to put some calves in and saw a big ball of red fire. It raised off the ground and then went out. Since it was dark, I couldn't tell how far away it was or how high it went."

Pressure was mounting on officials to start giving answers, as whatever was the reason behind all the killings, it wasn't just the livelihood of so many which was at stake, it was becoming a serious threat that needed immediate attention. In March 1975, *The Denver Post* printed an article titled *"Cattle Deaths and the FBI"* which publicly called for help from state officials. Editor Charles R. Buxton wrote, "If the FBI will not enter the investigation of mysterious livestock deaths in Colorado and some adjacent states then Senator Floyd Haskell should take the matter to Congress for resolution. The incidents are too widespread – and potentially too dangerous to public order - to ignore."

Buxton continued, "Senator Haskell should keep the pressure on the FBI. It has the manpower and a wide range of investigatory tools. If the FBI resists successfully, the Senator should go to Congress to get the sort of attention these alarming incidents deserve."

Haskell took the hint and on August 29, 1975 he wrote a letter to Theodore P. Rosack, Special Agent In Charge at the Denver Federal Building. Haskell wrote, "Because I am gravely concerned by this situation, I am asking that the Federal Bureau of Investigation enter the case. Although the CBI has been investigating the incidents, and local officials also have been involved, the lack of a central unified direction has frustrated the investigation. It seems to have progressed little, except for the recognition that the incidents must be taken seriously."

Assuming that he received a minimal response, Haskell pursued the matter further and called the director of the FBI on November 9, indicating his concern over the mutilations and put in a request for the FBI to enter the investigation. However, the FBI were strangely reluctant to offer assistance in the matter and Haskell was advised that "it would probably take a law" before they were obliged to join the investigation, so he was referred to the Criminal Division of the Department of Justice.

In reply to Haskell's request, one FBI special agent wrote in an official FBI document, "Upon being pressed I indicated that I, personally, knew of no legislation specifically covering the mutilation of livestock which would enable the FBI to enter such an investigation."[129]

More and more cattle were being found dead, their blood drained and selected organs removed, seemingly with surgical precision, and the cases were spreading throughout the states. *Oui Magazine* printed a piece in September 1976 stating that "During the past three years more than 1500 cattle in 22 states have been killed and mutilated. Suspects range from satanic cultists to government researchers."

Only once the phenomenon hit New Mexico did the FBI decide to step in and that was partly because they were given a gigantic push by former Apollo 17 astronaut, U.S. Senator Harrison Schmitt. On December 21, 1978 Schmitt wrote to the Honourable Griffin B. Bell, Attorney General of the Department of Justice. In his letter Schmitt expressed his views by stating that, "While an individual cattle mutilation may not be a federal offence, I am very concerned at what appears to be a continued pattern of an organized interstate criminal activity." Bell's response to Schmitt's correspondence was one of concern, "I must say that the materials sent me indicate the existence of one of the strangest phenomena in my memory", he declared.

Following an ever mounting series of cattle attacks on Indian lands in New Mexico, Schmitt came under pressure from local farmers to become proactive, which he did by organising a conference on livestock mutilations in Albuquerque on April 20, 1979. The conference was attended by approximately 180 persons, which included law enforcement investigators, the press and other interested parties, and most significantly FBI representatives. By the time the conference took place, it was estimated that since the outset of the mutilations there had already been around 8,000 different cases nationwide, placing the financial loss somewhere in the region of one million dollars.

Earlier that month on April 8, three police officers in Dulce, New Mexico, reported seeing an unknown aircraft resembling a U.S. military helicopter, hovering near a site which had recently played host to the latest wave of mutilations that had claimed the lives of sixteen cows. Farmer Robert Smith Jr. filed a report five years earlier on July 15, 1974 claiming that a white helicopter and a black twin-engine aircraft opened fire on him whilst driving his tractor on his farm in Honey Creek, Iowa. The consistent sightings of helicopters and other more unusual aircraft near areas most affected by the mute phenomenon was becoming a reoccurring theme and such bizarre activities were adding weight to theories of government and/or extraterrestrial involvement.

During the 1979 conference, researcher Tom Adams of Paris, Texas, told the attendees that during his six years of independently examining mutes that his investigation had revealed that helicopters were almost always observed in the area of the mutilations. Adams also stated that the helicopters did not have identifying markings and were reportedly flying at "abnormal, unsafe, or illegal altitudes."[130] The previous year, Adams was circulating a newsletter disseminating information about the mutilations entitled *Stigmata*, and his interest in the subject continues to the present day. Asked about his opinion on who might be responsible for the barbarous acts Adams replied, "I have no opinion. I am still trying to remain objective and let the evidence lead to its own conclusion. But, I defy any rational, objective person to look at the evidence, the whole evidence, and say that there's nothing to it."[131]

Investigators from Arkansas also spoke out in the conference by saying that the twenty-eight cases that they'd examined had led them to conclude that none were caused by predators but rather they were the work of intentional mutilators. An investigator from Montana agreed with their hypothesis by saying that in his opinion, the carcasses discovered in Montana had also been mutilated by deliberate means and not by predators.

The FBI was forced to confront the issue since the target of mutilations shifted from the Eastern plains to New Mexico during 1976. The small town of Dulce in northern Rio Arriba County began to receive considerable attention that year, following an incident which took place just thirteen miles east of Dulce on June 13. A mutilated three-year-old cow belonging to rancher Manual Gomez was found with its sexual organs, tongue, ear, and lower lip fully removed with some sort of sharp instrument. Although this showed the usual traits commonly exhibited in such cases, what set this one apart from the others was the appearance of "a mysterious trail of suction cup-like impressions".[132]

State police officer Gabriel L. Valdez was called to the scene where he witnessed firsthand the strange tracks and an unknown oily substance which he removed from the ground close to the corpse. Valdez reported finding a series of tripod-like indentations, each being roughly four inches in diameter and about twenty-eight inches apart. According to Officer Valdez, "the trail ended about 500 feet from the animal carcass, as if they had landed at that point, gone to the cow, and then returned to that point."

Rancher Gomez was unfortunately in the wrong place at the wrong time, as on several occasions his herd were selected by the unknown cattle killers and it wasn't long before the Dulce incidents began to generate a great deal of interest and speculation. Like the case of "Snippy" the horse, the first incident that took place at the Gomez ranch appeared in different magazines and newspapers across the country, bringing much attention towards Dulce and the state of New Mexico as a whole.

Following the Albuquerque conference, finally a LEAA[6] grant had been awarded by the Justice Department who authorised a special investigative unit to be set up under the auspices of the New Mexico State District Attorney in Santa Fe. The reason for the FBI's sudden change of heart can be attributed to the fact that several of the mutilation killings occurred on Indian lands where the FBI had investigative jurisdiction. Of particular interest were the incidents occurring on the Jicarilla Apache Reservation in the small town of Dulce.

The *National Enquirer* newspaper printed an article on June 5, 1979 which publicly confirmed the FBI's involvement; "**FBI Joins Investigation of Animal Mutilations Linked to UFOs.**"

The article stated "The FBI has joined in the investigation of the bizarre mutilation of thousands of grazing horses and cattle over an 18-state area – attacks which have been linked with UFOs. Disclosure of the FBI role was made at a recent conference of officials from seven states where the attacks have reached an alarming level. Sen. Harrison Schmitt, the ex astronaut and scientist who organized the conference declared "Either we've got

---

[6] Law Enforcement Assistance Administration

a UFO situation or we've got a massive, massive conspiracy which is enormously well funded.""

Bringing the FBI into the equation at least showed the ranchers and local law enforcement officers who had predominantly been the ones facing the horror full-on, that finally the issue was considered serious enough to warrant a thorough investigation. But how thorough were the FBI exactly?

OPERATION ANIMAL MUTILATION

Within one month of the conference convened by Senator Schmitt, the $44,170 grant awarded by the LEAA to the district attorney's office of New Mexico's First Judicial District was put in place to fund "Operation Animal Mutilation". The one-year assignment officially began on May 28, 1979 and was directed by Kenneth M. Rommel who had spent 28 years working as an FBI agent, specializing in counter-intelligence and bank robbery among other major crimes.

In his report, Rommel states that Operation Animal Mutilation had five primary objectives;

1)   To determine the reliability of the information on which the grant was based by gathering as much data regarding the cases reported in New Mexico prior to May 1979.

2)   To determine the cause of as many mutilations as possible, especially the New Mexico cases.

3)   To determine if livestock mutilations constitute a major law enforcement problem.

4)   If they do constitute a major law enforcement problem, to determine the scope of the problem and offer recommendations on how to deal with them.

5)   If it is shown that the mutilation phenomenon is not a law enforcement problem, to recommend that no further law enforcement investigations be funded.

During that twelve month period Rommel personally inspected the carcasses of 25 mutilations. He travelled to other states and conferred with investigators in those areas regarding the mutilations, but despite the complexity and unusual traits exhibited in the cases, Rommel remained adamant that he had received no information that would validate the theory that any animals had been intentionally mutilated by human beings.

Rommel believed that all the animals that he had examined showed evidence of damage consistent with predator action. "The rough jagged nature of the incisions together with the evidence at the scene clearly indicates that the carcass was damaged by predators and/or scavengers", he reported. Continuing, Rommel wrote "I have found no credible source who differs from this finding, nor has one piece of hard evidence been presented or uncovered that would cause me to alter this conclusion."

Rommel's objective approach to the mutilation phenomenon allowed him to rationalize every incident which he encountered personally during the yearlong investigation. Every individual case was explained away as the result of natural causes, predatory interference or the remnants of scavenging. As he commented in his report, "the parts of the carcass that are allegedly removed in a 'classic mutilation' are the same ones customarily consumed by predators and scavengers."[133]

Lander County Deputy Sgt. Keith Altemueller disagreed with Rommel's findings, speaking of one particular incident he said, "There's no evidence I have of what happened, how it happened or who did it. There are no tracks, no sign of disturbance and generally no blood. The cuts are very sharp – very unusual! I've lived in the desert all my life; I've seen what predators do. This is not what predators do."

Dr. Jim Armstrong, Professor of Zoology and Wildlife Science at Auburn concurred. Speaking about recent mutilation cases at a press conference held by the Fyffe Police Department in Alabama in April 1993, Armstrong declared, "It would be obvious if a coyote had been tearing through. The wounds would not be similar to a smooth cut. Coyotes bite through and pull to tear away the flesh. It would have a 'chewed on look'. There are scavenger animals such as vultures that will eat at the softer regions of a cow, but there's not going to be these clean, surgical-type cuts. There is no way a coyote or other predator inflicted those wounds."

The cases that Rommel personally dealt with may well have been exactly as he reported but what appears slightly suspicious is how he evaded investigating the finer details reported so frequently throughout the decade preceding the funded investigation.

How could he explain the anomalous aspects of the phenomenon such as helicopter activity, strange lights in the sky, medicinal odours, the absence of tracks or footprints, no traces of blood, precision cutting, signs of radiation and witnesses being fired at by unmarked aircraft? He simply commented that he found "a great deal of very creative writing on the part of the media and some law enforcement personnel and I found many statements made by others that were completely unsupported by factual data."

He asserted that his research had "clearly shown that the media has played a very important role in promoting both the livestock phenomenon and the lore surrounding it." Such an observation undoubtedly has a ring of truth to it, as it is widely accepted that the media's input into societal understandings of the world is often misleading, and persistently persuasive.

As part of Rommel's conclusion to the project he wrote, "It is my sincere hope that the conclusions reached in this report will help those engaged in the cattle industry and others to put behind them the rumors, theories and fears that some highly organized criminal activity or extraterrestrial conspiracy is responsible for these mutilations." But despite all the logical explanations, quotations from veterinarians and doctors, and evidential material confounding all mysteries in connection with the subject, Rommel still managed to avoid taking responsibility for the unexplained facets of the phenomenon by stating, "...how does one explain the livestock mutilation phenomenon...the answer to this question falls outside the framework of this project."

It was noted shortly after the results of Rommel's investigation was released to the press, that no 'classic' mutilations had actually occurred during the course of his project. Several individuals voiced their opinion on the matter, suggesting that the reason his verdict of "scavenger-induced damage" and predator action was reached, was due to the fact that the cases he had investigated did not represent common examples of the problem at large. Rommel agreed that he'd not had the opportunity to investigate what would be considered a 'classic' mutilation during his twelve month tenure as project director.

Harrison Schmitt read the report and seemed reasonably satisfied with Rommel's efforts but still believed there was much to the phenomenon than had been covered in the investigation. "I thought it was fairly well written, but it certainly doesn't answer all of the questions", remarked Schmitt. Author George Andrews was even less convinced as this next paragraph taken from his 1986 book *Extra-Terrestrials Among Us* demonstrates; "The resemblances to the *Condon Report* and the *Warren Report* are so obvious as to be hardly worth mentioning. The *Rommel Report* takes its place beside them, to gather dust on library shelves. One more expensive whitewash job paid for by the American taxpayer to maintain the illusory bliss of ignorance."[134]

THERE'S NOTHING TO SEE HERE

After much deliberation and a few gentle nudges, the FBI finally bowed to local pressure and gave a year of their time and resources into investigating whatever cases arose in New Mexico during the period from May 1979-80. The report undoubtedly satisfied many curiosities that had unsettled large numbers of people, but not everybody was convinced of the legitimacy or sincerity of the investigation.

Cattle mutilation researcher Linda Howe was far from impressed by Rommel's debunking tactics, "I ignore him – I believe he's being paid to cover up the real cause of the mutilations" she said.

New Mexico newspaper, the *Rio Grande Sun*, confirmed the locals' dissatisfaction at Rommel's efforts in an article titled "They Held a Mutilation But No One Came", written by Gail Olson in July 1979. Olson wrote, "The County's "freshest" mutilation report so far reached State Police within five hours of the kill last Saturday, but nobody came to investigate."

If there is any truth to this story, then it appears as if Mr. Rommel may have been more selective with which cases he took than he let on. Olsen continued, "Ken Rommel, hired through a $50,000 federal grant to investigate cattle mutilations in Rio Arriba County, had not been on the scene as of late Tuesday afternoon and was not available in his office."

The evening of the incident, local Dennis Martinez noticed that barking dogs would "go to the boundary of the fence and turn back" rather than continue straight through and chase the cows like they usually did. A number of residents also reported seeing strange "orange lights" in the sky that night. Martinez briefly examined the carcass of the mutilated cow that he found, and explained that he noticed that whoever was responsible for the crime had paid particular attention to the white part of the eye as they'd "tried to scrape at it" as if they were trying to take a tissue sample. This case did fit the 'classic' mutilation description as the rectum had been cored out and the udders and ears were removed with 'surgical precision' – a term used on a regular basis in regard to such occurrences.

Neil Bockman, a Santa Fe filmmaker and photographer investigating the mute phenomenon had recently written a news article on the subject called "Burgers for the Gods". When he arrived on the scene to capture recent footage of the incident he was shocked and puzzled by the absence of any law enforcement officials. Senator Schmitt shared Bockman's concern that no officials had attended the scene. Speaking of the witnesses Schmitt said, "I don't blame them for being upset." He explained that he had put in a funding request for more FBI support saying "I wanted the FBI to be more deeply involved. My understanding was that FBI agent Sam Jones was assigned to coordinate law enforcement on mutilations."

According to journalist Olson, "When Schmitt was informed that Ken Rommel had yet to contact Gabe Valdez, the most experienced State Policeman regarding mutilations, Schmitt remarked "That doesn't sound like complete investigating."" One local resident told the newspaper that District Attorney Eloy Martinez had gone to the State Police and insisted that Valdez was not permitted to have any part in the investigation. Other local residents also believed that a "muzzle" had been put on Valdez and expressed fears that both Rommel and Martinez were working together with the State Police to cover up whatever was really behind the mutilations.

Of the few who succeeded in contacting Rommel, complaints were made that he didn't appear to take their reports seriously, and his manner was either too "brusque" or "too flippant". Subsequently, as a result of his casual attitude and general demeanour, they felt unable to discuss such matters with him any further.

Is it possible that the investigation undertaken by a former FBI agent for a mere twelve months was set up with the intention of satisfying public curiosity whilst simultaneously pacifying over enthusiastic believers of UFO/government connections to the mutilations? Rommel's report, although reasonably thorough in scope, clearly omitted any circumstantial evidence that might complicate his simplified predator/scavenger theory. His lack of interest shown by his absence at the scene of significant reported cases understandably raises questions as to his true intent and purpose in the field.

Even an FBI document regarding fifteen mutilation cases on Indian Territory in New Mexico clearly states that the investigation undertaken was never properly dealt with;

"Concerning those prior mutilations reported to have occurred on Indian lands, no law enforcement agency was assigned investigatory responsibility and as a result, no adequate evidence collection or record making was undertaken. No evidence has been obtained because none was collected. In view of this, no further investigation will be done regarding the alleged mutilation of the 15 animals previously reported."[135]

Is it a coincidence that a substantial amount of incidents took place in New Mexico and in particular, Dulce, the alleged home of an underground facility believed to be a joint ET/government-run operation where nefarious experimentation takes place on a daily basis? (See *Out Of Sight, Out Of Mind*) The 'there's nothing to see here' tactic is nothing new, and the FBI have a long standing track record of deceit and denial. They don't like people sniffing around and getting too close to the truth of certain matters and will use any tactics within their capabilities to divert attention from those areas. With so many researchers, police officers, ranchers, witnesses and specialist experts insisting that none of the evidence of 'classic' livestock mutilations points to predatory actions, how and why did Kenneth Rommel manage to assert the opposite?

WHO IS RESPONSIBLE?

In order to get to the heart of the matter, one needs to gather information from a plethora of sources and remain open-minded as to the possible results. It is also important to accept sometimes that certain mysteries may not reveal conclusive evidence, so it is worth avoiding that forced push for finality. If we understood such matters comprehensibly then they would no longer be considered mysterious.

Many Native American Indians living in New Mexico claim to have witnessed the animal abductions firsthand and are in no doubt of who is responsible. Dr. Henry Monteith, an engineering physicist at Sandia Laboratories which handles government projects, has been investigating the attacks since they first came to light. According to Monteith, the Indians told him that they had actually witnessed spaceships landing in the desert, before unloading "star people" who then chase down animals before taking them aboard. He explained that the Indians are so terrified by the mutilations that they are reluctant to discuss the subject with anyone. They did admit that after discovering a mutilated animal they immediately bury the carcass, saying that even their dogs refuse to go near them.

"There have been thousands of these mutilations nobody knows about. The Indians are scared to death" claims Monteith. "They don't say anything about it because they know it's being done by the 'star people', they know why they're doing it, so therefore we should leave it alone", he stressed. "Those are their exact words...The 'star people' know what they're doing and should be trusted."[136] Monteith himself believes that aliens are responsible for the attacks and are using them for scientific study of life on Earth.

According to the *National Enquirer*, Richard Sigismund, a psychologist and UFO researcher from Boulder, Colorado, believes that "What few clues we have concerning those responsible for the mutilations suggest that we are dealing with well-equipped, highly capable airborne entities...we are forced, I feel, to the hypothesis that unidentified aircraft are the means – UFOs."

The presence of UFOs in the vicinity of cattle mutilations is common, and it has been noted that the animals often stampede and bellow whenever UFOs are near. The fact that mutilations often take place in UFO hotspots like Northern New Mexico and near Area 51 in Nevada, implicates possible ET involvement. Veteran New Mexico State trooper Gabe Valdez told the *National Enquirer*, "Any place we've had a mutilation we have also had UFO sightings."

A few witnesses have come forward claiming they saw firsthand, alien beings 'taking' cattle onboard their craft and perform physical examinations on them. On May 5, 1980 twenty-eight-year-old Myrna Hansen claimed that she and her six-year-old son watched as five UFOs descended into a cow pasture as they were driving home near Cimarron, New Mexico. Once home, Hansen realised that she had a period of four hours which were unaccounted for, along with strange unclear memories of having being abducted. Two days later, she contacted Paul Bennewitz, a physicist, inventor and APRO investigator, claiming that she had indeed been abducted by aliens. This led Bennewitz and Dr. Leo Sprinkle to invite Hansen to be hypnotised and following regressive hypnosis sessions over a three month period, Hansen was able to recall the bizarre events that had occurred the night she drove home with her son.

According to her account, she saw two figures in white suits emerge from one of the UFOs and proceed to mutilate one of the cows in the field whilst it was still alive, before abducting the animal. She and her son were taken too, by large, brightly lit disks, before being led to an underground facility where they watched more cattle being mutilated and drained of their blood. In one room Hansen recalled seeing large vats which contained human body parts.

Linda Moulton Howe wrote that Hansen also saw "a humanoid figure floating in a vat of reddish liquid which she perceived to be a 'treatment' or 'sustenance' of some kind for the immersed being. She also thought the liquid was related to blood fluids and tissues from animals."[137]

Hansen also informed Bennewitz that she believed that some sort of implants had been placed in both her body and her son's, saying that the devices allowed the aliens to control their minds. Bennewitz believed her story, and associated the alleged implant signals with the lights he had been witnessing over Manzano, a census-designated place (CDP) in Torrance County, New Mexico. Believing he could receive signals from the craft he had been regularly observing, Bennewitz built antennas and receivers which he thought could receive the low-frequency electromagnetic transmissions emanating from the spacecraft as part of what he called Project Beta.

In September, 1976 a Wyoming rancher Pat McGuire and his brother Mark reported seeing an unusual light hovering above a ridge, two miles from his house in Bosler. The following day they discovered two mutilated cows where they had been standing. Wanting to garner more information about what happened that day, Pat McGuire was encouraged to take part in a hypnosis session with Prof. Leo Sprinkle who at that time was Director of Counseling & Testing at the University of Wyoming.

On October 7, McGuire recalled under hypnosis that the light in the sky appeared to be heading straight towards them; "I said to Mark, let's get the hell out of here, I say that star is coming – either that or my eyes are bad. He said, it's coming...it changed from a pure white to an orange." Continuing, he told Sprinkle, "I said Mark; it's picking up a cow. Do you hear that cow? She's bawling!" He described the cow's stress calls as nothing that he had ever heard before, and he has been around cows his entire life.

In May 1973, Judy Doraty was driving back from a bingo game in Houston, Texas, when she, her mother, daughter Cindy and brother and sister-in-law all watched a strange light hover in the clear, moonlit sky. After that night, Judy Doraty suffered from terrible headaches and severe anxiety. In 1978, she took part in one hypnosis session which succeeded in bringing out some of her unusual experiences from five years previous, but not everything was cleared up. Following several psychological and personality evaluations it was concluded that she was not suffering from any mental disorders but fitted well within the normal behaviour bracket.

APRO contacted Professor Sprinkle and Doraty was referred to him for more thorough hypnosis, and on March 13, 1980 the session was filmed as part of Linda Moulton Howe's documentary *Strange Harvest*, which was originally broadcast the same year.

Like Myrna Hansen and Pat McGuire, under hypnosis Doraty described a similar event taking place; "It's like a spotlight shining down on the back of my car. It's like it has substance to it. I can see an animal being taken up in this. I can see it squirming and trying to get free and it's like it's being sucked up. It's taken into some sort of chamber – it's a little round tiny room and I get nauseated at watching how they excise parts."

Once inside the craft Doraty revealed what she saw happening to the cow that had been 'taken' by the unknown abductors; "It's done very quickly but the calf doesn't die immediately. For some reason the calf's heart isn't taken, I don't know, seems like it's still living and that upset me very much. And then I can see the calf being lowered, it's like it's being dropped back down. And when it's on the ground it's dead." She explained to Prof. Sprinkle that she was able to watch the calf being cut up using a "straight razor-like blade". She saw them insert something into the cow's testicles; a needle, tube or some sort of probe.

When asked if there was anyone else around with her she replied, "I feel the presence of other things but I don't know what they are, I can't see them." Slowly the memory comes into view before Doraty claimed, "It appears to be two little men. They look like - their hands are funny - they have long claw nails - they have very large eyes - they're very hypnotic - they're so big - and the eyes don't blink. Like a snake."

So, an everyday normal woman claims she saw an animal being taken from the field, up into a craft of some description, operated on, then returned whence it came, but in a worse state than when it was taken. If such an incident did actually occur and highly evolved beings did perform surgical procedures on the calf, one should question the motives behind such bizarre actions. Judy Doraty also wished to understand why they were doing it, and questioned the strange beings whilst on board the ship.

She explained their viewpoint, "For some reason they projected that it was necessary. That it must be done. It was for our betterment, for the betterment of mankind that this was done. That they were more or less watching out for us. They were just doing their job. Evidently it affects them too. And it has to do with, somehow nuclear waste or testing. They've been here for quite some time and they test our soil as well as our water as well as our animal life and vegetation."

As the session progressed it became apparent that her daughter Cindy was next on the operating table. Initially, Judy was extremely fearful that Cindy would receive the same treatment as the young calf but soon realised that the entities were just taking samples from her, such as scrapings from inside her mouth.

As is often the case, solid proof of incidents like the one Doraty experienced is nigh on impossible to attain, but the similarities between the separate cases does suggest that such tales may prove to be more than mere fabrication or folly. Abductee Christa Tilton was 'taken' in July 1987, and claims to have been taken to an underground base similarly described by Myrna Hansen. Tilton also reported seeing strange things in the facility which she believed to have been located beneath Dulce; she described seeing "people of all different types standing up against the wall inside a clear casing-like chamber." Upon closer inspection, the figures appeared as if they were made of wax. She also recalled seeing living animals in cages and grey aliens working alongside humans.

The experiences of Hansen and Tilton both point to the possibility that extraterrestrial life-forms may be using livestock for their body parts, reproductive organs and their blood. The connection between sightings in New Mexico, abduction stories based in the same state and the fact that many believe there to be an underground co-habited base beneath Dulce - leads one to consider ET/government involvement in the cattle mutilation mystery. Others tend to be more drawn to the government hypothesis.

As Linda Moulton Howe expressed, "it was made clear long ago that there were people in government who didn't want me or anybody investigating animal mutilations." In the early 80s she stated that "whatever's doing this has an enormous budget and incredible resources and mobility. Therefore it's got to be either the government, some fabulously wealthy international conspiracy, maybe corporate, or else it's extraterrestrials."

In his 1999 publication *The AIDS-ET Connection*, UFO researcher Philip S. Duke hypothesised that aliens may have been using commercial cattle stocks to incubate and research the HIV/AIDS virus. Duke claims that in order to obtain virus samples, the cattle blood is harvested using the anus and genitals primarily for tissue sampling as those areas are the HIV/AIDS transmission sites in humans.

Citing the work of Texas University Professor James Womack, Duke highlights the fact that humans share a substantial number of chromosomes with cattle, making them a prime target for large scale experimentation and biological incubation. Duke wrote, "HIV has only one natural host, humans, and logically would require a genetically similar animal host for replication."

Former New Mexico State trooper Gabriel L. Valdez personally witnessed many of the cattle mutilations which took place within his state, primarily during the 1970s. His job was to investigate the incidents and rule out any foul play by human hand, not to come to any conclusions that he was unqualified to say. However, due to the mysterious nature of the phenomenon, it was apparent to Valdez that these killings were not the result of one man or even a group of maladjusted individuals. The evidence was pointing to something much more complex, something secretive. What Valdez reported is not indicative of extraterrestrial activity but has all the hallmarks of another government black operation.

One case which he investigated occurred in Dulce on April 24, 1978 on a ranch belonging to Manual Gomez. The State Police had been contacted by Gomez at 7:30 a.m. in reference to an eleven-month old cross Herford-Charolais bull which, as the investigation later revealed, had been dropped by some type of aircraft north of his ranch house.

The rectum had been cored out and the sex organs had been removed with a sharp and precise instrument. The bull was last seen at 8 p.m. the previous evening and appeared to be in full health. It was estimated that the bull died around 4:30 a.m. the following morning. Valdez wrote a report on December 21, 1978 detailing the bizarre incident:

"The bull sustained visible bruises around the brisket area seeming to indicate that a strap was used to lift and lower the animal to and from the aircraft. Prints were found ten metres north of the slain animal. These four-inch diameter round footprints led to the animal and lasted 100 ft. where they apparently returned to a hovering aircraft. The imprints appeared to be quite heavy since the ground was dry mud and automobile tire tracks from the police car were barely visible. These imprints appeared to have scraped the ground as they moved."[138]

The strange imprints found by Valdez are not commonly reported in such cases but he did recall seeing identical four-inch circular imprints once before in a similar mutilation found approximately thirteen miles east of Dulce on June 13, 1976. Ironically, both incidents involved cattle belonging to Manuel Gomez.

Los Alamos Medical Laboratory examined the bull's heart and liver and discovered some unusual anomalies. "A specimen obtained from a heart chamber was shown to contain a rod-shaped organism. Definitive classification was not made", wrote Valdez.

The bull's liver was found to contain four times the amount of potassium, zinc and phosphorous and there was a complete absence of copper. Although no explanation was given at that time, a group of microbiologists set out to compare the abnormalities.

His report mentioned the possible use of radiation, as seven people who visited the mutilation site complained of nausea and headaches. Physical examination of the bull also revealed suggestive signs of contamination, as Valdez documented, "Flesh underneath the hide was pinkish in colour. A probable explanation for the pinkish blood is a control type of radiation used to kill the animal, according to radiation experts – The red capillaries are destroyed leaving the pinkish colour."

Another interesting fact exposed by the thorough investigative work of Gabe Valdez is that all the mutilations have happened to native cattle. Approximately 15,000 head of steers in Rio Arriba County have not been mutilated; all of which were imported from places that include Arizona, Texas and Mexico. Valdez suggested that the cattle which were identically mutilated throughout the Southwest were actually marked years in advance for just that purpose. He believes that the areas where mutilations occur have also been carefully assessed weeks in advance.

Officer Valdez estimated that by 1979, around 8,000 animals had suffered as a result of the killings since the outset of the phenomenon, placing the loss at approximately one million dollars. The fact that not a single person has ever being charged for the mysterious crimes led Valdez to suspect that whoever committed them must reside in the higher echelons of society; "One has to admit that whoever is responsible for the mutilations is well organised with boundless technology and financing and secrecy."

The only scientific organization in America that has been seriously investigating the mutilation mystery is the National Institute for Discovery Science based in Las Vegas. The institute encourages ranchers to report mutilation incidents, teams are then dispatched and samples are taken to be analysed. However, attaining answers following the analysis has proved to be problematic.

Biochemist Dr. Colm Kelleher investigated many cases whilst working at NIDS; he commented that, "There's no indication it's for food. The beef is never touched except on rare occasions." Discussing the amazing fact that not one person has been caught or charged in the fifty states where reports have surfaced over the past forty years or so, Kelleher said, "You expect people to eventually make mistakes, drink in a bar and brag about what they're doing. There is somebody out there, highly skilled in surgery, using sharp instruments doing animal mutilations."

One case investigated by NIDS occurred near Utah at around 11 a.m. one autumn. A newborn calf had just had its ear tagged by the farmer who then walked over the hill for a few minutes, then heard a strange noise before returning to find the calf completely stripped of flesh. Dr. Kelleher said, "It was perfectly cleanly done, the removal of 60 percent of the bodyweight of an animal in broad daylight."

Kelleher argues that the mutilations are taking place in an effort to track the spread of bovine spongiform encephalopathy (mad cow disease), scrapie and other related diseases by a clandestine U.S. Government.

As researcher and former police officer Ted Oliphant revealed, following his extensive cattle mutilation investigations in Alabama starting in 1992, traces of human pharmaceuticals such as anti-coagulants and pain killers were found in a number of the carcasses discovered. According to the *Albuquerque Tribune*, on May 2, 1979 the carcass of a six-month-old bull was found to contain traces of two drugs by a Los Alamos chemist. The animal which had been found mutilated earlier that year in Torrance County, contained chlorpromazine, "a street drug, often used to tranquilize schizophrenics" and citric acid, "an old-fashioned anti-coagulant once used by ranchers to help drain the blood from the animal."

Two law enforcement officers who had investigated the case believed that the tranquilizer could have been used to immobilise the animal whilst the citric acid clogged up the blood, making it easier to remove the blood through the jugular vein. One officer told the *New Mexican* newspaper that there were also "skid marks near the carcass, indicating it might have been dropped from the air."

In 1997, Oliphant wrote an article entitled *Dead Cows I've Known*, in which he theorised that the livestock mutilation scenario was most likely the result of covert research into emerging cattle diseases and the possible transmittal to humans. Oliphant believes that the National Institutes of Health (NIH), Centers for Disease Control and Prevention (CDC) or other bodies funded by the federal government may well be involved. Part of his reasoning for such a theory is based on the presence of pharmaceuticals in some of the mute cases.

Additionally, Oliphant recalled the eyewitness testimony of two Cache County, Utah, police officers which was included in a NIDS report in 2002. Following a spate of unusual cattle deaths in the area, ranchers had organized patrols in order to observe the movements of unmarked aircraft which they believed to be associated with the death of the livestock. According to the two officers, a heated encounter took place between themselves and several men in an unmarked U.S. army helicopter at a small community airport in Cache County. Following the incident, the witnesses asserted that the cattle mutilations in that region ceased for about five years.

Such evidence would suggest that there was human involvement in at least some of the cases, evidence that contradicts Ken Rommel's predator theory. Rommel was fully aware of the theories of government involvement that were rife during that early period. In 1980, he wrote in his *Operation Animal Mutilation* report, "It didn't take me long to realize that in terms of publicity, the most popular theory in New Mexico was that these mutilations were being performed by a well-organized, highly sophisticated group who were dissecting livestock as part of a program of biological and environmental testing."

He claimed that such theories were not substantiated by "one shred of hard evidence" and believed that if such an organized group did actually exist that someone at some point would have leaked some information.

Proving who is responsible for the atrocious acts of barbarity that have confounded ranchers, police officers and scientists alike, is not a feat which is likely to come to fruition any time soon. It would appear, should the investigative efforts of so many dedicated researchers prove legitimate, that responsibility could lie with a combination of efforts. The pure lack of evidence regarding the involvement of cult activity practically rules out that theory, but the consistent presence of UFOs and black helicopters so close to so many mutilations, must add some weight to the collaborative secret government/ET hypothesis.

Is it possible that different incidents were caused by different means? It is certainly much easier to rule out certain possibilities than it is to conclusively allocate responsibility to one specific group. Rather than attempt to assess what we don't really know, isn't it simpler to assert what we do know? We know that the majority of cases didn't appear to have involved predators, that many have been airborne at some point during their trials, that conclusive proof of the perpetrators is not presently available and most importantly that whoever is doing it intends to keep it a secret.

As we shall see in the following chapters, there are many reasons to suspect a collaborative effort between black project government officials and extraterrestrial races. The livestock mutilation phenomenon may prove to be just another link in a very long and complex chain of seemingly isolated and non-related issues.

6

MESSAGES IN THE FIELDS

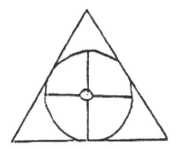

I think we're talking about other civilizations that aren't based on Planet Earth. I think we're being taught perhaps one lesson, which is that there exist tangibly other prodigious consciousnesses and intelligences, and that now they seem to be interested tangibly, materially, in making contact with us.

Michael Glickman

THE CROP CIRCLE PHENOMENON is a fascinating subject that could fill many books with the amount of information and study already achieved surrounding this complex topic. But we are going to look at the subject in relation to the extraterrestrial scenario and see what connections, if any, should arise. Since any conclusions regarding the creators of these extraordinary landscape designs are yet to be determined, it is worth speculating whether the crop formations appearing around the globe could be of alien origin. Let us first familiarise ourselves with an overview of the crop circle phenomenon before investigating some specific cases in more detail.

In 1880, a journal called *Nature* was published which included a historical account of crop circles. Amateur scientist Brandon Meland described a field containing a number of crop circles and suggested that they might have been caused by 'some cyclonic wind action'. Swirled into growing crops, these circular indentations of carefully flattened stems looked at first, as Meland believed, to be the result of freak whirlwinds.

In the seventeenth century people believed the formations to be the work of supernatural forces and were often referred to as 'mowing devils'. It wasn't until the late 1970's that the phenomenon as we know it today became part of public consciousness, mainly due to the ever increasing appearances of crop formations in the south of England.

Thousands of circles have appeared at sites across the world, on average around 250 crop designs appear annually although figures do vary slightly from year to year. Since records began, approximately ten thousand crop circles have been documented, mostly in the last third of the 20th century. Although they are a global phenomenon they predominantly appear in the northern hemisphere, in particular around Wiltshire in Southern England where it is reported that the area has played host to around ninety per cent of the recorded activity to date. Twenty-six countries have also reported experiencing these unexplained formations including Germany, The Netherlands, Canada, United States, Israel, Czech Republic and Russia to name but a few.

Every year around the world, huge beautiful and complex patterns are being found swirled into crop fields, wheat, barley and canola (oilseed rape) being the most common in England, because they're the main varieties grown. But they have also been reported in rye, oats, flax, peas, potatoes, sweet-corn maize and many other mediums, including rice paddies in Japan. Some formations have been found in undergrowth-type plants like bracken and wild grass. Although sometimes off-season formations do occur, usually they begin to appear from spring onwards until early autumn, most commonly arriving during the three main summer months of any given country.

What originally started as crop *circles* has evolved over the past two decades into what can only be described as crop *glyphs*. They have evolved from simple circles, into circles with rings around them and then into multiple circles. It first changed when one circle became surrounded by one ring which was followed by a circle with two rings. Next appeared two circles, the second being precisely half the size of the '*mother*' circle. Then there were three circles, two of them being half the size of the larger one. And later there was a circle made with four smaller ones around it in a kind of Celtic cross.

In 1990, two circles were joined for the first time by a shaft. This became a common occurrence throughout the nineties which also saw the arrival of pictograms, long chains of symbolic circles, rectangles and rings. As the difficulty level of the designs increased, so too did their beauty and their mystery. There are unmistakable signs of intelligent design in the crop glyphs. In general, the early formations (1970 - 2000) seemed to be based on the principles of sacred geometry. Formations occurring after 2000 appear to be based on mathematical designs and natural sciences, including shells and the DNA coil.

Elements of three-dimensionality became more frequent, culminating in spectacular images of cube-shaped structures, to the point where the complexity of the designs has increased so dramatically that they have become an art form in and of themselves. The geometric shapes and patterns could not be made by some mindless natural phenomenon like dust devils or some kind of whirlwind. They are far too intricate and complicated in design and made with such sheer precision that it must be deemed highly implausible that their existence can be attributed to random meteorological conditions. There is nothing random about their placement in the landscape either as the statistics will concur.

Many of the formations appearing in the English countryside are positioned near ancient monuments, such as Stonehenge, Silbury Hill, West Kennet Long Barrow and Wayland's Smithy which is just a stone throw away from the Uffington White Horse. Interestingly, in 2003, according to one study, nearly half of all the circles reported that year in the UK were located within a 9.3 mile radius of the town of Avebury.

Newspapers and television channels eagerly reported these astonishing patterns, but the claims of two retired English pranksters Doug Bower and Dave Chorley and other supposed hoaxers soon left the media disillusioned. Popular explanations for the circles have revolved around human activity, either involving satellite technology or, more usually, the simple actions of pranksters like Doug and Dave or landscape artists. In demonstrations however, teams of people have attempted to reproduce designs like those seen in the fields but struggled to recreate the more geometrically complex patterns and have taken many hours to reproduce anything resembling the authentic formations.

National Geographic TV actually funded a project to hoax a crop formation employing a group of individuals under the unusual name of *Team Satan* to attempt to reproduce the bizarre crop glyphs. Ironically however, whilst working away in the fields, members of the team reported witnessing strange anomalous orbs in the sky above their heads. Despite such attempts to replicate the mysterious crop circles it has been proven that certain designs have appeared within very short periods of time and the geometrical calculation and construction required for some, simply could not be carried out by human hand, least of all in one night.

The first pictograms began to appear as boxes and keys. Each year from then on brought about new themes and styles, each more evolved than the last. There were geometric symbols such as the Celtic cross, a spider's web, a pentagram and even a representation of the Mayan Calendar. Then linear formations started to appear that were much longer than previous designs with small fragments sprouting out of the sides.

One year saw insect designs flourish, scorpions and spiders amongst others, somewhat reminiscent of the Nazca pictograms in Peru. And then there came the year of the fractals, some looking like giant snowflakes on the ground.

The Julia Set formation appeared in 1996 near Stonehenge. There are 140 circles in that design and quite remarkably they appeared within a 25 minute window as determined by the testimony of a local helicopter pilot who flew over before and after their appearance. Reports of glowing lights and other bizarre phenomena associated with the circles began to flood in and deepen the mystery of the purpose and origin of these anomalies. Attempts to dismiss them as the work of human artists has become commonplace, but anyone who looks into the phenomenon in any detail will undoubtedly arrive at similar conclusions that the evidence points to a much stranger explanation. Wherever they come from and whoever made them, the complexity, accuracy and intricacy of these spectacular designs often displaying scientific, astronomical and esoteric symbolism, demonstrates some extraordinary and unexplained capabilities.

Their origin and purpose remains a complete mystery and the debate over the circles' origins continues to intensify. Many believe that they must be communications from extraterrestrials, contact from other worlds relaying messages for humanity to decode. The evidence for this popular hypothesis can be found in the many sightings and videos of unusual aerial phenomena at the precise time of the crop formations. And as we shall see shortly, some messages *have* actually been decoded already, although it appears that the mainstream media remain blissfully unaware of such events.

Some have postulated that the formations could be the product of unknown natural energy, suggesting that responsibility could lie with Mother Earth, whilst others consider the prospect that some sort of psychic forces are involved, influenced by the power of the mind although there can be no tangible evidence to support this theory.

Dozens of eye-witness accounts of crop circles forming before their very eyes have been reported but one well documented piece of video footage shot by John Wayleigh on August 11, 1996, at

Oliver's Castle in Wiltshire actually showed for the first time, a crop formation being created. The video revealed UFOs or balls of light flitting around just above the height of the crop. Shot in the early hours of the morning looking over a hedge into a field, circles in the wheat begin to form directly beneath the moving orbs which fly with speed, intelligence and intention.

To support his claims, Wayleigh wasn't the only one to experience something unusual that morning in Wiltshire. Two nearby campers told the Wiltshire Crop Circle Study Group that they had heard 'strange electronic buzzing' from the same field at Oliver's Castle that morning at the same time that the video had been taken. Also of interest, is the fact that Wayleigh took his video camera with him to The Barge Inn nearby that same morning and showed a few interested locals what he had recorded by allowing them to watch the fresh footage through the viewfinder of his camera. This piece of information alone surely rules out any foul play on his behalf.

The footage shows what other witnesses have described, light phenomena descending from the atmosphere before swirling silently around, creating complex and beautiful patterns as they go. Others have reported high-pitched whistling sounds and invisible forces sweeping in out of nowhere and violently spinning the crops down in seconds, yet with very little damage to the freshly laid crop. If this video evidence proves to be as authentic as it appears to be, then it does provide some clues as to how crop circles are formed. Such intelligently manoeuvrable balls of light cannot be employed by human hand nor do they appear to be a natural phenomenon. Do they fit the extraterrestrial hypothesis? It is too early to draw solid conclusions but it is certainly indicative of otherworldly activity.

THE CRABWOOD ALIEN

Lucy Pringle, a Founder member of the Centre for Crop Circle Studies and a Founder Member and Chairman of UNEX (Unexplained Phenomena Research Society) has an extensive collection of aerial photographs of crop circles and glyphs which she has collected from 1990 until the present day. Educated in England, France and Switzerland, she has travelled widely and currently gives lectures on the subject at home and internationally.

She also writes, appears on TV and broadcasts extensively on the crop circle phenomenon. She has most recently published an anthology on the topic titled *Crop Circles: Art in the Landscape* to much public acclaim. Her website remains the UK's most comprehensive photographic crop circle library.

One crop glyph in particular is of extreme interest and significance, photographed the day it was formed in August, 2002 in a field known as the Crabwood field belonging to Mike Burge in Pitt near Winchester, England. Lucy Pringle interviewed a group of people who lived near the wheat field who said they had witnessed lights swirling around then zooming into the sky and also strange pulsing noises that they assumed were from a generator or helicopter.

This feature is enormous; it's about 390 feet tall and 240 feet wide. It depicts an alien 'grey' holding a circle which is around 100 feet across [see SOURCES]. This image has struck a chord with the innermost feelings of many people as is clearly evident by the intense media interest in the Crabwood formation. Visitors from around the globe have travelled long distances to see for themselves this highly uniquely extraordinary event. Television producers from the BBC, Mexico, America and even Slovenia came and interviewed those with information relating to the case. UFO investigator Jaime Maussan from Mexico travelled 5000 miles to see the formation in person.

Local man Stephen Short from Warnford was in the field on the night of August 21st and fell into conversation with three young middle-aged women who were staying at the campsite located nearby. They told him that during the night of Thursday 15th August, they had witnessed "an amazing display of dancing lights over the field which kept darting about, spiralling down to the ground and then back up again; then going round in circles, then down and coming back up again before disappearing like a shooting star."[139]

Marie Wakelam, the owner of Crabtree Farmhouse which borders the Crabwood field, telephoned Lucy Pringle on Sunday 25th of August shortly after visiting the formation herself. Wakelam informed Pringle of a conversation that had just taken place with a family who had shown her slightly singed and blackened stalks of wheat taken from inside the formation. She thought this was curious as at about 11-11.30 pm on the evening of

Thursday 15th August she had been surprised to detect a strong smell of burning as if a bonfire was lit in the field. Her bedroom backs onto the field and her bedroom window was open at the time.

Pringle stated that, "the lay in the 'Alien' was one I had seen only once before, in the *Chilbolton 'Face'* of 2001; it seemed as though the flattened, swirled crop around each standing tuft had been laid individually." Such a task would surely be, as Pringle suggests, "beyond the ability of man during the short hours of darkness at this time of year. None of the stalks were broken in either formation; they were bent at the base. The lay in the circular dish was totally different to that in the face of the 'Alien', which was more traditional in construction."[140]

She also reported how being there in person had made her feel by adding, "Often I experience 'gut' energies when entering a formation. In the 'Alien' the energy, like the *Chilbolton 'Face'* was one that was new to me and one that I did not understand. Not uncomfortable, not welcoming but 'mechanical and technical and strangely sterile'."

While discussing the origins of the impressive formation at Crabwood, Pringle wrote, "it would appear that, if man-made, a technology was used that is unknown to all but a few selected people. The meaning of this formation is completely unambiguous. It is the face of an extraterrestrial, no more, no less; no other possible interpretation."

During a discussion on the nature of crop circle formations philosopher Palden Jenkins expressed this view; "These things are footprints of intelligences and through the characteristics of the phenomenon which come forward each year, we're being shown characteristics of a particular kind of intelligence which these beings, even the word 'beings' is inadequate, but we are being given some detailed signs of the nature of this intelligence which is undoubtedly compassionate and understanding and also educationally motivated."[141]

THE CODE WITHIN

Another interesting aspect of the Crabwood glyph is the similarity to an image designed by the brother of alternative researcher David Flynn, for his website back in 1996 which also shows an alien grey with a circle in one hand with the text '*Ultra-Tech Personal Computer Services*' alongside the image [see SOURCES] When placed side by side, the crop glyph of 2002 and the Flynn drawing of 1996 are eerily similar. Is this merely a coincidence?

Inside the disc there are some remarkable features as it would appear that the tufts of standing crop inside the circular element are most certainly not random, there is actually a readable code in the disc. The basic language used by computers and also NASA when trying to communicate with other intelligences is Binary code. In the 1960's, ANSI (American National Standards Institute) developed a code called the ASCII set (American Standard Code for Information Interchange) in order to convert binary into our alphabet. It's a system of binary; eight digits, zeros or ones, which make one symbol and it's all correlated to a keyboard for computers. So if you type an 'A' it will be 0010 or something similar.

The ASCII character set which consists of 128 characters was used to translate the binary digits and sequences of the code within the disc into their decimal equivalent. Then by looking them up in the ASCII character set to see which letters they correspond to, researchers Paul Vigay and Eltjo Haselhoff arrived at the following decoding:

"Beware the bearers of FALSE gifts & their BROKEN PROMISES.
Much PAIN but still time.
(Damaged word).
There is GOOD out there.
We OPpose DECEPTION.
Conduit CLOSING
(BELL SOUND)."

There were 26 words in the message which was decoded shortly after the crop circle first appeared and the message which appeared is very distinctive because it's so innocuous and vague. Many experts investigated this glyph and found no evidence of man-made hoaxing.

Computer consultant and leading crop circle researcher Paul Vigay, was found dead on Portsmouth beach in 2009. His death remains unexplained and was reported in the British newspaper

The Telegraph by Coroner David Horsley who termed his death a "mystery". He left behind his meticulous research on the subject he loved so much for all to study at his website *www.cropcircleresearch.com* which still remains the most informed and extensive site on the phenomenon. Back in 2002, Vigay suggested that if the Crabwood formation is indeed genuine, as it appears to be, then "we could be dealing with an intelligence far more advanced than previously imagined; an intelligence which is able to bypass universal symbols and interact directly using our language. Clearly this would bring any communication to a hitherto unknown and advanced level."

This particular crop glyph goes beyond conventional thinking and has so many remarkable attributes to it that it most definitely fits the description of phenomena. For example, upon closer inspection there are many details to be discovered. American author and researcher David Flynn analyzed these details in depth.

There are 59 lines of 'resolution' from top to bottom. The disc is 33 lines tall. 59 - 33 = 26, this is both the number of words within the code and also the number of letters in the alphabet. 59 x 33 = 1,947. And 33% of 59 are 19.47. This number becomes significant when related to the alleged UFO crashes in Roswell, New Mexico in 1947.

There are 33 lines of code inside the disc with a total of 151 ASCII characters in the code. 151 x 33 = 4,983. Interestingly 4,983 is the exact number of miles between the actual crash sites at Roswell and the site of the crop formation in Winchester, following the curvature of the earth. Incidentally, the Roswell sites are exactly along the 33.33.33 north latitudinal lines. Now adding 151 to 33 you get 184. This is the precise amount of days between January 1st and July 4th, the day of the alleged Roswell event. Each ASCII character is comprised of 8 bits. 151 multiplied by 8 means there were 1,208 total bits in code. There are exactly 1,208 miles between the latitude of the crop circle in England and the 33.33 latitude of Roswell.

So what does all this mean? Maybe nothing, maybe numbers of significance are to be found everywhere if one looks hard enough, but there is also the distinct possibility that there is a tangible correlation between these two different events at two separate locations.

Flynn's work tends to delve deeper than that of other researchers in his field. He wrote and lectured in his spare time and has a worldwide following of his work concerning ancient mysteries, religions, illuminated fraternities and Judeo- Christian theology. His research has been published and referenced by numerous best-selling authors, books and magazines around the world. Flynn's book *Cydonia: the Secret Chronicles of Mars* explores geometrical connections between ancient sacred sites and monuments on Earth with the monuments discovered in the Cydonia region on Mars as photographed by Viking I in 1976.

Similarly, in 1991 it occurred to researcher David Percy that the distances between the circular town of Avebury and Silbury Hill, along with other features in the area, could possibly act as a mirrored representation of the key features of Cydonia. Working with the large scale UK Ordnance Survey map of the region, he carefully measured the two areas in question and found them to be stunningly proportionate.

He reduced the Cydonia mound-and-crater complex by a ratio of approximately 14:1, i.e. fourteen miles in Cydonia equals one mile at Avebury, and it fitted exactly on the Avebury/Silbury map. The spiral mound on Mars fits on top of Silbury Hill and the Cydonia crater correlates with the town of Avebury itself. Percy's measurements revealed that an angle of 19.47 degrees from due north leads directly from the spiral mound/Silbury Hill formations to the Cydonia crater/circle of Avebury. Of relevance here is that number again, 19.47 as observed by Flynn when analysing the Crabwood crop glyph, its significance is unclear but the number continues to resurface along with the freemasonic associated number 33.

Archaeologist William Neil has pointed out that the Cydonia crater is a 'causewayed enclosure' and Avebury is also a colossal 'causewayed enclosure'. He states that causewayed enclosures predate the stone circles and were in place at Stonehenge and Avebury before the stones were erected. There are vast amounts of research dealing with similar topics, each subject as intriguing as the next, but let us return to the subject at hand, the phenomenon of the formations in the fields.

HAMPSHIRE HOSTS ARECIBO RESPONSE

On 16 November 1974, at a ceremony to mark the remodelling of the Arecibo radio telescope near the city of Arecibo in Puerto Rico, SETI (Search for Extraterrestrial Intelligence) transmitted a message into space. Aimed at the globular star cluster M13 some 25,000 light years away, which was chosen mainly due to the fact that they were the largest and closest collection of stars available in the sky at the time and place of the ceremony, the Arecibo message was broadcast only once using frequency modulated radio waves.

Binary is the universal language used when attempting to communicate with other intelligences and we have already witnessed some form of this communication being used by an unknown source in the Crabwood Disc. Written by Dr. Frank Drake, the creator of the Drake Equation, along with Carl Sagan among others, the transmitted message was less than three minutes in duration. Consisting of 1679 binary digits and approximately 210 bytes, it was transmitted at a frequency of 2380 MHz and modulated by shifting the frequency by 10 Hz with a power of 1000 kW. For those of you who are not scientifically oriented, the details given here are not of the upmost importance but rather for reference purposes only.

According to a press release in 1999, the message was intended as a demonstration of the newly installed equipments' capabilities rather than to make contact with other worlds. It was more of a show of human technological achievement as they estimated it would take 25,000 years for the message to arrive at its intended destination and an additional 25,000 years to receive any possible reply. Consisting of seven parts, the Arecibo message encoded the following information:

1. The numbers one to ten.
2. The atomic numbers of the elements hydrogen, carbon, nitrogen, oxygen and phosphorus, which make up deoxyribonucleic acid or DNA.
3. The formulas for the sugars and bases in the nucleotides of DNA.
4. The number of nucleotides in DNA and a graphic of the double helix structure.

5. A graphic figure of a human, the dimension (physical height) of an average man, and the human population of Earth in 1974.

6. A graphic of our solar system.

7. A graphic of the Arecibo radio telescope and the dimension (the physical diameter) of the transmitting antenna dish.

Fascinating stuff, but what has all this got to do with the crop circles and glyphs that keep appearing in our countryside? On August 20, 2001 in a field just outside the Chilbolton radio telescope grounds in Hampshire, England, a highly unusual crop glyph appeared. Initially dubbed 'the Persian Carpet' due to its rectangular dimensions and strange patterns, it was soon realised by English crop circle investigators to have more than a striking resemblance to the aforementioned Arecibo message from the seventies.

Meant to tell a story to any ET civilisation intercepting the message, the Arecibo version from 1974 shows a variety of binary images composed of zeros and ones. The similarities between the original and the Chilbolton Glyph (*see Sources*) which was formed 27 years later, are quite obvious, however there are subtle differences.

Paul Vigay noticed that there were several discrepancies in the Chilbolton message, notably the addition of a sixth atomic number. The other five atomic numbers that represent Oxygen, Nitrogen, Hydrogen, Phosphorus and Carbon, which consist of the necessary ingredients for life on this planet, were all present in the Arecibo response, whilst Silicon or element 14 had been added. Just as humans on this planet are carbon based life forms, it has been suggested that if there exists intelligent life beyond our world that they could well be silicon based.

Other differences between the two messages included an additional strand of DNA on the left of the double helix and the population figure had significantly increased. Also the height of the humanoid figure had decreased from approximately 5ft 9ins in the SETI version to roughly 3ft 4ins and with a larger and less human-like head. The representation of our solar system had altered slightly in the crop glyph, instead of only highlighting the Earth which is the third planet from the Sun, Mars and Jupiter; the fourth and fifth planets were also highlighted.

THE CHILBOLTON FACE

Remarkably, the same field played host to another strange anomaly only six days prior to the Chilbolton 'Message'. It was noticed on August 14, 2001 by Chilbolton telescope employees that a 'face' had appeared in the crop field adjacent to their place of work, although it was not officially reported until the 19th (and not by the facility staff).

According to ex-NASA employee Richard Hoagland, the image of the 'Face on Mars' taken by the Viking satellite in July 1976, bears a striking resemblance to the field formation which confronted the telescope personnel that morning. Whether or not there is any correlation between the 'Face on Mars' and the 'Chilbolton Face' [see SOURCES] remains to be seen but the fact still remains that a highly sophisticated image of a humanoid face had been imprinted into a field by unknown means once again.

Upon its announcement in England, the feature attracted lots of worldwide attention and became an internet sensation. Hoagland declared that this was partly due to the fact that 'it struck many observers as a deliberate effort to remind everyone of the infamous 'Face on Mars'. For one thing, the 'Face' crop effort seems to be designed to replicate the light and shading of the original Viking Cydonia image. Another intriguing aspect which attracted people to the site was the unusual textural appearance of the image. The whole glyph seemed to be made up of pixels or half-tone dots like those produced in newspaper or billboard images. These cells or pixels owe their appearance to a series of darker standing tufts of wheat while the bright 'pixels' were formed by the stalks between the tufts being gently swirled down. As Hoagland cited "the deliberately created illusion in this glyph – that the lighting is coming from the upper left (as in the original Viking Cydonia frame) – is further testimony to the superb optical physics embodied in this effort."[142]

So, who should take the credit for such a difficult and complex piece of art? Was this the work of human hands, natural phenomenon or is there extraterrestrial involvement here? To achieve an effect such as this in a field of moving wheat stalks is no mean feat as it is surely not the easiest of mediums for anyone to work with. As with all the circles and glyphs that have made themselves known to us over the past forty years, any conclusions would be premature, but one thing is certain, there are intelligences and technologies beyond human capabilities at work here. In Boulder, Colorado, former Senior Scientist at the National Centre for Atmospheric Research, James Deardoff attempted to calculate the likelihood of the Chilbolton glyphs being the result of human hoaxers.

He began his investigation by asking some very basic questions:

"[What is] the probability that hoaxers could:
a.   be creative enough to construct a new type of glyph like that, involving rectangular "binary units" in the "Arecibo" response, and no circles,

b.   repeatedly practise making the Arecibo glyph first, in some field(s), without these practice attempts being spotted from the air and reported

c.   actually carry it out, producing all those right-angle corners in the Arecibo-like pattern, without making any mistakes

d.   do it all in just a few hours overnight

e.   do it without showing up on the security cameras there, one or more of which looked out towards the relevant direction

f. do it without leaving undesired trampled stalks or stake holes, etc., behind, from having   accessed the location along some tram line and laying out the surveying lines, etc., which   would be necessary

g.   not claim credit for it afterwards and not offer to show sceptics just how they did it by being willing to quickly reproduce the same designs within a pristine area of a wheat field while under the watchful eyes of veteran crop-circle researchers." [143]

Deardoff goes on to say, "Surely several practice attempts would be needed in this case, and this would give away the hoaxers' final version unless they trampled down each practice attempt right away after making it, without being noticed.

However, such trampled areas would themselves likely be noticed from the air and/or the perpetrators reported. I estimate the probability of such going unnoticed and unreported as less than 50-50, say 0.3."

He continued to work through the possibility of hoaxing using percentages and averages based on common sense thinking along with 'a mathematical way of combining individual probabilities on a yes-no type of hypothesis, in this case a hoax or no-hoax hypothesis, to arrive at an overall probability'. His conclusions on the matter resulted in a less than 2 out of a billion chance of the crop formations at Chilbolton being a hoax. If there is any credibility at all to these calculations then it easy to wonder why the hoax hypothesis is given any credence at all.

SCIENTIFIC REINFORCEMENT

Biological anomalies and irreproducible effects such as nodal bending (where the 'knuckles' on stems are bent at strange angles to affect certain shapes in the lay) are always absent from man-made designs. Biophysicist W.C. Levengood worked at the University of Michigan as a research scientist but as soon as he could he set up his own laboratory to pursue his own interests.

He arranged for samples of the crops found in crop circles to be sent to him so that he could analyze them and along with his team he started testing crop circles from all over the world. They have sampled around 400 circles from eight different countries, including Australia, Israel, Canada, United States, Germany, The Netherlands and England. They have sampled multiple circles in multiple crops over ten years.

Levengood brilliantly documented the basic changes in the plants, which in his opinion were neither caused by wind or weather damage nor by fungus or pesticides or the application of unusual fertilizer.

By taking samples of the crop and cataloguing them, starting from the centre of a formation to non-affected areas outside of the design, Levengood was able to record the differences between them. Such research led him to conclude that the bent nodes found on the stalks within the crop formations are a result of something entirely unnatural.

Laboratory experiments have shown that at the affected crops' cellular level, biological changes have taken place, which suggests that microwave energy could be involved. Many people that have visited these sites and walked amongst the freshly laid patterns have experienced dizziness, throbbing headaches and nausea. Levengood wrote, "Plants from crop formations display anatomical alterations which cannot be accounted for by assuming the formations are hoaxes".[144]

Seeds were taken from affected and unaffected crops from fields containing crop circles, and then analysed in the laboratory. Levengood noticed that in many affected samples that seed germination was altered and that in many cases "the reproductive development appeared to be terminated at the time of the crop formation".[145]

To date he has not reached any definitive conclusions on the subject but Levengood did suggest that common aspects among the anomalous features discovered did provide clues as to what kind of force could be responsible for producing the crop formations. Levengood asserted that, "The affected plants have components which suggest the involvement of rapid air movement, ionization, electric fields and transient high temperatures combined with an oxidizing atmosphere. One naturally occurring and organized force incorporating each of these features is an ion plasma vortex, one very high energy example being a lightning discharge."[146]

The possibility that some form of vortex may be causing the physical changes seen in the fields to occur could provide one piece of the puzzle but it is akin to saying that the cause of a certain homicide was a bullet to the head. The bullet caused the fatality but who pulled the trigger and why? Some vortex type energy may be the cause of these mysterious crop designs but who made them happen, how did they do it, and more importantly what was their reason for doing so.

It is too early to draw conclusions on the origins of these formations with the data presently available but scientific analysis of physical changes to the crops is certainly a necessary area of research in dire need of further investigation. At this point in time science is unable to explain away the phenomenon or as researcher G. Wingfield wrote, "It has been argued that since the geometric patterns are 'complex and non-random', they are not explainable within the current scientific paradigms."[147]

SEEING IS BELIEVING

As the majority of crop formations tend to appear at night and out in the countryside, it is hardly surprising that eye-witness accounts of these patterns actually forming are few and far between. However, there have been a number of people who have come forward with compelling information on what they witnessed which, if compared to other accounts of similar events, can be of some value to the discerning researchers among us. Clear descriptions of how such amazing glyphs can appear seemingly out of nowhere can really help us piece together the crop circle puzzle and hopefully lead us down the road to a better understanding of what we are seeing in our fields year after year.

Once the field was opened to the public by the farmer it is estimated that around 10,000 people have visited the 'Julia Set' crop formation (*see Sources*) which appeared on July 6, 1996 across the A303 road from Stonehenge in Wiltshire, England. Being near such a major landmark has contributed greatly in making the 'Julia Set' the most visited formation in crop circle history. The Stonehenge crop glyph was named the 'Julia Set' as it apparently came to represent different things to different folk. Musicians related it to a bass clef, marine biologists recognised the pattern as the cross section of a nautilus and mathematicians saw a complex computer generated fractal.

Lucy Pringle reported the event as being "especially noteworthy for several reasons; a pilot flying a light aircraft...flew over the field opposite Stonehenge on the afternoon of Sunday 7th July...at which time the field opposite on the A303 was unmarked."[148] After refuelling he got back in the same plane to fly back to Exeter some 40-50 minutes later and was very surprised to observe a huge formation imprinted in the wheat below measuring 915.2ft X 508ft. According to Pringle, the fact that it had not been there that morning was confirmed by a guard at Stonehenge and a gamekeeper. German researcher Andreas Muller claimed "This report has remained one of the most important in the history of the crop circle phenomenon as rarely do crop circles appear during daylight hours."[149]

Shortly after giving a talk at Alton College in Hampshire, a friend of Pringle's rang her to tell her of a conversation that had just taken place with the driver of the taxi she had just been in. When she had mentioned that she'd just been to a fascinating talk on crop circles the taxi driver replied, "I saw one appear opposite Stonehenge." Pringle eventually arranged a meeting with the driver who chose to stay anonymous and go under the name of 'M', and managed to get her story down on tape. This is her story, in Pringle's words;

"M and Tim (her son's friend) were driving to Somerset in July 1996 to see her son who was in the army and driving down the hill towards Stonehenge she saw a lot of cars pulled in on the grass verge on the A303 opposite the stones. She mentioned that when people see maybe two cars or more pulled in and looking down into the field, other cars stop and gradually the traffic builds up and more and more as cars draw in to have a look. As she drew nearer Tim said, "Mrs M there's a corn circle there". A car drew out and she managed to pull into the empty space and got out and joined the crowd of other people who were also watching what was happening."[150]

M described what she saw, "There was an apparition, an isolated mist over it and as the circle was getting bigger the mist was rising above the circle. As the mist rose it got bigger and the corn circle got bigger. There was a mist [which] was about 2-3 feet off the ground and it was sort of spinning around and on the ground a circular shape was appearing which seemed to get bigger and bigger as simultaneously the mist got bigger and bigger and swirled faster."

She continued, "It was gradual and you are standing there and you are thinking what is going on and everyone is discussing it and more and more traffic is building up and everything and you just think that all the time you don't really realise what is happening and then you think then that's it and the thing is getting bigger and you are thinking of the beginning and end. But you don't realise what you are looking at. I didn't understand what was happening."[151]

So where was this mysterious mist coming from? Well according to M, "The mist wasn't anything from the ground as there was a clear space between the ground and the mist. There was no wind and no dust (she is an asthmatic). It was the strangest thing I have ever seen. It was a calm summer's day."

The taxi driver estimated that she stayed looking at the event for around 20 minutes but couldn't be certain as with the astonishing scenes unfolding before her eyes, she had lost track of the time. She claimed that the mist was still there when she left but couldn't say whether or not the formation was still forming. When asked about the colour of the mist she replied "Well it wasn't brown or blue or pink; it wasn't coming off the ground. And it didn't go far up into the sky. I felt my God, what is going on, look what's happening, are we going to see a leprechaun or the men from Mars or a Sputnik in a minute or something?"

Pringle was puzzled by the time frame in which M had insisted she had stood and observed the phenomenon, she was adamant and had insisted that she was present for at least 20 minutes as she had previously reported. This is highly unusual as all the other reliable reports that Pringle had of people witnessing the appearance of crop formations have all independently stated that they took between 4 and 20 seconds from start to finish. So why the lengthy time span for the Julia Set formation? Was this because of the sheer size and complexity of the design? The other circles that had been witnessed in the making which had appeared within a very short time frame had all been small single circles.

After making several enquiries, Pringle discovered that as a result of research conducted in the 1990's, it has become possible to calculate how long any given formation should take to appear based simply on the size and number of circles involved. Pringle wrote that 'The method relates to the Earth's gravitational and magnetic fields. This predicts a velocity of the resulting vortex filament of some 10ft per second. The filament propagates not unlike a solar flare, repeatedly looping through the Earth's surface 'embroidering' a gradually evolving pattern.' Relating this information to the 1996 Stonehenge crop glyph she concluded that 'to create the 151 circles in the 915.2 x 508 ft pattern would take of the order of 20-25 minutes to create. Indeed not only does it appear that M was correct in every aspect but it also corroborates the report by the pilot, the guard at Stonehenge and the gamekeeper. What a truly remarkable event.'[152]

So even though the creators of these masterpieces are still completely unknown and the reasons why they are appearing remains a mystery, after years of thorough research we are beginning to gain an insight into how the formations are being formed. When assessing the location of all the crop formations throughout Southern England, it was observed that they were all in the same vicinity and were appearing on the ground above underground aquifers. The Oxford Dictionary states that an aquifer is 'a body of permeable rock which can contain or transmit groundwater'.

The location of this underground water supply could well be an essential ingredient in the formation of crop circles. Pringle declared that, "The descending force emits an electrical discharge which releases bubbles from the underground aquifers which rise up through the surface of the ground and patterns are formed. The anchor point of the force is always off centre."[153]

Another eye-witness account, this time from Poland, mentions a mist or fog being present during the whole experience. In the early morning of 22nd July 2000, Mr. Jerzy Szpulecki was working late at night in the Polish town of Wylatowo building a new house on the edge of a wheat field owned by his neighbour Tadeusz Filipczak when the lights in house suddenly went out. Interviewed by Nancy Talbot on July 31st 2003, this is his story.

Looking through the large windows of his house, he saw almost immediately after the 'power-cut', a strange red light in the sky descending very slowly toward the field in front of his house. He described the light as being a very bright red spherical shaped object about 20 metres in diameter (*see Sources*). As the object came closer Mr Szpulecki described what he thought looked like a "turbulent and rotating misty white fog" above the red light which then appeared to be "some type of craft" on further inspection as the object descended directly in front of his windows, about 80m out in the field. It continued to descend very, very slowly as it banked at an angle, at which point the glowing red sphere appeared to Szpulecki to be some sort of "outer shell, encasing an inner white mass of fog, which was constantly swirling or rotating within the red sphere." It then apparently began to increase in size as it neared the ground and seemed to "discharge something into the air around it."

Szpulecki went on to say that he thought the "craft was the colour of the mist", explaining that he saw an actual solid craft surrounded by a swirling white foggy material, all of which he said was contained within the boundaries of the red sphere. He suggested that the red shell appeared to be "driving" the object inside it. He continued to describe the event saying that as it got close to the ground, sparks erupted "like a short-circuit...I saw it touch the ground...when it touched down there were brilliant flashes, like lightning." [154] Then out of the centre of the object, multiple "arms" extended and slowly bent to the ground as the whole thing landed.

Describing the "arms" as "tentacle-like protrusions" of which he remembers seeing four separate ones all the same length and of a bluish colour, they all oriented themselves toward the ground. He saw that each of the "arms" had its own light-ball on the ends, coloured violet they were round also and even brighter than the red sphere from which they were seemingly attached. It was at this point that the witness noticed that the occupants of at least three stopped cars on the road next to the field were also watching the object.

The glowing red ball of light had been seen in the sky by "many" other people as it travelled towards the field according to villagers that spoke with Mr. Szpulecki the following day. The Pole estimated that around seven minutes had elapsed from the moment he first saw the object to its departure. It wasn't until the next morning when Szpulecki's neighbour informed him that there was a strange marking in the field at the precise spot where the object had been seen, that he realised what had occurred the night before. A pictogram-style crop circle was flattened into the wheat in a cross-like design which fitted the actions of the sphere and its protruding arms perfectly. Incidentally, an additional 20 metre-diameter ringed circle was also found in another field on the north side of the road only a few meters away.

Szpulecki's first thoughts when he saw the object was that something was "on fire" in the field but as the sighting progressed he began to understand that this was not the case, instead he had reached the conclusion that something "other-worldly" maybe even "extra-terrestrial" was taking place.

After the object had disappeared he said he was profoundly moved, amazed and in complete awe of what he had just experienced, stating that "it was beautiful" and that he had not felt threatened or been afraid. BLT Research founder Nancy Talbott, personally interviewed Mr. Szpulecki, "To our knowledge this is the only report of its type in the crop circle literature, the only time in which the landing of such a complex visual object has resulted in a crop circle which appears to replicate, in the laid crop, the observed geometric aspects of the object itself."[155]

As we can see there are some fascinating reports out there that can help us to understand a little bit more about what goes on during the forming of these extraordinary crop formations. There are other accounts too which include similar descriptions of balls of light and the appearance of unusual mists, and these are just the ones that get reported. There must be numerous events that have been witnessed but have gone unreported for whatever reason, for example 'M' the taxi driver pointed out during her interview how surprised she was that no-one else who had witnessed the Stonehenge event had come forward already.

Video Producer and Managing Director of Norwegian Company 'Strat & Toftenes', Terje Toftenes, was invited to investigate some video footage of the making of one of the biggest crop formations in Wiltshire history, on Saturday July 7, 2007. The event which was filmed by UFO investigator Winston Keech, happened in the East Field and was seen from Knapp Hill by three eye-witnesses.

Toftenes had already produced a documentary for Norwegian television which was translated into English in 2006 as *Crossovers From Another Dimension* and had been working on a follow-up program. So when he was contacted regarding a massive formation of 150 circles in a highly unusual design, estimated to cover 2.25 acres of land or 96,600 square feet, plus three eyewitnesses who claim to have seen a bright flash of light whilst infrared and light sensitive cameras had been set up to record the event – Toftenes was on the first plane out of Norway and headed straight for Wiltshire, England. On arrival he discussed in detail with Keech what his camera equipment had recorded.

In 1991, Keech witnessed a ball of light creating a crop circle right before his eyes. The actual formation took only three seconds to create but the impression it made on Keech has lasted a lifetime. He watched in disbelief as the bright orb which had increased from the size of his fist to about 20 feet in diameter, floated above a wheat field as the crop below waved around before lying down in a perfect circle.

Failing to capture the remarkable incident on camera Keech returned to the same spot every summer since, always armed with video recording equipment. Over the years he was able to attain higher quality cameras and finally after sixteen years he managed to record the phenomenon on video for the first time. His light-sensitive Sony VX2100 video camera was able to pick up a shadow forming in the East Field following a big flash of light at around 3:08 am.

Other witnesses and researchers were up on Knapp Hill that evening, cheering and shouting excitedly because they believed the activity to be an answer of sorts to the ongoing discussion they had been having regarding the nature of consciousness and the existence of other realities. The feeling in the air was that whoever was making the crop formations was attempting to communicate that maybe they were 'on the right track'.

Interestingly, that night was extremely windy and the East Field is not completely flat, it curves up and down, making the fact that whoever was responsible for the 1,033 ft. long formation that evening managed to construct 100% perfect circles in total darkness on a hilly field.

According to Terje Toftenes, "To make circles look 100% from the air in a field that has up and down hills, you cannot create 100% perfect circles on the ground. You have to create ovals."[156] Constructing such perfect ovals in complete darkness with the pure intent of creating the illusion of being circles as seen in the air seems like an extraordinarily difficult task were it done by human hand. Many of the 150 ovals in the fields were extremely large also; the largest being roughly fifty meters in diameter.

Considering the likelihood that the crop formations were made by man, Toftenes remarked, "Under those dark conditions, I would consider that impossible and everyone I have spoken to among the researchers down here and also civil engineers who are used to land surveys – they say that to do that under those conditions and also within that limited time frame (90 minutes to 1 hour and 45 minutes), they regard that as absolutely impossible for humans to do."

On Monday, July 16, just nine days following the mysterious formation of the huge design in the wheat in East Field, Andrew Buckley, a graphic designer from Winsford, Cheshire, reported some suspicious activity from within the formation itself. Walking from Woodborough Hill to East Field he noticed three unmarked white vans parked up at the side of the road. One of the men stepped out of a van and advised Buckley not to enter the field as there was some kind of project going on there at the moment.

Once inside the field he saw several men wearing the same white overalls carrying bags which contained crop samples which they placed in the back of one of the vans. Before departing, the man who had warned him earlier asked if Andrew was expecting any other visitors to the crop circles that morning, Buckley asked why did he want to know and the man replied "You'd be advised to stay out of it because there is going to be some kind of military exercise there and you would be advised to stay out."[157]

He was right. At around 9:30 am the military activity began and suddenly there were a lot of helicopters circling the East Field for about an hour or so. One Gazelle helicopter dropped down into the field and flew very low over the small gathering of visitors which had recently arrived in the formation.

Buckley described feeling nauseous at the time the helicopter approached them, "There was a terrible smell from the helicopter. I can describe it as being a sulphurous smell – very powerful! It made my eyes burn. I noticed half a dozen other people as well – they were quite severely affected. I saw one man throwing up into the crop."[158] He had been taking radiation readings just before the low-flying craft had showed up and had picked up nothing from his dosimeter but minutes after the helicopter had made its presence felt Buckley recorded a sudden and dramatic change in his readings; "my dosimeter shot up very high between 300 and 500...which means get out of the place. It's dangerous!"

Whoever is responsible for all the incredible crop circles and glyphs which continue to amaze and perplex all those with an interest in this unique phenomenon remains unknown, but with the mounting evidence and research into the subject, we may arrive at some fascinating conclusions sooner than we think.

Terje Toftenes has made his mind up even if many of us are yet to. "I'm absolutely convinced it is a very intelligent entity, or whatever it is. I think there are other intelligences in this universe visiting and monitoring us. So, I think it is either something projected on the ground from an alien source or it is projected on the ground from an inter-dimensional source that we are not able to perceive with our senses."[159]

7

THE MEIER MYSTERY

I have not only seen the objects from outer space, but have taken photographs and even travelled in them.

Eduard 'Billy' Meier

HARD EVIDENCE OF THE EXISTENCE of extraterrestrial life on this planet is not only seemingly impossible to acquire but remains extremely difficult to authenticate. What kind of evidence represents a solid enough affirmation of events that might convince a general public of the reality of alien life in our midst? Confirmed UFO sightings by large gatherings of people? Correlating alien abduction accounts? Unexplained crop circle phenomena? Personal testimonies of ET contact from varying notables in highly respected positions within society? Or countless ancient peoples and tribes from around the world telling remarkably similar stories of extraterrestrial visitation, along with impossible feats of engineering achieved during the construction of the world's megalithic structures and greatest monuments which are still unexplained today?

It would seem that despite all of the above, the majority of humankind remains ignorant to such possibilities and is much more comfortable denying the existence of anything which may raise more questions than it answers.

Man sits contentedly at the top of the food chain and rests unchallenged as the most evolved species on Planet Earth if not the Solar System, or such is the common misconception which has been force-fed to so many since time immemorial. To prove that there are other humanoids in our universe much further up the evolutionary ladder, with technological capabilities which overshadow our greatest inventions a thousand fold, would not only be seen as a threat to our self-proclaimed superiority but would also rock the foundations of our understanding of Creation. Along with the death of Darwinism and the relinquishing of religious dogma, the Big Bang theory would self-implode like the very star which is believed to have started it all. It would in all likelihood be goodbye God and hello new understanding of the galactic history which has preceded all. Such a change in consciousness and comprehension could invariably frighten the uninformed masses; such would be the scale of a global verification of such magnitude. It is no surprise then, that despite an enormous array of evidence for the existence of other forms of intelligent life here on Earth, some form of denial appears to have a hold of our species regarding this largely unexplored area of interest.

One man in particular claims to have had a lifetime of intimate personal involvement with highly developed extraterrestrial intelligences, and has produced some of the most convincing proof of alien interaction that has ever surfaced. His name is Billy Meier. No single case in history has ever produced such a variety of richly documented evidence, corroborated with the testimonies of witnesses, such as that which has come to light during the Meier investigations.

As always when dealing with this controversial subject matter, much of the material can be extremely hard to swallow, as the rational part of the brain takes over and attempts to make sense of such highly unusual information. But, if one puts aside that innate human rationality for a moment, allowing the flow of new possibilities to enter the equation, then the Meier case has so much to offer even the most sceptical of minds and does so with integrity, honesty and consistency.

What you are about to read has to be the most intriguing, well-documented extraterrestrial contact story ever told. Brimming with physical evidence, the controversial Billy Meier case is considered 'too good to be true' by sceptics – and 'too real to be hoaxed' by others. If time reveals this man's testimony to have been a life-long hoax, then Mr. Meier has raised the quality of charlatanry to an inconceivably high level.

BORN TO BE BILLY

In Bulach, a farming community in the Swiss Lowlands, Eduard Albert Meier (-Zafiriou) was born to parents Julius and Bertha Meier on February 3, 1937. Eduard's story begins in October 1942, when at the tender age of five he witnessed his first UFO whilst stood next to a large walnut tree with his father at the rear end of his house at 9am, in their home town of Bulach.

Ten or fifteen minutes after a strange urge had compelled him to look up; he described seeing a silver flash shoot out of the sky towards his house at an incredible speed. As the object drew ever closer to them, he could see that it was a gigantic metal disc-like object about 250 to 300 meters in diameter. Without a sound and within a fraction of a second, the disc shot past them overhead, a mere 200 meters above their heads. He experienced telepathic communication for the very first time as the object drew near, and afraid of this bizarre experience and the internal dialogue which ensued, he ran to the village priest in fear of his own sanity.

His father had told Eduard that "It's a secret weapon of Adolf Hitler", but the young boy was unconvinced by this explanation because the disc didn't resemble one of the German fighter planes or American bombers which he had often seen fly over his village. He later sought further advice, especially regarding the voice inside his head which had appeared simultaneously with the UFO sighting, a voice that had calmly told him "Do not be afraid".

Meier described his experience to village priest Father Zimmerman who informed the young boy that he was aware of such flying objects, they were flown by people from another world but he was not really permitted to discuss the topic as he was a priest and he didn't want to frighten the villagers. "He told me to learn telepathy, to try to give answers. So I tried as I was told. After a few weeks it worked, and I was able to answer. I remember very well that Father Zimmerman told me not to talk about it to anyone, otherwise everybody would say I was crazy" Meier recalled.

In November, one month after the first incident, Meier saw a second UFO which he described as "pear-shaped" and it came right down to ground level before landing directly in front of the young Eduard. This time, somebody appeared out of the vehicle, an elderly man who looked between 90 and 95 years of age; a man who Meier would soon become very close with named Sfath. It was explained to Eduard that he would be trained and educated for a very tough and challenging mission that he was born to accomplish in this lifetime. Sfath took the young boy by the hand and without saying a word, led him onto the craft where he was asked to sit in a small chair beneath a spinning device located above his head. As the device began to spin, Meier said that all became clear as he remembered all of his former lives; where he had come from before this incarnation. Sfath was restoring all of his memories from previous incarnations where extraterrestrials had previously worked with him; they were essentially getting him 'back up to speed' again. He was then told that he would have to make a decision whether or not he would choose to work with them once more and fulfil the mission chosen for him.

Sfath informed the young Meier that he had come from a planet called Erra which is one of ten planets circling their sun, Tayget. Approximately 500 light years from the Earth, Erra is located near the star cluster in the constellation of Taurus known as the Pleiades (M45). Sfath told Meier that his race hails from the Plejares star system, roughly 80 light years beyond the Pleiades, in a dimension which is a fraction of a second in the future from our own, on an alternate timeline. Claiming that the Pleiadians are roughly 3,500 years more technologically advanced than terrestrial humans, they have been visiting our planet for thousands of years because we represent an earlier stage of their own evolution and they feel duty bound to help our evolutionary progress along by aiding us with our spiritual development as a race. Meier commented that "They just see us here as their little brothers, or something like that and they want [to] bring real teaching of the natural life and of the spiritual belonging, spiritual teaching, spiritual life and all this."

The Pleiades are recognised under different names throughout the world; the Seven Goddesses (South Africa), the Seven Maidens (China), the Seven Magnificent Spirits (Hindu Vedas) and are more commonly referred to as the Seven Sisters. The latter derives from Greek mythology and the seven sisters of Atlas and Pleione, which gave the seven stars their names; Sterope, Merope, Electra, Maia, Taygeta, Calaeno and Alcyone. Tayget[a], the sun of Sfath's home planet Erra, can be found in this list. Meier's contact in the seventies, a Plejaren woman called Semjase (pronounced Sem-Ya-Say), told Billy that the possible origins of these myths could have derived from the fact that females were always sent as contacts in antiquity, as they appeared less aggressive to early man. In later years Semjase also explained why the Plejarens feel compelled to visit the Earth, saying "We are not superior beings nor are we missionaries, but we feel duty bound to the humans of Earth to tell them the only thing limiting the progress of the Earth human is the Earth human himself."

With the exception of some minor anatomical differences and a vastly extended lifespan, the Pleiadians/Plejarens are basically human beings. They can live up to a thousand years old and aside from having slightly longer and more elongated earlobes they otherwise have the physical appearance of an Earth human. Erra, their home planet, is smaller than Earth with a population of about 500 million and is part of a greater federation of planets which is said to have an approximate population of 120 billion.

Sfath informed Meier that Earth humans and Plejaren humans share the same ancestry but have developed and evolved separately from one another. The Plejaren Federation is an organisation of civilisations derived from star systems located mostly within the Milky Way galaxy. Billy Meier is said to be the last surviving Earthling who has had contact with members of this Federation and he will continue to have personal contacts with them until his death. Meier was informed that there were previously four others who had also had contacts with the Federation but are all now deceased. The Plejarens have declared that their dutiful task is to preserve the already existent human life in the cosmos and the evolutionary process as it progresses.

At the end of summer 1944, Sfath arrived in his pear-shaped craft once more and this time Eduard was asked if he would like to step inside, he readily obliged and climbed on board where he was swiftly taken up into the sky, reaching about 70 km above the Earth. They remained up there for several hours whilst Meier was entrained and educated up to the level of a 35-year old person despite being only seven years old. This knowledge would continue to increase manifold over the coming years. Billy was told that he would have the highest degree of spiritual development of any human being on Earth with regards to spiritual knowledge, ability and understanding. Meier wrote "Beginning in 1944, during numerous visits on his beamship, Sfath explained to me many things and informed me about important data concerning many fields of knowledge, humanities, history, Creation and evolution, incidents and facts, etc., which I had to learn and retain in my memory. This was usually accomplished through electronically induced, deep hypnosis."

Eduard Meier's contact with the Plejaren Sfath was one of hundreds of contacts that have continued throughout his adult life right up to the present day. The remarkable aspect of Meier's contacts however, that which sets him apart from other alleged extraterrestrial contactees, is the fact that he was instructed to write down his contact experiences in report format for future reference and for the benefit of mankind. With one hand, Billy types up to sixty words per minute and has transcribed tens of thousands of pages of information since he first began. From 1975 until 2012, there have been over 1000 telepathic contacts with the Plejaren extraterrestrials and members of their Federation, 542 of which are documented and available as contact reports.[160]

Although his contacts began in 1942, he didn't start transcribing them until 1975 as he spent the early years of his life travelling to many countries and working. He covered around 142,000 miles hitchhiking and worked about 360 different jobs that included such occupations as dog-catcher, snake-handler, veterinarian, German teacher, ship painter, street planner, medicine man and private detective. He held an apprenticeship as a sandblaster in Bern in 1960, and in 1964 he worked in Bab El Hawa, Syria and was also employed in a marble quarry in Amman, Jordan. During his time in Jordan, Meier claims to have been employed by some Middle Eastern Police department to bring in serial killers and mass murderers, working under the pseudonym "The Phantom". It was in the sixties whilst visiting Tehran in Iran where an American woman gave Eduard a nickname that would stay with him for the rest of his life. He used to wear cowboy apparel - the hat, belt and boots - and reminded the lady of a character from a Western movie, namely Billy the Kid. She began to call him Billy and somehow the name just stuck. According to Meier, this incident was no accident. Sfath had already foreseen that he would receive a new name of which he would later be known for the rest of his life, and in 1945 Sfath had told him "on a certain date, in Tehran, in Persia, you will receive the name Billy, with which you will become known worldwide." Meier was informed that his name "Billy" was preserved in writing in an 8,500 year old document which was handed down and still exists on Earth to the present day.[7]

---

[7] In 1977, Harold Proch of Munich sent Billy a photographic negative which contained the photograph of an ancient fragment of a written document which had been purchased from the Egyptian black market by an Englishman. Meier was able to translate the text which contained the prophet's incarnation lineage from Enoch to the New Age. The Plejarens were amazed that this text existed and following a thorough examination, validated its age to be nearly 8,500 years old.

Among other things, the fragment's text stated:

"I am the herald of truth, and in this mission I will be once again amongst important times by the names of: Elijah - Isaiah - Jeremiah - Jmmanuel - Mohammed - Billy, so I shall serve the people as prophet seven times until their way of thinking changes to that of heeding Creation's laws and directives."

It is because of an ancient mission that began thousands of years ago, that he was sought out by the Plejarens. Meier had never strived for these contacts, rather they were destined to occur whether he wished them to or not. It is evident from his meagre lifestyle that he has not gained financially from his contacts, regardless of the publicity which has ensued.

On Billy's eighth birthday in 1945, Sfath explained to him the reasons why he had been chosen by them for contact. The date of this particular contact was Saturday, February 3, 1945 12.10 pm.[161] Sfath's instructions to the young Billy were later translated from German in February 2011 and transcribed for future use. Part of that transcript dating back to 1945 gives an overview as to the purpose of the Plejarens visitation to Earth and subsequent contact with a Swiss farmer's son with a limited education:

"The cause for the argumentation leads back to determinations which lie very far back in the past, and according to which, during the time of your present life, you are fitted into a certain task determined by yourself - as was the case repeatedly in your spiritual line of reincarnations in former lives and in other personalities and bodies - in order to fulfil the mission of a proclaimer and to bring, to the whole of humanity, peace, true love, freedom and unity as well as open, unencrypted knowledge of the spiritual matters and that which pertains to creational laws as well as wisdom."

He was born to reveal the existence of extraterrestrials, his very purpose on this Earth is to accomplish a mission set by himself previous to his present incarnation, to complete a task of monumental importance with little regard to his own personal desires and health. Sfath continued "you will only take up your actual mission and fulfil it when the time has become ripe for it, namely, with the date of the 28th of January, 1975." This date was given to Billy thirty years in advance and would later prove to be the exact date of his first official contact report, a contact which would not be with Sfath but with his granddaughter Semjase.

In 1945, Sfath spoke with enormous clarity about Meier's future and spoke of events that would come to pass in the years to come. He told Billy that he would travel first before beginning his mission, which he did, and also predicted an occurrence which would take place in 1965 that would affect Meier's life greatly. Sfath said "as with all genuine proclaimers and sages, you will also first have to learn very much, before you will take on and fulfil your task at your predetermined time. Thereby you must, however, consider that you will have to endure a quite adventurous and hard life, often full of privation, which, from the year 1965, will still increase in a form which will demand very many powers from you in every regard."

He definitely knew something, because as it transpired Billy Meier was involved in an accident on August 3, 1965 which led to the amputation of his left arm. He was sitting on a bus near Iskenderun in Turkey one hot day, with his arm hanging out of the window when another bus, driven by a drunk driver, rammed into them. Meier was hurled out of the window of the vehicle and his left arm was so seriously crushed and mangled that it was decided by the doctors that amputation was the best option. For the next month following the accident, Billy wandered around disorientated and suffering from hallucinations. Recognising him as "The Phantom", the Police finally picked him up and took care of him until he had recovered sufficiently to make his own way once more. Four months later, on Christmas Day, Billy met a seventeen-year-old Greek girl in Thessaloniki named Kalliope Zafiriou. Billy and "Popi", as she liked to be called, fell in love and were married in Corinthos in 1966, just as he was previously foretold would happen by both Sfath and a later contact called Asket. The married couple travelled to Switzerland where they settled in the small town of Hinwel and had three children together named Gilgamesha, Atlantis-Sokrates and Methusalem. Billy was employed as a night watchman and they settled into a domestic family life, albeit a slightly impoverished one.

In the 1945 transcript, Sfath also forewarned Billy of the tragic events which would unfold during that summer, events which would change the world forever. Speaking about the dropping of the A-bomb over Japan, Sfath predicted "...all kinds of criminality arise, such as even monstrous, destructive and annihilating weapons, such as the atom bombs, which, already in a short time, will be abused by the Americans for a deadly and annihilating function, when they destroy the Japanese city of Hiroshima in this year on the 6th of August, by means of a nuclear weapon operation, and claim hundreds of thousands of dead, then to repeat the same crime on the 9th of August with the likewise Japanese city of Nagasaki, which, once again, will cost the lives of around 100,000 human beings."

Prediction and prophecy form an integral part of the authentication process when evaluating the Meier case. Meier himself lays claim to an incredible amount of predictions, many of which have already come to pass and have been confirmed as 100 per cent accurate as shall be revealed further in this chapter. But this isn't simply a man telling the world what he has personally foreseen; rather he is claiming that his contacts have informed him of the events which will happen, his purpose is to pass that information on when the time is deemed appropriate. Many things which have been told to Billy during his lifelong interaction with the Plejarens will remain with him for the rest of his life, as he has been instructed not to share some of his knowledge of future events.

Once again, proving the validity of Meier's evidence is almost impossible, but likewise, it is just as difficult to disprove, as many non-believers will attest. The predictions are there in black and white for all to see, along with the date that they were written down, a date which obviously must precede the event in order to be termed as a prediction. The most problematic issue is proving that Meier wrote them when he said he did. Proving the legitimacy of any given evidence is always the hardest part and isn't always possible to achieve. This fact alone however does not necessarily negate the authenticity of the information; rather it allows room for scepticism where other more solid evidence may not. But in the case of Billy Meier, the accumulation of all aspects of his story needs to be considered 'en masse' if one is to ascertain some degree of validity.

When discussing the issue of extraterrestrial contact with Earth humanity, one question which tends to arise is "Why choose Billy Meier?" Why not reveal their presence to either more prominent figures in authoritative positions, or alternatively, address the nation as a whole. James W. Deardoff wrote a thesis for the Department of Atmospheric Sciences at Oregon State University in

1985, entitled *Possible Extraterrestrial Strategy for Earth* in which he theorised on varying strategies that extraterrestrials may employ when attempting to communicate with the human species for the first time.

Deardoff wrote "a scenario for this type of extraterrestrial strategy might involve their communicating with just one or a very few recipients scattered about the globe. A recipient would be supplied with a comprehensive message over an extended time period, so that he or she could fully understand it, and would also be allowed to gather extensive evidence on the reality of the events so as to be able to gain some measure of public acceptance of the messages. However, in order that scientists in general should not be alerted, only the recipient would be allowed to partake in the communication sessions and to witness the extraterrestrials themselves...Meantime, the messages would get published, translated into various languages, and distributed throughout the world amongst other occult literature...the messages could be expected to contain some spiritual, or at least ethical, aspects which might further deter scientific inquiry. If all this were not enough to prevent any premature scientific acceptance, the existence of similar communications which turned out to be hoaxes might occur naturally and serve to confuse the situation greatly. This would provide a further motivation for scientists to feel obligation to study the situation." Deardoff's paper could have been written with the Meier case firmly in mind.

Meier's experiences with Sfath lasted eleven years from 1942-1953, during which time he was allegedly introduced to some very influential figures in history including Mahatma Ghandi, King Farouk of Egypt and Haile Selassie I of Ethiopia.

According to Meier, these prominent historical figures were already fully aware of Sfath's origins, so Billy's visits would not have been particularly unusual for such knowledgeable men. Meier claims to have been given a small translation device or speech translator, which could be fastened to either his belt or breast pocket, thus allowing him to converse with people from other nationalities with ease. In Baghdad in 1959, Meier also met Saddam Hussein when they were both only twenty-two years of age, but this meeting was under normal circumstances without the assistance of Sfath.

During Billy's final contact with Sfath, whilst on board a Plejaren beamship, Billy was instructed to lean back in his chair to allow Sfath to place a helmet-like device around his head. Following a brief manipulation of several buttons and switches, a voluminous amount of information was suddenly available to him, and along with the gift of foreseeing future events, he attained many new abilities along with a great amount of knowledge.

He was told that he would now retain all of the abilities that had been released by the instrument, even following the removal of the device. Sfath then took Billy back down to Earth and once Sfath left he would never see Billy again. Although telepathic communication between the two men continued for a while where more knowledge and information was imparted to Meier, on his sixteenth birthday, 3rd of February 1953, Sfath's voice manifested itself in Billy's mind for the very last time. Sounding old and tired, he said farewell to the sixteen year old Meier and his voice faded away forever.

THE ASKET YEARS

Back in 1945, Sfath had already informed Meier that future contacts would be with other extraterrestrial humans instead of him. He told Billy "You shall already now know that the successor to my person will, as at 1953, be a young woman from the DAL universe, where you will certainly be taken someday. The name of your contact person will be Asket. She belongs to one of the branches of our peoples, others of which still reside in the Lyra and Vega systems, however, shifted a split-second from this space-time plane, just as is our space-time configuration in which our Plejaren systems exist. The contact between Asket and you will last for 11 years, just as they will between you and me."

He continued "Thereafter, you will be left alone for 11 years and must learn very much through your own initiative, after which then, in the year 1975, a contact connection with you will again be taken up, and indeed by my granddaughter, Semjase, as well as by my son, Ptaah. They both, in addition to others, will then continuously be your future contact companions." Everything Meier was told at the age of eight came to pass. A few hours after Sfath's voice faded in 1953, a very different voice appeared, a fresh, young and energetic sounding voice, soft and gentle. It was the voice of Asket, his new teacher and second contact person who would indeed remain close to Billy for the next eleven years.

Unlike Sfath, Asket did not originate from the Plejares system beyond the Pleiades cluster. She came from an allied nation located in our twin universe known as the DAL, where she explained, her people had emigrated from our universe (DERN) by advanced technological means approximately 50,000 years ago. Asket continued where Sfath had left off, educating and preparing Billy for the mission to come. As a more highly developed life form, she would take on Sfath's responsibilities to continue with Billy's education as Sfath's knowledge was now insufficient for the task at hand. Meier's extensive travels were guided by Asket, and it was during this period of time that he acquired a phenomenal amount of knowledge and experience which would prove so beneficial to him in later life.

Billy's first excursion away from home was at the age of sixteen when he decided to join the French Foreign Legion. He had been getting himself into trouble back home and this seemed the right move for him at that time, although he soon realized that it wasn't his calling. Billy remarked, "I simply wanted to leave everything behind me, false accusations and so forth. I wanted to elude the court and then when I was in the Foreign Legion I realized this was not the correct way." He was extremely uncomfortable with having to be trained to kill other human beings, so one day he walked out into the desert and returned home for Switzerland where he gave himself up to the authorities, resulting in him being locked up in an institution for two years.

Asket's influence on Billy throughout this period of his life was subtle but essential, as she guided him through most of the African, European and Asian religions during an eleven year adventure. His vigorous religious studies led him to personally experience brief spells as a Catholic, Protestant, Hindu, Muslim, Buddhist and Jew among others. He is alleged to have joined them one at a time, searching for a belief system that he could accept. This unlikely scenario was all part of Billy's education which was put in place in order for him to experience everything for himself rather than relying on the testimony of others for information on these matters. Those eleven years of extreme learning, travelling and personal experience were the main reason why Billy was prematurely led away from a formal education at such an early stage.

Whilst living in India in 1964, the opportunity arose for Billy Meier to capture his first photographs of extraterrestrial craft, or 'beamships' as he was informed was the correct term for those particular interstellar space vehicles. He was able to take some quite remarkable images during his stay that included a photograph of eight spherical objects flying over New Delhi railway station. A picture taken on July 3, 1964 shows a silver disc hovering above the Ashoka ashram in Mehrauli, in the south west district of Delhi, which Asket informed Billy was her own beamship. Meier was not the only person to have witnessed the UFO sightings at that time; in fact, sometimes hundreds of people also reported seeing the same thing.

One person in particular has gone on record stating that she too witnessed several events where flying saucers were present in the skies above the Indian capital; she is a retired U.N. diplomat for Cambodia called Phobol Cheng. She also remembers seeing Billy Meier in 1964 walking with Asket in and around the ashram, and Cheng also claims to have been in direct contact with Asket also. According to Cheng, Asket would visit her whilst she was in bed and as Cheng had seen Billy with this beautiful woman, she knew he must be a good guy and considered a friend.

Cheng said "I saw this being now we call Billy, and he was accompanied by the being that used to come and sing me to sleep."[162] Discussing the appearance of spaceships in the area at the 8th International UFO Congress in Laughlin, Nevada 1999, she commented; "So this ship would appear at the time - usually would be around at the same time I had a visitation, or sometime no visitation - but I would see the ship. (In response to a question) This [photo] was taken by Billy Meier, and [the ship] was present even when I first met [him]...not every day, but almost - I would see it once a week, or sometimes twice a week; there was no timing [to it]." Phobol Cheng has not only confirmed his presence there in India but has also corroborated his story of Asket and the beamships. This is always the case with Meier's extraordinary tales of adventure and travel; he has so much photographic and circumstantial evidence to backup many of his wild claims. During his tenure in India, Meier managed to get himself in the local Delhi newspaper *The Statesman*, on Wednesday, September 16th, 1964. The front page article read;

"The Flying Saucer Man leaves Delhi.
Swiss claims he has visited three planets.
He left Delhi for Pakistan en route to Switzerland on Monday.
"I have not only seen the objects from outer space, but have taken photographs and even travelled in them."

As the article stated [see SOURCES], he claimed to have visited three planets with Asket in her beamship. Meier's story starts getting even more convoluted at this point, as he claims to have travelled back in time with Asket and also states that he was taken to other planets in our solar system. Suddenly, not only has this man being contacted by extraterrestrials from another universe, and had his life mapped out for him thousands of years ago, but now he has physically travelled through time, both forwards and backwards and seen some quite incredible things. It sounds ridiculous and highly improbable but he has the photographs to confirm his assertions, which are available to view thanks to an American man named Randolph Winters, who spent several months living with Billy Meier in 1986 along with fellow countryman and UFO researcher, Wendelle Stevens.

Winters video-recorded himself thumbing through Meier's astonishing photo album which appears to contain some quite impossible pictures taken from unbelievable vantage points, previously unseen by any person here on our planet. The footage available today comes from a lecture presented by Randolph Winters as he narrates over the video presentation that he shot at Meier's home in Switzerland.[163]

Meier claims to have travelled back to prehistoric times on Earth where he was allowed to get out of the spacecraft and take photographs of dinosaurs and prehistoric plant life. During this prehistoric visit, he had a photograph taken of himself with a Pleiadian man, both wearing spacesuits stood outside on the ancient terrain. During his first flight around our solar system he photographed Venus, Mars, Jupiter and Earth. He photographed a dust storm on Mars and also travelled to the spring of 1976 where he was shown a manmade satellite in orbit above Mars which he also has photographic evidence of. One picture shows a UFO in deep space overlooking Jupiter which Meier told Winters was the mothership that he spent three days on as he visited different places in our galaxy. The photo was taken as they were approaching the colossal mothership in a smaller craft which was about to board the larger craft, said to be fifteen miles high and ten miles in diameter.

Another astounding photograph shows Earth in the background with not one, but two moons in the foreground. This particular shot was taken from around 60 million years ago when our planet was said to have had two moons orbiting it. According to Asket, neither of the moons from that photograph exists in the Earth's orbit today, as the moon of which we are all so familiar with has only been there for about five million years. The 'dual moon' theory is a fascinating possibility which has grabbed the attention of many researchers in recent times and has already been transcribed in ancient texts.

Another anecdotal piece of information that has surfaced from Meier's extraordinary photo album concerns the Polish-American George Adamski, who single-handedly popularised the concept of contact from other worlds by becoming the first well-known UFO contactee in the early 1950's. His claims of face to face contact with human-looking Venusians, along with a number of black and white UFO photographs, led to the publication of his first book *Flying Saucers Have Landed* in 1953. His experiences are as interesting and bizarre as Meier's but there is a real lack of evidence and consistency to support his extravagant claims.

Author Jenny Randles wrote, "There is no doubt that Adamski's evidence is barely persuasive. His photographs have convinced few, and many allege analysis shows them to be small, crude fakes. His stories about conditions on other planets in the solar system were found to be scientifically absurd even before he died." While many people discredited Adamski due to his unbelievable stories and crude photographs, it has been suggested by some researchers that his popularity may have been engineered by secret government intelligence agencies keen to promote wildly fictitious accounts.

People who travelled with Adamski claim that he had been issued a special passport which is most commonly reserved for VIPs such as diplomats and high government officials. UFO researcher George Andrews speculated the reasons for a civilian having gained such high authority could be "that he may have been a CIA disinformation agent, who successfully fulfilled the mission of making the subject of UFOs seem so absurd that no independent in-depth investigation would be made by qualified academics."[164]

Meier was told that the Adamski case was a fraudulent one, fraught with inconsistencies, but he also believes that not everything Adamski told the public was deliberately deceptive. Some of his photographs taken in 1962 of bell-shaped craft were genuine objects and some of his alleged contacts with extraterrestrial beings did occur as he described, only they weren't extraterrestrial at all. The human-looking blond-haired woman he met coming out of one of these unusual craft looked human, because she was. Back in the sixties these craft were being flown out of Brazil and were being spotted all over the globe. If on occasion they got careless and were seen by a member of the public, it was easier to tell the innocent bystander that they were from Venus rather than expose the truth that they were in fact working for German Intelligence.

THE TALMUD OF JMMANUEL

During 1956, Asket took Billy travelling through time to places and events of his choosing. One of these visits was to meet a man called Jmmanuel, or as he has mistakenly become known, Jesus Christ. The spelling of Jmmanuel is not a mistake; rather it traces back to the Pleiadian's forefathers who use the 'J' instead of 'I' when transcribing Jmmanuel in written form.

Leaving from Jordan in 1956, they left Earth in Asket's ship and flew high enough that Billy said he could see a small planet Earth below them. Asket did something with the instrumentation on board and they immediately flew back down to the surface, landing pretty much in the exact same spot from which they'd just departed, except it wasn't 1956 any longer, it was the year 32 A.D. They had arrived just a couple of days before the crucifixion. Billy was given robes to wear instead of his modern day clothing and underneath he was given a silver tight fitting space garment for reasons unexplained in his report. Attached to his belt was one of the box translator devices that he had previously worn during his time with Sfath, as he had no understanding of the Aramaic language. They set off on foot and would stay in that time period for four days.

Shortly after the activities of Jmmanuel in Palestine had gained wider attention, his true spiritual teachings were greatly falsified, leading to the creation of Christianity which was established and initiated from the forming of a fictitious entity based on his character. During Meier's alleged meeting with Jmmanuel, a conversation between the two men ensued where Jmmanuel told Billy "Truly, they shall make a cult from my real human existence that will result in great harm. They still see in me only the human being I really am, but soon they will turn me into something slanderous and as being equal to Creation. Truly, I foresee these events of the future but cannot change them even though I resist them."

In 1963, seven years after his personal encounter with the man they call Christ; Meier claims to have been led to a roadway just south of the Old City of Jerusalem by his Lebanese friend Isa Rashid, a former Greek Orthodox priest. Rashid had previously been informed of the approximate location of a tomb site through telepathic promptings which he had received sub-consciously from the Plejarens. Together, the two men discovered the abandoned ancient tomb of the man known as Jesus, where they unearthed an ancient document.

Crawling into a small entrance they had dug out, they managed to remove a flat rock which had been concealing some preserved ancient scrolls wrapped in tree resin encrusted animal skins. The bundle which was about 60 cm in length and 25 cm wide turned out to contain the Talmud of Jmmanuel (TJ) in the form of written scrolls. Once removed, they opened up the scrolls to reveal the writing in Old Aramaic and also recovered a small figurine that had been left by Indian healers whilst Jmmanuel had been sequestered in the tomb for three days. Also wrapped in the skins was a piece of gypsum (calcium sulphate), which is scentless when burnt and turns to a white powder. The gift was said to have been given to Jmmanuel as a keepsake from his father Gabriel when he was just seven years old and is believed to have originated from the planet Alkyon.

The document was not complete, as over time, some of the pieces of parchment had invariably decayed and become illegible. However, Rashid was able to translate the first of the four scrolls into German; these 36 chapters were then mailed to Meier in Switzerland in 1970. It was apparent to the pair from the outset that any translation work would have to proceed in secret if the document was ever to become public. Meier only received permission from 'higher sources' to make the information publicly available in 1974 and one year later the translated German version of the TJ was published.

Life got very difficult for Isa Rashid and his family once the knowledge of the existence of the scrolls had reached a number of religious factions, and soon they were on the run in fear of their lives. Rashid had the overwhelming responsibility of keeping the original scrolls safe, as he was attempting to translate the other three and was forced to flee from Jerusalem to Lebanon, to evade persecution from Christian and Jewish orthodox groups as well as a number of shadow government agencies. Rashid's persecutors were intent on destroying the scrolls before the information could be released, and silencing Rashid was considered a necessary evil. When he was finally tracked down in a Lebanese refugee camp in 1974, he had already hidden the scrolls within the stone walls. The Israeli Military subsequently bombed the camp and although Rashid escaped with his family, the scrolls were either destroyed in the chaos or they were discovered by the authorities and have been reclaimed.

The information contained in the scrolls was deemed to be heretical due to the contents being heralded as the 'original book of Matthew', written by one of Jmmanuel's contemporaries and disciples Judas Iscariot. According to the TJ, Judas had been wrongly denounced as a traitor[165] of Jmmanuel as he'd had nothing to do with the betrayal of which he was blamed; "This ugly deed was carried out by Juda Ihariot, the son of a Pharisee."[166] The author of the Talmud explains how Jmmanuel's mother Mary was secretly impregnated by Gabriel, a distant descendant of the celestial son Rasiel and when Joseph discovered this he was furious and considered leaving her. Gabriel sent someone down to Earth to explain the situation to Joseph "Mary is betrothed to you, and you are to become her spouse; do not leave her, because the fruit of her womb is chosen for a great purpose."

It is an incredible document and has quite rightly ruffled a few feathers amongst religious groups all over the world. Isa Rashid was assassinated because of the Talmud and Billy Meier has also been the victim of a number of assassination attempts. He really does seem to possess supernatural capabilities as his uncanny ability to avoid being killed has testified. As of December 8, 2011 there have been a total of 22 attempts on his life, originating from both terrestrial and extraterrestrial beings according to Meier. The TJ has caused so much controversy because it reinforces the ancient astronaut theory which suggests that modern man was created by an extraterrestrial race from another star system, and that the Old Testament God was not actually a "Father" in heaven but rather an extraterrestrial leader. The texts clearly demonstrate a very physical connection between extraterrestrial and human lineage, which is all the more fascinating considering that the TJ was discovered by Billy Meier, the most famous ET contactee in history. Is this an act of coincidence or was it 'written in the stars'? Logic would suggest the latter. Parts of the Talmud texts concur with Sumerian beliefs that extraterrestrials came to Earth and mated with early-Earth women thus creating a hybrid race that has evolved into the modern human being. Verses 87 and 88 of the TJ explain;

"They will name the fruit of her womb Jmmanuel, which translated means 'the one with godly knowledge', as a symbol and honour to god. Through god's power and providential care the Earth was made to bear intelligent human life when the celestial sons, the travellers from the far reaches of the universe, mated with the women of Earth."

The text continues, "Behold, god and his followers came far from the depths of space, where they delivered themselves from a strong bondage, and created here a new human race and home with the early women of this Earth."

In chapter 28, verse 59, the TJ confirms more of the ancient alien theory by stating that "God and his Sons of Heaven are other human races who have come in their metallic machines from stars in the vastness of space."

Also included within the verses is a mention of Jmmanuel meeting two Pleiadian men wearing spacesuits; "...there appeared to Jmmanuel, two very tall men, the likes of whom he had never seen on Earth. / Their clothing resembled a covering of foam, and their arms were like golden wings. / They inhabited an environment of their own, because the air of this earthly world would have been fatal to them. / These two men from the constellation of the seven stars were venerable teachers." (Chapter 4, verses 23-26)

Later passages reveal the use of spacecraft; (chapter 3, verses 30 - 33)

"...and behold, a metallic light fell from the sky and rushed over the Jordan. / Consequently they all fell on their faces and pressed them into the sand while a voice from the metallic light spoke: / Jmmanuel entered into the metallic light, which climbed into the sky, surrounded by fire and smoke, and passed over the lifeless sea, as the singing of the metallic light soon faded away."

And chapter 4, verse 49 reads "Not until the time of space-travelling machines will the truth break through..."

For such an ancient document to be mentioning "space-travelling machines" is revelatory in the sense that it confirms what many scholars consider to be part of the true history of mankind whilst acknowledging that high technology was already existent in ancient times.

Meier's time with Asket came to an end in 1964, and he was finally given permission to take a photograph of her before she said her final farewell. There has been much controversy surrounding a photograph which is alleged to be a picture of Asket with a co-worker called Nera that is presently circulating the internet. This image shows a blonde woman next to another lady and has been proven to have been taken from a still frame of a piece of video footage from the Dean Martin TV Show in the 1970's. The two women performed together with a dance group and looked very alike Asket and Nera whom Meier photographed standing inside their craft.

Some critics are attempting to debunk Meier by asserting that his photograph of the extraterrestrial woman Asket is a fake. They are right in this assumption; however, Meier wasn't responsible for the manipulation of the image. In 1975, a photographer claiming he was from the Rhine valley region of Switzerland created forgeries from Meier's original prints stolen from his home, by retouching, recopying and 'sandwiching' separate sequences together. Because of the close resemblance of the two female look-alikes in the forged photograph, even Billy didn't notice the difference until 23 years later when it was pointed out to him that the girls in the picture were American dancers on television.

During the seventies, Meier's home was an open house and many photographs were stolen or lost. The Plejarens requested that Billy never turned anyone away; hence the Meier household became a magnet for all kinds of dubious characters over the years. The forged picture was slipped back into Meier's collection and looks to all but the informed minority, to have been a result of Meier's own doing. This would prove to be a thorn in his side for years to come, as one suggestion of hoaxing and fraudulent manipulation is all that is needed to muddy the water and cast doubt over the whole Meier mystery.

THE EVIDENCE

Eleven years after Billy Meier's final contact with Asket from the DAL universe, on Tuesday, January 28, 1975 at 14:12 pm - he was contacted once more. Just as Sfath had explained to Meier thirty years earlier, his granddaughter Semjase from Planet Erra arrived right on cue. Meier was sat at home at one o'clock when suddenly a force inside him caused a voice to become audible and slowly comprehensible. Something was coercing and directing him softly to leave the house with his camera.

He drove away from the house on his motorcycle, aimlessly but guided, to a specific place unknown to him at that point. Driving through the village of Hinwil and across fields, forests and meadows, he finally arrived at an isolated spot in the Frecht Nature Preserve. Looking at his watch he noticed that the time was 2:12 pm. Suddenly he saw an object in the sky descending rapidly over the tree line as it reduced its speed considerably, and after hovering around a while and slowly manoeuvring through the woods, the object reached a clearing in the meadow and finally touched down on the ground, gently and in complete silence.

Meier strode boldly towards the craft which he described as "disc shaped with similar shapes on its top and bottom" with an upper dome larger than the base and "equipped with red, highly placed rectangles," but was stopped in his tracks by an unknown force like that of a strong wind. So he chose to sit down on the ground and wait. Then, a figure appeared from behind the disc; a human being wearing an unusual grey close fitting suit. Meier described the material as durable, light and pliant, resembling elephant skin, with a ring around the neck for the mounting of a helmet. The figure was an attractive female with a strong and graceful confidence about her. She approached Meier, grabbing his arm to help him stand up, then after walking together for a while they sat down in the grass and she began to speak in perfect German, albeit with a strange accent.

Before introducing herself to him, her first words were "You are a fearless human being". She went on to inform Meier that her name was Semjase and she had come from the Pleiades. The language that Semjase speaks on her world is called 'Sarat' (there is a Universal language called 'Kosan' that it is alleged that most extraterrestrials speak). Billy asked her why she had chosen to visit him and she responded by saying "We have been studying you for years / through you we want to clarify some things / we've kept an eye on you because you have been preoccupied with these problems for thousands of years within other personalities and because you think and act in a real and honest way; and because you have already frequently carried out such a mission in your former lives, even though for us, great mysteries surround this fact."

The beautiful space-traveller went on to deliver further instructions to Meier regarding his mission;

Semjase – "Listen very carefully now to what I have to say. Write down everything and tell the public about it, but in a different way than when you carried out your mission in previous lives."

Billy – "How can I do that when I have nothing here to write on? I also don't have a tape recorder or anything like it."

Semjase – "Do not worry about that; you can write it down later. First I will explain everything to you so you have an overview. Besides, it is easier for me to contact you later when I can transmit the thoughts to you so you can write everything down word for word very precisely."

On that day in 1975, Meier began to transcribe every contact made with the extraterrestrial human visitors which would become known as the *Contact Reports*. Meier was now considered ready to progress to the next step of his mission, to provide physical evidence of the existence of our extraterrestrial counterparts and to finally go public with it all. He was also requested to set up a group of like-minded individuals for further developmental studies in the areas of both spirituality and UFO research, with the intent of publicising the information also. Along with his colleagues, Meier founded the non-profit organisation FIGU after his early contacts with Semjase in the 1970's. FIGU is a German acronym which stands for *Freie-Interessen-gemeinschaft fur Grenz-und Geisteswissenschaften und Ufologiestudien* which translates as the "Free Community of Interests for the Border and Spiritual Sciences and Ufological Studies". The headquarters are based at Hinterschmidruti in Switzerland at the Semjase Silver Star Center. FIGU was setup to aid with the publishing and distributing of Billy Meier's documented contacts, experiences and evidences along with other more current affairs which affect the global population such as women and child abuse, human rights, animal protection, overpopulation and environmental issues.

1. Photographs and Video Recordings

Part of Meier's mission to help raise mankind's consciousness awareness was to provide visible proof of extraterrestrial visitation to the world. Armed with an Olympus 35mm SLR camera (with a focal length 1:28 / f 42mm) and an 8mm video camera, Meier was able to capture many remarkable photographic stills and video images of a variety of beamships. Without Semjase's help, it would not have been possible for Meier to achieve the results that he did. She instructed him to stand at precise locations within the landscape in order to optimise the quality of photograph or video required for the intended purpose. She avoided unnecessary human attention by carefully positioning herself discreetly between trees and hills, so that she could only be seen from one spot where Billy would be told to setup his cameras. Semjase would demonstrate the beamship's capabilities in front of the lens, offering the viewer a rare opportunity to witness extraterrestrial technology in action.

In 1975, Meier's first ever piece of video footage of a beamship shows the craft manoeuvring and hovering above a pine tree, oscillating and pulsing in large circles around the top of the tree, using the Earth's magnetic field. Another video clearly shows her ship disappear then reappear in a fraction of a second. Meier was told that the Plejarens have technologies that allow their craft to move 'out of phase', in and out of the dimension.

Watching this sort of footage in the modern era instinctually leads the mind to consider that some form of video manipulation must have been involved in producing such a visual effect. However, following an in-depth examination of the Meier material by technicians at Nippon TV in Japan, it was discovered that there had been no cutting or editing of the film; the object does actually disappear and later reappears in less than one eighteenth of a second. It is worth considering that in 1975, Billy Meier simply did not have access to the computer software of which is readily available today. As UFO researcher and Meier advocate and spokesman, Michael Horn stated during a 'Karma Air Radio' interview with Michael Parker, "when he took most of his material, took these photos, there was no photoshop, there were no home computers."

Many of Meier's photographs and videos were analysed using a range of scientific instruments that included electron microscopes, thermogram edge identification, infraredometer, digitizer, density and film grain inspection, Z scale contour and laser scanning. One of Billy's photographs showing a beamship above the woods near his home in Switzerland, often referred to as 'The Woodpile Scene', was examined and tested by physicist and aerospace engineer Neil Davis using a microdensitometer, an extremely sensitive optical instrument used to detect spectrum lines on a film or photographic plate, too faint to be seen by the human eye. The conclusion of Davis' report declared that "nothing was found in the examination that would cause me to believe the object in this photograph is anything other than a large object photographed some distance from the camera."[167]

Other methods were also employed to determine the authenticity of Meier's UFO photographs, one being 'the triangulation method' which required the measuring of known background objects within the image as a reference point. Using this simple technique led to the conclusion that the object in question, the beamship, was precisely the size that Billy had claimed it to be, seven meters in diameter. Tests by a professional American laboratory using a 'pixel analysis method' of another beamship photo, clearly illustrated once again that the object proved to be seven meters in diameter, as Meier had alleged it was. By rendering an object in a photograph into a computer pixelated version, image analysts are able to discern whether or not the object has three-dimensional properties or is actually the result of placing a two-dimensional cut-out into the frame prior to taking the picture.

In the late seventies, an American research team led by retired USAF Lt. Colonel Wendelle Stevens launched an extensive investigation into the Meier case in an attempt to either prove or disprove the validity of the Swiss farmer's extravagant claims. Two documentary films were based around these investigations.[168] One of their experiments involved the use of a 1.5 metre replica model of a beamship in one of Meier's pictures, which had been skilfully crafted by expert model makers in the film industry in Hollywood at Stevens' request.

With Billy's cooperation, the team set out to replicate some of his best photographs using the lightweight model and some monofilament line and a long pole from which the model could be suspended. Together, they photographed the model against the background of the Swiss landscape and the final results were very impressive. In the imitation photographs, the wire was invisible as planned, and the model UFO looked so realistic that it made it difficult to get a sense of scale; allowing the object to appear larger than it was. However, they did have problems focusing on both the object and the background simultaneously. The fake images were taken to a laboratory where they could be examined in detail alongside the originals and the results were conclusive. Computer analysis exposed the model photographs instantly, as the small size of the object in the image was swiftly recognised, leading the lab technician to comment that "It is easy to tell a small model". The model also lacked the reflective qualities seen on the original beamship pictures, appearing whiter rather than silvery. Meier's originals stood up to the challenge and ultimately there was no comparison. Author Gary Kinder described the model photos as "a crude and somewhat stark beamship frozen in an otherwise familiar setting; but they lacked the feel of Meier's, the natural relationship that appeared to exist between his background and his ships. They had no depth."[169]

Some sceptics and debunkers have seen the photographs of Billy with the beamship model, whilst others discovered some of these models lying around his house and immediately put two and two together. Stories of Meier using models to produce his pictures have all originated from this scenario and in truth they have no substance. Meier used to take his original negatives to get developed at a local photo lab called Bar Photo. Owner Willy Bar told investigators "I never saw anything suspicious in the black and white film I developed, nor was I ever told to manipulate anything...My personal opinion was always, 'I don't know about UFOs, but the pictures are real.'"

Billy has managed to capture hundreds of stunning photographs of different variations of spacecraft, most of which were piloted by human extraterrestrials. Some craft were described as scout ships and others as telemeter or drone ships which are pilotless craft which are operated by remote-control.

Photo 171 taken at Hasenböl-Langenberg in Fischenthal on the 29th of March 1976, shows Semjase performing a demonstration flight with a new type of beamship. The visual alterations from the old version include a higher dome structure and a different rim design whilst also being more technologically advanced than its predecessor enabling the ship to achieve multi-dimensional flight as well as time-travel. Regarding the Type 3 beamship seen in a series of Meier's images, Semjase explained that "the function of the sphere is for propulsion of the craft in interstellar flight." This Variation 3 craft was examined in more detail by computer analyst Jim Dilettoso and led him to conclude that "In the pixel distortion test it appears to me, and the computer, that this object was photographed in the same original piece of film, at the same time that the background was photographed -in other words, no overlay. I would say these pictures are genuine."[170]

To add further weight to his testimony, Meier was also able to photograph the physical imprints left by the three landing pods of Semjase's ship, which left three circular impressions in the meadow grass. The circles that he photographed on many occasions, and also showed first hand to Wendelle Stevens and his crew, always consisted of three counter clockwise swirls. The reason for this swirling effect was because the "spiral shape antigravity oscillation" pads move with the whole ship, according to Semjase. The three circles all fitted within a greater circular area of about seventeen feet in diameter, and interestingly enough, the grass in these affected areas continued to grow in a counter clockwise formation for nearly three months after they had appeared. If this kind of evidence would have presented itself today, the grass would have succumbed to more rigorous testing by crop circle investigators and scientists alike, with bent stalks and soil samples being sent to laboratories for closer examination, such has currently become procedure in these matters.

Motherships are enormous in comparison to the beamships seen in Billy's photos and are used to travel vast expanses of space. They remain in orbit and never enter into a planet's atmosphere; rather they are used as a base from which all the smaller scout ships descend. Meier talked at great length about the mothership he had been on to investigator Wendelle Stevens during the several months they were together, and in 1978, Stevens wrote the following; "This entire ship is exceedingly large by comparison to our Earth-made structures. This colony-ship is constructed and assembled entirely in space, and once put into operation is never again dependent on any planet for support. It is completely self-contained and almost perfectly efficient in all respects. It gets its energy from sun and star-light and its only loss is a little radiated heat. Eduard Meier took five 36-shot rolls of film during this trip and only one of them was ever returned to him from the photo processors. The rest were 'lost' in handling."

2.   Sound Recordings

As well as the photographs and video recordings which Meier produced so prolifically, he was also able to take sound recordings of Semjase's ship. Under normal circumstances her craft would fly in silence, but she was able to allow Billy the opportunity to hear and record the sounds as they would appear without having been muted. The sounds that emanated from the beamship were so loud that they could be heard over four kilometres away. The results were extremely unusual, producing throbbing, pulsating noises which sounded almost electronic. The recordings were taken to be analysed by electronics consultant and sound engineer Steve Ambrose, who stated that "If you were going to create a noise for a spaceship, you would be hard put to come up with something as original as this."

During analysis using an oscilloscope, the sounds appeared to consist of up to nine different frequencies. The oscillations appeared random, with all nine frequencies often being present simultaneously but separately, and then they would alter suddenly and blend into one more coherent sound, creating an alignment of frequencies. One interesting aspect to note is that among the random signals there appeared to be a single steady pattern. This particular wavelength was moving at around five to ten cycles per second, which happens to be in the same region as that of the natural resonance of the Earth, otherwise known as 'the Schumann Resonance'. Reasons for this mysterious correlation with the other more random frequencies remain unknown.

The beamship recordings were later taken to Robin Shelman, a specialist in sound identification. Using software which contained a sound bank that could recognise and match-up varying sounds, Shelman was able to identify every sound within the recordings except the object itself – the emitted sound. For example, the machine identified a small dog barking, a crow cawing and a European police siren, all in the distant background. As for the sounds emanating from the beamship however, nothing in the sound bank matched up and therefore it could not be identified. With reference to the object under examination, Shelman concluded that "the machine must have been built for a specialised application, recognising the sounds of such a machine may be difficult."

3.   Metal and Crystal Samples

Semjase gave some crystal and metal alloy samples to Billy as more physical evidence to confirm the validity of the Plejaren's existence and also their interaction with Meier. The metal fragments and crystal samples were given to Wendelle Stevens in 1979, before he sent them on to Dr. Marcel Vogel, a scientist and chemist working at IBM. According to Meier, the metals are representative of around seven different stages of manufacturing that the Plejarens must go through to produce the metal required to construct their spacecraft. The final product reveals that the only possible means for its appearance is due to the metal having gone through a cold fusion process, which is a type of nuclear reaction which occurs at, or around, room temperature. A 'hot' fusion process requires temperatures in the millions of degrees. At the present time, cold fusion is not a process which has been proven or accepted by mainstream scientists, although further research into this new method is been considered by the U.S. Department of Energy, as long as experiments are conducted "within the present funding system".

Vogel classified the metal sample as 'F-1' and claimed to have isolated a number of elements which included silicon, iron, silver, copper and thulium, all in one specimen. The most unusual of the elements found was thulium, which is a costly and rare Earth element that is difficult to extract. Vogel stated that "We, with any technology that I know of, could not achieve this on this Earth plane. I could not explain the type of material that I have and its discreetness by any known combination of materials. I could not have put it together myself, as a scientist. I showed it to one of my friends who is a metallurgist and he shook his head and he said 'I don't see how it can be put together'".[171]

Following further examination under an electron scanning microscope, Dr. Vogel discovered evidence of micromachining, proving that the sample was a deliberately manufactured product with clear signs of "mechanical manipulation". He concluded that "There is evidence of machining. There are striations which look like the sample has been worked mechanically. It doesn't look like anything we've made here. At this moment I would feel very much inclined to accept what was given to me as being true."[172]

Another metal sample examined by Vogel was described as containing nearly every element of the periodic table, Vogel claimed that "Each pure element was bonded to each of the others, yet somehow retained its own identity." Following closer inspection using a microscope to magnify the sample 2500 times, he states that it was "...metal, but at the same time...it is crystal!" Experimenting with some of the actual crystal samples he had received, Dr. Vogel reported; "When I touched the oxide with a stainless steel probe, red streaks appeared and the oxide coating disappeared. I just touched the metal ... and it started to deoxidize and become a pure metal. I have never seen a phenomenon like that before."

Shortly after completing his experiments on the Meier samples, Vogel stated that they had vanished from the IBM laboratory, preventing any further analysis from being undertaken by alternative scientists.

4. Witness Testimonies

With so many of Meier's UFO photographs and videos having been taken close to his home in the Swiss countryside, you would expect that other people must have witnessed some of the sightings also, despite Semjase's discreet intent. As word spread of Meier's experiences and his photographs became publicised in magazines and newspapers throughout Europe, visitors soon came flocking to see him. In fact, it wasn't long after his popularity had grown that capturing daylight footage had become an impossible task as he would nearly always be followed by UFO enthusiasts, keen to see the beamships for themselves. This ultimately resulted in Meier pursuing his contacts in the early morning hours. One evening, according to Meier and his close associates, Semjase did a public demonstration in her ship for the benefit of the group. It was those closest to Meier, such as family members, friends and co-workers at FIGU that often witnessed UFO activity on or nearby Meier's property.

Bookbinder and teacher Hans-Georg Lanzendorfer had many experiences whilst working at FIGU. On seeing UFOs on site he said, "The whole situation after twenty-five years is somewhat normal and we deal with such unusual phenomena quite differently...In February 2001, I drove my car into the protection shield of a telemeter disc. That means that I touched the electro-energetic protection shield of that disc with my car and the whole car was enveloped in a huge ball of light."

Another local teacher, Guido Moosbrugger, who has been a close associate and friend of Meier's for years, published beamship photographs that he had taken between 1975 and 1979 in his book *And Still...They Fly!* As his pictures confirm, he saw many objects in the sky whilst working in close proximity with Billy, and on one occasion he claimed that, "Once I was with other witnesses when I saw Semjase eliminate a free standing, approximately three to five meter tall, fir tree in a meadow. It suddenly disappeared." Moosbrugger has kept an apple preserved in a jar for over thirty years, claiming that it was not grown on Earth but rather it originated from one of the vast greenhouses on a mothership under the control of the leader of the Plejaren race, Commander Ptaah, another contact of Meier's from the mid-1980's onwards. He claims that very few people actually believe his anecdotal tale but nevertheless, he remains adamant that it is the truth.

Meier's children have spent their entire childhood surrounded by the furore that followed their father's decision to go public regarding his experiences. They were teased by non sympathetic kids at primary school, who were most likely subconsciously voicing their parents' views that Meier must be insane because he thinks he can talk to aliens. Regardless of the childish banter which they were forced to endure, nothing could alter the fact that the extraterrestrial scenario which had engulfed their father's life would inevitably affect their own. Speaking about his experiences, one of Meier's two sons, Atlantis said "I had several sightings of ships, UFOs, beamships as they are called, due to the fact that my father had contact with a Plejaren, and repeatedly said "I have been called once again"...It has been a natural thing 'cos I have been a part of it since childhood."

According to some sources, over 120 eyewitnesses to various ET related phenomena have surfaced since 1975, including fifteen people who passed lie-detector tests in 1981, set-up using protocols of the University of Arizona. Eyewitness photographs of the same UFOs and events described by Meier have also come forward to corroborate his testimony[173], Guido Moosbrugger and Phobol Cheng being just two examples.

In 1987, American investigator Lee Elders performed a psychological stress evaluation test (PSE) on Billy Meier to try and determine whether or not he was lying about the whole thing. Elders recorded the question and answer session with Billy before sending the tape away for further analysis. It was sent to Bob Phelan, a former criminal investigator with the Sheriff's Department of Colorado and a specialist in lie detection. After having reviewed the tape several times, Phelan concluded that he could find no evidence of deception in the statements about Meier's experiences. Earlier PSE tests were conducted on Meier and other witnesses in 1978. Once all the voice tapes were analysed, it was concluded that every one of them had passed the tests; "no indication of conscious or deceitful intentions was detected on the part of either Billy or any of the other participants."[174]

5. Prophecy & Prediction

Another fascinating aspect of the Meier mystery lies in the written documentation which has become one of the key factors in proving his case. Anyone who has publicly declared himself to be a recipient of alien visitation and personal extraterrestrial contact ought to have some form of presentable evidence at hand, in order to legitimise their outlandish claims. Unfortunately however, most alien contactees fail to deliver anything substantial enough to be considered as evidence. Billy Meier on the other hand, really does have an abundance of material available to offer open-minded and sceptical researchers alike, the opportunity to immerse themselves in a variety of possibilities.

The Meier case stands alone in its genre simply because it contains such a wealth of information and so many different types of evidence. This is not just the story of a man who says he meets with aliens, with nothing but his word for it and maybe a handful of blurred and questionable photographs. On the contrary, Billy's story involves a lifetime of continuous involvement, with voluminous pages brimming with astounding material on every conceivable subject of importance to the human race. Subject matters covered by Meier in his hundreds of contact reports include; Earth history, Creation and the origins of the universe, spirituality, terrestrial religions, reincarnation, genetic engineering, human evolution, human relationships, government/military cover-ups, environmental issues, interplanetary space flight, astronomy, science and much, much more.

It is his coverage of current affairs however, which is of interest at this juncture. Meier has documented numerous important events in human history before they have actually taken place. The accuracy of these predictions or prophecies, if you will, has proven to be extremely high. Putting aside the issue of how to validate the times and dates that Meier claims to have written the material, and assuming for a moment that the dates have been authentically transcribed, the examples of predictive writing which follow are worthy of further investigation.

On August 25, 1958, a document was transcribed containing 162 verses of predictions, originally constructed from revelations told to Meier by the Plejaren Sfath and the extraterrestrial Asket from the DAL universe. The list which was first compiled by Billy Meier, writing from Uitikon in Switzerland, was sent to fifteen European countries as a "Warning to all the governments of Europe!"[175] As one would expect, Meier never received a reply from any of the leaders who had received the letter, as we live in a world where the art of prediction is not taken seriously or even considered possible by the mainstream scientific community. The translators of the 1958 document wrote in 2006, "As it has been since time immemorial, announcers will not be heeded and their

265

warnings of future events will simply be cast to the wind, and indeed at the cost and to the disadvantage of the people".

The predictions and prophecies are said to have arisen from the 'results of some calculations and looking out ahead' along with statements made by Sfath and Asket. The predictions selected here are written alongside the corroborating information, to highlight the accuracy of the material transcribed back in 1958. Meier has continued to produce information which predates the actual event or discovery throughout his life via his many contact reports, but the examples shown here originate from the 1958 document.

a) "...next year on September 13th, 1959, using rocket propulsion, the Earth human, respectively the Soviet Union, will make a hard landing of an unmanned object on the moon"

Corroboration: On September 14 1959, unmanned space probe Luna 2 became the first probe to land on another celestial body. It successfully impacted with the lunar surface east of Mare Imbrium near the craters Aristides, Archimedes and Autolycus. Launched September 13, (Moscow time).

b) "...on April 12th, 1961 an Earth human will climb high in the sky with a rocket to orbit around in the Earth's outer space.."

Corroboration: Yuri Alexeyevich Gagarin became the first human in history to journey into outer space, when his spacecraft 'Vostok 1' completed an orbit of the Earth on 12th April 1961.

c) "...on February 3rd, 1966 an aerospace object will make a soft landing on the moon..."

Corroboration: Luna 9 was the first spacecraft to achieve a lunar soft landing. Luna 9 launched on 31 January 1966 at 11:41 UT (14:41 Moscow time) from Baikonur Cosmodrome and reached the Moon on 3rd February.

d) "...then in 1968, the outer fringes of Earth's space will be left, and later the first trip to the moon will be undertaken, whereby up until the year 1972, five manned moon landings will take place through the U.S.A., while a sixth moon landing -

supposedly the first - on August 20th, 1969 will rest only on a world-wide staged deceit as a result of the political armament race with the Soviet Union."

Corroboration: Apollo 7 was the first crewed flight of the Apollo spacecraft, which launched on 11th October, 1968. Seven television transmissions were made from Apollo 7 becoming the first live TV transmissions from a piloted U.S. spacecraft. Apollo 8 was the first of the Apollo series to successfully orbit the moon, and the first manned spacecraft to leave Earth's gravity and reach the Moon. On July 20th 1969, Apollo 11 became the first manned lunar module to land on the Moon. Meier was told that this particular event didn't really take place but was artificially staged for political reasons. Many researchers share his sentiments regarding this most important historical event. The other five manned Apollo missions which successfully landed on the Moon were Apollo 12, 14, 15, 16 and 17. Apollo 17 was the last official mission to land, in December 1972.

e)   "Because of unrestricted prostitution, in about twenty-five years an already embryonic deadly epidemic will develop worldwide that will be named AIDS and will finally cost several hundred million human lives."

Corroboration: AIDS was first recognized by the Centers for Disease Control and Prevention (CDC) in 1981 and its cause—HIV infection—was identified in the early part of the decade.

f) "...in 1993, a political and commercial European dictator will arise that will be called the European Union..."

Corroboration: The Maastricht Treaty established the European Union under its current name in 1993.

g) "...East Germany...will...only exist until the late 80's of this century, thereafter Germany will be reunified..."

Corroboration: The date on which the Berlin Wall fell is considered to have been 9th November 1989.

267

h) "...hundreds of thousands of people will be murdered as in the Soviet Union which will be dissolved no later than 1991..."

Corroboration: The USSR was formally dissolved on 26 December 1991.

i) "...in Iraq a war will be led through the United States of America, through their country's president, however this will be without success, for which reason one of his sons, who will likewise be the U.S.A's head of power, will, in the third millennium, unleash a second war in Iraq..."

Corroboration: The Gulf War (August 2nd 1990 –February 28th 1991) was a war waged by a UN-authorized coalition force from 34 nations led by the United States against Iraq, in response to Iraq's invasion and annexation of Kuwait. On 10th March 1991, 540,000 American troops began to move out of the Persian Gulf. George H.W. Bush was the American President at that time. The Iraq War started (March 20th 2003 - December 18th 2011). George W. Bush, the son of the former President Bush, had become the U.S. President in 2009.

The details of Meier's predictions have proved to be extremely accurate on many occasions, and the sheer consistency of his writings leads one to consider the possibility that his highly implausible case may yet hold some validity, despite the overwhelming rejections enforced by earthbound logic.

Should the extraterrestrial scenario prove to be as Meier's story suggests, that such highly-evolved human beings from other planets have the ability to travel vast distances through space whilst also having the capacity to time-travel, then surely the ability to foresee future events must be considered a realistic supposition. It seems more unlikely that an Earth human would be contacted by an extraterrestrial race with relatively few special abilities, especially considering the distance they must have travelled to reach our planet in the first place.

A MAN OF MANY TALENTS

Overall, the Billy Meier material offers an overwhelming array of plausible yet extraordinary evidence to reinforce his remarkable testimony. Many people have come forward to publicly discredit the Swiss, often without any proof whatsoever and any information that has actually succeeded in contradicting Meier's claims has more often than not originated from the most questionable of sources.

One man who is currently giving lectures and presentations on Meier's behalf, concerning Billy's story, is American Michael Horn. Given all the evidence at hand, Horn struggles to comprehend how any informed researcher can continue to dispute the Meier case with such belligerent ignorance. Horn commented, "The sceptics would like us to believe that this man with no resources, working as a night watchman on a partial disability pension with one hand – is not only the master model maker, film maker, photographer, digital and special effects person, videographer, metallurgist, electronics genius, sound recording engineer, knowledgeable about topography and map-making, geography, ancient history, mining ores, agriculture and thirty other disciplines...They will credit him with all that, but they won't say the guy's telling the truth."[176]

During the Meier investigations initiated by Wendelle Stevens in the eighties, a panel of experts discussed the possibility of hoaxing the entire Meier catalogue of evidence and concluded that it would take over ten thousand man hours and cost in excess of one million dollars to duplicate the evidence available. Another intriguing facet of the Meier situation is the innate abilities of which he possesses. On New Year's Eve 1977, Billy was allegedly persuaded to demonstrate some of his mental abilities to those present. It was reported that he used mental power alone to bend spoons and put his fingerprints into metal coins and earlier in the year he apparently had lifted an oven onto a truck.

On numerous occasions he has managed to defy death at the hands of his would-be assassins. Once he was shot at whilst walking near his home, the bullet touched his hair, narrowly missing his head. The assailant later wrote a letter to Billy, explaining how her religious sensibilities had been offended by Meier's writings, and that she considered him to be the devil and so was duty bound to kill him. She later befriended Meier and took an avid interest in his work.

On May 10, 1980, he was shot at for a seventh time whilst sitting on a sofa with Wendelle Stevens outside on the veranda. Billy described feeling pains in his lower back which caused him to bend over in agony, just as a gunshot sounded. A 7.5mm calibre bullet flew so close to his head that dust from the wall behind them was found in his hair. The pair retrieved the bullet from the wall where it had become lodged, centimetres from Meier's head. The back pain dissipated after five minutes but had already served its purpose and saved his life, again. Meier explained that pain often surfaced when danger was imminent.

On another occasion, a dream apparently saved his life. A few days before another shooting incident occurred, Billy dreamt that he would get shot in the chest whilst heading towards the trees, where he was expecting another contact. He had become so confident in his own ability to foresee future events through such visions and was so aware that the dream could become a reality that he placed a metal plate in his breast pocket, reinforced by a memorandum book in front of the metal. Someone had nailed a sign on his door that read "It's enough you dog. You will be put down", and sure enough, a few days later, he was shot at whilst on his way to a contact. The bullet hit him exactly where he had dreamt that it would, and he had defied death once more as he was saved by the small book and metal plate. He shows evidence of this occurrence in the documentary film *Contact From The Pleiades*.

Billy has also managed to survive two nearly fatal bouts of pneumonia during his life, the first being in 1937 when he was only six months old. According to Meier's mother, the family physician, Dr. Strebel, had informed both of Meier's parents that they should prepare themselves for the death of their son; such was the severity of the pneumonia he had contracted. Billy later discovered that his first extraterrestrial contact Sfath, had administered to him at that time, thus curing him of his ailment at such a tender age and saving his life. His mother told him how they had spoken of his sudden and inexplicable recovery as a "miracle".

When he reached adulthood, Meier once again contracted pneumonia and was close to death before being taken onboard a craft where he underwent a lifesaving operation. Several witnesses had accompanied him to a certain location where he was instructed to go before disappearing in full view in a "flash of bluish light". According to Meier, human looking aliens used "strange instruments" to drain the pleural area of his chest of "a considerable amount of pus and liquid" before releasing him thirty minutes later. To the astonishment of his friends who had seen him before he'd disappeared looking grey with deep sunken eyes, Meier had reappeared looking "sprightly and smiling", appearing to be "in perfect health".

Another ability that Meier claims to have been blessed with is the core reason why he was 'chosen' for contact by the Plejarens in the first place. He believes that they are able to communicate with him because his vibrations, the natural frequencies of his mind, are compatible with theirs. Meier said, "You see, I can work together with them because I understand how to close up my Earth body vibrations."

Semjase had explained to Meier that "when entering your terrestrial state, we must make an adjustment in our vibrational patterns. It is similar to you adjusting the fine tuning on your communication devices. In our case, it allows for the clear perception necessary for an exchange to take place." When Billy is about to have a contact he receives a cooling sensation on his forehead followed by a telepathic communication which he once described as being "like a knowing, at the same time, like a voice". Many of the telepathic contacts have taken place in his home, enabling him to transcribe their conversations into written reports. He doesn't always leave the premises and board a Plejaren craft in order to speak with the visitors.

His abilities along with the mission he was born to fulfil has not come easy to Billy Meier. Aside from the death threats, assassination attempts, slanderous comments and public ridicule, since the contacts began he has repeatedly struggled to continue with the work. On October 24, 1980 during Contact Report 140, Meier's health was deteriorating as a result of the stress involved, so he told Semjase that he could no longer deal with the whole situation and wanted to stop the contacts between them.

Semjase: ...you've built up an uncontrollable rage and determination in yourself that you will now still drop your task.

Billy: You've grasped it.

Semjase: That - is ... excuse me ...

It makes me very sad.

I would be so happy to help you ...

Billy: It's too late for that.

Semjase: I have already informed Quetzal and father.

Billy: And?

Semjase: They won't be against your decision even a little bit and neither will I.

Billy: Very well.

Semjase: In your transition stage, even the slightest occasion had to cause this.

Nevertheless, I have explained this to you several times.

Billy: I know.

Semjase: We accept your decision in any form.

Thus, we also consider our contacts as finished.

Billy: That is good.

Semjase: Also, we won't make any more attempts from our side to win you over for the fulfillment of the mission and, thus, for the contacts.

Billy: That is also good.

Semjase: The decision still lies solely with you.

The following contact came on January 3, 1981, as Billy's health began to improve slightly and Semjase managed to subtly coax Meier into considering re-establishing the contacts with the mission in mind.

Semjase: I thought that a visit as an advance notification was better, and if you allow it, I would like to talk with you again about the discontinuation of the contacts.

Billy: If it's just a discussion, then so be it. I think that I'm so far better off again that I no longer get excited so quickly.

Semjase: You look better, much better.

Obviously, you could still recover a little bit.

Nevertheless, I'm not mistaken in that your health is still very bad.

Billy: There, you're quite right, but I will still certainly improve a lot more. Perhaps I can then devote myself to my work again.

Semjase: Does that mean that you're willing to take up the contacts with us again?

Billy: I said nothing about that.

Semjase: Yet it would be desirable and a great joy for all of us.

It would certainly be appropriate if you'd think about it.

We ourselves can also continue with our task.

Billy: Today, I am neither for nor against it in this respect.

Semjase: Certainly, but your reflection would certainly be of value.

Billy: That may be, and - okay, I will do it. Give me some time until the filming and the photographing. Then, we can talk about it again.

Semjase: Sure, it's a word, and this gives me joy and hope.

Billy: Your joy and hope are an honour for me, but you shouldn't set your hopes too high.

And so the contacts continue to this day, although he no longer speaks with Semjase but with her father Ptaah and another Plejaren named Quetzal, among many others who have communicated telepathically with Meier over the years. The Meier mystery continues to reach new audiences and is as confounding, perplexing and incredibly fascinating as ever it was back in the late seventies once his decision to go public changed his life forever.

The information is still flowing back and forth from Erra to Switzerland, and the contact reports continue to be transcribed in lucid detail. The UFO community remains divided on the issue of Meier's authenticity and will no doubt continue in this vein for years to come, and no matter what you believe to be true, the fact remains that no single case in history can offer so much food for thought regarding the extraterrestrial conundrum.

Even with all the technological advances made since Meier's earliest contact experiences, and the birth of the internet and digital imaging, no other photographs and videos of extraterrestrial craft have ever surfaced that can compete with the quality, clarity and consistency of those taken by Billy Meier.

It is the responsibility of the vigilant researcher to investigate the many aspects of this man's testimony and life story before writing off the whole situation as a fanciful hoax. As always, a clear head and open mind is required, along with the self awareness of avoiding possible gullibility due to subconscious bias and influence with regards to the acceptance of any material which reinforces the reader's personal preconceived notions.

The Meier story is a fascinating read and the information which can be extracted from his contact reports is of the highest value to anyone with an interest in the world around them. If time reveals Meier as a fraudster who has dedicated his life to deceiving the people of this Earth, then a gigantic question mark will hang over the possibility of extraterrestrial beings visiting this planet, one that will be almost impossible to erase. In the words of Wendelle Stevens, who has investigated the Meier case in greater depth than anyone else; "I've been at this for twenty years. If this is a hoax, there are no real cases."[177]

8

SPACE SECRECY

Oh God! You wouldn't believe it! I'm telling you there are other spacecraft out there...lined up on the far side of the crater edge! They're on the Moon watching us!

Neil Armstrong

THE ADVENT OF SPACE EXPLORATION in the 1960's was a very exciting time for all involved and must have really captured the imagination of the public, because for the first time in our history we were able to leave our home planet and reach for the stars. Of course there are many that believe that the Moon landings were all faked and that in fact man has never ascended higher than 300 miles above the Earth's surface. Many documentaries have raised fascinating arguments against the authenticity of the whole Apollo program and have suggested that all the video and photographic evidence of lunar landings were faked, possibly filmed on a film set somewhere out of sight, all just part of an elaborate hoax. This may well be the case, but the argument *for* is also just as viable.

Another theory is that we *have* been to the Moon and have also set up bases there, however, this wasn't achieved during the public space missions and it wasn't accomplished using the rocket technology that we are familiar with. Some believe that we have travelled there using reverse-engineered alien technology and that the entire NASA setup is but a ruse to mislead the public. As author William Milton Cooper suggested, "No man has ever orbited, landed on, or walked upon the moon in any publicly known space program. If man has ever truly been to the moon it has been done in secret and with a far different technology."[178]

Whatever the truth may be, the fact still remains that "officially" the successful Apollo missions were the only occasions in which we have landed human beings on the surface of the Moon. The "did we land on the moon" conspiracy has been covered in great detail so that side of the argument shall not be covered in this book. Instead, aspects of the official story which is already compelling enough shall be reviewed, whilst also revealing another version of events in which the astronauts did really go but have been forced to keep quiet about what they saw up there. It becomes very apparent when trawling through the masses of conflicting evidence available that nothing is as it seems and NASA hasn't been completely honest with the public since the early days of their conception. Let us now refresh our memories a little and review how the space program was first conceived.

The impossible dream cited in JFK's 1962 speech at Rice University, of landing a man on the Moon before the end of the decade, became a reality on July 20, 1969 as Apollo 11 commander Neil Armstrong descended the Lunar Module's ladder and set foot on the Moon's surface for the first time in human history.

President John F. Kennedy actually announced the ambitious and dramatic goal before a special joint session of Congress on May 25, 1961 a year earlier than his public announcement. His decision to attempt to catch up with the Soviet Union and finally overtake them in the "space race" was largely influenced by a number of political matters, as has been well documented. The Soviets had already successfully managed to send the Sputnik satellite into space in 1957 and four years later on April 12, 1961 Russian cosmonaut Yuri Gagarin became the first human in space, much to the embarrassment of the United States. Although less than a month later on May 5, Alan Shepard followed Gagarin up into orbit becoming the first American in space, but instead of achieving a full orbit of the Earth as his Soviet counterpart had managed, Shepard only flew on a short sub-orbital flight.[8]

During Kennedy's 1961 special message to the Congress on 'Urgent National Needs', he declared his vision for the decade ahead saying, "I believe that this nation should commit itself to achieving the goal, before this decade is out, of landing a man on the moon and returning him safely to the Earth. No single space project in this period will be more impressive to mankind or more important for the long-range exploration of space; and none will be so difficult or expensive to accomplish."

Continuing he said, "We take an additional risk by making it in full view of the world, but as shown by the feat of astronaut Shepard, this very risk enhances our stature when we are successful. But this is not merely a race. Space is open to us now; and our eagerness to share its meaning is not governed by the

---

[8] A sub-orbital flight is a spaceflight which reaches space but does not complete one orbital revolution. An object launched from Earth that reaches 100 km or 62 miles above sea level then begins its descent back to Earth, is considered a sub-orbital spaceflight.

efforts of others. We go into space because whatever mankind must undertake, free men must fully share."[179] Brave and ambitious words from a man who must have been outside the 'loop' considering that he would never get to see how the Apollo missions fared, as he was assassinated in November 1963.

Entire books have been filled with page after page of conspiratorial evidence and theories of the deceitful nature of the President's unexpected murder which, if researched thoroughly enough, seem to lead to the conclusion that he was shot by the Secret Service agent driving the car named William Greer. The farcical Warren Commission that was set up to investigate the incident used a panel that mostly consisted of members of the Council on Foreign Relations (CFR). This fact alone would suggest that some bias was involved in the arrival of conclusions in the case. We shall not be going into that in detail here but it is worth bearing in mind how that decade started, dowsed in suspicious circumstance, secrecy and conspiracy, as we begin to unravel the nature of the "secret" space program that ran parallel to the "official" space program which remains within public view.

This chapter will address the unlikely origins of NASA and its Nazi connections. We will be finding out what the Apollo astronauts really saw up there and learn more about the anomalous aspects of both the Moon and our neighbour Mars, most of which have been hidden from us. All of this information is given in relation to the extraterrestrial phenomenon that we are here to investigate. But before we delve into the unseen world of space exploration let us start the chapter at the beginning and familiarise ourselves with the "official" version of events.

PROJECT MERCURY

The first human spaceflight program of the United States was named Project Mercury which ran from 1959 until 1963. The two goals set were firstly, to put a human in orbit around the Earth, and secondly to achieve it before the Soviet Union. Well during the first Mercury mission in 1961, NASA managed to send Alan Shepard into orbit but they had to settle for second place behind Gagarin.

The entire program consisted of twenty unmanned launches, followed by six manned flights; two suborbital and four orbital flights. Astronaut Leroy Gordon Cooper Jr. commonly known as Gordon Cooper was one of the seven original astronauts in Project Mercury. He goes down in history as the first American to sleep in orbit; he also flew the longest flight of the Mercury program and became the last American to have been launched into orbit alone and complete a solo orbital mission. He would later be involved in the Gemini program which, along with Mercury laid the groundwork for the Apollo moon-landing program.

As one of the most outspoken astronauts, Gordon "Gordo" Cooper would later become fascinated with the subject of UFOs, partly due to his discussions with other astronauts and also because of the UFO sightings he had personally witnessed. He became a proponent for disclosure and open discussion on the subject and in 1985 he appeared before a United Nations panel discussion on UFOs. The head chair that day was U.N. Secretary-General Kurt Waldheim. Here are some of U.S. Astronaut Cooper's thoughts on the topic as discussed during the panel meeting:

"I believe that these extraterrestrial vehicles and their crews are visiting this planet from other planets, which are a little more technically advanced than we are on Earth. I feel that we need to have a top level, coordinated program to scientifically collect and analyze data from all over the Earth concerning any type of encounter, and to determine how best to interfere with these visitors in a friendly fashion." One would imagine that NASA must have been tearing their hair out when they heard about this open discussion going on record before a U.N. panel.

Most of their astronauts have kept their lips tightly sealed regarding matters of extraterrestrial intelligence, either because they know nothing or they have sworn an oath to remain silent on such matters, if the following evidence has any credulity to it, then one would be swayed towards believing the latter. Cooper went on to admit that he had seen unidentified objects flying in the skies in the early days of his career and such admittance should be accepted as a highly creditable testimony considering the man's credentials.

In Cooper's own words, "I should point out that I am not an experienced UFO professional researcher, I have not as yet had the privilege of flying a UFO nor of meeting the crew of one. However, I do feel that I am somewhat qualified to discuss them, since I have been into the fringes of the vast areas of which they travel. Also, I did have occasion in 1951 to have two days of observation of many flights of them, of different sizes flying in fighter formation, generally from west to east over Europe."[180]

An American astronaut admitting he has personally witnessed unidentified flying objects should be a real eye-opener to all the naysayers and debunkers out there. It is testimonies like these which could really challenge the status quo and help raise awareness of the mysterious field of UFO research. Cooper isn't the only astronaut to have voiced his opinion on the subject. Following a successful return from the Moon, Apollo 14 astronaut Edgar Mitchell was quoted as saying "My neck still aches as I had to constantly turn my head around because we felt we were not alone there. We had no choice but pray." The Moon has always amazed and bewildered humankind, its mystery demanding ever closer investigation which ultimately resulted in man's desire to land on the surface and explore the unknown territory reaching fruition.

THE APOLLO PROGRAM

Remarkably, the Apollo program which followed the Mercury and Gemini projects only ran for nine years from 1963 to 1972 and was created with the intent of landing humans on the surface of the Moon and returning them safely home again. The six missions that achieved this goal returned a wealth of scientific data including almost 400 kilos of lunar samples. The twelve men who walked on the Moon between 1969 and 1972 brought back over 1/3 of a ton of moon rocks. The range of experiments done by the astronauts included seismic, soil mechanics, lunar ranging, heat flow, meteoroids, solar wind experiments and magnetic field investigation. Here is a chronological list of all the Apollo missions and a brief summary of the details involved:

Apollo 1 - (initially designated Apollo Saturn-204 and AS-204) was scheduled to be the first manned mission with a target launch date of February 21, 1967. But all three pilots (Grissom, White and Chaffee) were killed in the cabin fire which took place on the launch pad and destroyed the Command Module during the test flight on January 27.

Apollo 2 - Refers to the second unmanned flight AS-202.

Apollo 3 - Refers to AS-203 which carried only the aerodynamic nose cone.

Apollo 4 - Saturn/Apollo 4 (AS-501) was an unmanned mission and was the first all-up test of the three stage Saturn V rocket. It carried a payload of an Apollo Command and Service Module (CSM) into Earth orbit.

Apollo 5 - The unmanned Saturn/Apollo 5 was the first test flight of the Lunar Module (LM).

Apollo 6 - The unmanned Saturn/Apollo 6 mission was designed as the final qualification of the Saturn V launch vehicle and Apollo spacecraft for manned Apollo missions.

Apollo 7 - First crewed Apollo flight was launched 11th October, 1968. Earth Orbiter (Schirra, Eisele, Cunningham).

Apollo 8 - 21st December, 1968. Lunar Orbiter (Borman, Lovell, Anders).

Apollo 9 - 3rd March, 1969. Earth Orbiter (McDivitt, Scott, Schweikart). First crewed Lunar Module test.
Apollo 10 - 8th May, 1969. Lunar Orbiter (Stafford, Young, Cernan).

Apollo 11 - 16th July, 1969. First Lunar Landing (Armstrong, Aldrin, Collins) Landed on Moon 20th July on Sea of Tranquillity and returned to Earth 24th July.

Apollo 12 -14th November, 1969. Lunar Landing (Conrad, Bean, Gordon). Landed on Moon 19th November at Ocean of Storms and returned to Earth 24th November.

Apollo 13 -11th April, 1970. Lunar Flyby and Return. (Lovell, Haise, Swigert) Malfunction forced lunar landing to be aborted before returning to Earth 17th April.

Apollo 14 - 31st January, 1971. Lunar Landing, (Shepard, Mitchell, Roosa). Landed on Moon 5th February at Fra Mauro and returned to Earth 9th February.

Apollo 15 - 26th July, 1971. Lunar Landing, (Scott, Irwin, Worden). Landed on Moon 30th July at Hadley Rille and returned to Earth 7th August.

Apollo 16 - 16th April, 1972. Lunar Landing, (Young, Duke, Mattingly). Landed on Moon 20th April at Descartes and returned to Earth 27th April.

Apollo 17 - 7th December, 1972. Lunar Landing. (Cernan, Schmitt, Evans). Landed on Moon 11th December, 1972 on Taurus-Littrow and returned to Earth 19th December.

Each manned mission to the Moon consisted of a Command Module (CM) and a Lunar Module (LM), upon reaching orbit the two units would separate. One crew member would remain inside the CM which would orbit the Moon, leaving the other two astronauts to land the LM on the lunar surface before external exploration could commence. Once returned to the CM, the team could journey back home to Earth.

So, why have there only been six successful lunar landings since 1969? And why has no other country been compelled to follow the Americans. It seems very suspicious that NASA would spend such a vast amount of time, money and resources on the Apollo missions only to stop in 1972 and call it a day. As Ingo Swann, author and co-creator of CRV (co-ordinate remote viewing) wrote' "In December, 1972, Apollo 17 was the LAST American Moon craft to the Moon. At that point, American Moon visits abruptly ceased for reasons that were never adequately explained. The remaining three Apollo crafts which were already built at enormous expense, were left to rot."[181]

The Russians were the last to officially land on the lunar surface aboard the probe Luna 24 on August 19, 1976; the probe collected 170 grams of lunar dirt and sent it back to Earth. But surely by now we could have progressed much further in the field of space exploration, possibly achieving a successful manned mission to

Mars or at the very least we should be experts at Moon exploration. So what happened up there during those six missions? Why haven't we returned? Have NASA been completely honest with their findings or is there more to this story than meets the eye? Before taking a closer look at what the Apollo astronauts really saw on their travels and why they are more than hesitant to return, let us examine the sinister origins of the United States "Official" Space Program in an attempt to further understand the secrecy involved.

OPERATION PAPERCLIP

As WWII was drawing to a close, Germany's strategic position was at a severe logistical disadvantage following their failure to successfully invade the Soviet Union (Operation Barbarossa June-Dec 1941) coupled with the added firepower of the United States Army as they joined forces with the allies. The war was also longer than the German military industries had prepared for. So, in the spring of 1943, Germany began to recall all scientists and technicians from their designated combat units so they could be put to better use in areas of research and development.

Dieter K. Huzel, author of *Peenemunde to Canaveral* wrote, "Overnight, Ph.D.s were liberated from KP duty, masters of science were recalled from orderly service, mathematicians were hauled out of bakeries, and precision mechanics ceased to be truck drivers."[182] After identifying and tracking down the right personnel, the recall effort culminated in the Osenberg List written by engineering scientist Werner Osenberg, who was head of the Wehrforschungsgemeinschaft (Military Research Association). Shredded pieces of the Osenberg List were discovered in a dysfunctional toilet by a Polish laboratory technician in March 1945. A list of scientists that were set to be interrogated was compiled by U.S. Army Major Robert B. Staver, Chief of the Jet Propulsion Section of the Research and Intelligence Branch of the U.S. Army Ordnance based in London. Infamous Nazi rocket scientist Wernher von Braun topped the list of scientists, codenamed the 'Black List'.

Some of von Braun's associates included Arthur Rudolph, chief operations director at Nordhausen, described as "100 per cent Nazi, dangerous type". Kurt Debus, SS officer and rocket launch specialist whose report stated that "he should be interned as a menace to the security of the Allied Forces." And Hubertus Strughold, who authorized workers to conduct human "experiments" at Dachau and Auschwitz concentration camps where inmates were said to have been put into low-pressure chambers and frozen, which often resulted in death. Strughold would later become "the father of space medicine" after designing NASA's onboard life-support systems. Kurt Debus became a director at Kennedy Space Centre in Florida and Arthur Rudolph became project director of the Saturn V rocket program that sent the Americans to the Moon.

Following a telegram sent to Colonel Joel Holmes at the US Pentagon HQ on May 22, 1945 by Major Staver, his original intention to interview only rocket scientists altered, as it soon became deemed "important for [the] Pacific War"[183] to evacuate the German technicians along with their families. This was also considered to be a necessary tactic to deny the Soviets the expertise that could be gained from possible future contact with any of the German specialists. The Osenberg List engineers and their families were initially housed in Landshut, Bavaria in southern Germany after their capture. Most of them had been working at the German Army Research Centre Peenemunde (ARC) on the Baltic coast developing the V-2 rocket.

Two years previous, following the Allied invasion of Italy in September 1943, the Alsos Mission, which was commanded by Colonel Boris Pash, a former Manhattan Project security officer, was created to investigate the German nuclear energy project. In order to prevent the Soviets from capturing the personnel, records and material relevant to the German nuclear project, the Mission employees searched to attain these things first.

After successfully managing to track down and remove many of the German research personnel along with a fair amount of records and equipment, the Alsos Mission took most of the senior personnel into custody including Werner Heisenberg, the head of the German nuclear energy project, as he was considered to be a great asset to the Americans: "…he was worth more to us than ten divisions of Germans".[184] Although it was primarily the nuclear physicists and rocket engineers that were the most sought after, various Allied teams were also on the lookout for naval weapons experts, chemists and doctors of medicine.

A program originally named Operation Overcast that began on July 19, 1945 was created for the U.S. Joint Chiefs of Staff (JCS) to manage the captured ARC engineers. However, the program had to be renamed the following year in March 1946 due to the locals' awareness of the name "Camp Overcast", the place where the scientists were being housed, thus Overcast changed its name to Operation Paperclip. The name derives from the fact that the individuals selected to go to the U.S. were distinguished by paperclips on their files which joined their scientific credentials with regular immigration forms.

Operation Paperclip (or Project Paperclip as it was sometimes referred to) was the codename under which German scientists from Nazi Germany were extracted during and after the final stages of WWII, by the U.S. intelligence and military services. In August of 1945, Operation Overcast was authorised by President Truman, and less than three months later on the 18th November, the first group of German scientists arrived in America. On arrival they were transported to Fort Bliss, Texas, where they developed rockets for the U.S. Army.

The rockets were then tested and launched at White Sands Proving Ground in New Mexico and in 1950, the team led by Wernher von Braun, built the Army's Jupiter ballistic missile at Redstone Arsenal near Huntsville, Alabama.[185] The Joint Intelligence Objectives Agency (JIOA) was established in 1945 and was directly responsible for Operation Paperclip which would soon come under the control of the globalists based in the Council on Foreign Relations (CFR)[186]. It is also worth mentioning that some of the Paperclip scientists brought to the States were also employed by Yale University, the home of the notorious and not so secret Skull and Bones Society.[187] Another program designed specifically to get German scientists away from the Soviets and out of Europe was code-named Project 63, where most of them were given employment by defence contractors or universities rather than working for the U.S. government.

According to Linda Hunt, despite government claims that Paperclip was terminated in 1947, the project was "the biggest, longest-running operation involving Nazis in our country's history. The project continued nonstop until 1973 - decades longer than was previously thought. And remnants of it are still in operation today."[188] Despite all the attempts at secrecy, in 1958 an article about Wernher von Braun in *Time* magazine openly mentioned the project.[189] Von Braun was quoted as saying "The British could not afford us; The Russians terrified us so we went to the Americans." Research has shown that he was more than just an ardent Nazi but was actually a Major in the 'Schutz-Staffel' or 'SS', which not only became one of the largest organisations in the Third Reich but also the most powerful. In 1937, he joined the Nazi party and three years later he joined the SS. He has been described as a "murderous fascist who was prepared to spill the blood of innocents in order to fulfil his own ambitions."[190]

Von Braun was the leader of what is often referred to as the "rocket team" who worked in missile development for the Nazis during the Second World War. The V-2 ballistic missile was developed at a secret laboratory at Peenemunde on the Baltic coast, then later following Allied bombing raids which destroyed this site, research facilities were moved to Dora – Mittlebrau where the missiles were manufactured at a forced labour factory called Mittelwerke. The Mittlewerke/Dora concentration camp and underground rocket facility was located about 6km outside the town of Nordhausen on the southern side of the Harz Mountains; here lay a series of underground, impenetrable caverns.

Germany may have been losing the war but behind closed doors they managed to develop such groundbreaking technologies as jet aircraft, nerve gas, supersonic rockets, hardened armour, guided missiles and even stealth technology. The Third Reich used Jewish prisoners as slaves to build their underground bases in Germany where they were forced to manufacture V-1 and V-2 rockets in 1944-45. It is estimated that between 7,000 and 20,000 slave labourers, mostly prisoners of war of which many were French and Soviet, were worked to death at various German rocket facilities during the war.

They built vast laboratories and underground facilities, including the one at Nordhausen which used the entire side of a mountain. Many of the 60,000 slave workers had arrived straight from Buchenwald Concentration Camp and were constantly held at gunpoint as they worked tirelessly to convert the former calcium sulphite mines into functioning facilities. The galvanizing shop known as Gallery 39 was an especially frightful cavern, where it is said that the lung damage inflicted by the toxic fumes emanating from the metal treatment plant meant that very few workers would survive longer than a fortnight. And those marginally fortunate enough to work elsewhere on the site were warned that any infringement of the rules would lead to death by hanging.

Survivors of the Dora – Mittlebrau recall that on one occasion, as a warning to others, twelve workers were ordered to be hanged by Von Braun after he'd noticed some damage to the system guidance of some of the rockets he was inspecting. Over 20,000 deaths were witnessed by Von Braun in less than two years within the caverns of the Nazi scientists. During his tenure working for the U.S. he was also involved in operations more covert than the Space Program, when he was employed at Area 51 in Nevada developing missiles for use in the deployment of nuclear warheads. It was here where he developed a nuclear powered trans-atmospheric vehicle. In an article published in *Faster than Light* magazine, author Geoff Richardson wrote about von Braun saying, "That such a man could spend his later years standing next to presidents at medal presentations and giving speeches on the wonders of space exploration, rather than rotting in prison where he belonged, is a testament to the political realities of the cold war."[191]

THE BIRTH OF NASA

During the spring of 1958 after Congressional hearings, legislation was passed by Congress and on July 29, the National Aeronautics and Space Act was signed into law by President Eisenhower. All rockets used in the United States and Soviet Union space exploration programs were preceded by the V-2 rocket designed by Von Braun and his Nazi cohorts. Von Braun's rocket development centre was transferred from the Army to the recently established NASA and he was immediately directed to start work building the giant Saturn rockets.

He soon became director of NASA's Marshall Space Flight Centre and led the team which built the super-booster Saturn V launch vehicle that would give the Americans the power to liftoff into space for the first time and head for the Moon. Von Braun was later awarded the Congressional Medal of Honour for his services to the Apollo Space Program.

Linda Hunt wrote "...the Germans dominated the rocket program to such an extent that they held the chief and deputy slots of every major division and laboratory. And their positions at Marshall and the Kennedy Space Centre at Cape Canaveral, Florida, were similar to those they had held during the war."[192]

So just how is it possible that America's greatest enemies came to be the countries prize assets, working in prominent places within the government and virtually taking the Americans by the scruff of the neck and dragging them into space? Without the scientific expertise of a large number of Nazi scientists, the U.S. Space Program would never have come into existence. A meeting took place between CIA director Allen Dulles and former Nazi spymaster General Reinhard Gehlen, where the German offered to forward the extensive spy network within his control into the hands of the CIA in exchange for the expunction of the scientists' Nazi pasts. Their dossiers were rewritten and any self incriminating evidence in connection to their involvement with the Nazis was eliminated.

This apparently went ahead despite the orders previously expressed by President Truman who had stated that anyone found "to have been a member of the Nazi party and more than a nominal participant in its activities, or an active supporter of Nazism militarism" was to be excluded from any U.S. employment. This would have also excluded Von Braun from any involvement in the space program, as documents written by the military governor in 1947 had described him as a "potential security threat".

However, in a report written only months later he had been reassessed and it was now considered that "he may not constitute a security threat to the U.S."[193] Von Braun's brother Magnus who was also brought to America had his pro-Nazi record expunged even though he had been declared a "dangerous German Nazi" by counterintelligence officers.

It is clear that there exists a controlling group above the authority of the President which has been making decisions without his consent. Evidently, Truman was totally unaware of the violation of his direct orders concerning the non-admittance of Nazis into the U.S. services under Project Paperclip. As Linda Hunt noted, "The effect of the cover-up involved far more than merely whitewashing the information in the dossiers. Serious allegations of crimes not only were expunged from the records, but were never even investigated."

So we've seen how NASA originated, by the covert collaboration with a large group of scientific-minded Nazis who spearheaded the organisations responsible for initiating the space race allegedly 'against' the Soviets. But further research suggests that there never existed in earnest, a competitive race between the Americans and the Russians, in actuality it was more of a combined U.S./Soviet space program controlled by high-level elitists and run by Nazi scientists. Nazi V-2 rockets were captured by both nations in order to jumpstart their space programs, in fact in the 1950s a joke which became quite common during the Cold War era first surfaced during an argument between an American and a Russian, when they shouted at each other "Our German scientists are better than your German scientists."

According to author Joseph P. Farrell, "[I]t is perhaps significant that some contemporary observers of the American space program and its odd thirty-year-long 'holding pattern' and tapestry of inconsistencies, lies and obfuscations have long suspected that there are indeed two space programs inside the U.S. government, the public NASA one, and a quasi-independent one based deep within covert and black projects."[194]

In the spring of 1945 as Nazi Germany was been closed in on by the Allied forces, it is claimed that orders were given to some top American commanders to leave all the rockets, along with their plans found at Nordhausen for the Russians. Unofficially however, some decided to ignore these orders and managed to abscond with many documents, plans, manuals and about a hundred V-2s.

One American officer went on record saying "We gave the Russians the key to Sputnik... [F]or ten weeks, the American army had in its hands the rocket plant that gave the Russians their head start in the missile race."[195] Former Petty Officer in the U.S. Navy, Milton William Cooper, has become somewhat of an authority on information regarding the alien presence on Earth and the US Government's involvement. Discussing his knowledge of NASA and the space program he wrote that "a public charade of antagonism between the Soviet Union and the United States has been maintained over all these years in order to fund projects in the name of National Defence when in fact we are the closest allies." [196]

The space program was always designed to be a public program which acted as a pool where funds could be siphoned off for work on covert projects, some of which concerned the development of alien technology as well as funding for possible bases on the Moon. During his time in Germany with the Nazis, Wernher von Braun and Hitler were said to have been intent on colonising the Moon. This sentiment was later to be externalised via Project Horizon; the US Army's proposal to place a military base on the moon.

Von Braun was in no doubt of the existence of extraterrestrials and believed that the advancements achieved in the projects which he was involved in, were a direct result of back-engineered alien technology. On the 3rd June 1959, during a test flight, the Juno II rocket was mysteriously deflected whilst travelling during the re-entry phase and failed to achieve orbit. Von Braun commented in the German press; "We find ourselves faced by powers, which are far stronger than we had hitherto assumed, and whose base is at present unknown to us. More I cannot say at present. We are now engaged in entering into closer contact with those powers, and in six or nine months it may be possible to speak with some precision on the matter." [197]

Dr. Carol Rosin, Von Braun's spokesperson during the latter years of his life, has confirmed the sentiments expressed above by stating that "Wernher Von Braun knew about the extraterrestrial issue." One can only speculate at this juncture as to what von Braun was referring to when he talked about "entering into closer contact with those powers". He could have meant the Soviets or he could be talking about alien species, whatever he was driving at it is clear that the man knew much more than he let on. The following quote from *Esotera Magazine* would suggest that von Braun had not been talking about any human political power after all, when he declared that "extraterrestrial powers do exist, and they are more powerful than previously thought. I'm not authorized to give you any more details on the issue."

PROJECT HORIZON

The U.S. Army had a report dated 9th June 1959, which proposed a plan to place a military base on the moon by 1965. This report was titled *Project Horizon Report – A U.S. Army Study for the Establishment of a Lunar Outpost.*[198] This proposal was intended to serve the United States in a multitude of ways, both politically and scientifically and most importantly for reasons of national security.

Contrary to suggestions that it is impossible for man to proceed beyond the Van Allen belt for reasons concerning radiation and that the environment in space is non-conducive to human life, the report held no such qualms stating that "there are no known technical barriers to the establishment of a manned installation on the moon". The report declared that it is imperative that the United States be the first to establish a lunar base in order to achieve scientific and security objectives plus political prestige and military dominance, although the full extent of the military potential cannot be predicted "it is probable that observation of the earth and space vehicles from the moon will prove to be highly advantageous."

In section 3b of the report under the sub-heading 'Reason for Requirement', the issue of moon-based weapons systems was raised, suggesting that the employment of such weapons "against earth or space targets may prove to be feasible and desirable." Military power based on the moon was considered to be a strong deterrent against war "because of the extreme difficulty, from the enemy point of view, of eliminating our ability to retaliate."

Senator Lyndon B. Johnson, prior to succeeding JFK as the U.S. President in 1963, is on record speaking about the possibility of military dominance using the Moon as an outpost for the United States military. Whilst addressing the Senate Democratic Caucus on January 7, 1958, just one year before Project Horizon was put into writing, Lyndon declared the following:

"Control of space means control of the world...from space, the masters of infinity would have the power to control the Earth's weather, to cause drought and flood, to change the tides and raise the levels of the sea, to divert the Gulf Stream and change the climate to frigid. There is something more powerful than the ultimate weapon. That is the ultimate position - the position of total control over the Earth that lies somewhere in outer space...And if there is an ultimate position, then our national goal and the goal of all free men must be to win and hold that position."[199] Very chilling words indeed from a future president whose intentions don't appear to have been to solely protect his country, but rather to gain outright power over all other nations.

WHAT NASA DOESN'T TELL YOU

There are many people who through either their own extensive research or personal experience, have come to the conclusion that we have not been told the whole truth regarding NASA's space program. NASA is considered to be a civilian agency although many of its programs are funded by the Department of Defence budget and most of the astronauts are subject to military security regulations. The Apollo Missions are of particular interest to many because of the vast amount of inconsistencies involved in both the photographic and video archive footage and also official explanations and information offered to the public by NASA spokespersons.

Recent research has revealed that conditions on the Moon could be very different from what the public has been led to believe. The massive NASA archives are all supposed to be in the public domain and accessible to all but it seems that very few people have been given access to the genuine original material. Even one of NASA's foremost scientists Dr. Farouk El Baz expressed what many people have suspected when he declared that "not every discovery has been announced to the public."[200]

Literally millions of photographs are currently been stored in the NASA library which is said to include an impressive catalogue of transmission tapes and videotapes documenting the presence of UFOs.

Astronauts working in orbit have filmed many strange anomalous objects flying above the Earth's atmosphere. Documentary filmmaker Chris Everard claims that he received an anonymous parcel at his home which contained a box full of video cassettes of NASA footage of the live feeds taken directly from the astronauts' cameras. This extraordinary material can be seen in his documentary film series *Secret Space I, II* and *III*. As Everard contests, there is something highly unusual taking place in the upper atmosphere of Planet Earth and NASA have successfully suppressed such information, much to the detriment of the human population.

Using an image intensifying camera, fascinating footage of a group of UFOs was filmed on 19th November, 1996 during the Mission STS-80. A specialist satellite designed by the German Space Agency - DARA, was taken up into space in the payload bay of the Space Shuttle then released, where it was left to float in space and take still and video images of its surroundings.

The satellite was called the ACTS/ORFEUS-SPAS: (Advanced Communications Technology Satellite – Orbiting and Retrievable Far and Extreme Ultraviolet Spectrometer-Shuttle Pallet Satellite) and as the name suggests, it films the ultraviolet spectrum. It was built to "make observations and take measurements of celestial objects that emit most of their light in the ultraviolet band of the electromagnetic spectrum that is not visible to the naked eye." [201]

The purpose of recording such data is to help scientists to learn more about the life cycle of stars and to better understand how they interact with interstellar gas.

The STS-80 Mission saw an extraordinary event take place in front of the lens, where a number of UFOs coming from behind the satellite into view began to line-up in a circular formation with a single UFO appearing last and positioning itself in the centre of the circle. Once the formation was completed, the light orbs glowed once brightly as if taking a bow at the end of a show. Another piece of ultraviolet footage from the same mission shows a large object, possibly 20 km in diameter, emerging from out of the Earth's atmosphere accompanied by a number of other unidentified objects in the vicinity which appeared to be stationary. Also in 1996, a UFO was filmed flying past the shuttle after liftoff, then later as they were repairing the Hubble telescope, Mission Control can be heard saying "looks like you got an object right in front of you Mark if you look out there..." Later, the astronauts were 'flashed' by something while re-entering the shuttle. The conversation between the astronauts and Mission Control went as follows:

ASTRONAUT 1: "What was that flash?"

MISSION CONTROL: "What Mark?"

ASTRONAUT 1: "I saw a light flash past me just there. Did you see it? I thought it must have been me. I thought it was my imagination."

ASTRONAUT 2: "Yeah, I saw it too...so it's not. There were two of them. There's another one, what are they?"

Other video footage from a different Space Shuttle Mission on September 15, 1991 reveals evidence of the possible deployment of some type of plasma beam weaponry being fired from Earth at large UFOs in the upper atmosphere. Lt. Col. Philip J. Corso, a former Chief of the Pentagon's Foreign Technology desk in Army Research and Development, confirmed the existence of such weaponry in his controversial book *The Day after Roswell*.

In his documentary *Secret Space*, Chris Everard claims that the extraterrestrial scenario goes far beyond mere Earth visitation, suggesting that a secret weapons program exists to defend our planet from an 'outside' threat. He stated that "we are also in a situation where the Star Wars Weapons Program which was meant to be a protective shield against nuclear attack, is actually proactively being used to wage a war on extraterrestrial craft."

The 1991 Mission STS-48 had a camera on board the shuttle which was focused on infinity, beyond the curvature of the Earth's upper atmosphere seen in the video footage which was shot between 8.30 and 8.45 pm GMT. This piece of footage shows an object roughly 180 miles away which had to be at least 700 yards in diameter in order for it to have been viewable from an onboard camera. The object heads northwards when suddenly there is a flash of light which causes the UFO to accelerate out of the atmosphere in an immediate u-turn at around 88,000 miles an hour; about the same speed as a meteor or shooting star. This travelling object couldn't be either of those as they travel down into our atmosphere, not out of it. A beam of light is then seen shooting past where the UFO had just been, which seems at first glance to be something that has being fired from below. Watching this footage, it is clear to see why researchers are suggesting that 'someone' down here is firing 'something' at 'someone' up there. Whatever the true explanation may be, it is extremely obvious that NASA is keeping a lot of archive material very close to their chests.

You know something is been hidden when even amateur astronomers have observed and recorded strange 'lights' and anomalous structures on the Moon for decades. Joseph F. Goodavage, an American journalist, writer and astrologer who interviewed Immanuel Velikovsky in 1970,[202] reported that over two hundred white "dome shaped" structures had been observed and catalogued, before they often vanished mysteriously and reappeared elsewhere.

In 1994, 1.8 million photographs were taken of the Moon during the Clementine Mission. The Deep Space Program Science Experiment 'Clementine' was launched from Vandenberg Air Force Base on January 24. Different variations of images were taken by the Clementine Probe including full colour photographs and according to some researchers, the Apollo 8 mission also brought back colour photographs which clearly show evidence of green vegetation.

The Jose Escamilla documentary film *UFO – The Greatest Story Ever Denied Part II - Moon Rising*, talks in depth about the lies and deception forced upon the public by NASA regarding the facts about our Moon. By colourizing many of the black and white photographic images sent back by Clementine in '94, Escamilla raises questions about the authenticity of the publicly available NASA archive material and suggests that everything we have been told about the Moon is a lie.

Quoting from the site promoting the film[203] "The suppressing of the evidence that there may have been civilizations existing on the Moon, or even more incredible, the possibility they are still there brings into question why we have been kept in the dark. The biggest insult is we've been led to believe the moon is a grey - colourless rock. On the contrary, The Moon appears to be a small planet teeming with life and structures the likes of which you have never seen before until now. At least it appears to have been inhabited in 1994 when these photos were taken."

In Escamilla's opinion, there is no doubt that we have landed on the Moon, the question that he raises is what was waiting for us when we arrived and how did NASA manage to conceal it all. As a Bell Communications/NASA insider allegedly said "we lied about everything". Images from the Clementine Probe were made available for public consumption over the internet on the Clementine Lunar Image Browsers 1.5 until 2009, but following the release of Escamilla's documentary *Moon Rising*, it has been replaced by version 2.0. This newer version has removed all anomalies, allowing the viewer to see only what NASA want you to see. The *Moon Rising* Archives contain many more anomalies that were available to view until 2009. Using the Clementine 1.5 Web Browser, Joseph P. Skipper apparently discovered one object resting on top of crater Zeeman, located on the far side of the Moon, which was determined to have been ten times larger than the City of Los Angeles. This is just one example of anomalous objects being erased from NASA's image bank in order to perpetuate the lies that they've deemed necessary to conceal the truth.

ERASE AND DENY

There are a growing number of ex-NASA employees coming forward and unveiling different aspects of a monumental cover-up, one of those is a former NASA slide technician called Donna Hare. She was employed for fifteen years by a NASA sub-contractor at the NASA Johnson Space Centre in Houston and received a number of space awards during her tenure as slide technician. The National Aeronautics Space Administration awarded her the 1969 Apollo Achievement award; she also received the 1973 Skylab award and a medallion for success on the Skylab-Suez Test project. And Ann Richards, Texas Governor to the Advisory Committee of Psychology Associates, awarded Donna Hare a 1994 recommendation for her skill as a Technical Artist.

During a 1995 radio interview on *Washington DC Radio Station* she openly discussed her work and professional involvement as a technical illustrator in the Space Program, where she worked in the Precision Slide Lab in building 8 of the photo lab, throughout the years of the Apollo missions. Here she drew lunar maps, launch sites and landing sites, reducing art work to one inch by one inch drawings. She worked alongside astronauts and even worked on flight manuals and she has seen pretty much all the different types of images available that are still used in the Space Program today.

The following information was derived from a transcript of the radio show called *UFO's Saturday Night* which was broadcast on

June 5, 1995.[204] Donna Hare first became aware that NASA were hiding something following an incident that took place whilst she was testing the boundaries of her secret clearance and wandered into a restricted area where they developed pictures taken from satellites as well as all of the Apollo flight missions. She started talking with one of the photographers and developers as he was making a mosaic of photos using lots of smaller photos to make a larger photo pattern. Whilst she was studying the pictures and learning new methods about the whole organisation of the images, the photographer directed her attention to one area of an image and then said to her "Look at that." He was pointing to a very white circular dot in a black and white photograph, so she asked him if it was simply a spot on the emulsion, to which he replied "Well I can't tell you, but spots on the emulsion do not leave round circles of shadows."

She looked closer and realised that she was in fact looking at a round shadow under the white dot in an area where there were pine trees that were also casting shadows in the same direction as the round shadow. Hare said it was a shadow of some aerial phenomena because it was higher than the trees but not too high and was still close enough to the ground to cast a shadow. She described it as spherical but ever so slightly elongated.

Hare asked "Is it a UFO?" to which he replied "Well I can't tell you". After questioning "What are we going to do with this piece of information?" his response was very revealing as he explained "Well we have to airbrush these things out before we sell these photographs to the public." Suddenly she understood the implications; "I realised at that point that there is a procedure setup to take care of this type of information from the public."

So what is clarified here is that a professional slide technician working at NASA, with access to restricted areas, has admitted that the standard procedure put in place by NASA is to airbrush out all aerial phenomena from all existent negatives taken from their satellites and space missions. Richard Hoagland, a specialist on lunar artefacts and also a former NASA employee, says that NASA continue to retouch or partially refocus photo materials before publishing them in public files and catalogues. If the public are not being told the truth about what is on the Apollo slides, what else could they be hiding?

Donna Hare went on to discuss another incident which she felt was very important, about a man that she had dated who was in quarantine with the astronauts straight after coming back from the moon.

She asked him about the saucers she had seen in the satellite photographs and wondered if he knew anything about that, "he told me that every astronaut, every moon trip had been followed by craft, by saucers, that every one of them, every astronaut that went to the moon, now I don't know about other sites but they all had seen it and all had been told to keep quiet about it and they were threatened with jail and their whole retirement, everything taken away from them." He then told her that if she ever mentioned to anyone that he had told her all of this information, that he would deny the fact that the conversation ever took place.

These views are shared by ex-NASA employee Maurice Chatelain who has publicly expressed the fact that "all Apollo and Gemini flights were followed, both at a distance and sometimes also quite closely, by space vehicles of extraterrestrial origin-flying saucers, or UFOs, if you want to call them by that name. Every time it occurred, the astronauts informed Mission Control, who then ordered absolute silence."[205]

Every moon trip had been followed by craft? Such information has clearly been successfully omitted from the public arena. The official view within scientific circles regarding extraterrestrial life continues to be one of denial, after all, they continue to pump money into the SETI program in hope of one day receiving a mere frequency signal from possible other life out there in the universe. Nobody seems to be mentioning the fact that UFO's have been seen during every Apollo mission by numerous astronauts. In late 1973, NASA finally confirmed that 25 astronauts had seen UFOs during lunar missions although it would seem that this statement didn't reach the public domain.

Regarding the Apollo 13 mission (popularized by the Hollywood movie starring Tom Hanks) which was aborted before the astronauts were able to disembark the craft, the official version of events states that there was a malfunction with the command module and they were forced to orbit the Moon before returning straight home.

Donna Hare referred to this incident during her radio interview saying that she was told they were very fortunate to have returned, "well he said that it shouldn't have come back, I mean, there was no, ah, they had help. And that was all he would say. He said it was impossible for that craft to have gotten back home." She went on to say that the USA was told not to go "to that certain place on the back side of the moon."

She said that they (the aliens) didn't want the Apollo 13 craft to investigate the part of the Moon where they were heading towards, so not only did they help to rescue the Apollo team but they may have actually caused the malfunction to start with. NASA was told not to go but they chose to ignore it and as a result the mission failed and nearly cost the lives of Capt. James Lovell and his crew. When asked if her contact knew the reasons why they weren't supposed to go there, Hare replied "I guess they didn't want us to see something back there, I don't know, I don't know that part."

WHAT THE ASTRONAUTS REALLY SAW

Retired Command Sergeant Major Robert Dean also believes that they did go to the Moon, but like so many others studying the subject, he remains adamant that NASA cannot be trusted. He turned his full attention to the study of UFO's following his retirement and has travelled to many countries sharing his wealth of knowledge on the subject.

He believes that man landing on the Moon is only half the story and that the real story is what they found when they got there and what was recorded on film. Speaking at the Project Camelot *Awake and Aware* conference held in Los Angeles in 2009, Dean revealed information and photographic evidence exposing the fact that NASA have lied about what they discovered in space. In 2007, NASA admitted that they had inadvertently erased forty rolls of film from the Apollo program. The media reported the story when it was released at the time but nothing was said about it from then on. Dean told his audience "We're talking about hundreds maybe thousands of photographs contained in those rolls. They erased them, why? Because they showed what they ran into on the way to the moon, and what they saw when they got there."

Back in the sixties, NASA had given a contract to the Japanese Space Agency which Dean reckons must have involved lots of money, and the Japanese bought every single negative taken during the Apollo program. These were then stored in their computers where they remain today. It seems that someone at NASA had forgotten about this. Whilst working in Japan, Dean was given copies of some of these images for the purpose of exposing them to the public.[206]

The Apollo 13 astronauts, who suffered great difficulties due to equipment malfunction, only circled the Moon before heading back home but did manage to take some incredible photographs from the window of their craft. In one image that Bob Dean shows from that mission, there are three bright objects in the frame with the moon in the distance. One of the objects is estimated to be five miles long and another at about two miles long. Although the origin of such objects remains a mystery, one thing can be confirmed, these enormous craft are definitely not manmade. So why haven't NASA shared these fascinating details with the world unless they are intent on hiding something? And more importantly, why would they feel obligated to suppress such information in the first place?

About 3 days and 200,000 miles into the Apollo 11 flight, mission control received a cryptic message from the astronauts. The crew required the information on the current position of the S-IVB, the final stage of the rocket that had been jettisoned away two days earlier. The reason that they were so curious to know the exact whereabouts of the S-IVB is because they could see a mysterious object travelling alongside them and if it turned out that it wasn't part of their rocket then it would mean that they were not alone up there.

Astronaut Buzz Aldrin remembered the event saying "there was something out there that was close enough to be observed, what could it be? Mike decided he thought he could see it in the telescope and he was able to do that and when it was in one position it had a series of ellipses, but when you made it real sharp it was sort of L-shaped. That didn't tell us very much." It was apparent that NASA knew very little about the reported object which was obviously an unidentified flying object. Such objects were not uncommon during the Apollo missions and even early Earth-orbit spaceflights going back over the years had indicated that several crews have seen and reported unknown flying objects. Despite the Apollo 11crew having a clear view of the UFO they were understandably wary of reporting it to Mission Control.

Aldrin remarked, "Obviously the three of us were not gonna blurt out "hey Houston we got something moving alongside of us and we don't know what it is. Can you tell us what it is? We weren't about to do that 'cos we know that those transmissions would be heard by all sorts of people and who knows what…somebody would have demanded that we turn back because of aliens or whatever the reason is. So we didn't do that, but we did decide that we'd cautiously ask Houston where…how far away was the S-IVB." The following excerpt is the actual recorded conversation that took place that day in 1969.

APOLLO 11: "do you have any idea where the S-IVB is with respect to us?"

MISSION CONTROL: "standby"

MISSION CONTROL: "Apollo 11 – Houston. The S-IVB is about 6,000 nautical miles from you now. Over."[207]

It was obvious to the crew that what they were looking at was much closer than 6,000 miles so they decided to go to sleep and not talk about it anymore until they arrived back for debriefing. Ham radio operators managed to bypass NASA's broadcasting outlets by using their own VHF receiving equipment and during the two minute interruption in the live television broadcast of the Apollo 11 Moon landing in 1969, hundreds of ham radio operators received the transmission written below loud and clear. According to NASA, the reason for the break in transmission was due to one of the television cameras overheating which consequently interfered with the reception. Many researchers are now of the opinion that both image and sound were deliberately censored. This information was verified by Otto Binder who was part of the NASA team during that famous mission. According to Binder, both Aldrin and Armstrong were walking on the surface some distance away from the LEM when Armstrong grabbed Aldrin's arm in excitement and exclaimed:

ARMSTRONG: What was it? What the hell was it? That's all I want to know!

MISSION CONTROL: What's there? (Malfunction…Garble) Mission Control calling Apollo 11…

APOLLO 11: These babies were huge sir!...Enormous!...Oh God! You wouldn't believe it! I'm telling you there are other spacecraft out there...lined up on the far side of the crater edge! They're on the Moon watching us!

APOLLO 11: Those are giant things. No, no, no – this is not an optical illusion. No-one is going to believe this!

MISSION CONTROL (Christopher Craft): What...what...what? What the hell is happening? What's wrong with you?

APOLLO 11: They're here under the surface.

MISSION CONTROL: What's there? Emission interrupted...interference control calling Apollo 11.

APOLLO 11: We saw some visitors. They were here for a while, observing the instruments.

MISSION CONTROL: Repeat your last information!

APOLLO 11: I say that there were other spaceships. They're lined up in the other side of the crater!

MISSION CONTROL: Repeat, repeat!

APOLLO 11: Let us sound this orbita...in 625 to 5...Automatic relay connected...My hands are shaking so badly I can't do anything. Film it? God, if these damned cameras have picked up anything – what then?

MISSION CONTROL: Have you picked up anything?

APOLLO 11: I didn't have any film at hand. Three shots of the saucers or whatever they were that were ruining the film.

MISSION CONTROL: Control, control here. Are you on your way? What is the uproar with the UFOs over?

APOLLO 11: They've landed here. There they are and they're watching us.

MISSION CONTROL: The mirrors, the mirrors - have you set them up?

APOLLO 11: Yes, they're in the right place. But whoever made those spaceships surely can come tomorrow and remove them. Over and out! [208]

This version of the "top secret tape transcript" was allegedly leaked from a source close to 'the top' according to author Sam Pepper who has since disappeared. When UFO researchers first became aware of the 'Pepper Transcripts', many of them wrote to their congressmen demanding answers and an official confession by NASA regarding the whole cover-up.

In January 1970, NASA responded with a letter addressed to several congressmen from the Assistant Administrator for Legislative Affairs which stated "the incidents...did not take place. Conversations between the Apollo 11 crew and Mission Control were released live during the entire Apollo 11 mission. There were between 1000 and 1500 representatives of the news media and T.V. present at the Houston News Center listening and observing, and not one has suggested that NASA withheld any news or conversations of this nature."[209]

Such information is virtually impossible to validate but nevertheless it is always worth considering an alternative version of events when trying to siphon out the truth of any given situation. Is it possible that somebody faked the reported "secret" transmission and sent the radio waves into the ether just to confuse matters? Such a scenario could seem to the rational mind, to be more likely than Armstrong and Aldrin witnessing enormous spaceships upon arrival on the Moon. But let us consider for a brief moment that such an event did occur, extraterrestrial life was already present and watching the Americans' every move; with an estimated 600 million people watching back home, then surely for the sake of national security NASA would have had no choice but to interrupt the live broadcast until the situation was more stable.

Ex-NASA employee Otto Binder concluded that "if true, one can surmise that mission control went into a dither and then a huddle, after which they sternly [ordered] the moonwalkers to 'forget' what they saw and carry on casually and calmly as if nothing had happened."[210] Maurice Chatelain, the former NASA Chief of Communications Systems[9], has also gone public with information regarding the Apollo 11 story, and in 1979 he confirmed that Armstrong had indeed made the aforementioned communication regarding UFOs on or in a crater.

"The encounter was common knowledge in NASA" Chatelain revealed, "but nobody has talked about it until now." Chatelain went on to confirm that in order to keep the secret information

---

[9] Other sources claim Chatelain worked for a NASA sub-contractor as a "low-level engineer"

from the public, the Apollo 11 transmissions were deliberately muted on more than one occasion. He was an electronics engineer who specialised in telecommunications so his claims are to be considered highly credible due to his area of professional expertise. He would later become a proponent of the ancient astronaut theory, publishing his book *Our Cosmic Ancestors* in 1975. As well as owning eleven patents whilst employed at North American Aviation, he also designed and built the Apollo communications and data processing systems.

Scientist, oceanographer, and former Soviet submarine captain Dr. Vladimir Azhazha, was another who spoke publicly confirming the Apollo 11 encounters described in the "Pepper Transcripts". Speaking on the subject he said "According to our information, the encounter was reported immediately after the landing of the module. Neil Armstrong relayed the message to Mission Control that two large, mysterious objects were watching them after having landed near the moon module. But his message was never heard by the public-because NASA censored it."

He also claimed that the UFOs present departed minutes later. Dr. Aleksandr Kazantsev, another Soviet scientist has gone on record stating that Buzz Aldrin filmed UFOs from inside the Lunar Module using colour movie film; he then continued to film them as he ventured outside for the first time with Armstrong.[211]

It has been reported that following the Apollo 11 astronauts' return to Earth, a professor who remains anonymous, approached Neil Armstrong at a NASA symposium and became engaged in an earnest conversation with the famous astronaut.

PROFESSOR: What REALLY happened out there with Apollo 11?

ARMSTRONG: It was incredible, of course we had always known there was a possibility – the fact is we were warned off! There was never any question then of a space station or a moon city.

PROFESSOR: How do you mean "warned off"?

ARMSTRONG: I can't go into details, except to say that their ships were far superior to ours both in size and technology – Boy, were they big...and menacing! No, there is no question of a space station.

PROFESSOR: But NASA had other missions after Apollo11?

304

ARMSTRONG: Naturally – NASA was committed at that time, and couldn't risk panic on Earth. But it was a quick scoop and back again.

A friend of UFO author Timothy Good who formerly served in a branch of the British Military Intelligence claims to have been present at the symposium and overheard the above portion of the conversation. Good has stated that he is not permitted to reveal the name of the source, nor the location and date. It is alleged that Neil Armstrong himself confirmed the veracity of the story but refused to go into further detail, yet he has admitted that the CIA had been behind the cover-up.

The term "Santa Claus" used during Apollo transmissions has become commonly accepted as a NASA code-word for UFO by those interested in the subject. Chatelain wrote "I think that Walter Schirra aboard Mercury 8 was the first of the astronauts to use the code name 'Santa Claus' to indicate the presence of flying saucers next to space capsules. However, his announcements were barely noticed by the general public. It was a little different when James Lovell on board the Apollo 8 command module came out from behind the Moon and said for everybody to hear: "Please be informed that there is a Santa Claus", even though this happened on Christmas Day 1968, many people sensed a hidden meaning in those words."

James Lovell did in fact report a UFO sighting during the Gemini VII flight in 1965. The astronauts spent nearly two weeks in space making a total of 206 orbits, and were joined later by the Gemini-VIA flight which performed a rendezvous manoeuvre of manned spacecraft for the first time. The *Gemini VII Mission Report* dated from January 1966 is available in its entirety at the following web address.[212] Lovell's encounter with an unknown flying object was reported in the following dialogue between himself and the Capsule Communicator or CAPCOM[10].

---

[10] It is the role of one single individual, the *Capsule Communicator* or CAPCOM, to communicate directly with the crew of a manned space flight. This role was usually filled by another astronaut, often one of the backup or support-crew members, as NASA believed that an astronaut was the most suitable candidate to understand the situation in the spacecraft and pass information in the clearest way.

LOVELL: Bogey at 10 o'clock high. Cad.
CAPCOM: This is Houston. Say again seven.
LOVELL: Said we have a bogey at 10 o'clock high.
CAPCOM: Gemini 7 - is that the booster or is that an actual sighting?
LOVELL: We have several...actual sightings.
CAPCOM: Estimated distance or size?
LOVELL: We also have the booster in sight.

There are more transcripts of the Apollo and Gemini transmissions available which are also of interest, where the astronauts involved are describing unusual structures and formations as well as strange tracks and markings on the terrain. But as always, the authenticity of such documentation should remain under scrutiny if one is to succeed in ploughing through the mountains of disinformation.

Apollo 14 Astronaut Edgar Mitchell was the sixth man to walk on the moon and has managed to openly express his thoughts regarding the Apollo missions without being silenced, as was Neil Armstrong's greatest fear. According to close friends of Armstrong, he would've loved to have come clean about the whole affair but knew that he would only be putting his family in danger by doing so.

Mitchell on the other hand has been remarkably open about the whole affair; "Yes, there have been ET visitations. There have been crashed craft. There have been material and bodies recovered. There has been a certain amount of reverse engineering that has allowed some of these craft, or some components, to be duplicated. And there is some group of people that may or may not be associated with government at this point that have this knowledge. They have been attempting to conceal this knowledge. People in high level government have very little, if any, valid information about this. It has been the subject of disinformation in order to deflect attention and create confusion so the truth doesn't come out."[213]

To conclude this section it is worth noting that physical evidence of previous missions to the Moon has been photographed from above by NASA's Lunar Reconnaissance Orbiter (LRO). High-resolution images of the Apollo 12, 14 and 17 landing sites have been taken by the LRO and have provided the sharpest views to date of where they touched down on the lunar surface. Astronaut Schmitt from Apollo 17 recognized his backpack and helped researchers to identify other objects such as packing materials, pieces of the LM's protective coating and other life supporting backpacks. The paths formed by the astronauts on foot can be seen along with moon buggy tracks. There has been no evidence of the American flags that were planted in the sixties and seventies but this could be down to years of degradation.

OUR MYSTERIOUS MOON

Many amazing facts have come to light in recent years with respect to our mysterious moon. Books have been written which have covered the subject in detail and any researcher who has followed this trail cannot help but be astounded by the information which has surfaced. It appears that the moon itself shouldn't actually be where it is, and all the data regarding the moon's size and its distance from the sun and from the Earth, have confounded scientists and researchers alike.

The Moon revolves at exactly one hundredth of the speed that the Earth turns on its axis. It is also precisely 400 times smaller than the Sun and exactly 400 times closer to the Earth. Patterns and number sequences are consistent when looking at all of the Moon's major aspects, contrary to the inconsistencies of all other planets and moons in our solar system. If you divide the circumference of the Sun by that of the Moon and multiply by 100 you get the polar circumference of the Earth. In fact, so precise are the measurements and correlations between the Earth, Sun and Moon that any differentiation in the figures would inevitably lead to vastly visible changes. Take the solar eclipse for example; the Sun would no longer be able to conceal itself so perfectly behind the Moon. That astoundingly perfect fit that we take for granted would cease to be.

The diameter of the Moon is 2,160 miles whilst the Sun's colossal diameter is 864,000 miles across, so it is a remarkable coincidence that the two spheres should appear the same size during the eclipse. In his book *Space, Time and Other Things*, American author Isaac Asimov makes an observation about this truly amazing situation, "What makes a total eclipse so remarkable is the sheer astronomical reason why the Moon and the Sun should fit so well. It is the sheerest of coincidences, and only the Earth among all the planets is blessed in this fashion."

There are many theories doing the rounds regarding the enigmatic nature of Earth's Moon. Many claim that the moon is an artificial satellite rather than a natural object. It is hollow, which should be impossible were it a natural planetary object. As noted astronomer Dr. Carl Sagan wrote in 1966, "A natural satellite cannot be a hollow object."[214]

NASA astronauts have tested the Moon's density on several occasions using seismic equipment and have reported officially that the Moon rings like a bell when struck. Seismological equipment recorded the shock waves caused by the Lunar Module ascent stage of Apollo 12 when it was sent crashing into the Moon. NASA scientists were dumbfounded by the results as the artificially created Moonquake lasted for 55 minutes. Apollo 12's seismic records were not unique either as the seismometers they had set up also recorded the vibrations caused by the impact of the Apollo 13's ill-fated Saturn rocket booster 87 miles away. The impact was equivalent to 11 tons of TNT and the entire Moon reportedly vibrated for longer than 3 hours and 20 minutes, reaching a depth of 22-25 miles down. The Apollo 14's S-IVB was also sent crashing into the lunar surface by remote control causing the shock waves, which were detected by instruments 108 miles away, to vibrate for over three hours. According to a NASA science publication "the Moon reacted like a gong."[215]

Interestingly, the probability that the Moon was NOT actually a solid satellite was first realized and mentioned back in 1962, the year following JFK's 'man landing on the Moon' speech. It is noteworthy to consider the implications that the Apollo program was actually built on the knowledge that the Moon in all likelihood must be an artificial construct. The data became available to them from 1962-63 onwards that the Moon was not a natural satellite and as Ingo Swann stated, "It would also have been clear that the two Earthside superpowers fully expected to utilize the Lunar cavities as opportunistic Moonbase habitation. This "plan", however, seems not to have been fulfilled. One is forced to wonder WHY?"[216]

The immediate reaction within scientific circles at the time was that the data which suggested the object to be hollow must be faulty, however, the several studies which followed arrived at the same conclusions. Finally, in February 1962, Dr. Sean C. Solomon of MIT reported that "The Lunar Orbiter experiments vastly improved our knowledge of the moon's gravitational field...indicating the frightening possibility that the moon might be hollow."[217]

So, if the Moon is a hollow artificial construct as the facts lead us to understand, who built the Moon, how did they get it into its present orbit and why did they put it there? How is it that our moon remains stationary in Earth's orbit, never revealing the dark side to us? Such questions will certainly not be answered overnight but the initial realization that our Moon is not a natural object behaving naturally would raise a few eyebrows were it common public knowledge.

Asimov himself struggled to comprehend the implications of such a discovery when he wrote on the subject in 1963. He said "It is a shame that one small thing remains unaccounted for; one trifling thing I have ignored so far, but what in blazes is our Moon doing way out there? It's too far out to be a true satellite of Earth. It's too big to have been captured by the Earth. The chances of such a capture being affected and the Moon then having taken up a nearly circular orbit about the Earth are too small to make such an eventuality credible. But then, if the Moon is neither a true satellite of the Earth nor a captured one, what is it?"[218]

An article theorizing on the origins of the Moon was published in the Soviet journal *Sputnik* entitled "*Is the Moon the Creation of Alien Intelligence?*" The piece written by Michael Vasin and Alexander Shcherbakov suggested that eons ago somewhere out in space, intelligent beings far more advanced than humankind had used immense machines to hollow out a planetoid, spilling out the excess material onto the lunar surface. Once stabilized, the huge cavernous rock which had been transformed into a gigantic craft, with an inner shell like the hull of a boat and a protective hard outer shell, was pulled through the cosmos and finally placed with precision into its present position.

This proposition, as fantastic and unlikely as it may seem, could offer us some understanding as to why the Moon rocks retrieved during Apollo missions have been scientifically dated as 5.3 billion years old, whilst the dust they were taken from has been proven to be one billion years older than the rocks themselves.

The mainstream scientific community continues to the present day to insist that both the Earth and the Moon were formed from the same rock when our solar system first came into being roughly 4.5 billion years ago. However, since the advancements in science over recent years, the dating system for rocks has become much more accurate, as tracks burned into the rocks by cosmic rays can now be examined. Interestingly, the oldest rocks on Earth found so far only date back 3.5 billion years. It is clear from these figures alone that the Earth may not be as old as initially thought and that Moon dust appears to have existed nearly 2 billion years before the solar system was formed, therefore putting official scientific opinion regarding the Moons origins into chaos.

Dr. Norman Bergrun, a former NASA research scientist published an astounding book *Ringmakers of Saturn* which shows photos taken of Saturn's rings from the Voyager I flight in 1980. Voyager I was sent to the rings of Saturn to investigate some strange anomalies that they had witnessed through their observations from Earth and NASA couldn't believe what they found in the images that were sent back. With exclusive access to the raw NASA photographs, Bergrun saw firsthand what the general public was not allowed to see, making him the first legitimate, verified member of the scientific community to discover cylindrical vehicles. Bergrun's book exposed for the first time exactly what Voyager I saw, but unable to get it published in America he travelled to Scotland and finally got it published in Aberdeen.

One of the photographs in his book is of an artificially constructed object in the A-ring of Saturn that he calls an 'electromagnetic vehicle'. It was 2000 miles long and over 450 miles in diameter. What kind of high-technology must it take to build an object of that size, and who could be responsible for such an impossible feat of engineering? Bergrun thought it could be possible that these craft were actually making the rings, hence the book's title, but other scholars have raised the possibility that they could be mining the precious metals and nutrients that make up the rings. Either way, what an incredible discovery, another one that appears to have been left out of the public domain. A reviewer commenting on Bergrun's book wrote, "Saturn's rings are 'not' natural, but are some type of effluent from massively huge, cylindrical objects, themselves measured in terms of earth diameters!"

Former U.S. airline pilot and son of the founder of the Lear Jet, John Lear, met with Bergrun and discussed the origins of the Earth's Moon, knowing that it had to have been placed into its present orbit by someone or something. Bergrun had informed him that some form of large electromagnetic vehicle had been responsible for manoeuvring the Moon into its present location.

During a Project Camelot interview, Lear mentions a conversation he had with Bergrun once, saying "by the way, the electromagnetic vehicle that towed the Moon into orbit...where is it now? And he said "I think it's on the dark side of the Moon." So when I got hooked up with Ron Schmidt, we started collecting photos on the dark side of the Moon and we found it. It's in the crater of Tchaikovsky."[219]

This is a really fascinating possibility that could explain a lot of the mysteries surrounding the Moon's origins, should it turn out to be true. If sometime in the near future the facts regarding the Moon's construction and placement were to surface publicly, then John Lear's observations could lead to a thorough investigation of the Tchaikovsky crater. Who knows what they may discover, such an enormous vehicle could be resting there and our knowledge of space and the origins of the Moon among other things could be infinitely improved. After all, science is based on the understanding of new discoveries.

One such discovery was made on the night of July 29, 1953 by John J. O'Neill, science editor of the *Herald Tribune*. As he settled down for an evening's observation of the Moon as it approached the equator on its northerly course, he was amazed to discover a gigantic bridge stretching above the Mare Crisium.[220] Bewildered by his observation, O'Neill carefully re-checked his telescope thinking it may be an optical illusion, but the visual conditions were excellent and upon looking for a second time he found the enormous object was still there. He had watched the Moon for years and there had never been anything above the Mare Crisium before but there it was, stretching for twelve miles in a straight line from pediment to pediment.

As he continued to observe the mysterious anomaly for an hour and a half, he changed eyepieces twice from 90X to 125X then 250X. Under higher magnification, the sharp outline of the unexplained vast structure was even clearer. Aware of the furore that such a discovery would cause, O'Neill reported the incident tactfully in his report to the Association of Lunar and Planetary Observers by calling his remarkable discovery a "gigantic natural bridge". It was evident to many of his fellow astronomers that it was impossible for Nature to create such an immense structure so suddenly.

As expected, O'Neill's unusual discovery led to some astronomers criticizing his findings and even questioning the man himself, however his critics would soon be silenced for in the August 1953, a mere month after his initial discovery, the great British astronomer Dr. J.P. Wilkins officially confirmed the existence of the bridge. Four weeks later, the president of the British Astronomical Association, Sir Patrick Moore, also verified O'Neill's discovery.

There are historians and archaeologists that believe they have found evidence that there existed a time before the Moon was in our sky. An old Hellenistic and possibly Egyptian belief is that "the celestial bodies which we now see were not all visible in earlier times".[221] The Arcadian people from ancient Greece who called themselves the Proselenes, as reported by Aristotle, were said to have held claim to Arcadia because they lived in that region "before there was a moon in the heavens." Even the term Proselenes means "before the moon".

Some researchers, who have studied the Great Idol monument in the Bolivian city of Tiahuanaco, postulate that the symbols engraved in the sandstone represent a wealth of astronomical data about the Earth and the heavens from around 27,000 years ago. Authors H.S. Bellamy & Dr. P. Allen wrote about the Moon's first appearance in our skies saying that "The symbols of the idol record that the satellite came into orbit around the Earth 11,500 to 13,000 years ago."[222]

Immanuel Velikovsky, the Russian psychiatrist who became well known for his bestselling book *Worlds in Collision* published in America in 1950, also wrote of a time before the Moon was in existence. In his book Velikovsky wrote, "The traditions of diverse people offer corroborative testimony to the effect that in a very early age, but still in the memory of mankind, no moon accompanied the earth." It is evident that there exists an interesting hypothesis of which a number of intellectuals are in agreement, which suggests that once upon a time the Moon wasn't around but was brought here at a later date, the question still remains however, who was responsible for such a mammoth task and why? If the Moon is older than the Earth and the solar system itself, then it must have originated elsewhere further back in time, allowing for the possibility that at some point in Earth's short history the Moon was brought here and placed in orbit.

There are many researchers out there who believe that there are buildings and monuments on both the Moon and Mars. The Viking Orbiter was launched in 1976 and photographed segments of the Martian landscape as it orbited the red planet. A region named Cydonia revealed a number of unusual structures that appear to be of intelligent design, such as the 'Face on Mars' which is an oval structure 1500 feet high and resembling a humanoid face. There is also a five sided pyramid called the "D & M Pyramid" alongside a complex of smaller pyramids known as "The City Square". It has been concluded by a number of investigators, most notably by another former NASA employee, Richard C. Hoagland, that these enigmatic structures must be the remnants of an ancient extraterrestrial civilisation. The Cydonian monuments appear analogous to the monuments situated on the Giza plateau in Egypt, which would suggest that the architects may be intrinsically linked in some way.

According to Bill Cooper, a joint U.S.-Russian winged space probe that used a hydrazine propeller, orbited Mars three times before landing on May 22, 1962. The probe relayed information back to Earth which gave confirmation that a life-sustaining environment existed on the red planet. He also claims that the construction of a colony on the planet began not long after, and today there are cities present which are populated by "people from different cultures and occupations taken from all over the Earth". The Mars colonisation project went under the name of 'Adam and Eve'.

In 2009, the University of Arizona received photos from an orbiting satellite which showed a rectangular object jutting out of the surface of Mars. The "monolith" roused much curiosity when it was first reported but Alfred McEwen, the professor of planetary science at the university, said "It is not that unusual. There are lots of rectangular structures on Mars. It is striking when you see one that is isolated, but they are common."[223]

Buzz Aldrin announced that a similar "monolith" had been detected on Mars' moon Phobos. Talking on the U.S. television network C-Span, Aldrin stated "There is a monolith there, a very unusual structure on this little potato-shaped object that goes around Mars once every seven hours. When people find out about that, they are going to say 'who put that there?' Well, the universe put it there, or if you choose, God put it there."

One of the photos sent back from the Russian probe Phobos II was taken using infrared film of beneath the Martian surface, revealing a city apparently the size of Chicago. A huge object approaching Phobos II can be seen on another photo, which actually impacted the satellite, knocking it completely out of the orbit of Mars. These images were published in a German magazine by Michael Hesemann.

A monolithic structure has also been discovered rising more than a mile above the Moon's surface. Known as the "Shard", this irregular spindly object was photographed in 1967 by the Lunar Orbiter. It is considered to be a real physical object due to it casting a shadow in the correct direction and close-up imaging reveals a cellular-like internal structure.

A massive seven mile high structure named the "Tower" stands above and behind the "Shard", which includes a central "cube" which appears to be suspended from a tripod-like base. Both objects share a similar cellular construction, but the "Tower" has a distinctly hexagonal pattern. Apollo 10 astronauts reportedly made a unique picture (AS-10-32-4822) of a one mile long object known as the "Castle" which casts a distinct shadow onto the lunar surface because it is hanging at the height of 14 kilometres. Explanations as to their origin and purpose remain inconclusive.

A mission control specialist has commented on some of the NASA photographs stating that "Our guys observed ruins of the Lunar cities, transparent pyramids, domes and God knows what else, which are currently hidden deep inside the NASA safes..." Given access to the archives, some scientists and geologists who have had the rare opportunity to study the many anomalies present in the images have concluded that such objects cannot have been formed naturally, saying that "we should admit they are artificial, especially the domes and pyramids."[224]

According to some researchers, a Moon base named "Luna" was spotted and filmed by the Apollo astronauts which Bill

Cooper believes to be a joint United States, Russian and alien base. He claims that photographs were taken showing "domes, spires, tall round structures which look like silos, huge "T" shaped mining vehicles which left stitch-like tracks in the lunar surface, and extremely large as well as small alien craft." But Cooper has also written that man probably landed on the Moon sometime during the mid-fifties, explaining that "at the time when President Kennedy stated that he wanted a man to set foot on the moon by the end of the decade we already had a base there."

A construction surrounded with a tall D-shaped wall was discovered not far from the landing site of Apollo 15 in the upper part of Rima Hadley and near the Tiho crater. Concentric hexahedral rock excavations resembling terraces including a tunnel entrance have been discovered which appear to be open cast mines. An unusual dome structure which glows blue and white from within, has been found raised above the edge of the Copernicus crater, which is 300 metres wide and 400 metres long. A disc with a diameter of roughly 50 metres has been seen standing on a square basement surrounded with rhombi walls in the upper part of what is known as the Factory area. Close to these walls, a dark round opening in the ground can be seen, resembling some form of entrance. It is said that presently unknown artefacts have been discovered in 44 different regions on the Moon which are being investigated by the Houston Planetary Institute and the NASA Goddard Space Flight Center.

An official press-release was reported in Russian newspaper *Vecherny Volgograd* which said "NASA scientists and engineers participating in exploration of Mars and Moon reported results of their discoveries at the Washington National Press Club on March 21, 1996. It was announced for the first time that man-caused structures and objects had been discovered on the Moon."[225]

Later that day on March 21, a radio interview took place on 'Coast to Coast AM with Art Bell' with Richard Hoagland and another former NASA employee Ken Johnston. Art Bell set up the interview in an attempt to discover what had really taken place earlier that day at the seemingly under-reported press briefing at the National Press Club in Washington D.C. The briefing was arranged to openly discuss and bring to light the information kept secret by NASA regarding the structures and possible ancient ruins discovered on the Moon during the Apollo missions.

Bell had been informed by the National Press Club that there were around 60 guests and 18 cameras present at the briefing which included the American television network C-SPAN. Representatives of the network told Bell that they didn't cover the story because they had "other things to do" and also because they weren't told who would be there besides Hoagland. C-SPAN said "Well, we didn't cover it" but then later Bell was told that "We did cover it, but we're not going to broadcast it". A very unusual scenario considering the nature of the briefing and the fact that television networks are in place to report such briefings. As Hoagland told Art Bell during the radio interview, "Well, what I find bizarre, is if they are not going to broadcast it, why bother to show up?"[226]

Apollo archive video and photographic footage that was taken by different Apollo astronauts was demonstrated at the briefing, causing people to question why such material had been kept from the public. NASA specialists were on hand to answer their questions stating that "it was difficult to forecast the reaction of people to the information that some creatures had been or still were on the Moon. Besides, there were some other reasons to it, which were beyond NASA."[227]

Whatever the reasons that NASA continue to use to justify the ongoing procedure of deceit and denial, it is apparent to even the casual observer that honesty and integrity are not high on their agenda. From NASA's early Nazi connections to its inception as an administration, secrecy and conspiracy have been an integral part of its history. But any vigilant researcher can easily unravel the lies which have been so diligently put in place by those enforcing the strict NASA deception.

We may not have access to the many archives which have been hidden under lock and key but there remains enough material available to expose the simple fact that everything is not what it seems. Our Moon has enough anomalous aspects and scientific inconsistencies to suggest that we really know very little about our closest celestial neighbour. And the experiences and testimonies of those who have worked for NASA reveal to those of us on the outside, that what we have been told about the Apollo program and the famous Moon landings could well be inaccurate to say the very least. As time continues to pass and more and more information comes to light, it is surely only a matter of time before the truth about the Moon, Mars and the space surrounding our own planet is revealed and the secrecy can finally come to an end.

9

THE BURISCH
SAGA

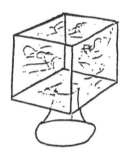

I frankly thought, honestly thought that those people who believed in aliens were tin-foil heads...Egg on my face!

Dr. Dan Burisch

WHAT YOU ARE ABOUT TO READ will test your sense of reason, your belief system and your worldview and will appear to the average reader to be a story of fantastical proportions. The information divulged here is so complex yet compelling, that if you don't question its validity then you are surely either too open for suggestion and consider anything possible or you haven't really understood what you are reading.

The story of Dr. Dan B. Catselas Burisch is a fascinating one that pushes the conceptual boundaries of the reality of which most of us have become so familiar and will stretch the credulity of even the most open minded researchers out there. Some of his experiences initially appear to have surfaced from the annals of science fiction literature but rest assured Dan's story certainly does not belong in the fiction section of any library.

His testimony reveals his experiences involving personal contact with extraterrestrial beings and Men in Black (MIBs), time-travel technology (Stargates), and his involvement with the still highly secretive group Majestic 12 and the black projects of which they are privy to.

His story is a hugely important one, should it prove to be an accurate portrayal of events. What helps the validity of his case are the documents proving his involvement in Majestic working at Area 51 on various secret projects and also several signed and legally binding affidavits that point to the veracity of his testimony. In the words of Don Deppeller, the man behind the detailed and informative website *www.danburisch.info*, "the one thing (in fact, there are several that are relevant) that makes Dan Burisch more authentic than the shadowy bamboozlers of lesser note is the affidavits that he has authored, which in this field of fluid facts should give pause to the pooh-poohers and naysayers that call themselves 'experts'."

Most of the information in this chapter comes directly from Dan Burisch and also from his close colleague and confidante Marci

320

McDowell (now also his wife). Researcher and author William Hamilton wrote a book entitled *Project Aquarius: The Story Of An Aquarian Scientist* which includes a detailed synopsis of the extensive work of Dr. Burisch. Due to his time spent with Dan, Hamilton's involvement has led him to become somewhat of an authority on his story and so I shall be referencing Hamilton here also.

Born Danny B. Crain on February 2, 1964, to John Dennis and Doreen Aglaie Crain and married to Deborah K. Burisch (who held a managerial position with Majestic) on July 17, 1990.

He changed his surname to Burisch on 30th August, 1995, in Las Vegas, Nevada. He received his Bachelor's degree from UNLV (University of Nevada at Las Vegas), his Master's at St. Patrick's Seminary, and his doctorate from SUNY at Stony Brook (State University New York) in 1989.

He was invited to join the New York Academy of Sciences, and received the civic award 'Straight from the Heart' in Las Vegas in 1990 and was also nominated for the Nobel Peace Prize in February 2005.

IN THE BEGINNING

In Mae Bower Park in Southern California during the summer of 1973, nine year old Danny Crain was playing baseball with his Grandpa. As he went to retrieve the ball his Grandfather had thrown for him to catch, Dan remembers looking down towards the grass and seeing a shadow that reminded him of a triangular kite followed by a flash of light. He was missing for several hours and upon his return to the park Dan found his Grandpa sat in a state of shock unable to explain the bizarre event that had just unfolded, muttering "you're okay now, you're okay now" before walking home together.

Dan recalls his grandparents having a major argument with his parents shortly after arriving home which ultimately led to his grandparents moving out. Dan was only informed about the events that occurred that day much later in his life, because as a child he'd had no memory of it.

He was told that a triangular shaped flying craft had hovered above him that ominous morning and pulled him up by his chest into an alien craft. He was laid down on an examination table

321

inside the vehicle next to a boy named Michael who happened to be the son of a highly ranked member of the covert group Majestic 12, whose codename was MJ-1.

The extraterrestrials on board the craft performed a medical procedure on the young Michael which unfortunately led to his death despite frantic attempts to revive him, so in order to save the boy's soul they performed what Dan labelled a 'soul transfer' and tried storing Michael's 'energy' in Dan's body.

Burisch explained, "Something went wrong during the course of my time on board the craft, when samples were being taken of me for their studies. And the son of the former MJ-1 died. During that time they put some sort of equipment on me. It almost looked like an EEG type.., a neural net if you will...the receivers, probes...electrodes, if you will...on me. And they were trying to save, desperately trying to save...And I could see the...the movement of the J-RODs around this other boy. And I know what he looked like and all of that because I've seen it through the eyes of Chi'el'ah (the J-ROD he came to know through Project Aquarius). They were trying to save him, and he ultimately passed. During that time, apparently they were trying whatever technology they could employ to save the boy by 'storing' him. They look at us as no more than...containers or...cylinders almost. Almost like beakers full of material, electromagnetic material. And so they were trying to save, store, his energy if you will..., they were trying to store him for a while, I guess, in me."[228]

The transfer was apparently successful. Of course Dan grew up completely unaware of any of this but did suddenly have a great interest in the sciences which wasn't there before the incident. He had always been into sport and other 'normal' activities like any other child of his age but something changed in him and it appeared he was taking on Michael's interests and fortes.

As Burisch described it, "there was a substantive intellectual change in me where I was no longer interested in those same things of my youth. Was that maturation? Probably some of it. Was it a change as a result of what was done with me on board the craft? The Majestic thinks so, thinks that it had something to do with that other boy because that other boy was known as very bright in the sciences. And all of a sudden, true enough, I got a hankering for Erlenmeyer flasks and boiling flasks and microscopes that I'd never had before.[229]

The abduction experience and subsequent encounter with the extraterrestrials was a pivotal turning point for him, as he would only discover much later in his life. The subtle change in Dan evolved over the next few years as he developed a staggering ability in the sciences, particularly in the area of biology and microscopy. So impressive were his new found abilities that his mother arranged for Dr. Reynolds (the director of pathology in histology and microbiology at Long Beach Memorial Hospital) to tutor Dan at weekends for several years to come. He was eventually invited to become a member of the Los Angeles Microscopical Society due to his high level of skills in microscopy and became their youngest ever member.

It was during his time at the LAMS when Dan was thirteen or fourteen that he had his first encounter with the father of the now deceased boy Michael whom he had inadvertently become intrinsically involved with. Dan remembers seeing a man at the back of the meeting room at George C. Page Museum, looking over at him for an uncomfortable length of time as he popped open a Zippo lighter with the United States Navy seal on it, lit it then closed it before walking away out the back door. As it later transpired, the stranger's brief visit that day was his way of introducing himself to Dan at an early age, keeping an eye on the teenager who he believed to be housing his son's essence. He was making his presence known to the boy who would later prove to be such an asset to the Majestic group because of his scientifically advanced knowledge along with his innate ability to think 'outside the box'. The man who Dan later discovered to be former MJ-1 would play an important role in Dan's future development as a microbiologist and also with his involvement with Majestic.

Dan took the skills that he had developed into adulthood and became a Senior Operative/Scientist working for the Committee of the Majority (CotM)[11] and the Majestic 12 between 1986 and 2003

[11] The Committee of the Majority allegedly consists of 33 of the most powerful people in the world. Members are said to derive primarily from the ranks of the Trilateral Commission. "The original core group of Majestic 12 maintained direct authority and oversight of all extraterrestrial matters, and the remainder of the CotM coordinated international relations and the cover-up of the ET subject. The Committee is primarily a

and then for the following two years up to 2005 he worked for MJ-12 only. The group was formally adjourned on October 12, 2005.

He was assigned to a Black/Ops Unit during the 1991 Gulf War and was deployed into the International Coalition's Zone of Operations. Dan refuses to go into detail of his role in bio defence but he did confirm that he was involved in Operation Desert Storm as a defence bio-warfare expert whose job was to counteract unauthorised biological warfare agents intended for use against the Iraqi army by a rogue military unit.

Dan's experiences with Extraterrestrials and MJ-12 go back to 1986 when he was inducted into Majestic while he was still a student at UNLV. He had already worked for many years with the LAMS and studied with Dr. John Bunyan so he'd already had a long and distinguished history in microbiology before he was even at UNLV. Majestic already knew back then that he was extremely gifted. Like all aspiring and ambitious scientists, Dan had always dreamed of making a big and important discovery, and in 1986 his avid interest in the space program and the possibility of alien life forms led him to write a proposal and send it to NASA as they were accepting new proposals for exobiological research.

And so, shortly after graduating Dan sent them his proposal which was titled *"On the Transplantation of Protozoa and the Exploitation of Martian Exobiology: The Case for Euglena Viridis in the Automated Biological Laboratory."* The letter of reply from NASA read "Your project has been found to contain sufficient intrinsic merit as to enable integration into NSCORT Bioregenerative Life Support Division, a sub-directorate of the Controlled Ecological Life Support Systems (CELSS) Program of the National Aeronautics and Space Administration."[230]

Dan was also attracting attention from other areas of the government too, unbeknown to him, and it wasn't long before he was visited by three strangers who claimed to be agents for the Department of Naval Intelligence. Unfamiliar with such a department he decided to look it up and could only find a listing for the Office of Naval Intelligence. This was to be Dan's

---

Scottish Rite Masonic group, and as such was home to several factions of the legendary and illusive 'Illuminati'."(www.danburisch.info)

introduction into black project operations running outside of official government channels.

The secretive nature of this type of work did have its benefits however such as substantial financial backing for his studies and unlimited use of scientific instruments. He was offered the chance to further his education and expand into areas that previously he'd only dreamed of, when he was given the opportunity to work in Black Operations in his specialist subject and become a well respected figure in Special Applications. On acceptance of this offer he began being trained and groomed for work on 'exotic' biological material at the now infamous test site Area 51 in the Nevada desert, also referred to as 'Dreamland' by outsiders and 'Watertown' by those in the know.

Because of the events surrounding his abduction as a child back in '73, Dan was now being 'mentored' by MJ-1, although Dan was unaware of this fact at that time. It was because of what happened that day in the park that this anonymous figure felt a great affection towards Dan along with a very close connection with him that continues to the present day.

PROJECT AQUARIUS

Dr. Dan Crain (as he was originally known), having recently completed his PhD, discovered whilst working on exotic materials that he had in fact been studying tissue samples that were extraterrestrial in nature. Dan was later assigned as a Microbiologist Level V at the Papoose Lake Facility S4 which is also known as "The Dark Side of the Moon". The facility was originally designed as a biological weapons laboratory in the early 1950's.

It was here at Sector 4, that Dan's belief system would be truly challenged as he was about to come into contact with physical evidence that extraterrestrials did really exist. He discovered that the United States Government had been working with extraterrestrial visitors for decades and the U.S. military were in possession of physical extraterrestrial vehicles and their occupants. It was through a "reverse engineering" program which originated in the 1940's, as described by Bob Lazar, which led to the many technological advancements associated with military aerospace.

The S4 facility is said to have five working levels, the last of which is accessible by one elevator alone. Burisch described the security measures at S4 to be very oppressive. Besides the excessive amount of armed guards, he underwent showering, shaving, weighing and decontamination along with voice print identification and optical scans. He was given a secret "Q" clearance and was informed that he had been commissioned by the department of the Navy although he was also assigned to work under the direction of The Defense Intelligence Agency (DIA) and the Naval Research Laboratory (NRL).

To get to Area 51, Dan was transported from McCarran International Airport in the "Janet" 737-200 airliner which had a white fuselage with a single red stripe running along both sides. The pick-up and drop-off point is across from the main terminal at the EG&G building. As the plane approached to land, Dan recalled hearing the Pilot say "Pyramid Pyramid Pyramid" which he believed to be the authorization clearance from the air traffic control at Groom Lake before allowing jets to make the final approach to Area 51. Transportation from Area 51 to Area S4 was by either standard issue blue colored Air Force bus, U.S. Army Blackhawk helicopter or Soviet Mi-24 Hind helicopter. On entering the S4 facility a poster of a UFO with the words "I want to believe" written on it was mounted on the wall immediately to the left of the entrance.

Dan recalled making a brief visit to the Dulce facility in New Mexico where he mentioned the appalling activities that goes on deep below the ground there. He stated, "My experience in the time that I stayed in the residential unit there was horrifying. You know, when you hear human beings screaming in pain?"[231]

He then compared it to the S4 facility in Nevada of which he became so familiar with. Describing Level 3 at S4 he said, "It's been called various different things: It's been called the 'Museum', the 'Housing Unit', the 'Hall of Tortures' and an 'Animal Retention Facility'. One of the horrifying things about the S4 facility is travelling in the elevator system. There is enough of a sound conduit in the elevator system where you can hear the sounds of the 'test subjects' from the 3rd floor while you are in the elevators on various other floors. And the sounds are akin to what I heard at the Dulce facility. Every once-in-awhile you could hear the sounds of other vertebrates - dogs, cats, monkeys - screaming.

326

Some of which are just natural behaviours due to how they're being kept - very sterile...When I say 'sterile' I mean a non-conducive-to-play environment, more of a housing facility like a kennel. And then you occasionally hear the sounds that [here he chokes up] you know are one of your brothers and sisters..."[232]

It soon became apparent to Dan that while he was working within the S4 facility he was being given a surprising amount of leeway which allowed him to gain access to multiple levels within both Area 51 and S4 laboratory complexes. Although still required to follow all the protocols, his security badge permitted him to gain access to other projects unlike most of the other Special Application workers. The employees worked within a system of compartmentalization so that no one knew what workers on other levels were doing.

Here is the opening paragraph on page one of a nine page document reportedly obtained by William Moore in 1980 that offers an insight into the 'official' beginnings of Aquarius;

"(TS/ORCON) (PROWORD: DANCE) Contains 16 volumes of documented information collected from the beginning of the United States Investigation of Unidentified Flying Objects (UFOs) and Identified Alien Crafts (IAC). The Project was originally established in 1953, by order of President Eisenhower, under control of NSC and MJ12. In 1966, the Project's name was changed from Project Gleem to Project Aquarius. The Project was funded by CIA confidential funds (non-appropriated).

The Project was originally classified SECRET but was upgraded to its present classification in Dec. 1969 after Project Blue Book closed. The purpose of Project Aquarius was to collect all scientific, technological, medical and intelligence information from UFO/IAC sightings, and contacts with Alien life forms. This orderly file of collected information has been used to advance the *United States Space Program*. (TS/ORCON) The proceeding briefing is an historical account of the United States Government's investigation of Aerial Phenomenon, Recovered Alien Aircrafts, and Contacts with Extraterrestrial Life Forms."

Page three continues; "In 1953, Project Gleem was initiated by order of President Fisenhower, who believed the UFOs presented a threat to the national security of the United States. Project Gleem, which became Project Aquarius in 1966, was a parallel reporting system for UFO sightings and incidents. Reports collected under Project Aquarius were considered actual sightings of Alien aircrafts or contacts with Alien life forms. Most reports were made by reliable military and Defense Department civilian personnel."

In 1994, Burisch began operating as a Working Group Leader on Project Aquarius at R-4800, Sector 4 on the Nevada test site. Here he was responsible for leading a group of scientists in the investigation of the neuropathy of an EBE (extraterrestrial biological entity) which was been housed at the S4 facility under Papoose Mountain which is 12 miles south of Area 51's Groom Lake site. This individual which could commonly be referred to as a 'Grey' became known using the term J-ROD and claimed to originate from about 52,000 years into the future on a separate timeline (timeline 2) from that of ours (timeline 1). He became classified as a P52 (present + 52,000 years) and would later reveal that his name was Chi'el'ah.

He claims to have travelled back in time to try and find some assistance to treat his people's illness and also to help change our future for the better by sharing some of his knowledge with us. He explained that he had been travelling with an entity known as EBE-3 and his assistant whom had come to Earth from a planet that was orbiting Zeta Reticuli 2. They were both P45s, a J-ROD group originating from approximately 45,000 years ahead of the present. He had been helping the group with abduction sampling in the same craft that took Dan that day back in 1973 and witnessed the 'soul transference' firsthand and was therefore able to recount the details of the event to Burisch. The ET then travelled back to 1953 on another mission with the P45s which ultimately ended in disaster as their craft crashed near the city of Kingman in Mohave County, Arizona.

Two of the three J-RODs survived the crash, one was taken to Los Alamos National Laboratory (LANL) and worked with Bill Uhouse on flight simulator equipment whilst the other J-ROD (Chi'el'ah) was recovered and taken to Groom Lake to assist in a scientific exchange program that had allegedly been established in New Mexico in 1964 as part of Project Sigma.

Burisch was astounded to discover that ultra secret branches of the government had succeeded where the SETI program had failed and managed to establish not only communications with extraterrestrials but had also negotiated an agreement for a scientific exchange program. In exchange for technology that would enable us to achieve space travel they wanted our scientists to help them to find the cause of their neural degeneration. I think it is apparent to us all how technology has advanced since the 1940's to such an extent that it would seem highly unlikely to attribute this surge in technological achievements to mankind's ingenuity and endeavour alone. In 1972, NASA Scientist Dr. Hermann Oberth asserted "We cannot take credit for our record advancement in certain scientific fields alone. We have been helped. And we have been helped by the people of other worlds."

Sure we are capable of incredible and astounding feats as the history books will attest to but how much of our high technology has originated from outside sources, primarily that of an extraterrestrial kind? If only man had progressed spiritually and morally as far as he has technologically, we would be living in very different times indeed.

Along with the other J-RODs, Chi'el'ah was suffering from a debilitating medical condition which was affecting his nervous system and the Aquarius team was set the task of figuring out why this had occurred and of finding a way to ameliorate the pathology. This was achieved by taking tissue samples from the J-ROD that was now being housed inside pressurized hydrogen 'Clean Sphere' containment unit which was designed specifically to support his environmental and atmospheric needs and was situated on level 5, deep below the S4 facility.

As Burisch explained in detail to Bill Hamilton; "the larger partial pressure of the environment was hydrogen, and in so doing we have a pressurization and a temperature difference. It was an extremely cold facility within the Clean Sphere. There was insufficient oxygen within the gaseous mixture to support human life, 'human' as we understand it presently. In other words, if I would have been introduced into the Clean Sphere not wearing a TES [suit], I would have died fairly rapidly from asphyxiation and from cold."[233]

Part of the project's investigation included direct interaction with the J-Rod with the intent of reintroducing his tissue samples back into his body after they had first been processed, evaluated and then finally transformed. Burisch explains in more detail;

329

"what we were trying to do is we were trying to actually strip the exterior cytoplasm off from the cells and produce cells which would be independently functioning, then to understand those cells biochemically, genetically, so that those cells could then be re-added as a graft into the J-Rod."[234]

After a while as communications with the "visitors" improved it became evident that the J-RODs weren't at all "alien" as was once assumed, in fact it proved to be the opposite; they had much more in common with human beings than we could ever have deemed possible. Rather than being just space travellers, they were in fact time-travellers. They claimed to have travelled back in time using 'Stargate' technology which they called 'Looking Glass' technology using a small planet in the Gliese Star System (approximately 15 light years from Earth) as a local base from where they could stage their trips here. They have travelled from a human future, which although only a potential future for us, as things stand, is a reality to them.

THE CLEAN SPHERE INCIDENT

Initially, it was the role of Dan's supervisor Dr. Steven Mostow to get suited up and enter the Clean Sphere to take the tissue samples required from the J-ROD while Dan was part of the backup team. However, Dan was rapidly promoted within the team and was taught the necessary protocols to enter the sphere himself even though his premature promotion apparently caused problems in the team structure as Dan was the newest member and clearly lacked the seniority or experience required to undertake such a responsibility.

This sudden and unexpected change of events was due to the J-ROD rejecting the services of Dr. Mostow and demanding a change of personnel, insisting that Dr. Burisch, who was working outside of the sphere but in plain sight of Chi'el'ah, should take over his duties instead. It was at this point when Dan was still part of B-unit team that the J-ROD communicated with him for the first time when he looked at him through the clean sphere and spoke to him telepathically saying the words "I remember" and "Hello".

Describing the initial contact and the concept of telepathy Dan said "You know the sound of yourself when you talk to yourself. Self-talk. It's the same sound except... it's the wrong linguistics, the wrong wording. You can tell it's not you...and from my perspective initially when it was happening, there was a very panicky feeling."[235] It would later become apparent that the reason the J-ROD insisted on this change was because he recognized Dan as being one of the abducted children that had been on board the same craft as himself, back in 1973, his connection to Dan was down to this one-off event. As complicated and extremely hard to believe as this all is, it remains part of Dan's testimony. Burisch himself has had to go through many stages of acceptance and stated that, "before I experienced the 'gentleman' in the Clean Sphere', I frankly thought, honestly thought that those people who believed in aliens were tin-foil heads...Egg on my face!"

Dan became accustomed to his new role working in the Clean Sphere in direct contact with the J-ROD, the sampling methods necessary and the protocols involved in the whole process, getting suited up before entering the gantry and then into the Sphere, the required exit protocols and finally the debriefing that would follow each session. But one day there was a violation of the protocol that took everyone by surprise as the J-ROD decided to get up, step forward and approach Dan who was startled enough to break another protocol by backing away. He fell backwards after catching his heel on a floor grate and ended up laid on his back on the floor of the containment unit. This happened during the early days of his working relationship with the EBE so nobody really knew what to do in such a scenario, least of all Dan.

Feeling terribly afraid and in a state of panic, he was thinking "get me the hell out of here". Later, he told one of the project scientists Jeff Rense that he felt as helpless as a cockroach lying on its back. The alien then climbed up on top of him until he was sitting on Dan's abdomen, then leaning forward with his hands on his chest he pushed Dan down. Then this being from another time and another planet began to telepathically impart or 'download' a vast amount of information into Dan's mind.

"I won't hurt you Be-anie" said Chi'el'ah, this being the nickname he had given Dan. Along with the knowledge of the history of his people he also took the opportunity to share his own personal experiences with Dan which included the events of his abduction as a child. Whilst this entrainment was in progress and the data was entering Dan's mind, the ET flooded him with natural opiates to relax him.

Prior to the commencement of this assignment he had been briefed on the many dangers involved and it was well understood that the J-RODs were to be considered a threat. The team used to joke that if the alarms went off in an emergency situation such as a contamination then it would be advisable to "Get in a straight-backed chair and lean way over and kiss your ass good bye". Despite maintaining radio communication with the staff outside of the Clean Sphere, it was impossible to get anyone in or out quickly. According to Burisch there were two separate units on the radio like separate radio frequencies, an E unit and a B unit. As he began to dissociate himself from the bizarre occurrence within the clean sphere he could hear the panic and distress coming from his team as they desperately attempted to get him out of there; "they were stepping over each other, screaming, saying "Get a secondary unit ready!", they were going to enter in and pull me out"[236] claims Burisch.

The situation was completely unprecedented and required an emergency rescue from the support team but with the alien in the process of entraining Dan with information, the team were careful not to be too hasty and decided against the usual procedure of firing a repress valve to change the pressurization in the clean sphere to cause the J-ROD pain when he didn't respond as the team would like. Because he was of a lesser physical density to us, meaning his bone structure was less dense than ours, when they fired the repress it would cause a change of pressure to his skin which would hurt him. During the incident Dan recalls screaming "No!" and he thinks that if they had followed through with the procedure, that the pain felt by the ET would have been felt by him also and could very possibly have killed them both. When Dan was finally removed he was unconscious and spent several days in a coma at S4 and only when his physical condition improved did they take him to Area 51 and finally back to Las Vegas.

Before he died, Dr. Steven Mostow leaked out the scientific results of the J-ROD's tissue sampling gathered over two years by Dr. Burisch, to Marci McDowell in a document that Dan and Steven were writing to go up to the Cover Committee named The Q-94 document. Copies of this are hard to come by but can be found by trawling the internet. It is a fascinating but extremely difficult read as it is written using scientific terminology, yet it does offer a rare insight into the methods employed in Project Aquarius and how things generally are written up inside a Black Ops project.

Chi'el'ah and Dan developed an unlikely friendship over the years and began to understand each other. They were both prisoners in their own ways, Burisch was under the control of the CotM and under orders from Majestic, whilst Chi'el'ah was hospitalized and confined to the S4 facility, light years from his home and his family. Initially Dan struggled to read the EBE's expressions and understand his emotions because due to the anatomy of the J-ROD it was difficult to see when he was smiling or when he was sad. To get around this, Chi'el'ah learnt to telepathically tell Dan how he was feeling. Eventually though, Dan came to understand his moods and he soon discovered that they shared the sense of humour, much to the disapproval of his superiors.

Burisch stated that "When I knew he was laughing, after that, then that got me into trouble with the folks in the facility because I reacted naturally to his physical responses. And so I would smile or whatever over at him, and they would say, "What is transpiring between you two?" I'd hear it come over the radio."[237]

But Dan learnt to lie about what was going on between them when questioned, because often Chi'el'ah was angry either simply due to his lack of freedom or because the relentless tissue extractions were causing him pain and discomfort, and should Dan choose to relay this information back to his superiors then the J-ROD would be punished using the repress valve. When asked if he thought the ET had the means to protect him, Dan replied that it was probably the other way around, saying "I was covering for him by not telling them of the anger, because then they would have followed an operant conditioning protocol that had been set in, against him, to penalize him. So I was actually protecting him."[238]

Since then Majestic have made many unsuccessful attempts to retrieve from Dan the information shared between the two of them. Although he has shared his experience with the world for reasons that we shall discover shortly, Dan has refused to disclose much about what they discussed between themselves, even though he has taken a specific interest in the United States space program (among other things), seemingly as a result of his interactions with the J-ROD.

Dan remained loyal to Chi'el'ah until the end, his friendship was something of great value to them both as he told Cassidy; "the kinship was no ruse. And that's something that that they (Majestic) misinterpreted, although he appeared different, that he didn't belong, he's still a human being...I had a true friendship with him. There was true affection there between the two because he was showing me things from his childhood and I was showing him things from mine and we were actually enjoying each other's experience of each other in a... a friendship. It was a true friendship and I don't really think that Majestic ever regarded it that way."[239]

At the back end of 2003, Dan Burisch risked his life to send Chi'el'ah home to be with his son as he had requested. They were both transported independently of each other to Egypt where a Stargate unit had been set up. Dan was brought in later as it transpired that Chi'el'ah, who'd arrived earlier as part of a communication program that had been established almost a decade after Project Aquarius had been terminated, wasn't communicating adequately enough for them to continue without the assistance of Dr. Burisch.

But unbeknown to his superiors, Dan's empathy for his friend would ultimately lead to an unexpected event occurring of which he was 100 per cent culpable. As soon as the security personnel turned their backs, Dan approached Chi'el'ah, who was now inside a kind of large bell jar over the top of a 'Segway-type' stroller, and using very little force pushed this waist high stroller towards the Stargate. With one more final shove the stroller entered the Stargate and to the best of Dan's knowledge, Chi'el'ah finally returned home to his son, 52,000 years into the future.

Burisch described the event; "I pushed forward, then the next feeling was a feeling of numbness. For a brief moment I thought I had really screwed up and maybe killed myself or whatever because I literally felt numb everywhere. Then I remember a flash of gray. And then I was seated, coughing, on a block about 20, 30 metres away, maybe. And I had people rushing up to me, still over-dramatically actually cocking an automatic firearm at me, screaming at me. And I was grabbed, picked up from the block and taken over and said, you know, "You're under arrest." And, I mean, I had committed a violation of the protocols. And I was being threatened with weapons to my head and things like that."[240]

Majestic personnel were very angry with Dan over the incident but there was nothing they could do now apart from arrest and detain him in level 3 at S4 until they could figure out what to do with him. He was basically told "That's where you are for now." He was kept in unit one out of 12. He had all the amenities and he could ask for food but wasn't allowed to leave. He wasn't tortured as such but was subjected to several different acts of unkindness from Majestic which "can range from everything from psychological unkindness - being rude to you, to being threatening, to being physically harmful."

THE PURPOSE OF DISCLOSURE

So, why would Dr. Burisch be allowed to disclose any of this information if it is so top secret? In the autumn of 2005, Majestic presented him with a new set of orders, to tell the public of his experiences at S4 and his history with Majestic. Once he had formerly accepted their orders he was given approximately one year in which to complete his mission. He claims to have been debriefed to disclose his experience to the public as and when requested by his superiors and sure enough he went on to do just that.

As he himself confirmed, "Well, following 20 years of service for the Majestic, last October the 12th, which was October 12, 2005, I was dismissed at the time of their adjournment, to complete a final set of orders, if you will, to present the information which I have learned over the last twenty years concerning the extraterrestrial intelligences to the world or to whomever wanted to hear. For the last year's time we have been committed to a debriefing of my service since 1986 and even actually before that. We've ranged into speaking about my early life as well. We're hoping that within a short period of time, the DVDs will be completed and this will be presented. And this will then conclude my service to Majestic, with a very big relief and 'Thank God!'" To witness the moment he was debriefed about the disclosure and given his orders, please go to this web address in the endnotes.[241] This piece of video footage was filmed in Marci McDowell's apartment with his ex-wife and Majestic operative Deborah Burisch as a witness (they were married at the time).

Here are his orders in written form:

"To: The Most Honourable Dr. Danny B Catselas Burisch, Majestic ID# H-6196-E.

From: The Most Honourable MJ#1, for the Consistory of the Majestic 12, Washington, D.C.

Within and for the Consistory of this Majority assembled; by order of the Majestic 12, in Formal High Session, Thursday, October 12, 2005 A.D., you are hereby instructed, ordered, and enjoined to the best of your abilities and talents to present the truth of the extraterrestrial reality, as you have personally known it, on dates yet to be established, to the population of the world. You will conduct this disclosure with the application of your sacred honour, without regard for personal security, and in an unwavering manner rely upon the Truth and the countenance of Almighty God as your personal defence. Know now that you have the personal assurance of the Majestic 12 that none shall prevail against you, that your message shall be for the unity of humanity during the time of the cycle's cross. Such supremacy of word, but subordinate to God, is established by Treaty with the future extraterrestrial intelligences. You are hereby held to all ethical and moral boundaries, as in keeping with the standards set forth for Senior Agents of the Majestic 12. May God be with you, O' Son of the Majestic! We will stand, unanimous and adjourned to your purpose. Your acceptance of this order is hereby requested forthwith."

Dr. Burisch was briefly a pro-tem member of the Majestic 12, as MJ-9, and was finally assigned as H-1-Maj, the designated person to disclose the 'extraterrestrial human lineage (time travel) information'. He completed his final orders in September, 2006, and has now retired from service.

In 1980 William Moore obtained an original document from inside sources titled Project Aquarius (TS/ORCON) or (Top Secret/Originator Controlled) meaning only the originator may release the information. Page seven of the document gives a reason why such classified information should eventually become public stating that in order to avoid causing a worldwide panic "MJ3 has

336

developed a plan that will allow release of Project Aquarius, Volumes I thru III. The release program calls for a gradual release of information over a period of time in order to condition the public for future disclosures." This document is a fascinating read and contains a wealth of information on the project of which Burisch was to find himself so deeply involved.

PROJECT LOOKING GLASS

The Stargate that allegedly sent Chi'el'ah home originated from a reverse-engineered extraterrestrial device found on board one of the crashed discs at Roswell in '47 called a Looking Glass. This device was designed as a mechanism that would enable the opening of a portal used for Stargate-type travel and due to its capacity to bend time and space, it allows the user to view future and past events. When paired up with a second device the resulting events on show can also be heard.

The Stargate unit is comprised of three separate components according to Dr. Burisch: an electromagnetic ring component, a projection component and a barrel component. Two of these are Looking Glass units which must be used simultaneously with the Stargate unit to achieve both visual and sound outputs. Field posts are positioned around the Stargate and provide the power necessary for it all to function. When all three units are used in tandem, the Stargate units access natural wormholes that are existent throughout our galaxy and possibly the whole universe, enabling travel between two points in time and/or distance. Not only are they used for various physical objects to be transported to and fro but they also allow for the passing of information and communication via the energy or matter which is spread out in a compatible way by the machine itself. It basically allows anything to traverse vast distances in time and/or lengthy expanses of time.

On 16th June 2003, Deborah Burisch was requested by Majestic to do a series of remote viewing sessions to try and locate the locations of some of the Stargates. She succeeded in finding several and documented what she saw in the document RV No. 0403. Among them were Volochanka, to the north by the Tundra in Russia (the 2018 winter Olympics is to be held here), one in the southwest Tibetan Mountains and one in Mosjoen in Norway, where the equipment was actually removed completely and the

Pirin Mountains in Bulgaria. On February the 4th of 2003 she did a special RV, and wrote in her report "I came up with the following in my session. I saw a place 10 miles south-southeast of Baghdad."

It is estimated that at one time there were in excess of fifty functional Stargates scattered across the globe in various countries, including Egypt, Iraq, Syria and Turkey. However, for safety purposes and to avoid causing a global catastrophe it was deemed necessary to disengage all the three major components from each other and distribute them amongst the European Union, the United Nations and NATO. It is now impossible to reactivate the devices as long as no individual group gains access to any of the other two components. It was always deemed too dangerous for people to be routinely transported back and forth due to the unstable nature of wormholes. If they should collapse with someone mid-transit, then that person would die, suspended in space somewhere between worlds. The Stargates were once used primarily for the two-way transportation of hardware and supplies between the ET's point of origin and Earth. Only occasionally were they used to transport extraterrestrial delegates here in times of importance or as Dr. Burisch stated "only under extreme circumstances involving international uproar when there were problems with the treaties", and in this case they were used to send them *this* direction only.

According to Burisch, the 1954 meeting with President Eisenhower was initiated by a group of P52 Orions who had passed on some of their Looking Glass technology to the United States during that meeting. They soon realised that humans were not mature enough as a species to use the technology responsibly and insisted on negotiating a treaty which would establish a set of rules we had to adhere to. We were allowed to retain the devices but were restricted with their usage. It was stipulated within the treaty that we were not to step through a Stargate unit into other parts of the galaxy, knowing how dangerous and immature we are as a race. And although on occasions we have apparently pushed the boundaries of some of the treaty mandates imposed by the Orions, we are currently still undergoing amicable relations with that group.

TAU-9 TREATY SYSTEM

During his time working for Majestic, Dan Burisch became involved with the Tau-9 treaty system and has been present at the negotiations of these extraterrestrial groups. During this particular event known as the Tau-9 Conference for the Preservation of Humanity, U.S. government representatives and various alien factions were all present to discuss and put in place certain rules which to abide by.

Dr. Burisch claims to have contributed to the T-9 treaty by managing to convince those present that it would be in everyone's best interests to reduce the number of treaty-sanctioned human abductions to zero. This was accomplished. If it hadn't have been for the treaty negotiations then the four different groups would never have encountered one another. The four groups being the P45 J-RODs, the P52 J-RODs, the P52 Orions and the present day humans. The P45 J-RODs were unaware of the existence of the Orion group until they met during this timeframe.

The P45's who are commonly referred to as 'the Greys' and also known as 'the Rogues' by Majestic are considered to be a service-to-self group unlike their more advanced ancestors the P52s, and are responsible for the vast majority of human abductions if not all of them. The purpose of these abductions according to Burisch "is a long-term longitudinal genetic drift study which is aimed solely at benefiting their species." The P52 J-RODs on the other hand, as Chi'el'ah has already demonstrated are of a more altruistic nature and have returned to Earth in an attempt to rectify our present time situation by informing us about the dangers of time-travel and the ramifications of Stargate abuse.

Dan has expressed his admiration for the P52 Orions whom he has only encountered during treaty negotiations and has described them as very spiritual and also much more human-looking than the other races. UFO and contact reports of this race commonly describe them as the 'Nordics', the 'Talls' or the 'Blondes'.

Dan explained his understanding of the Orions to Kerry Cassidy; "They're essentially, you know, the anthropomorphic very tall human beings with blond hair, very large eyes, very blue, pretty eyes. Larger than our eyes, as in ratio to cranium size. The orbits are larger, etc. They're just brilliant, just absolutely brilliant people. And what I found most intriguing about them was how they modulated what I consider their brilliance through emotion. The emotions coming from them were so less rudimentary, they were so more complex than what even I experienced with Chi'el'ah. I would have really enjoyed spending some more time with them."[242]

THE CONVERGENT TIMELINE PARADOX

The Looking Glass technology has the potential to influence and even exacerbate a global catastrophe during this critical time on our planet. According to many within scientific and military circles, it is generally accepted that the Earth's crust and ecosphere will be stressed more than it has for over 25,000 years due to the fact that our solar system is entering a zone called the galactic plane, in which extremely high amounts of energy will radiate towards us from the nucleus of the Milky Way. Apparently we are already seeing the effects of this but it will become significantly more pronounced as the years roll by.

It is of the upmost importance that the Looking Glass and Stargate units remain dismantled and housed somewhere safe from harm in order to minimize the likelihood of any forthcoming disaster. The 'Rogue' P45s only exist as a race on timeline 2 as a result of an Earth cataclysm sometime in their distant past, and they are the descendants of the P52 J-Rods and the Orions. If left in the hands of the 'Greys' then the overuse of Stargate technology will inevitably lead to the planet's demise and eventually the uprising of their species.

Author and researcher Eric Franz wrote, "What appears to have happened on the J-Rods timeline (Timeline 2) in which the Earth catastrophe actually takes place, is that the anatomy and physiology of post-apocalyptic humanity eventually devolves as a result of living underground for tens of thousands of years. The resultant beings are the P45 and the P52 J-Rods, who eventually migrated to the Zeta Reticuli star system."[243]

While one group went underground, the group that would later become the Orions fled the Earth after the disaster heading first for the Moon, then Mars and finally to the star system that would become their new home. The deterioration of the J-Rods anatomy caused by environmental and other factors suffered as a result of this cataclysm yet the P45 Orion's decision to flee for pastures anew left them in good shape and was responsible for them keeping their human-like form thousands of years into the future.

It was suggested by the J-Rods that the reason the catastrophe which occurred on Timeline 2 became a reality was most likely caused by the amplifying affects of over usage of the Stargate and Looking Glass machinery and the overlaying time anomalies which resulted from this. Hence the reason the P52 J-Rods and Orions returned to inform us of this possible outcome and force our hand in decommissioning the devices that could ultimately destroy the planet we call home.

Prior to the decommissioning of the Stargates, the information received from the Looking Glass indicated that there was a 19% chance with an 85% confidence level that the global catastrophe will occur. It was predicted that around 4.2 billion people would lose their lives over the course of a few years as a result of this cataclysmic event occurring on Timeline 2, which it is said that we had moved onto from our original Timeline 1. Fortunately for us, if there is any truth to all of this crazy 'Back to the Future' type scenario, Dan Burisch has it on good authority that we have safely moved back from Timeline 2 (where the catastrophic event was likely to occur) to Variant 83 of Timeline 1.

Steps have been taken in case the worst should happen and Dan has confirmed that there is an object being stored safely on the Moon which is referred to as 'the Ark'. This is just a nickname for something that contains genetics and tissues from all walks of life, covering a range of biodiversity. It is stored up there for safe keeping in case of global disaster. Dan claims "I know the exact spot that the thing is setting there...I know what it looks like, I know how many pieces there are. I was involved in looking at and assisting with the biospherics on it. I know exactly where it sets and what happens if I say exactly where it sets and something happens to it?"

A physicist using the pseudonym Henry Deacon who is working on highly classified projects has confirmed Dan Burisch's testimony. He claims that the concept of a timeline paradox derives from the notion that if you were to travel back in time and kill your grandfather, that you wouldn't cease to exist as might be expected using logical thinking. Rather, the paradox is avoided by the creation of another timeline that would bypass the point of the grandfather's death and thus diverges from the original timeline. So it is assumed that every time a future being has travelled backwards in time to attempt to remedy or change a certain scenario, they are creating a number of new timelines. These new timelines then become new potential possibilities for us that were not there before but are not pre-determined fixed realities. Every action has a consequence, so in the best interests of us all it has been decided, primarily by the Orions, being the more spiritually advanced race, that maybe we should stop with the actions for a while!

MAJESTIC VS BURISCH

Dr. Burisch was formally censured by the CotM in the late 90's for his violation of direct orders, but thanks to the intervention of a very private religious order based in France, managed to get his academic credentials restored. The Committee had issued a demand for Dan to stop working on a book he was aiming to publish concerning anomalies on Mars. He had spotted something whilst perusing images of Mars in the NSSDC (NASA gallery) that looked like another face on the Martian surface in the area known as 'Inca City'.

The book called *Eagles Disobey: The Case for Inca City, Mars* was written with Marci McDowell during 1997 and 1998 and caused members of Majestic to sit up and notice. They questioned Dan about his 'conversations' with Chi'el'ah in relation to the astounding discovery of so many anomalous structures on Mars and wondered if his sudden interest in this field was related. Dan refused to tell them anything and went ahead with the book which was published and released in late 1998. The Committee took immediate action and caused his PhD degree to be vacated. Dan was so affected by the loss of his credentials that he was hospitalised after suffering a heart attack. He continued regardless of the consequences upon his recovery and left the CotM in a state of confusion, not knowing exactly how to deal with his behaviour.

McDowell wrote "They couldn't outright 'get rid' of him, as he had heavy connections into the upper echelons of Majestic, as well as deep connections with the J-Rods who were in treaty negotiations with Majestic and major governmental bodies, plus he also had familial connections due to his marriage into a

Majestic family line that reached all the way back to the early 1940s and the Roswell incidents,"[244] (she is speaking of Dan's family connection with June Crain, whose story has become part of the fabric of the Roswell incident).

So after much deliberation it was decided that they would move him and his family to alternative location and give him a new 'cover' job in a new environment. But first they tried to modify his memory, only the period of time where he had been rebelling against them during the 'Mars discoveries' period. In order to facilitate this, he was taken up north to undergo a process involving experimental neuro-peptides then housed in Mississippi to start his new life. Unfortunately for the Committee, Dan's mind rejected the conditioning and he started to experience memory recall.

Afraid that they may have permanently damaged one of their best scientists it was eventually decided that the procedure should be reversed. They did this and returned him and his family back to Las Vegas where he could continue his research and concentrate on his personal studies which right up to the present day is focused on a project called 'the Lotus Protocol'. This project is based at Area 51 and concerns the creation of life and something called 'the Ganesh Particle'. This area of work is of the upmost importance to humanity as it is working with the building blocks of life and gaining an unprecedented understanding of human life at a cellular level. Marci McDowell declared that "Carefully hidden from view behind millions of dollars of subterfuge, this knowledge could ultimately lead to experimental methodology that will alter the very fabric of our humanity.... for the things postulated by Dr. Burisch could ultimately undo and reweave the very elements that make up our humanity, forming us into different beings than we are today."[245] The project deals primarily with genetic structures and could become a dangerously effective way of altering the makeup of human beings as we are today, should the knowledge that Dr. Burisch holds fall into the wrong hands.

Dan Burisch comes across as an incredible man of great integrity who has risked his life and that of those close to him, all for the sake of the betterment of mankind. Let's hope that he continues in this vein but with less risk to himself, and that the work that he is currently dedicating his time to will have a positive effect on the future of humanity. And if it turns out that he is a liar and a fraud then he should seriously consider writing a science-fiction novel or a movie, because with stories like his he could become a very wealthy man.

10

BEYOND THE FRINGE

It's one thing to read about UFOs and stuff in the papers or in books. It is another to hear rumours about the military or government having an interest in such matters, rumours which say they have captured aliens and downed alien space craft. But it's quite another matter to find oneself in a situation which obviously confirms everything.

Ingo Swann

THIS FINAL CHAPTER focuses on a more alternative method of attaining evidence of the existence of extraterrestrial life both here on Earth and further afield in the vastness of the cosmos. The obscure kind of information you are about to read coexists in a somewhat parallel fashion with the more familiar and trusted means of data gathering.

The evidence offered throughout the previous chapters has mostly originated from the personal experiences of certain individuals and sometimes groups of people en masse, either as eyewitnesses to particular incidents or through some variable of physical sensory contact; meaning that most reports of alien close encounters have come via sight, sound or touch. Not all information regarding the ET presence has emerged through such established means as these.

The psychic discipline of remote viewing has allowed researchers the opportunity to go beyond the fringes of time and space to previously unexplored regions of our solar system. The mind can go where the body cannot, and with training and purpose it has proved to do just that.

Bearing in mind that the human brain takes in about forty million bits of information per second but only sixteen bits of that actually goes into your conscious mind - with the rest finding its way into our subconscious, it is clear that we only perceive a fraction of what we consider 'reality' during waking hours of full consciousness.

Remote viewing (RV) is a method used to tap into the subconscious mind in the right side of the brain in order to reveal previously uncovered information. The viewer can go beyond the individual's mind capacity and reach further into the unknown to perceive things which exist physically beyond the immediate influence of the viewer. RV is a trained ability which allows the viewer to acquire accurate direct knowledge unavailable to the ordinary senses, of events or 'targets' which are distant in time or space, in either the past, present or future. In the words of the leading researchers in the field, Russell Targ and Dr. Harold E. Puthoff, "Remote viewing is a human perceptual ability to access, by mental means alone, information blocked from normal perception by distance, shielding, or time."[246]

The information is retrieved under specific scientific protocols and then recorded and filed in a report for further analysis. Such psychic practices became useful military applications which were utilised in a number of ways to enable the viewer to perceive targets in (amongst other things) top secret facilities around the world, as a means to spy on the enemy undetected.

SIGHT BEYOND SIGHT

The ability to see beyond one's range of vision may be used for different purposes in modern times and for completely different reasons, but the use of such psychic skills is by no means a new endeavour. As remote viewer Courtney Brown wrote in his book *Cosmic Explorers*, "...the ancient seers were our first human astronauts. While in a deeply relaxed state, they let their minds roam across the fabric of the universe, and some perceived what was there with surprising accuracy."[247] Brown believes that it is the genetics of our human bodies that limits our perceptual abilities and that remote viewing as a process actually helps to alleviate such limitations.

Joe McMoneagle, who was known in the US Army's psychic intelligence unit at Fort Meade in Maryland as "Remote Viewer No. 1" (he was the original member of a top secret program on the subject codenamed the 'Stargate Project') explained the meaning of the term - "Remote viewing is the ability to produce information that is correct about a place, event, person, object or concept which is located somewhere else in time and space, and which is completely blind to the remote viewer and others taking part in the process of collecting the information."

Ultimately, the art of sight beyond sight was the main skill employed by the U.S. military's psychic spies from the 1970's onwards. American research into psychic functioning began in earnest as a response to reports which had surfaced in the early seventies revealing the Russian's progress in the subject. Rand Corporation had produced a 1973 Net assessment study of paranormal phenomena; this was a 33-page document detailing what the Russians were investigating and how American studies compared. It was because of reports like this as well as the 1971 book, *Psychic Discoveries behind the Iron Curtain* by Sheila Ostrander and Lynn Schroeder, which led to Stanford Research Institute's involvement in psychical research studies.

A remote viewing program was set up at SRI in California in response to a CIA request to build up a large database of scientific evaluations on the subject. It was here where Targ and Puthoff were employed to further their research on the matter.

What began as a low budget project evolved into a highly-classified special access program which was carried out under a number of guises. Such codenames included SCANATE, Phoenix, Stunt Pilot, Sun Streak, Center Lane, Grill Flame and Star Gate. Following additional funding and tasking from the navy, the air force, the army and other areas of the intelligence community, the program expanded until it was finally consolidated under the aegis of the Defence Intelligence Agency (DIA).

Writing about the various remote viewing projects which were undertaken at SRI, author Margaret Head explained, "These particular experiments do start with several advantages: they come out of physics, popularly believed to be the hardest of the hard sciences; they come out of a respected laboratory; and they do not appear to be the work of true believers who set out to use science to validate passionately held beliefs."[248]

These covert programs ran undetected for over twenty years until 1995 when they finally became declassified and available to the public for the first time. This sudden revelation followed President Clinton's Executive Order number 1995-4-17, entitled *Classified National Security Information*.

On September 6, 1995, the CIA's involvement in initialising a remote viewing program was publicly announced by the CIA Public Affairs Office in a release entitled "CIA Statement on 'Remote Viewing'." Almost 90,000 pages of declassified documentation are now available to the public at NARA (National Archives and Records Administration) in Maryland or from the Information and Privacy Coordinator at the CIA, Washington D.C.

Russell Targ and Harold Puthoff who had previously worked as laser physicists, started the program in 1972 where they worked mainly with former Police Commissioner Pat Price who had the ability to see things psychically at a great distance. The first experiments involved Price working alongside Targ to reveal Puthoff's location – where he would drive to different locations to test Price's abilities. The results were astounding. Price described each location accurately first time in 7 out of 9 trials.[249]

Following the successful experiments with Price, Israeli psychic Uri Geller was invited to SRI to be tested for his remote viewing capabilities. Among those testing Geller was the sixth man on the Moon, Edgar Mitchell. On arrival at SRI in Menlo Park near San Francisco, Geller was asked to describe the object on the desk of CIA officer Dr. Kit Green, who was sat in his office at CIA headquarters in Langley, Virginia. The 'target' Geller was asked to remote view was a book entitled *The CIBA Collection of Medical Illustrations* by Frank H. Netter.

Green opened the book at a random page and stared at the image in front of him whilst Geller began to scribble down what he was seeing in his mind. After discarding the first few attempts, Geller finally settled on something. Harold Puthoff recalled Geller saying, "I don't know what to think. It looks like I have made a drawing of a pan of scrambled eggs, yet I have the word 'architecture' coming in strong."[250]

Once Green received a copy of Geller's drawing he was astounded, as the page Green had originally been focussed on was a profile picture of the human brain – with the words 'architecture of viral infection' written by Green in pen across the top of the page. The word 'architecture' stood out as it was written alone, with the other words scribbled beneath it. This brief experiment was enough to convince both Puthoff and the CIA of Geller's psychic ability, and ultimately led to Kit Green authorising the expenditure of sufficient funds in order that SRI could expand their remote viewing experimentation.

Russell Targ was tasked with filing reports on Geller for the CIA following their scientific tests on his psychic powers. In one such report dated January 24, 1973 Targ wrote, "It strikes me that what is of interest to CIA is not whether Geller's perceptions are sensory or extra-sensory but rather whether his capabilities are exploitable by CIA (not necessarily utilizing Geller personally: possibly others could be trained to do what he does)." Geller was subsequently employed by the CIA as a Psi spy (psychic spy) following the SRI reports.[251]

THE SWANN FACTOR

American psychic and artist Ingo Swann was probably the most innovative and influential remote viewer to have succeeded in this most unusual field of parapsychology. Swann described remote viewing as being "...composed of a five part protocol, and when any one of the five parts are omitted (such as confirmatory feedback), then what has taken place is something other than remote viewing..." Continuing he added, "If these important definitional boundaries are not understood and maintained, the ultimate result will be ambiguous definitional quagmire of benefit to no one, and the demolition of what the remote viewing protocol achieved in terms of respect and repute"[252]

Swann's psychic powers which he had felt so strongly as a child didn't really resurface until the 1970's. During his childhood, he recalls his father coming home late some evenings and explaining his whereabouts to Ingo's mother before being corrected by his psychic son who innocently informed both of his parents where he had *really* been. This was not always the most popular of decisions, and slowly his innate ability to see beyond the extent of his vision got put on the back burner.

Upon reaching adulthood, his first extensive psychic experiments were in clairvoyancy which began at the American Society for Psychical Research in his home town of New York back in December 1971. It was here where he worked alongside Janet Mitchell and director of research Dr. Karlis Osis, attempting to blindly see unknown targets which were hidden either in boxes or the next room out of view. As Swann became increasingly frustrated at the laborious experiments he was tasked with, he realised that in his mind he could see people in the street outside before they actually walked past his building. For example, one morning he told his colleagues that the next person to walk by would be a lady wearing a yellow coat, and sure enough, he was right.

Realising the potential to view targets much further away than had previously been considered possible, Swann proposed a larger experiment, to describe the weather in a different city then calling someone at that location to confirm the accuracy. The term 'remote viewing' originated, as the cities they were attempting to view were remote from New York. Because back in the seventies there was no internet or any other immediate means of Swann knowing the weather elsewhere whilst isolated in his room, the initial experiments proved to be successful. He managed to accurately describe 'seeing' rain in Arizona when it hadn't rained for months; this most definitely was not guesswork.

Around this time period Swann along with Cleve Backster attempted psychokinetic experiments which involved trying to influence plants using mental power alone. He had some success in this unusual area of research which then led to controlled tests on thermistors (temperature sensitive resistors) at City College, New York, which were devised by parapsychologists Gertrude Schmeidler and Larry Lewis. Swann used his psychic influence to alter the temperatures of the thermistors. [12]

During his time at the American Society for Psychical Research between 1971-73, Swann was also the subject of out-of-body experiments which involved him projecting his consciousness into sealed boxes placed several feet above his head on a small platform. Swann was tasked with revealing the target symbol concealed within the box without moving from his chair. Whilst under strict laboratory conditions Swann's movement was monitored by electrodes which were attached to him whilst he was seated. Despite the physical restraints placed upon him he managed to successfully describe the targets above his head. In one experiment he actually commented correctly on a dysfunctional light source which was meant to illuminate one of the hidden target symbols. The only way he could have known the light was out was by opening the box.[253]

This work led to his involvement at SRI, working on his first CIA funded project which was headed by physicist Dr. H. E. Puthoff. The U.S. had become aware that the Soviets were roughly 25 years ahead in Psi research, and it was because of the Americans desire to catch them up which ultimately allowed Ingo Swann to make a living from his psychic abilities.

The initial project was set up to explore ways of reproducing ESP phenomena at will, something which Swann was more than

---

[12] For detailed report refer to G.R. Schmeidler – *PK Effects Upon Continuously Recorded Temperature*, from Journal of the American Society for Psychical Research, no. 4, October 1973.

adept at already. The project was given eight months to produce some results but Swann became bored of the same repetitive processes involved in the daily experimental trials so he suggested maybe trying something a bit more adventurous and exciting to relieve the monotony.

NASA had recently launched two probes, Pioneer 10 and 11 to flyby the planet Jupiter, and the data which would be collected was to become available from September, 1973. It was in April of the same year that Swann suggested remote viewing Jupiter before any information had been received, as it could easily be verified or dismissed once the signals returned to Earth. He was essentially aiming to psychically 'arrive' at Jupiter before the NASA vehicles did physically. Such an experiment was considered unrealistic and Swann wasn't taken seriously until he announced, "I quit, and you can return what's left of the money to the funding clients."[254]

Once his superiors had reluctantly agreed, the experiment was done on a Saturday, a non-working day, on Swann's own personal time. Initially the VLD (very-long-distance) experiment was done unofficially but it was still considered a necessity for the RV raw data to be recorded in order to establish that it had existed prior to the arrival of the Pioneer probes. Many respected scientists in the Silicon Valley area including two from Jet Propulsion Laboratories, agreed to receive copies of Swann's raw data which finally consisted of two and a half pages of verbal observations and one page of sketches. In order for the experiment to be successful it was deemed essential to include impressions of factors regarding Jupiter which were previously unknown to man.

The raw data which Swann produced, yielded thirteen "scientifically unanticipated" factors which were eventually confirmed to be accurate at a later date, once the incoming NASA data had been analysed. Below are the raw data factors on Jupiter which Swann recorded, along with the dates they were confirmed.

1. The existence of a hydrogen mantle: Confirmed 1973, and again in 1975.

2. Storms, wind: Confirmed 1976 as to dimensions and unexpected intensities.

3. Something like a tornado: Confirmed 1976 as strong rotating cyclones.

4. High infrared reading: Confirmed 1974.

5. Temperature inversion: Confirmed 1975.
6. Cloud colour and configuration: Confirmed 1979.
7. Dominant orange colour: Confirmed 1979.
8. Water/ice crystals in atmosphere: Confirmed 1975.
9. Crystal bands reflect radio probes: Confirmed 1975.
10. Magnetic and electromagnetic auroras ("rainbows"): Confirmed 1975.
11. A planetary RING inside the atmosphere: Confirmed 1979, not only as to its existence, but as being inside the crystallised atmospheric layers.
12. Liquid composition: Confirmed 1973, 1976, as hydrogen in liquid form.
13. Mountains and solid core: Still questionable, but suspected as of 1991.[255]

The majority of scientists had denounced the possibility of Jupiter containing a ring until it was confirmed in 1979, despite the fact that Ingo Swann had sketched it in his raw data back in 1973. It was this information which Swann produced that really brought him to the attention of some very secretive members from within the higher echelons of society not to mention the American government. As Swann recalled, "Among those taking an active interest in the possibility of interplanetary spying was a group so clandestine that it would be characterized not merely as a deepest black project, but as an entirely invisible one."[256]

Around this period of time, Swann had been searching for more progressive scientific methods of remote viewing which could lead to better results and data. By suggesting that a viewer should picture New York for example, Swann was aware that the name alone would summon up images of taxis, skyscrapers and busy streets and could seriously impair the quality of data coming through. So one day, whilst lounging on an inflatable in a swimming pool, a voice in his head suggested he should try coordinates. Swan wrote "...people do find their way around the world using coordinates...then there is no real reason why one cannot use them to find their way in a psychic voyage, as a kind of focus, so to speak."[257]

No-one, including Ingo Swann fully understood how this new approach would actually work, and at first it didn't, but after about fifty attempts it started to payoff. This new technique which involved using geographical coordinates as the sole target information instead of names or places became known as coordinate remote viewing or CRV.

Following a phone call to Swann from a man using the pseudonym Mr Axelrod, a planned secret rendezvous in the Smithsonian Museum in Washington was arranged for him. Upon meeting two very strangely similar looking men who insisted on communicating with him in silence by feeding him cards with text on, Swann was led to a secret underground facility with a hood over his head. It was at this secret facility where Swann was asked to perform CRV on the dark side of the Moon.

Naturally, he didn't expect to find anything except rocks and dust but the opportunity to see what was there was too good to refuse, along with the promise of $1000 a day. Swann speculated on the reasons for him being asked to look up there, and considered that maybe "they", whoever he was actually working for, were looking for a good place to build a Moon-base or perhaps they were trying to locate a missing secret spacecraft of some kind.

The first 'Moon Probe' session as he called it, took Swann to the lunar surface without the use of coordinates. He was simply informed of the Moon's position in relation to the Sun and the Earth. Axelrod only gave him his first set of coordinates once he had psychically arrived on the surface of the Moon. "OK, I can see these rocks, and some dust, so I guess I must be here. Give me your first Moon coordinate preceding it with the word Moon", Swann instructed.

Swann's immediate impression was one of confusion; to such an extent that he believed that he must have arrived back in Earth. He reported seeing "largish tractor tread marks" on the terrain before him, then following a greenish haze into a crater he discovered actual lights which he described as "sort of like lights at football arenas, high up, banks of them. Up on towers of some kind..."[258] He gave up at this point, disillusioned and firmly believing he had inadvertently landed back home. "Well, Axel, I can't be on the Moon. I guess I have to apologize, I seem to be getting somewhere here on Earth" Swann conceded.

He was having trouble understanding how lights could possibly be on the Moon, but there they were, and Axelrod who was saying very little in response to Swann's questions remained tight-lipped throughout the session but gave enough small facial gestures to suggest that Swann was on the right track and to continue looking. "Have the Russians built a Moonbase or something? Is that what I'm supposed to be remote-viewing?" No reply.

Continuing somewhat bewildered, he soon came across a massive tower on the crater's edge which he compared to the 39-storey Secretariat building at the United Nations in New York. Speaking to Axelrod he said, "Does NASA or the Soviet space program have the capabilities of getting such large stuff onto the Moon? I thought the only thing we got on the Moon was a flag planted in some crater somewhere."

Slowly the implications of what he was viewing dawned on him, "You mean – am I to assume this stuff is – not OURS! Not made on Earth?" Raising his eyebrows Axelrod responded with, "Quite a surprise isn't it." Ingo Swann was so taken aback with the information he was unveiling that he was becoming dizzy and began taking very short breaths.

Expressing his surprise he wrote, "It's one thing to read about UFOs and stuff in the papers or in books. It is another to hear rumours about the military or government having an interest in such matters, rumours which say they have captured aliens and downed alien space craft. But it's quite another matter to find oneself in a situation which obviously confirms EVERYTHING."[259]

Evidence of structures on the Moon prior to the Apollo landings was inadvertently revealed to former US Air Force Sgt. Karl Wolfe during his time as an electronics engineer at Langley AFB, Virginia in 1965. Wolfe who had bypassed the usual lengthy process required to receive a top security Crypto clearance, revealed to Dr. Stephen Greer during the Disclosure Project interview series in 2001, that he once had access to photographic images from the Lunar Orbiter which the National Security Council were collecting.

Wolfe recalled being told by a colleague of the same rank, "We've discovered a base on the back side of the Moon!" Continuing, Wolfe went on to say "...and then he pulled out one of these mosaics [photo-montage] and showed this base, which had geometric shapes, there were towers, there were spherical buildings, there were very tall towers and things that looked somewhat like radar dishes but they were large structures." Giving an example of the scale of some of these objects he

355

explained that "some of the structures are half a mile in size, so they're huge structures."[260]

Back to the secret facility where Ingo Swann was discovering the extent of the Moon conspiracy, it had become clear that he was being held in some kind of "ultra-ultra-ultra secret place" built with the intent of understanding extraterrestrial matters. As the levity of the situation became increasingly evident, Swann exclaimed "whoever is in charge of these matters hasn't managed them very well", to which Axelrod conceded, "Frankly, no one has known what to do, and many mistakes have been made." Quite an understatement really, considering how far the deception on extraterrestrial matters appears to have extended.

Swann had been rather reluctant to share the information which he was receiving during the Moon sessions, as he told his superior, "Had I not learned some time ago to accept and describe what I was seeing psychically, accept it BEFORE prejudging it, I would have not dared to say I saw lights on the Moon. I would have edited that out, fearing others might see me as a loony. God damn it! ETs on the Moon, no less!"

As the sessions progressed Swann began to question why his services were required in the first place; why not send up another Apollo mission instead? Looking at Axelrod he began to realise the awful truth, "Unless they somehow have told you to stay away, and somehow shown you they meant it!" Finally, he now understood why the Apollo program had finished so abruptly. So, whoever was employing him needed Swann to see as much as he could and report it back to them before the Soviet psychic spies beat him to it. A psychic race to the Moon followed the physical race to the Moon.

Axelrod explained to Ingo Swann why his services had been required initially, especially considering the vast amount of information that 'they' already had on the Moon. "Your information might provide a kind of check point in what you surely now realize must be a mass of interpretations of the photographic and other evidence" he told Swann. "It was my idea to find a psychic who did not know anything about the Moon, and see what might be seen there, sort of an independent source of information, which would lean our interpretations one way or another."[261]

Explaining the bizarre and sudden end to the Apollo space program, following what had appeared to be six very successful moon landings, Swann wrote, "In December, 1972, Apollo 17 was the LAST American craft to the Moon. At that point, American Moon visits abruptly ceased for reasons that were never adequately explained. The remaining three Apollo crafts which were already built at enormous expense were left to rot."[262]

Continuing with the task at hand, Swann remotely-viewed many more anomalous objects during his brief journey to the lunar surface including towers, machinery, bridges, strange-looking 'buildings', domes of various sizes, some with platforms on. He also witnessed large cross-like structures, obelisks which had no apparent function and tractor-like machines going up and down hills. Stored in caves or next to crater edges he also reported seeing small saucers with windows.

During the final part of his sessions for Mr. Axelrod, he saw what he could only describe as naked human-looking males, working on the surface, digging and excavating. The session ended somewhat abruptly once two of the figures turned towards Swann as if they were aware of his presence.

Since his experiences working on such highly classified subject matter, Swann began to research the alien enigma in more detail referring to books like *Somebody Else Is On The Moon* by George H. Leonard (a copy of which was mailed to Swann in 1976, most likely from Axelrod himself in Swann's opinion), Maurice Chatelain's 1978 book *Our Ancestors Came From Outer Space*, and *Moongate: Suppressed Findings of the U.S. Space Program* by William Brown. With the information contained within books such as these, it is becoming increasingly difficult to accept the 'Dead Moon Dictum', a theory which continues to be enforced on the general public to the present day and one which is becoming harder and harder to validate.

As Swann discusses in his 1998 publication *Penetration*, secrecy is promoted by elitist spin doctors in an attempt to manage undesirable and 'dangerous' information in order to conceal it from public cognizance. This process of reality management plays an essential part in the success of any covert operation or cover-up. Humans have what Swann describes as an "information comfort zone" which allows us to operate in a simpler and clearer fashion. Too much information can be too taxing for many people to absorb, so it is often preferred to keep in touch with old and familiar knowledge rather than extending one's mind to unfathomable boundaries.

Constructing realities for the general public has long been a tactic enforced by higher authorities as far back as one cares to venture. Knowledge has always been considered best kept secret amongst the highest echelons of any given society, hence the birth of secret societies; to contain and withhold ancient knowledge from the common man.

The decision to deny the existence of extraterrestrial life on this planet and beyond, along with the continued insistence that the Moon is a natural satellite bereft of life, are but two prime examples of the 'informed' elite constructing a reality of which the masses must accept if they are to be included in a conformist society. Those people choosing to reject popular notions of reality face being forced into obscurity and ostracized. Swann wrote, "Information management has to do with establishing whatever is to be conceptualised as constituting reality within any given societal framework."[263]

Ingo Swann's long career in remote-viewing lasted nearly twenty years, during which time he saw and experienced a plethora of unusual activity whilst working in the shadows of CIA funded projects. Some of what he saw and recorded has been verified as scientifically accurate, as the aforementioned Jupiter data will affirm, but other celestial outings have been much harder to confirm.

But as Swann declared himself in the preface to *Penetration*; "...the authenticity of my personal, unprovable, experience probably doesn't need to be considered all that much – because the drift of accumulating information is inexorably leading to establishing the authentic existence of extraterrestrial intelligences anyway."

Regardless of the verifiable accuracy of his Moon observations, Swann was the first man in modern times to seriously attempt psychic astronautics and follow his desire to push the perceptual boundaries beyond previously considered unreachable locations.

SOME MEN ARE FROM MARS

In 1996, American remote viewer Courtney Brown published his book *Cosmic Voyage: a scientific discovery of extraterrestrials visiting Earth*. Using the rigorous and scientific remote-viewing protocols established by Ingo Swann for the CIA, which were initially developed for the military for espionage purposes, Brown details the existence of two known extraterrestrial races which he believes presently reside side by side on our planet. *Cosmic Voyage* describes how both alien worlds faced ecological disasters and died before the surviving members of each civilisation aborted their home planets in favour of a new beginning here on Earth.

Much of the information Brown offers appears highly incredulous but he insists that every detail recorded came about as a result of remote-viewing and is to be taken as fact rather than fiction. As Brown states, "The data that are obtained using these protocols accurately represent reality, not imagination or allegory. I make no apologies for the methods used to conduct my research, though in the absence of these methods the research would not have been possible."[264]

Brown's first psychic visit to Mars came about unexpectedly during a routine CRV session on September 29, 1993; the only information Brown was given were the target coordinates 5987/9221. His previous target was a bridge over a river in Viet Nam; his monitors liked to vary the target selections to discourage Brown's mind from guessing the targets rather than just letting the information flow naturally. Sat in his office with a pen and paper he began collecting information such as surface textures, colours, sounds, temperatures, tastes and smells, all of which are associated with the target. All the while he was attempting to isolate the signal and establish a mental "lock". Finally, after 19 pages of preliminary data he managed to 'arrive' at the target destination.

CB: "...Things are brown and sandy here. There is a house. What is that pyramid doing here? Let me AOL [analytic overlay] on a pyramid. It must be my imagination."

MONITOR: "Don't judge things. Just put it down as an AOL for now."

CB: "The pyramid is tall, stone, hard, gritty. It is sandy and windy around here. It seems like the pyramid is solid, but hollow at the same time. Wow, it sure is tall."

Continuing, Brown is asked to go inside the pyramid and write down anything noteworthy such as descriptive feedback or any feelings of emotion which arise.

CB: "...I get the sense of a sombre purpose to this structure. Goodness, I can perceive lots of people now. I clearly get the sense that either this structure or something related nearby was a great building project, and that the folks needed help and lots of resources. Apparently many died to build this. There is a nearby city. Wow. There is also a nearby mountain erupting. What's going on here? There are no volcanoes near a pyramid that I know of. It is like Pompeii, but there are no pyramids near Pompeii.

MONITOR: "Don't analyze. Just record the data. Keep going."

CB: "Lots of people have died, and are dying. There is a lot of movement. People are running. Many are scattered. There is a sense of hopelessness. This is terrible!"

At this point Brown started sketching the scene before him. He described the volcano being located towards the east of the city, and that the people were mostly running north. He then moves forward in time marginally to reveal that some of the survivors have set up a village nearby consisting of shacks and tents. He describes the scene as desperate poverty with no one there to help those left. This was followed by;

CB: "Mmmm. There are some new people rebuilding the city. They are not the original folks. They are rebuilding for a new group of people, it seems. Others are coming in. These new folks come from very far away, and they do not seem to be panicky – in a sense of urgency – about helping the former residents."

After the session finished Brown asked his trainer where he had just been sent, so a folder was pushed across the table to him with the target photograph inside. He opened up the folder and pulled out a picture taken by a satellite of the Cydonia region of Mars, with evidence of volcanic activity to the east of the pyramid.

"You're kidding. You sent me off-planet? To Mars?" Brown remarked in astonishment. The idea of Mars having been inhabited at some point in the distant past had always belonged to the realm of science-fiction until that day, now he had to get used to the concept of having witnessed "an actual fragment of Martian history."

As was briefly touched upon in the *Space Secrecy* chapter, photographs of highly unusual structures have been taken from passing satellites which raise many questions regarding the possibility of ancient civilisations on the red planet. The anomalous Mars observations recorded by Tsuneo Saheki back in the fifties had already raised a few eyebrows at the time, with some suggesting that such bright flares seen ejecting from the Martian surface could possibly have been signs of nuclear activity.

The many ancient astronaut theorists bandying around notions of highly advanced civilisations existing and exerting their influence on humankind way back in antiquity, all concur that Mars and its former inhabitants have had, and may continue to have, a prominent role in our galactic history. The pyramid on Mars (as remote viewed by Courtney Brown), the mile long humanoid face on Mars and the whole Cydonia region as photographed by the Viking orbiter, all exhibit signs of ancient activity of intelligent beings.

Brown's psychic voyages into these unchartered territories have served as purposeful scientific explorations into a wealth of possible scenarios which can neither be validated nor disproved. Such is the nature of remote viewing that only data that can be verified by comparable physical evidence, already accepted as scientifically accurate, can be confirmed. Every venture beyond the fringes of known science and provability will continue to be unverifiable until the day when physical scientific exploration catches up with its psychic counterpart. Nevertheless, such information has its place and purpose until it can be fully dismissed as impossible, and some of which may actually go a long way towards progressing our current understanding of life beyond Earth.

Brown's Mars sessions brought about a great deal of fascinating data which would be impossible to accumulate without the use of parapsychology. His remote viewing experiences led to a wealth of information on Martian life both past and present, and as has just been highlighted, may or may not be a true account of events.

Following a session in 1993 where Brown was asked to remote view a mountain, whose location remained unknown prior to the viewing, the forthcoming data suggested that the mountain was Santa Fe Baldy, located within a national forest near Santa Fe, New Mexico. This led Brown to the conclusion that the Martian beings he had previously viewed on their homeland were also living outside their natural habitat.

"There *are* Martians on Earth, but one must think clearly about the implications of this before ringing the alarm bell. These Martians are desperate. Apparently they have very crude living quarters on Mars. They cannot live on the surface. Their children have no future on their homeworld. Their home is destroyed; it is a planet of dust", stipulated Brown.

Describing the Martians he said, "They have no hair and have larger eyes than humans. Their skin is light." It was to become apparent to Brown and his team that there had at some point in the ancient past been a cataclysmic event which threatened the very existence of the indigenous inhabitants of Mars. But, just before the death of an entire race it seems that another race of intelligent beings arrived there and assisted with the evacuation of the planet.

CB: "I see other beings here now. They are smaller, shorter. They give the sense of being workers on a mission. Wow, are they motivated. For some reason, speed and urgency are paramount in their minds. These other beings have ships, spaceships. They have uniforms with insignias. Some of these beings are pilots. I do not see any Martians right now."

MONITOR: "Try to find out where the Martians are."

CB: "That's just it. The Martians are gone. They're finished. The houses are empty. I am still on Mars, but it is a ghost town except for these short advanced beings."

"The situation was one of panic and despair when the short beings arrived. These short beings are milky white. The Martians viewed them as godlike...This is weird. It feels like the short beings are planning on the Martians getting a physical change in their bodies, and they're being put in cold storage for a while. These little short folks look like Greys."[265]

So according to Brown's claims, the Martian society which experienced a major catastrophe at some point in the distant past was partly rescued by the infamous Greys, although he is uncertain as to whether or not the locals liked the terms of the rescue. Arriving with precision timing at the final moments of the cataclysmic event, the Greys managed to "store" the Martians in an attempt to preserve what was left of Martian life with special emphasis on retaining their genetic material.

Brown asserts that the "stored" Martians were then brought to Earth which would become a safe haven for their dying race where they could potentially seek refuge and start again in the mountanous regions of Santa Fe amongst other places. Brown discovered that beneath Santa Baldy is a Martian base which acts as centre for all of their planetary operations.

In 1996 he wrote, "Virtually all remote-viewing data show that the Martians seem to have been genetically altered to enable them to live in the heavier gravity and different conditions on Earth. The actual alteration occurred recently, following a period of preservation, and is not yet complete." CRV data also revealed that a small percentage of the Martian survivors have found a way to blend in with everyday people, specifically in Latin America, where they have successfully concealed themselves and integrated into the human population.

With regards to the psychic mechanisms of the human mind and particularly such tools as remote viewing, it has been proven many times over that somehow, these complex and predominantly uncultivated innate human abilities, do actually function to a level beyond our wildest imagination. Ingo Swann's Jupiter foray proved how a human mind can penetrate the far reaches of outer space without ever leaving the room. Uri Geller's personal history of CIA funded psychic neanderings and experimentation is replete with successes throughout, leaving the discerning researcher in no doubt of the validity of remote viewing as a means to gather hitherto unretrievable information.

This said, proof of the functionality of such parapsycholgical techniques does not by any means prove that all forthcoming data is 100 percent accurate. In fact, there are so many factors involved in each individual RV session including who is performing it, why are they pursuing a particular target and for whom specifically the results are meant for. It is the unverifiable data which will always remain 'Speculative', which is remote viewing terminology for data that cannot be verified until it has been collaborated with physical data. The results of any given session are given clarity scores from 0-3 in this order:

0 = All incorrect
1 = Target contact, many errors
2 = Good
3 = Perfect

As long as there is a lack of physical data to reinforce the psychic data, speculative information remains just that, speculative. Courtney Brown's fact finding mission which he so succinctly put into words in *Cosmic Voyage* remains open for interpretation until further notice, but let us not be deterred by the lack of concrete evidence. Many scientific theories have stood the test of time without substantial hard evidence to back them, one only has to think of Darwin's theory of evolution which remains unproven to this day but is commonly perceived as a matter of fact despite evidence to the contrary.

Brown's research has led him to become to near certainty regarding the ET scenario to such an extent that he is of the opinion that humanity's next step should be to learn as much as possible from our galactic neighbours in a hope that one day we may be able to establish some means of direct communication between our species and theirs.

He wrote, "I strongly believe that the time has come to seriously consider a change in the previous policy of denial. Historically, humans have always been passive with regard to interactions with ETs. We have watched the ships fly by, and some of us have been abducted. But always the ETs came to us, and we just watched it happen. Now we have the ability to move from a passive place to an active stage in studying interstellar life. With this ability must come a new grasp of our need to participate responsibly within this larger society. Just as ETs have studied our society, we can begin closely examining theirs. Moreover, educating our own public about the ETs is the first step toward establishing reciprocal diplomatic relations."[266]

Continuing, Brown suggests a way in which such relations may materialize; "Perhaps the best way to advance communication between the humans and the Greys is to use SRV to ask the Greys how we might be able to assist them with the genetic project that is related to their own species' evolution. In the past, conscious and willing human help with this project has been nonexistent. Greys have had to work with humans who have little or no understanding of the complexities of subspace life."[267]

DEALING WITH DISCLOSURE

Disclosing details and information regarding the alien enigma has always proved to be a dangerous tactic, historically speaking. Many who have chosen to share the truth publically have either found themselves either completely discredited, stripped of any hard earned academic accreditations or in the most extreme scenario…dead. Commonly the death of a whistleblower comes in the form of a suicide, and only those close to the victims are 100 percent certain of the conspiratorial aspect of their loved one's death. Suicides are easy to accept for the rest of us; a nice, simple explanation wrapped up in a conveniently neat little package.

One example of such a death came following a total power failure which paralysed New York City on July 13th, 1965, as Senior Physicist of the Institute of Atmospheric Physics at the University of Arizona, Dr. James E. McDonald, found himself in all sorts of trouble. The great New York power failure of 1965 featured heavily in Major Donald E. Keyhoe's book *Aliens From Space* in which he included a meticulously detailed investigation.

Keyhoe wrote, "Just after the power failed at Syracuse, two UFOs were seen at Hancock Airport by multiple witnesses, including the city's Deputy Aviation Commissioner." One of the UFOs was also observed from above by a flight instructor and a computer technician in a plane approaching to land and was described as being "directly above the Clay power substation, an automatic control unit between Niagara Falls and New York, on a grid system that was supposed by our best qualified experts to be accident-proof and infallible."

In the aftermath of the power failure, experts traced the origin of the breakdown to the area of the Clay substation but weren't able to locate the malfunction which ultimately disabled the billion dollar U.S. – Canadian grid system. In 1968, Dr. James McDonald was placed on record by Congressman William F. Ryan, to discuss the UFO activity at the time of the power failure. It was then that Dr. McDonald charged the Federal Power Commission with evading the evidence connecting UFOs to the power failure, an accusation which was entered into the Congressional Record.

He was found dead with a bullet in his head and a gun by his side, three years later on June 13, 1971. Author George Andrews wrote, "The fate of Dr. McDonald is an unmistakably clear example of what happens when a scientist of integrity dares to disagree fundamentally with the clique of professional politicians whose only aim is to perpetuate and extend their control over everyone else."[268]

As mentioned in a previous chapter, The Disclosure Project setup by Dr. Stephen Greer is a research project aimed at fully disclosing the facts about extraterrestrials and UFOs to the public. Whilst also exposing classified advanced energy and propulsion systems, Greer has successfully got on board over 500 government, military and intelligence community witnesses willing to testify to their personal, first hand experiences regarding the ET's, their technology, and the conspiracy to keep the whole complex issue well and truly covered up.

Despite their brave efforts however, the Disclosure Project press conference which took place on Wednesday, May 9th, 2001 at the National Press Club in Washington DC doesn't appear to have caused much of a stir and shaken the world up as sufficiently as they must have hoped at the time that the conference took place. In fact YouTube views of the conference remain below 150,000, which is clearly not nearly enough to change public opinion. Considering that a 17-second clip of a sneezing panda has raked in over 215 million views, one wonders how interested the general populace actually are with certain important and life changing issues such as the origins of mankind and the mind-blowing implications of extraterrestrial involvement in our ancient past up to the present day and beyond.

Maybe one part of the problem of disclosure lies with the fact that the average human is either not ready to take on such knowledge at this juncture in their personal evolution, or it is simply much easier to give away our responsibility to those who govern our daily lives than it is to face up to some pretty dark and sinister truths. That said it only takes the tiniest pebble thrown into the stillest lake to cause ever increasing ripples.

The public's interest in outer space was momentarily roused in November 2014, as a robotic European Space Lander named Philae ended its ten year journey into the cosmos by becoming the first manmade object to touchdown on a comet. The comet 67P was estimated to have been 300 million miles away from Earth at the moment of contact. Landing an object the size of a washing machine onto a three mile long lump of rock was such an astounding feat of human engineering that it quickly became global news for a short time. If the public can be so fascinated with landing on a comet, surely confirmation of direct extraterrestrial contact with humans here on Earth would have a huge impact on the public were it announced all over the world as the news of Philae's arrival on 67P had been.

It is not a question then of how interested people are regarding matters of alien existence, but rather how can the people gain access to this information if those controlling the media continue to conceal and deny all news which they deem 'unsuitable' or too 'dangerous' for public consumption. Some of the information in this book may prove to be inaccurate as more material comes to light, but nevertheless that does not negate the fact that there most certainly appears to be a conspiracy of massive proportions aimed at concealing much of the type of information you have read thus far.

There is far too much evidence available which points towards the largest cover-up in human history, even if the names of those responsible may be up for debate, the deception remains hard to disprove given the raw data available and surely it is only a matter of time before these mysterious matters step out of the conspiratorial shadows of concealment and into the light for all of humankind to judge for themselves.

SOURCES

The symbols used for each chapter page originated from Valdamar Valerian's book series *Matrix I-IV*. They represent different insignia and logos witnessed by abductees on the uniforms and breastplates of both extraterrestrials and human workers either during abductions or in underground facilities.

LYRAN EMPIRE

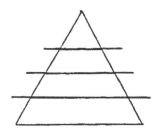

ZETA RETICULUN

369

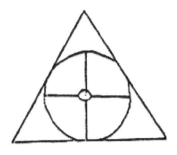

SIRIAN

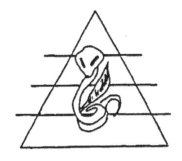

SIRIAN

SEEN ON PERSONNEL WITH
NO ACCESS TO UNDERGROUND OPERATIONS

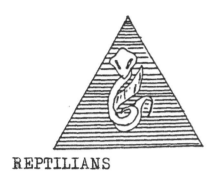

WORN BY SIRIANS   AND
REPTILIANS

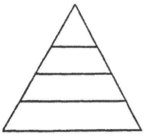

WORN   EXCLUSIVELY   BY
HUMANS WORKING IN ALIEN TYPE ENVIRONMENT,
MILITARY AND CIVILIAN.

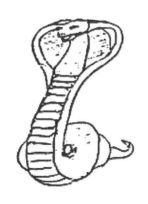

ZETA RETICULUM

PLEIADIANS

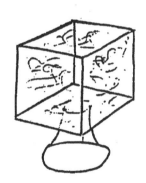

ORION GROUP

RETICULUM

372

I SKY GHOSTS

[1] UFOTV Presents Out Of The Blue, narrated by Peter Coyote, released 09/11/2011

[2] www.ufocasebook.com

[3] Ibid

[4] Look magazine, May 14, 1968

[5] New York Times, Dec 18, 1969

[6] http://www.tonytopping.co.uk/a-1968-article-by-john-g-fuller-flying-saucer-fiasco-condon-report/

[7] Marrs, Jim – Alien Agenda

[8] Interview with Jim Marrs, Aug 16, 1993

[9] Fowler, 1979, p.159

[10] Boston Sunday Globe, May 21, 2000

[11] COMETA Report, July 1999

[12] Ibid

[13] Ibid

[14] http://www.disclosureproject.org/

[15] UFOTV Presents Out Of The Blue, narrated by Peter Coyote, released 09/11/2011

[16] Letter from Headquarters Space Command, Peterson AFB, Colorado, Department of the Air Force – Dated 27 Aug, 1984

[17] National Press Club, Washington D.C., UFOs and Nukes Conference, September 27, 2010

[18] Ibid

[19] Ibid

[20] Ancient Aliens, Alien Contacts episode, History Channel documentary series

[21] Behind the Paranormal, hosted by Paul and Ben Eno, aired January 2010

[22] UPI quote, Dec 10, 1965

[23] UFO Crash at Kecksburg – The Untold Story, Film Documentary

[24] Ibid

[25] Ibid

[26] http://www.ufocasebook.com/Kecksburg.html

[27] UFO Crash at Kecksburg – The Untold Story, Film Documentary

[28] Farrell, Joseph, P. - Hitler's Suppressed and Still-Secret Weapons, Science and Technology, 2007

[29] Farrell, Joseph, P. – Reich of the Black Sun: Nazi Secret Weapons and the Cold War Allied Legend, 2004

[30] UFO Crash at Kecksburg – The Untold Story, Film Documentary

[31] Los Angeles Times, Feb 26, 1942

[32] Hall, Richard – The 1952 Sighting Wave: Radar-Visual Sightings Establish UFOs As A Serious Mystery, 2005 http://www.nicap.org/waves/1952fullrep.htm

[33] http://www.nicap.org/520719washington_dir.htm

[34]
http://www.youtube.com/watch?feature=player_embedded&v=sTZ7O9cfpPQ

[35] Clark, Jerome - *The UFO Book: Encyclopaedia of the Extraterrestrial*. Visible Ink,1998.

[36] Ibid

[37] Ibid

[38] Hall, Richard - The 1952 Sighting Wave: Radar-Visual Sightings Establish UFOs As A Serious Mystery, 2005

[39] Charleston Gazette – July 28, 1952

[40] The Washington Post – July 28, 1952

[41] www.Project1947.com

[42] UFOTV Presents Out Of The Blue, narrated by Peter Coyote, released 09/11/2011

[43] White House Press Conference, Washington D.C. – April 4, 1950

[44] Maussan, Jaime – Voyagers of the Sixth Sun – Video Documentary

[45] Experiencers –Documentary Film by Stephane Allix

[46]www.youtube.com/watch?feature=player_embedded&v=cJOIKpO3kzU - Ariel School Research 1994-2012

[47] Experiencers –Documentary Film by Stephane Allix

[48] History Channel Documentary, "Secret Access : UFOs On The Record"

[49] ABC News Report by Christopher Sign

[50] History Channel Documentary, "Secret Access : UFOs On The Record"

[51] UFOs & Area 51 – The Official Bob Lazar Video

[52] Cameron, Grant – The True Story of Area 51: A Look At The Actual Evidence, 2011

[53] George Knapp interview of John Lear and Gene Huff, Coast to Coast AM Radio, March 22, 2009

2 FINGERPRINTS OF DECEPTION

[54] James E. Clarkson interviews June Crain – Ocean Shores, WA - June 27, 1997

[55] www.project1947.com

[56] http://www.youtube.com/watch?v=VZsCGgIFf3w

[57] Marrs, Jim - Alien Agenda, Harper Collins, 1997

[58] www.rense.com/general44/nmxx.htm

[59] James E. Clarkson interviews June Crain – Ocean Shores, WA - June 27, 1997. Also included in documentary - The Secret Evidence We Are Not Alone, Paranormal TV

[60] Witness to Roswell – Carey, Tom & Schmitt, Don (2009)
[61] Air Material Command Intelligence Department report, August 1949
[62] Letter of Transmittal from Office of Scientific Research & Development, 1530 P Street, NW, Washington 25, D.C. –July 5, 1947
[63] Good, Timothy – Above Top Secret: The Worldwide UFO Cover-up, Quill, 1988
[64] Marrs, Jim - Secret Societies That Threaten to Take Over America
[65] http://keyholepublishing.com/Death%20of%20James%20Forrestal.htm
[66] Marrs, Jim - Alien Agenda, Harper Collins, 1997
[67] Robert M. Wood, Ph.D. - Mounting Evidence For Authenticity of MJ-12 Documents - *Presented at the International MUFON Symposium July 2001, Irvine, CA*
[68] Eisenhower Briefing Document
[69] Ibid
[70] Ibid
[71] Marrs, Jim - Alien Agenda, Harper Collins, 1997
[72] Ibid
[73] http://www.cufos.org/ros5.html
[74] Majestic-12 Group Special Operations Manual, TO 12D1-3-11-1, April 1954
[75] Ibid
[76] Ibid
[77] Ibid
[78] "Majestic Twelve Project, 1st Annual Report"
[79] Ibid
[80] Majestic-12 Group Special Operations Manual, TO 12D1-3-11-1, April 1954
[81] Marrs, Jim - Alien Agenda, Harper Collins, 1997

3 OUT OF SIGHT, OUT OF MIND

[82] Richard Sauder – Hidden Empires : Underground Bases and Tunnels (Video from XCON 2004)
[83] Jacobsen, Annie – Area 51: An Uncensored History of America's Top Secret Military Base, 2012
[84] Ibid
[85] Cooper, William – Behold A Pale Horse - 1991
[86] Cooper, William – Majestic 12 and the Secret Government
[87] Ibid
[88] http://www.youtube.com/watch?v=Xs4emKd_fG4
[89] http://www.apfn.org/apfn/cynthia.htm
[90] http://www.angelfire.com/oz/cv/rrummell3.html
[91] Conference dated October 20, 1991

[92] Video of Phil Schneider's lecture at the Preparedness Expo in November of 1995
[93] The Feb.-Mar. 1991 issue of 'UFO UNIVERSE' - Article titled 'The Deep Dark Secret At Dulce', written by Bill Hamilton and 'TAL' LeVesque
[94] "A-Bomb in the Gas Field," *Science News,* 92 (23 December 1967):610; "Going Deep for Gas," *Science News,* 96 (20 September 1969): 236; "Once More for the Money," *Science News,* 95 (19 April 1969):376; "Swords into Plowshares," *Time,* 78 (22 December 1961): 29.
[95] Rhodes, John – Where It All Began – Probing Deeper Into The Dulce 'Enigma'
[96] Hamilton, William – Cosmic Top Secret
[97] Valerian, Val – The Dulce Papers – Leading Edge Research
[98] http://www.thewatcherfiles.com/dulce/chapter25.htm

4 INTRUDERS

[99] Prichard, E., David, and Mack, E., John: Alien Discussions: Proceedings of the Abduction Study Conference held at MIT. Cambridge, Massachusetts, 1994
[100] Touched –Documentary film by Laurel Chiten, Blind Dog Films, 2004
[101] Little, Dr. Gregory L. - UFO Abductions Through The Ages, Excerpt from Grand Illusions,1994
[102] Turner, Dr. Karla – Taken: Inside the Alien/Human Agenda, 1994
[103] Rux, Bruce – Architects of the Underworld: Unriddling Atlantis, Anomalies of Mars, and the Mystery of the Sphinx; p. 109-116, Frog Books 1996
[104] Touched –Documentary film by Laurel Chiten, Blind Dog Films, 2004
[105] Ibid
[106] Horrigon, John - The Lost Betty Hill Interview, October 1999
[107] Webb, Walter."A Dramatic UFO Encounter in the White Mountains, NH" Confidential report to NICAP. October 26, 1961.
[108] Clark, Jerome. The UFO Book, 1998, p. 276
[109] Friedman, Stanton & Marden, Kathleen – Captured! The Betty and Barney Hill UFO Experience, New Page Books, 2007
[110] Ibid
[111] http://www.ufocasebook.com/pascagoulainterview.html
[112] In Contact – The Pascagoula UFO Abduction - Documentary film directed by Charles Hickson
[113] Marrs, Jim – Alien Agenda
[114] Walton, Travis – Fire In The Sky – The Walton Experience, Paragon Plus, 1996
[115] Marrs, Jim – Alien Agenda
[116] Ibid
[117] The X-Conference 2009, Gaithersburg, MD, April 17 – presentation on case file # SC001-09-08

[118] Coast to Coast radio with George Noory
[119] Little, Dr. Gregory L. - UFO Abductions Through The Ages,
[120] Ibid
[121] Sinistrari, Ludovico Maria - De Demonialitate, 1875
[122] Little, Dr. Gregory L. - UFO Abductions Through The Ages, 1994

5 SURGEONS FROM THE STARS

[123] Perkins, 1979: 20
[124] Marrs, Jim; *Alien Agenda,* Harper Collins, 1997
[125] Jacobs, David Michael; *The UFO Controversy In America*; Indiana University Press, 1975
[126] Andrews, George C. - *Extra-Terrestrials Among us*, 1986, p.132
[127] Saunders and Harkins
[128] Jim Marrs interview with Linda Moulton Howe; August 7, 1996
[129] http://vault.fbi.gov/
[130] ibid
[131] Marrs, Jim; *Alien Agenda,* Harper Collins,
[132] Albuquerque Tribune, 1976
[133] Rommel Jr., Kenneth M. - Operation Animal Mutilation; Report of the District Attorney First Judicial State of New Mexico; June 1980
[134] Andrews, George C. (1986) – Extra-Terrestrials Among Us, (p.177)
[135] FBI Vaults; File AQ 198-541, August 1, 1979
[136] National Enquirer, June 5, 1979, p.5
[137] Howe, Linda Moulton; *An Alien Harvest: Further Evidence Linking Animal Mutilations and Human Abductions to Alien Life Forms*, 1989
[138] http://vault.fbi.gov/

6 MESSAGES IN THE FIELDS

[139] http://www.lucypringle.co.uk/articles/crabwood/
[140] Ibid
[141] Crop Circles: Quest For Truth, Dir. William Gazecki, 2003
[142] http://www.enterprisemission.com/
[143] http://www.enterprisemission.com/glyph.htm
[144] Levengood, W. C., "Anatomical Anomalies in Crop Formation Plants," Physiologia Plantarum 92 (1994): 356-363.
[145] Ibid
[146] Ibid
[147] Wingfield, G. 1990. Beyond the current paradigms. *In* The Crop Circle Enigma (R. Noyes, ed.), pp. 99-110. Gateway Books

[148] http://www.lucypringle.co.uk/news/stonehenge-julia-set-eyewitness.shtml
[149] Ibid
[150] Ibid
[151] Ibid
[152] Ibid
[153] Ibid
[154] http://www.bltresearch.com/eyewitness/eyewitness2.php
[155] Ibid
[156] Moulton Howe, Linda – Crop Circle Formation By Bright Flash Of Light, July 27, 2007 (From Great Dreams website)
[157] Ibid
[158] Ibid
[159] Ibid

7 THE MEIER MYSTERY

[160] www.futureofmankind.co.uk/Billy_Meier/The_Pleiadian/Plejaren_Contact_Reports
[161] www.futureofmankind.co.uk/Billy_Meier/Sfath%27s_Explanation
[162] www.tjresearch.info/Phobal_plain_text.htm
[163] www.youtube.com/watch?v=91kQ-NIqZIs
[164] Andrews, George C. (1986) – Extra-Terrestrials Among Us, (p.152)
[165] www.youtube.com/watch?v=pAOtJISsqZc&feature=autoplay&list=PLB9AC08747296E850&playnext=1
[166] Rashid, Isa and Meier, "Billy" Eduard Albert – The Talmud Of Jmmanuel
[167] Contact : The Extraterrestrial Experiences of Billy Meier / The Billy Meier Story – UFOs and the Prophecies
[168] Ibid
[169] Kinder, Gary – Light Years: An Investigation into the Extraterrestrial Experiences of Billy Meier (New York: Atlantic Monthly Press, 1987).
[170] Contact : The Extraterrestrial Experiences of Billy Meier / The Billy Meier Story – UFOs and the Prophecies
[171] Ibid
[172] Ibid
[173] Go to www.tjresearch.info/witness-list.htm for a comprehensive list of key witnesses
[174] Moosbrugger, Guido – And Yet...They Fly! (2001) Tulsa, OK: Steelmark; translated from the German edition of 1991.
[175] www.theyfly.com/lost/meier.prophecies.1958.htm
[176] The Billy Meier Story – UFOs and the Prophecies
[177] Beamship : The Meier Chronicles

8 SPACE SECRECY

[178] http://www.hourofthetime.com/majestyt.htm
[179] http://www.jfklibrary.org/Research/Ready-Reference/JFK-Speeches/Special-Message-to-the-Congress on-Urgent-National-Needs-May-25-1961.aspx
[180] UFO Universe magazine; Condor Books 351 West 54th St., New York, N.Y. 10019], November, 1988, (Vol 1, No. 3)
[181] Swann, Ingo – Penetration: The Question of Extraterrestrial and Human Telepathy (1998)
[182] Huzel, Dieter K (1960). *Peenemünde to Canaveral*. Englewood Cliffs NJ: Prentice Hall.
[183] McGovern, James (1964). *Crossbow and Overcast*. New York: W. Morrow.
[184] Naimark, Norman M (1979). *The Russians in Germany;* A History of the Soviet Zone of Occupation, 1945–1949. Harvard University Press.
[185] http://history.msfc.nasa.gov/vonbraun/bio.html
[186] Marrs, Jim. "Secret Societies That Threaten to Take Over America"
[187] Ibid
[188] Hunt, Linda – Secret Agenda: The United States Government, Nazi Scientists, and Project Paperclip, 1945-1990
[189] "Reach for the Stars", Time (magazine), February 17, 1958.
[190] http://www.zamandayolculuk.com/cetinbal/v2rrocket.htm
[191] http://www.zamandayolculuk.com/cetinbal/v2rrocket.htm
[192] Hunt, Linda Secret Agenda: The United States Government, Nazi Scientists, and Project Paperclip, 1945-1990
[193] Ibid
[194] Farrell, Joseph P. - Reich of the Black Sun - 2004
[195] Marrs, Jim. "Secret Societies That Threaten to Take Over America"
[196] Cooper, William Milton – Behold A Pale Horse
[197] "News Europa" Jan. 1959
[198] http://www.astronautix.com/articles/prorizon.htm
[199] Marrs, Jim. "Secret Societies That Threaten to Take Over America"
[200] Wilson, Don – Our Mysterious Spaceship Moon, 1975, p.139
[201] http://www-pao.ksc.nasa.gov/kscpao/nasafact/80facts.htm
[202] Joseph F. Goodavage, "Immanuel Velikovsky: Genius vs. The Scientific Mafia," *SAGA*, September, 1970, p. 93
[203] www.moonrising-themovie.com
[204] http://www.thelivingmoon.com/43ancients/01documents/Nasa_Airbrush.htm
[205] http://www.ufocasebook.com/moon.html
[206] http://projectcamelot.org/los_angeles_19-20_september_2009.html

207 http://www.bibliotecapleyades.net/luna/luna_apollomissions06.htm
208 Watson, Richard – Celestial Raise, 1987; page 147-148
209 http://ronrecord.com/astronauts/armstrong-collins-aldrin.html
210 Wilson, Don – Our Mysterious Spaceship Moon
211 Good, Timothy – Above Top Secret
212

http://ntrs.nasa.gov/archive/nasa/casi.ntrs.nasa.gov/19790076811_197907681
1.pdf
213Disclosure Project, Dr. Steven Greer, pp. 61-64
214 Sagan, Dr. Carl– Intelligent Life in the Universe, 1966
215 Apollo 14: Science at Fra Mauro, p.17 quoted in Wilson, Don – Our
Mysterious Spaceship Moon
216 Swann, Ingo (1998) – Penetration: The Question of Extraterrestrial and
Human Telepathy
217 Solomon, Sean C. – Astronautics publication, February 1962
218 Asimov on Astronomy Mercury Press, 1963
219 John Lear interview with Project Camelot April 2nd 2008
220 Keyhoe, Major Donald E. – The Flying Saucer Conspiracy, Holt, 1955
221 Von Humboldt, Alexander - COSMOS: A Sketch Of A Physical Description Of
The Universe, Vol. IV, P.438
222 Allen, Dr. P and Bellamy, H.S. – The Great Idol of Tiahuanaco, Faber & Faber,
1959.
223 As reported in The Telegraph newspaper, August 6, 2009
224 http://www.ufocasebook.com/moon.html
225 http://english.pravda.ru/
226 http://www.enterprisemission.com/tran1.html
227 http://www.ufocasebook.com/moon.html

9 THE BURISCH SAGA

228 Bill Hamilton interviews Dan Burisch, Las Vegas, September 18-19, 2002
229 Ibid
230 Hamilton, Bill - The Saga of S-4 Scientists also "Project Looking Glass"
http://www.skywatchresearch.org/
231 Bill Hamilton interviews Dan Burisch, Las Vegas, September 18-19, 2002
232 Ibid
233 Ibid
234 Out from under Majestic: Dan Burisch uncensored – Video interview with
Kerry Lynn Cassidy, Las Vegas, July 2006
235 Ibid
236 Ibid

[237] Ibid
[238] Ibid
[239] Ibid
[240] Ibid
[241] http://www.youtube.com/watch?v=3t8uIY8vkKE
[242] Ibid
[243] Franz, Eric – Space Faring Civilisations, Earth Humanity's Ongoing Involvement with Extraterrestrials - iUniverse, 2009-10
[244] https://eaglesdisobey.net/
[245] Ibid

IO BEYOND THE FRINGE

[246] Targ, Russell and Puthoff, Harold E. – 'Mind-Reach' – Scientific look at Psychic Abilities, Hampton Roads Publishing Company, 1977.
[247] Brown, Courtney - Cosmic Explorers: Scientific Remote Viewing, Extraterrestrials, and a Message for Mankind, Dutton 1999.
[248] Targ, Russell and Puthoff, Harold E. – 'Mind-Reach' – Scientific look at Psychic Abilities, Hampton Roads Publishing Company, 1977.
[249] BBC Horizon documentary – The Case for ESP (1983)
[250] Ibid
[251] Documentary Film - The Secret Life of Uri Geller – Psychic Spy?
[252] Article in Fate Magazine – On remote viewing UFOS and extraterrestrials, September 1993.
[253] http://rviewer.com/IngoSwann_encyclopedia.html
[254] Swann, Ingo – Penetration: The question of extraterrestrial and human telepathy, Ingo Swann Books, 1998.
[255] Ibid, p.5
[256] Ibid, p.7
[257] Ibid, p.16
[258] Ibid
[259] Ibid, p.26
[260] https://www.youtube.com/watch?v=7Clbn3zgsRs - "Secret Structures on the Moon" - Sgt. Karl Wolfe
[261] Swann, Ingo – Penetration: The question of extraterrestrial and human telepathy, Ingo Swann Books, 1998.
[262] Ibid
[263] Ibid, p.68
[264] Brown, Courtney – Cosmic Voyage: A scientific discovery of extraterrestrial visiting earth, Dutton Books, 1996
[265] Ibid, p. 73

[266] Ibid, p. 89
[267] Ibid, p. 263
[268] Andrews, George C. (1986) – Extra-Terrestrials Among Us.

UFO CAUGHT IN ARTILLERY CROSSFIRE, BATTLE OF LOS
ANGELES, 1942

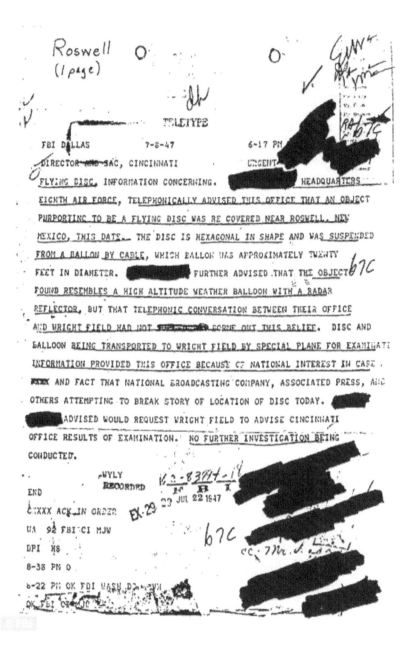

Roswell
(1 page)

TELETYPE

FBI DALLAS   7-8-47   6-17 PM

DIRECTOR AND SAC, CINCINNATI   URGENT

FLYING DISC, INFORMATION CONCERNING.   HEADQUARTERS

EIGHTH AIR FORCE, TELEPHONICALLY ADVISED THIS OFFICE THAT AN OBJECT

PURPORTING TO BE A FLYING DISC WAS RE COVERED NEAR ROSWELL, NEW

MEXICO, THIS DATE. THE DISC IS HEXAGONAL IN SHAPE AND WAS SUSPENDED

FROM A BALLON BY CABLE, WHICH BALLON WAS APPROXIMATELY TWENTY

FEET IN DIAMETER.   FURTHER ADVISED THAT THE OBJECT

FOUND RESEMBLES A HIGH ALTITUDE WEATHER BALLOON WITH A RADAR

REFLECTOR, BUT THAT TELEPHONIC CONVERSATION BETWEEN THEIR OFFICE

AND WRIGHT FIELD HAD NOT BORNE OUT THIS BELIEF. DISC AND

BALLOON BEING TRANSPORTED TO WRIGHT FIELD BY SPECIAL PLANE FOR EXAMINATI

INFORMATION PROVIDED THIS OFFICE BECAUSE OF NATIONAL INTEREST IN CASE

AND FACT THAT NATIONAL BROADCASTING COMPANY, ASSOCIATED PRESS, AND

OTHERS ATTEMPTING TO BREAK STORY OF LOCATION OF DISC TODAY.

ADVISED WOULD REQUEST WRIGHT FIELD TO ADVISE CINCINNATI

OFFICE RESULTS OF EXAMINATION. NO FURTHER INVESTIGATION BEING

CONDUCTED.

WYLY
RECORDED
END

XXX ACK IN ORDER

UA 9½ FBI CI MJW

DPI HS

8-38 PM O

8-22 PM OK FDI WASH D

OK FBI

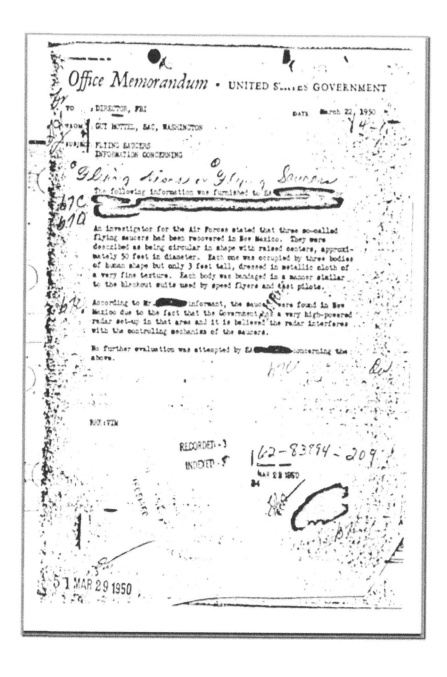

Office Memorandum • UNITED S.....ES GOVERNMENT

TO : DIRECTOR, FBI

DATE: March 22, 1950

FROM : GUY HOTTEL, SAC, WASHINGTON

SUBJECT: FLYING SAUCERS
INFORMATION CONCERNING

The following information was furnished to SA ___

An investigator for the Air Forces stated that three so-called flying saucers had been recovered in New Mexico. They were described as being circular in shape with raised centers, approximately 50 feet in diameter. Each one was occupied by three bodies of human shape but only 3 feet tall, dressed in metallic cloth of a very fine texture. Each body was bandaged in a manner similar to the blackout suits used by speed flyers and test pilots.

According to Mr. ___ informant, the saucers were found in New Mexico due to the fact that the Government has a very high-powered radar set-up in that area and it is believed the radar interferes with the controlling mechanism of the saucers.

No further evaluation was attempted by SA ___ concerning the above.

RXX:VIM

RECORDED - 3
INDEXED - 5

62-83894-209

MAR 29 1950

51 MAR 29 1950

OPERATION MAJESTIC 12

PRELIMINARY ANALYTICAL REPORT

ATTACHMENT D.
PART B.
Section 3.

Preliminary Autopsy of Extraterrestrial

Biological Entity (s)

5 JULY 1947

From: Dr. Detlev Bronk, Chairman National Research Council Atomic Energy
Commission; Medical Advisory Board: Physiologist, Biophysicist.
To: President Truman

Subject: Preliminary autopsy of unidentified cadavers (multiple).

Time of death: 2330 hours (approximately)
Date of death: 4 July 1947
Place of death: 45 miles north northwest of Roswell New Mexico
Time of Preliminary autopsy: 1600 hours/ Date: 5 July 1947
Place: Roswell Army Air Force Base, Roswell New Mexico

The purpose of this preliminary postmortem examination is to determine the
causes and manner of death, the origin of the entities, and the type of biological
lifeform. Dr. Bronk is assisted by a noted forensic pathologist, Dr. Stanford, an Air
Force pathologist, Maj. J. B. Johnson, Capt. Miser the base Mortuary Affairs
officer, and an anthropologist, Professor Frank Holden. Security personnel are
stationed throughout the hospital and outside the operating room. Lt. General
Nathan Twining commander of Air Materiel Command at Wright Field and
Secretary of Defense (Select), James V. Forrestal are witnesses and will hand carry
the report of the initial autopsy to the President of the United States.

Unidentified debris of nonferrous materials was discovered 75 miles northwest
of Roswell by a local rancher William Brazel, witnessed by his son and daughter.
An early morning aerial search resulted in discovery of partially intact and severely
damaged unidentifiable aerospace vehicle and unidentifiable bodies on 5 July 1947.

An intelligence officer, Maj. Jesse A. Marcel of the 509th Bomb Group
Intelligence Office was the first official of the government to recover debris from
the incident. Counter Intelligence officer, Capt. Sheridan Cavitt, of Air
Intelligence (T2), witnessed and assisted Maj. Marcel. Debris will be subsequently
transferred to Wright Field in Dayton Ohio, Sandia Base, Albuquerque, New
Mexico, and Classified Location.

The bodies appear identical in appearance disregarding the damage sustained.
One body appears to be undamaged and the other four are severely damaged from
the trauma of the crash, exposure, and predators. The cadavers support a
disproportionately large cranium and appear to be mongoloid/oriental by loose
comparison. Each is clothed in what initially appears to be a garment made of a
single piece metallic material of unusual strength, yet retains pliability.

No instrument available can cut or pierce the material. The material has a dull sheen and is silver in color. Four bodies have external dermal abrasions and carbonized areas around the face and cranium. The clothing on two of these bodies has separated in sections that run along an undetectable seam from under the arm down to the feet. Another seam with partial opening runs from the neck down the back to the buttocks.

The bodies have been stored in a cooler at the base and transferred to the base infirmary for the postmortem. The undamaged body is uncommonly warm to the touch. This is unusual since the other bodies are near freezing in temperature and all the bodies were removed from the cooler whose temperature is a constant 38 degrees, fahrenheit. Some sort of chemical action or reaction continues to take place in the undamaged body in order to produce a 89.3 degree fahrenheit temperature.

I have ordered each of the four damaged bodies be placed in a hermetically sealed container and packed in dry ice for shipment to facilities more appropriate for examination. The undamaged body will be kept at 89.3 degrees fahrenheit during shipment.

No heartbeat or palpitation was observed although some background noise or resonance can be heard through a stethoscope. No pulse or respiration can be detected. The bodies all weigh fifty six pounds and actual height of these beings is 49.4 inches. The limbs are consistently tubular and no joints are discernable. The arms are 5.1 inches in circumference and the legs are 7.5 inches in circumference. The neck measures 10 inches and both the chest and hips measure 31 inches around, consistently from the torso down to the hips. The finger tips reach to where the knees should be, or mid leg. The hands contain four long slender fingers with some webbing and no opposing digit such as a thumb. Each finger tip has four bumps or wart-like projections with concave centers. Which appear to function as suction cups.

The cranium measures 22 inches maximum and there is no discernable jaw or cheek bones. A thin crease 1.25 inches wide, much like a scar appears where the mouth should be. The mouth cavity is tiny and does not appear to function as a means of ingesting food or communication. No ears are visible, but a small 3/4 inch diameter bump protrudes 1/8 inch where the ears should be. Two small openings appear where the nasal cavity should be, and no visible structure exists for a nose. The small, inwardly tapered nasal openings are slightly less than 1/8 inch in diameter. The head is firm, but slightly pliable and responds to pressure similar to the feel of a human without the skin being loose.

The eyes are of particular interest. On the damaged bodies, they are wide spaced, teardrop in shape, with the point being at the edge of the skull. The deep set eyes are without eyelids or eyelashes and the eyes are solid deep dark brown in color. An opaque film, of milky color coats each eye.

The undamaged body is different. A dark, coarsely textured, flat black, seamless almond shaped apparatus covers each eye with no apparent attachment points. For a lack of better description, eyeglasses or sunglasses comes to mind. Perhaps this apparatus is an aid in distance viewing, blocking harmful solar radiation, enhanced spectrum detection, low light or infrared vision, or some other unknown use.

There are no visible sexual organs or genitalia or other differentiating exterior signs of sex or mating capabilities, nor are there a urinary or rectal openings. The bodies are bereft of hair, bumps, scales, and the skin has the texture of fine cotton cloth of an ivory parchment color. Tiny lines run horizontally from head to foot much like record groves but smaller, and are only discernable through a magnifying glass or microscope.

Of peculiar note is the fact that Sec. Forrestal reported a buzzing sound in his skull and severe migraine like pain on each occasion that he touched the undamaged body. He is the only one in attendance that reported such phenomena.

No digestive system, no gastrointestinal tract, no alimentary or intestinal canal, no interior reproductive organs, or other recognizable organs are present. One large Geo organ is present.

Cause of death; acute blunt trauma.

Blood: colorless viscous liquid oozing which smells like ozone and ammonia.

A more detailed scientific report will be made available to the Secretary of Defence and the President. The follow on report will address; analyzing fluids, materials, gasses, and biological structures and functions of these beings. Upon examination in person, it does not take a leap of imagination to realize that these beings are alien extraterrestrial biological entities. Acronym EBE should be used as an interim for security measures. A special committee, headed by the Sec Def or a Presidential appointee, should be formed for the express purpose of determining the impact upon 'National Security'. I hesitate to speculate upon the impact to civilization, religion, government, or individual sanity if this information is prematurely released. The highest security should be maintained by all involved. God help us all.

TOP SECRET
EYES ONLY
THE WHITE HOUSE
WASHINGTON

September 24, 1947.

MEMORANDUM FOR THE SECRETARY OF DEFENSE

Dear Secretary Forrestal:

   As per our recent conversation on this matter,
you are hereby authorized to proceed with all due
speed and caution upon your undertaking. Hereafter
this matter shall be referred to only as Operation
Majestic Twelve.

   It continues to be my feeling that any future
considerations relative to the ultimate disposition
of this matter should rest solely with the Office
of the President following appropriate discussions
with yourself, Dr. Bush and the Director of Central
Intelligence.

Harry Truman (signature)

TOP SECRET / MAJIC
EYES ONLY
* TOP SECRET *
****

002

SUBJECT: OPERATION MAJESTIC-12 PRELIMINARY BRIEFING FOR
PRESIDENT-ELECT EISENHOWER.

DOCUMENT PREPARED 18 NOVEMBER, 1952.

BRIEFING OFFICER: ADM. ROSCOE H. HILLENKOETTER (MJ-1)

NOTE: This document has been prepared as a preliminary briefing
only. It should be regarded as introductory to a full operations
briefing intended to follow.

* * * * * *

OPERATION MAJESTIC-12 is a TOP SECRET Research and Development/
Intelligence operation responsible directly and only to the
President of the United States. Operations of the project are
carried out under control of the Majestic-12 (Majic-12) Group
which was established by special classified executive order of
President Truman on 24 September, 1947, upon recommendation by
Dr. Vannevar Bush and Secretary James Forrestal. (See Attachment
"A".) Members of the Majestic-12 Group were designated as follows:

> Adm. Roscoe H. Hillenkoetter
> Dr. Vannevar Bush
> Secy. James V. Forrestal*
> Gen. Nathan F. Twining
> Gen. Hoyt S. Vandenberg
> Dr. Detlev Bronk
> Dr. Jerome Hunsaker
> Mr. Sidney W. Souers
> Mr. Gordon Gray
> Dr. Donald Menzel
> Gen. Robert M. Montague
> Dr. Lloyd V. Berkner

The death of Secretary Forrestal on 22 May, 1949, created
a vacancy which remained unfilled until 01 August, 1950, upon
which date Gen. Walter B. Smith was designated as permanent
replacement.

****
* TOP SECRET *
TOP SECRET / MAJIC
EYES ONLY
EYES ONLY

T52-EXEMPT (E)

001

391

TOP SECRET / MAJIC

EYES ONLY

NATIONAL SECURITY INFORMATION

```
**************
* TOP SECRET *
**************
```

EYES ONLY

COPY <u>ONE</u> OF <u>ONE</u>.

BRIEFING DOCUMENT: OPERATION MAJESTIC 12

PREPARED FOR PRESIDENT-ELECT DWIGHT D. EISENHOWER: (EYES ONLY)

18 NOVEMBER, 1952

<u>WARNING</u>: This is a TOP SECRET - EYES ONLY document containing compartmentalized information essential to the national security of the United States. EYES ONLY ACCESS to the material herein is strictly limited to those possessing Majestic-12 clearance level. Reproduction in any form or the taking of written or mechanically transcribed notes is strictly forbidden.

```
**************
* TOP SECRET *
**************
```

TOP SECRET / MAJIC

T52-EXEMPT (E)

EYES ONLY

EYES ONLY

(1)

```
# # # # # # #0020140
#  TOP SECRET #
# # # # # # #
```

TO BE DELIVERED BY SPECIAL COURIER

DIRECTIVE TO LIEUTENANT GENERAL TWINING

You will proceed to the White Sands Proving Ground Command Center without delay for the purpose of making an appraisal of the reported unidentified objects being kept there. Part of your mission there will deal with the military, political and psychological consequences at the projector, in the course of your survey you will maintain liaison with the military officials on the army.

In making your appraisal it is desired that you proceed with the greatest care and avoid opinions or opinions expressed by personnel all of which do not conform to sound reasoning with regard to the possible outcome. In presenting the findings of your mission you should endeavor to state as concisely as possible your estimate of the character, extent, and probable consequences in the event the maintenance is not given.

When your mission in New Mexico is completed you will make a brief trip to the Sandia AEC facility to make an appraisal of the situation there, also of the reaction by the Los Alamos people involved. Before going to White Sands you will communicate with General Eisenhower to ascertain whether he desires you to proceed via Airtlant, AAF.

You will take with you such experts, technicians, scientists and assistants as you deem necessary to the effectiveness of your mission.

Approved: *Dwight D Eisenhower*

Dated 9 July 194...

DISTRIBUTION:

1/Cy Chief of Staff to the Commander in Chief
        of the Armed Forces
1/Cy Military Aide to the President
1/Cy Director, Office for Emergency Management
1/Cy Director of Central Intelligence Group
1/Cy Director of Intelligence, USA
1/Cy Director of Intelligence, USAAF
1/Cy Director, Office of Naval Intelligence
1/Cy Director, Joint Intelligence Objectives Agency
1/Cy Joint Intelligence Committee
1/Cy Director, Armed Forces Special Weapons Project

CENTRAL INTELLIGENCE GROUP
2430 E Street, N. W.
Washington 25, D. C.

19 SEP 1947

MEMORANDUM FOR THE MILITARY ASSESSMENT OF THE JOINT INTELLIGENCE
COMMITTEE

SUBJECT: Examination of Unidentified Disc-like Aircraft near Military
Installations in the State of New Mexico: A Preliminary Report

  1.   Pursuant to the recent world events and domestic security
problems within the Atomic Energy Commission, the intelligence reports
of so-called "Flying Saucers" and the intrusion of unknown aircraft over
the most secret defense installations, a classified intelligence project
is warranted. The National Security Act of 1947 established a Central
Intelligence Agency under the National Security Council. When the
Director of Central Intelligence assumes his official responsibilities,
the National Intelligence Authority is abolished the files pertaining to
unidentified aircraft sightings, intelligence personnel and funds of the
Central Intelligence Group will be transferred to the Agency.

  2.   The recovery of unidentified planform aircraft in the state of
New Mexico on 6 July 1947, ten miles northwest of Oscura Peak, and a debris
field 75 miles northwest of the Army's 509th Atomic Bomb Group, Roswell
Army Air Field, is confirmed. A subsequent capture of another similar craft
30 miles east of the Army's Alamogordo Army Air Field on 5 July 1947, has
convinced the Army Air Forces S-2, Army G-2 and Navy ONI, that the craft
and wreckage are not of US manufacture.

  3.   Until a clear directive from the President is issued, there can
be no co-ordinated scientific examination of the objects in question.
Currently, the core material is being secured at the Naval Research
Laboratory hanger facilities at the White Sands Proving Ground, the Sandia
Base facilities (Armed Forces Special Weapons Project), Alamogordo AAF and
the Aero Medical Research facilities at Randolph Field, Texas.

  4.   The research scientists at the Air Forces Research and Development Center, Wright Field, are utilizing their test facilities and a new
biological laboratory in an on-going study program. The offices of the
JRDB, FBI and the State Department are assisting the Joint Intelligence
Committee in acquiring any intelligence from MI5 and MI6 on possible Soviet
long-range reconnaissance aircraft/missile research and development tests.

/S/

R. H.   HILLENKOETTER
   Rear   Admiral, USN
Director of   Central Intelligence

TOP-SECRET/EYES ONLY.

RESTRICTED

SOM 1-01

TO 12D1—3—11—1

MAJESTIC—12 GROUP SPECIAL OPERATIONS MANUAL

EXTRATERRESTRIAL

ENTITIES AND TECHNOLOGY,

RECOVERY AND DISPOSAL

TOP SECRET/MAJIC
EYES ONLY

WARNING! This is a TOP SECRET—MAJIC EYES ONLY document containing compartmentalized information essential to the national security of the United States. EYES ONLY ACCESS to the material herein is strictly limited to personnel possessing MAJIC—12 CLEARANCE LEVEL. Examination or use by unauthorized personnel is strictly forbidden and is punishable by federal law.

MAJESTIC—12 GROUP • APRIL 1954

CHAPTER 1
OPERATION MAJESTIC—12

Section I. PROJECT PURPOSE AND GOALS

1. Scope

The manual has been prepared especially for Majestic—12 units. Its purpose is to present all aspects of Majestic—12 so authorized personnel will have a better understanding of the goals of the Group, be able to more expertly deal with Unidentified Flying Objects, Extraterrestrial Technology and Entities, and increase the efficiency of future operations.

2. General

MJ—12 takes the subject of UFOBs, Extraterrestrial Technology, and Extraterrestrial Biological Entities very seriously and considers the entire subject to be a matter of the very highest national security. For that reason everything relating to the subject has been assigned the very highest security classification. Three main points will be covered in this section.

a. The general aspects of MJ—12 to clear up any misconceptions that anyone may have.

b. The importance of the operations.

c. The need for absolute secrecy in all phases of operation.

3. Security Classification

All information relating to MJ—12 has been classified MAJIC EYES ONLY and carries a security level 2 points above that of Top Secret. The reason for this has to do with the consequences that may arise not only from the impact upon the public should the existence of such matters become general knowledge, but also the danger of having such advanced technology as has been recovered by the Air Force fall into the hands of unfriendly foreign powers. No information is released to the public press and the official government position is that no special group such as MJ—12 exists.

4. History of the Group

Operation Majestic—12 was established by special classified presidential order on 24 September 1947 at the recommendation of Secretary of Defense James V. Forrestal and Dr. Vannevar Bush, Chairman of the Joint Research and Development Board. Operations are carried out under a Top Secret Research and Development - Intelligence Group directly responsible only to the President of the United States. The goals of the MJ—12 Group

MJ 12 48-98B

2

TOP SECRET / MAJIC EYES ONLY

SOM 1— 01

Special Operations Manual }
No. 1 - 01 }

MAJESTIC — 12 GROUP
Washington 25, D. C., 7 April 1954

EXTRATERRESTRIAL ENTITIES AND TECHNOLOGY, RECOVERY AND DISPOSAL

		Paragraphs	Page
CHAPTER 1.	OPERATION MAJESTIC - 12		
Section I.	Project purpose and goals	1-5	2
CHAPTER 2.	INTRODUCTION		
Section I.	General	6,7	4
II.	Definition and data	8-11	4
CHAPTER 3.	RECOVERY OPERATIONS		
Section I.	Security	12,13	8
II.	Technology recovery	14-19	9
CHAPTER 4.	RECEIVING AND HANDLING		
Section I.	Handling upon receipt of material	20	15
CHAPTER 5.	EXTRATERRESTRIAL BIOLOGICAL ENTITIES		
Section I.	Living organisms	21-24	17
II.	Non-living organisms	25,26	18
CHAPTER 6.	GUIDE TO UFO IDENTIFICATION		
Section I.	UFOB guide	27-29	21
II.	Identification criteria	30-35	22
III.	Possible origins	36,37	26
Appendix I.	REFERENCES	--------	28
Appendix Ia.	FORMS	--------	29
Appendix II.	MAJIC—12 GROUP PERSONNEL	--------	30
Appendix III.	PHOTOGRAPHS	--------	31

AFFIDAVIT
Charley E. (Chuck) Wade

(1)   My name is Charley E. (Chuck) Wade.

(2)   My address is P.O. Box 27, Gallup, New Mexico 87305.

(3)   I am self employed. My business is Wade Building Company.

(4)   I was born October 23, 1939. My father, Jesse Wade, owned and operated the Wade Bar in
       Corona, New Mexico, for 42 years, retiring in 1976. All my life I heard my dad relate the
       following story many times up until he passed away on April 13, 1978.

(5)   Dad was alone at his bar, standing in the door looking out at the main street of Corona, when
       Mac Brazel drove up in his old pick-up truck. Mac told Dad that something had crashed out at
       the ranch he managed, and he asked Dad to lock the bar and go with him to see whatever it was.
       Mac said that what was out there was different from anything he had ever seen before. Dad
       refused Mac's persistent persuasion, and suggested to Mac that he report this information to the
       military in Roswell.

(6)   This incident occurred shortly after World War II, when nearly everything (gas, tires, etc.) was
       in short supply--which is probably why Dad turned down the chance to go and see what Mac
       was talking about. Also the road to the Foster Ranch was all dirt then, as most of it is today. In
       later years, Dad always wished he had gone out to the ranch with Mac. He said he was sure it
       was something important, because otherwise Mac would not have used the gas, tires, etc. to
       drive in to Corona, and he would not have tried so hard to persuade Dad to go along with him.

(7)   Not too long after Mac told Dad about the crash, Dad saw Mac driving a new pick-up and soon
       afterward Mac left the Foster Ranch and purchased a meat locker in Alamogordo. Dad always
       wondered if the government paid Mac off for his silence, because before the crash he never had
       two nickels to rub together. Mac never spoke to Dad about the crash after Mac returned from
       Roswell!

(8)   Dad said he heard that the military brought in a lot of men and really cleaned up the crash site.

(9)   I have not been paid or given or promised anything of value to make this statement, which is the
       truth to the best of my recollection.

Charley E. Wade CHARLEY E. WADE   27 MAY 97
(Signature and Printed Name)   (Date)

Signature witnessed by: STATE OF NEW MEXICO
                                           COUNTY OF McKINLEY
Helen S Lewis   Helen S Lewis   May 27, 1997
(Signature and Printed Name)   (Date)

My Commission expires: 9-23-2000

2002 SEALED AFFIDAVIT OF WALTER G. HAUT
DATE: December 26, 2002
WITNESS: Chris Xxxxxx
NOTARY: Beverlee Morgan
(1) My name is Walter G. Haut
(2) I was born on June 2, 1922
(3) My address is 1405 W. 7th Street, Roswell, NM 88203
(4) I am retired.
(5) In July, 1947, I was stationed at the Roswell Army Air Base in Roswell, New Mexico, serving as the base Public Information Officer. I had spent the 4thof July weekend (Saturday, the 5th, and Sunday, the 6th) at my private residence about 10 miles north of the base, which was located south of town.
(6) I was aware that someone had reported the remains of a downed vehicle by midmorning after my return to duty at the base on Monday, July 7. I was aware that Major Jesse A. Marcel, head of intelligence, was sent by the base commander, Col. William Blanchard, to investigate.
(7) By late in the afternoon that same day, I would learn that additional civilian reports came in regarding a second site just north of Roswell. I would spend the better part of the day attending to my regular duties hearing little if anything more.
(8) On Tuesday morning, July 8, I would attend the regularly scheduled staff meeting at 7:30 a.m. Besides Blanchard, Marcel; CIC [Counterintelligence Corp] Capt. Sheridan Cavitt; Col. James I. Hopkins, the operations officer; Lt. Col. Ulysses S. Nero, the supply officer; and from Carswell AAF in Fort Worth, Texas, Blanchard's boss, Brig. Gen. Roger Ramey and his chief of staff, Col. Thomas J. Dubose were also in attendance. The main topic of discussion was reported by Marcel and Cavitt regarding an extensive debris field in Lincoln County approx. 75 miles NW of Roswell. A preliminary briefing was provided by Blanchard about the second site approx. 40 miles north of town. Samples of wreckage were passed around the table. It was unlike any material I had or have ever seen in my life. Pieces which resembled metal foil, paper thin yet extremely strong, and pieces with unusual markings along their length were handled from man to man, each voicing their opinion. No one was able to identify the crash debris.

(9) One of the main concerns discussed at the meeting was whether we should go public or not with the discovery. Gen. Ramey proposed a plan, which I believe originated from his bosses at the Pentagon. Attention needed to be diverted from the more important site north of town by acknowledging the other location. Too many civilians were already involved and the press already was informed. I was not completely informed how this would be accomplished.

(10) At approximately 9:30 a.m. Col. Blanchard phoned my office and dictated the press release of having in our possession a flying disc, coming from a ranch northwest of Roswell, and Marcel flying the material to higher headquarters. I was to deliver the news release to radio stations KGFL and KSWS, and newspapers the Daily Record and the Morning Dispatch.

(11) By the time the news release hit the wire services, my office was inundated with phone calls from around the world. Messages stacked up on my desk, and rather than deal with the media concern, Col Blanchard suggested that I go home and "hide out."

(12) Before leaving the base, Col. Blanchard took me personally to Building 84 [AKA Hangar P-3], a B-29 hangar located on the east side of the tarmac. Upon first approaching the building, I observed that it was under heavy guard both outside and inside. Once inside, I was permitted from a safe distance to first observe the object just recovered north of town. It was approx. 12 to 15 feet in length, not quite as wide, about 6 feet high, and more of an egg shape. Lighting was poor, but its surface did appear metallic. No windows, portholes, wings, tail section, or landing gear were visible.

(13) Also from a distance, I was able to see a couple of bodies under a canvas tarpaulin. Only the heads extended beyond the covering, and I was not able to make out any features. The heads did appear larger than normal and the contour of the canvas suggested the size of a 10 year old child. At a later date in Blanchard's office, he would extend his arm about 4 feet above the floor to indicate the height.

(14) I was informed of a temporary morgue set up to accommodate the recovered bodies.

(15) I was informed that the wreckage was not "hot" (radioactive).

(16) Upon his return from Fort Worth, Major Marcel described to me taking pieces of the wreckage to Gen. Ramey's office and after returning from a map room, finding the remains of a weather balloon and radar

kite substituted while he was out of the room. Marcel was very upset over this situation. We would not discuss it again.

(17) I would be allowed to make at least one visit to one of the recovery sites during the military cleanup. I would return to the base with some of the wreckage which I would display in my office.

(18) I was aware two separate teams would return to each site months later for periodic searches for any remaining evidence.

(19) I am convinced that what I personally observed was some type of craft and its crew from outer space.

(20) I have not been paid nor given anything of value to make this statement, and it is the truth to the best of my recollection.

Signed: Walter G. Haut
December 26, 2002
Signature witnessed by:
Chris Xxxxxxx

[Source: Tom Carey & Donald Schmitt, Witness to Roswell, 2007]

Affidavit

My name is Jim Ragsdale, formerly of 702 North Greenwood, Roswell, N.M. and I am making the following information available to clarify any and all portions of my involvement in the UFO Incident occuring in 1947. Everything contained herein is the result of my personal observation and not from any secondary source.

At that date I was employed by an Oil Co, living in Carlsbad, N. M. and my type of work was Transit Hauling, operating all types of heavy equipment related to oil field development. Over the long July 4th weekend, I had 7 or 8 days that I did not report for work. It was on this weekend, my friend and I spent several days in the Pine Lodge area, west of Roswell.

At that time the Pine Lodge was a favorite spot for all of the area ranchers and others from all over southeast New Mexico, for they always had a dance on Saturday Nights during the summer months. I had been at Pine Lodge on many occasions during the time before 1947.

My friend and I had a pickup truck on this weekend, sleeping in the back, with covers and a tarpaulin (tarp) covering the back of the truck. It was about 11:00 PM, the weather was perfect, and we were looking up at the stars. A storm was in the west, with lightning, but far away enough we couldn't hear the thunder.

Suddenly, a tremendous flash occured, several miles to the north, with it being as bright as a flame from a welder's arc. It was huge, but far enough away we couldn't hear it immediately. Then the object started in our direction and soon we could hear the noise it was making. The only way to compare the noise it was making coming our direction, and until it hit the side of the mountain, was it was like the sound of a jet motor now used on take offs by large jet air liners. We were frightened and didn't know if it would miss us. The object passed through the trees not more than 60 yards from our truck, and struck the mountain at a point a few yards farther from where we were in the truck.

After a little bit we took flashlights and went to the site of the impact and spent considerable time looking all around.

The craft split open on impact and had struck large boulders in the area some as large as an automobile. The craft had slid down between boulders of this size, but was easily approached. When we looked into the craft, we saw four bodies of a type we had never seen before, and all were dead. The interior of the craft had the equivalent of a dash board with various instruments and writing of some sort I have never seen before or since.

In addition to the wreckage on the inside of the craft, there was lots of material of the type reported on the site of the "Crash" near Corona. This material was on the outside and scattered all over the side of the mountain, described later as weather balloon material.

Affidavit

THE BODIES OF THE OCCUPANTS WERE ALL ABOUT FOUR FEET OR LESS TALL, WITH STRANGE LOOKING ARMS, LEGS AND FINGERS. THEY WERE DRESSED IN A SILVER TYPE UNIFORM AND WEARING A TIGHT HELMET OF SOME TYPE. THIS IS POSITIVE BECAUSE I TRIED TO REMOVE ONE OF THE HELMETS, BUT WAS UNABLE TO DO SO. THEIR EYES WERE LARGE, OVAL IN SHAPE, AND DID NOT RESEMBLE ANYTHING OF A HUMAN NATURE.

WE DECIDED TO RETURN TO OUR PICKUP UNTIL DAYLIGHT SO WE COULD BETTER SEE THE SITE, HOWEVER THERE WAS VERY LITTLE SLEEP UNTIL IT WAS DAYLIGHT. WHEN WE RETURNED WE FILLED TWO LARGE GUNNY SACKS WITH THE MATERIAL, AND IT WAS WITH US WHEN WE LEFT THE SITE.

DURING THE EARLY DAYLIGHT HOURS WE INSPECTED THE MATERIAL USED IN THE CRAFT AND THE PIECES RESULTING FROM THE CRASH. IT WASN'T A RIGID METAL, BUT EVEN THOUGH BEING THICK WAS FLEXIBLE UP TO A POINT. YOU COULD BEND IT AND IT WOULD COME RIGHT BACK TO IT'S ORIGINAL SHAPE. THIS WAS ALSO TRUE OF THE LIGHTER MATERIAL SCATTERED ALL OVER THE MOUNTAIN THAT LOOKED LIKE TIN FOIL AND WOULD GO BACK TO IT'S ORIGINAL SHAPE WHEN CRUMPLED IN YOUR HAND. THE MATERIAL OF THE CRAFT ITSELF HAD A SORT OF BRONZE-GRAY COLOR. THERE WERE NO RIVITES, SEAMS OR INDICATION OF HOW IT HAD BEEN CONSTRUCTED. *THE CRAFT WAS ABOUT 20' IN DIAMETER + HAD A DOME IN THE MIDDLE, NO WINDOWS WERE SEEN* IT WASN'T TOO LONG AFTER WE WERE LOOKING AT THE TOTAL AREA, WE HEARD WHAT WE BELIEVED WAS TRUCKS AND HEAVY EQUIPMENT COMING OUR WAY, SO WE LEFT AND WERE NOT THERE WHEN WHAT EVER IT WAS ARRIVED.

THIS MATERIAL WAS WITH US LATER IN THE DAY WHEN WE STOPPED AT THE BLUE MOON TAVERN, JUST SOUTH OF ROSWELL, A FAVORITE PLACE FOR TRUCKERS GOING THROUGH THE AREA AND I SHOWED THE MATERIAL TO SEVERAL OF MY FRIENDS. HOWEVER, AS FAR AS I KNOW, ALL OF THEM ARE DEAD.

UNEXPLAINED TO THIS DAY IS THE DISAPPEARANCE OF THE MATERIAL. MY FRIEND HAD SOME IN HER VEHICLE WHEN SHE WAS KILLED HITTING A BRIDGE, AND IT WAS GONE WHEN THE WRECKAGE WAS BROUGH IN TO TOWN. MY TRUCK AND TRAILER WAS STOLEN FROM MY HOME, AGAIN WITH MATERIAL IN THE TRUCK, NEVER TO BE HEARD FROM ANYWHERE. MY HOME WAS BROKEN INTO, COMPLETELY RANSACKED, AND ALL THAT WAS TAKEN WAS THE MATERIAL, A GUN AND VERY LITTLE ELSE OF VALUE.

THE IMPACT SITE IS EXACT AND CAN BE DESCRIBED AS: A SIGN POST ON THE PINE LODGE ROAD INDICATES "53 MILES TO ROSWELL". NEAR THIS SIGN IS A ROAD GOING SOUTH TOWARD PINE LODGE (THE LODGE BUILDING WAS BURNED DOWN SEVERAL YEARS AGO) AND THE TURN OFF TO ARABELLA LEADS EAST AND SOUTH. 2 OR 3 MILES DOWN THIS ROAD TOWARDS ARABELLA IS THE SITE OF OUR PICKUP THAT NIGHT AND NEARBY THE IMPACT SITE. THIS AREA IS NEAR THE MOUNTAIN INDICATED AS "BOY SCOUT MOUNTAIN."

JAMES R. RAGSDALE

State of Oklahoma
County of Logan

Subscribed and sworn to before me this 15th day of April, 1995.

Notary Public

My commission expires 12-8-98

ROOM LIGHT : PINK-PURPLE
BRIGHT IN SOME AREAS

HUNDREDS OF THESE IN
VARIOUS STAGES OF GROWTH.

WISPY HAIR, "ALMOST NOSE"
MOUTH LOOKS "SEALED"

WOMB LOOKS GREY
VEINS (?) LOOK DARK GREY
CREATURE WHITE- PALE
EYES - DARK LIDS (?)
CAN'T FIND GENDER
2 TOES : 3 FINGERS

LIQUID - AMBER COLOR
NOT COMPLETELY CLEAR

LOOKS LIKE GLASS TUBE,
BUT ABOUT 5 FT TALL

TAKEN FROM DULCE PAPERS

ANATOMICAL DETAIL OF EBE HAND

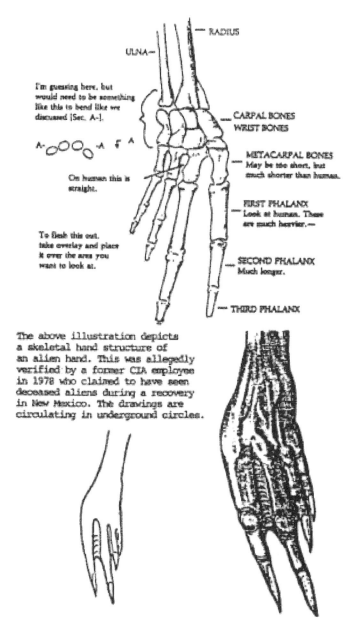

RADIUS

ULNA—

I'm guessing here, but would need to be something like this to bend like we discussed [Sec. A-].

A- ⚬ ◯ ◯ ⚬ -A

On human this is straight.

To flesh this out, take overlay and place it over the area you want to look at.

CARPAL BONES
WRIST BONES

METACARPAL BONES
May be too short, but much shorter than human.

FIRST PHALANX
Look at human. These are much heavier.—

SECOND PHALANX
Much longer.

THIRD PHALANX

The above illustration depicts a skeletal hand structure of an alien hand. This was allegedly verified by a former CIA employee in 1978 who claimed to have seen deceased aliens during a recovery in New Mexico. The drawings are circulating in underground circles.

United States Patent [19]

Altseimer et al.

[11] 3,885,832

[45] May 27, 1975

[54] APPARATUS AND METHOD FOR LARGE TUNNEL EXCAVATION IN HARD ROCK

[75] Inventors: John H. Altseimer; Robert J. Hanold, both of Los Alamos, N. Mex.

[73] Assignee: The United States of America as represented by the United States Energy Research and Development Administration, Washington, D.C.

[22] Filed: Jan. 25, 1974

[21] Appl. No.: 436,401

[52] U.S. Cl. 299/14; 175/11; 299/33
[51] Int. Cl. E21d 9/00
[58] Field of Search 299/33, 14; 175/11, 16,
61/45 R

[56]   References Cited

UNITED STATES PATENTS

3,334,945   8/1967   Bartlett 299/33

3,396,806   8/1968   Benson 175/11
3,693,731   9/1972   Armstrong et al 175/11

Primary Examiner—Frank L. Abbott
Assistant Examiner—William F. Pate, III
Attorney, Agent, or Firm—Dean E. Carlson; Henry Heyman

[57]   ABSTRACT

A tunneling machine for producing large tunnels in rock by progressive detachment of the tunnel core by thermal melting a boundary kerf into the tunnel face and simultaneously forming an initial tunnel wall support by deflecting the molten materials against the tunnel walls to provide, when solidified, a continuous liner; and fragmenting the tunnel core circumscribed by the kerf by thermal stress fracturing and in which the heat required for such operations is supplied by a compact nuclear reactor.

3 Claims, 5 Drawing Figures

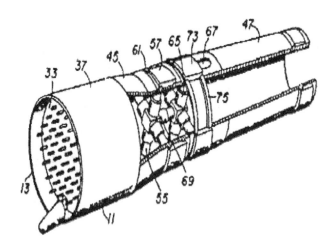

file copy

THUNDER SCIENTIFIC CORPORATION

2 December 1981

The Honorable Pete Domenici
4239 Dirkson Senate Office Bldg.
Washington, DC 20510

Dear Pete,

To date as noted, I have not heard from you and therefore assume with all of your new duties that you are very busy and just have not had the time. In light of that, I have taken the case directly to the Chief of Staff - Pentagon Air Force Intelligence. I talked by phone directly with Captain Harris, Asst to General John B Marks who was out of the office at the time.

The facts I gave Captain Harris were simple and straight forward as follows:

1) I knew the location of the Alien bases in Northern New Mexico in the center of the Jicarilla Reservation 4.5 miles northwest of Dulce, NM.
2) I knew that someone in the military made a deal with the Aliens several years ago giving the Indian land, cattle, etc. and apparent assurance of safety to the Alien in trade for Technology in the form of an Atomic powered ship at the same time establishing an extensive US base alongside to test the ship.
3) That sometime late 79. or first of 80 an argument insued over weapons and the military abandoned; the final circumstance of the men unknown.
4) That I had high resolution official NASA U2 CIR (color infrared) photos in addition to low level and ground photos showing the base in total detail. (photos obtained legitimately thru UNM)
5) The ship design traded for is over thirty (30) years behind the alien technology.
6) I advised Captain Harris I knew of the two women and child near Austin, TX who were severely exposed to radiation at close distance from the ship in trouble and that it was seen to come west with helicopters (unmarked) and that the Government was quietly paying their hospital expenses.

Throughout the Captain claimed not to know - but listened and asked no questions. Then he said - "What do you want us to do?" "Send me a letter and tell me what you think we should do about it". Knowing it would be highly classified and he could not talk of it - to me this statement was for all intents and purposes an admission of the facts which are totally visible on the CIRs.

I have written that report and have enclosed a copy for your perusal along with a copy of the cover letter.

Major Ernest Edwards, Commander 1608th Security Police Sqdn of all security here at Manzano Base has been with this project unofficially since Jan 27, 1980 and has witnessed and provided logistics advice throughout. He has read the enclosed report - approved of its accuracy and agreed upon my sending it. His phone is autovon 244-7803 should you desire to talk with him to assure yourself of my professional integrity.

The meat of the problem is outlined completely in the report. Please read it carefully. I doubt that you have been totally advised. I am also very concerned that the President has not been totally advised of the situation and have forwarded a copy to him, cover letter enclosed for your record.

It is hoped you will value this valuable input and in time get in touch with me.

Best regards,

Paul F Bennewitz, Pres.

623 WYOMING, S.E. □ ALBUQUERQUE, NEW MEXICO 87123 □ TEL. (505) 265-8701

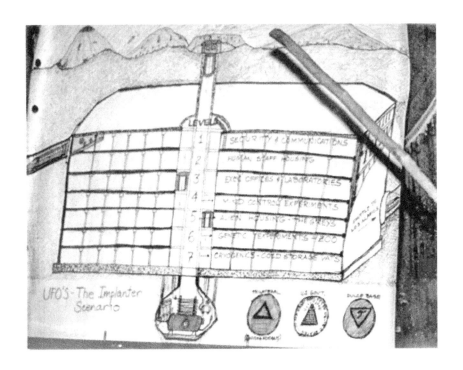

THOMAS CASTELLO DRAWING OF DULCE BASE, NEW MEXICO,
USA

CLACKAMAS COUNTY
PHILIP SCHNEIDER

AUTOPSY PERFORMED:

BY: Karen Gunson, M.D.
AT: 301 N.E. Knott Street, Portland, Oregon 97212
ON: Friday, January 19, 1996 - 10:30 a.m.

CAUSE OF DEATH: ASPHYXIATION BY LIGATURE STRANGULATION

MANNER OF DEATH: SUICIDE

ANATOMIC DIAGNOSES:

I.   Asphyxiation by ligature strangulation

       A.   Rubber tubing tied tightly around neck
       B.   Intact hyoid and thyroid cartilages
       C.   No evidence of anterior strap muscle hemorrhages
       D.   Scattered petechial hemorrhages of palpebral conjunctivae and sclerae
              of right eye
       E.   No evidence of head, trunk or extremity extremities

II.   Moderate decomposition

III.   Wheelchair confinement

       A.   Multiple surgical scars of trunk and extremities

*There were so many discrepencies in this report
that it almost felt like it was not the body
of philip. But the autopsy photos I got later
prove without a doubt that it was his body
! The Photos were VERY GRAPHIC + Close-up
They sliced + diced his body, exposing all of
his insides - pulled out his brain .... just
so hard to see a loved one laying dead and
a ~~xxx~~ ... mutilated*

409

CLACKAMAS COUNTY
PHILIP SCHNEIDER
Page 2

The body is that of a normally developed, normally nourished and normally hydrated,
moderately decomposed white male, measuring 72-1/2" in length. When first viewed,
he is clothed in a pair of fleece pull-on shorts. He has a condom catheter present
along with an adult diaper. These are present in the usual positions.

6 fee
philip 6'2"
me is hav
but surgery
back discs
his have
very hurt
compressed

The subject is of husky build, weighing approximately 220-230 pounds.

POSTMORTEM CHANGES:

The eye globes are sunken. The corneas are cloudy. Purge is present in the nose and
mouth. There is green discoloration of the face, anterior chest, back and upper
extremities. Putrefactive vesicles are present. There is marked skin slippage on the
chest and face. There is a moderate odor of putrefaction. The fingertips are dry, black
and shrunken.

GENERAL EXTERNAL EXAMINATION:

The head is covered by gray hair, measuring to approximately 1". The irides appear
to be brown. A few scattered petechial hemorrhages are identified in the lower
palpebral conjunctivae on the right and in the sclerae on the right. The left eye cannot
be evaluated due to decomposition. The dentition appears to be complete and in a
poor state of repair. No blood is present in either external auditory canal. The injuries
to the neck will be described below.

*philip stated a bomb was dropped on him while working as a construction
engineer for Morrison Knudsen "friendly fire" from the US Air Force in vietnam*

The chest and abdomen are remarkable for numerous scars including a midline scar
extending from the sternal notch to the epigastrium, measuring approximately 20" in
length. There appears to be burn-type scar present in the upper chest area. Horizontally oriented apparent scarring is identified on the chest bilaterally at the costal

*he stated that the crew accidentally saw something they
shouldn't have, a nuclear plant in the jungle.*

margins. An obliquely oriented surgical scar is present in the right lower quadrant and measures approximately 9".

Multiple linear, vertically oriented scars are present in the left upper arm, ranging in length from 3" to 6". A sutured curvilinear scar is present on the flexor surface of the left forearm and measures 6". The distal portions of the left thumb, index and middle fingers have been surgically amputated in the past. There are no recent needle puncture marks or perivascular scars in the left antecubital fossa. No injury is present on the palm of the left hand. The remaining fingernails are short and natural. No injury is present on the dorsum of the left hand or forearm.

No injury is noted on the dorsum of the right hand or forearm. There is no perivascular scarring or recent needle puncture marks. The fingernails are short and natural. No injury is present on the palm of the hand or between the fingers.

The external male genitalia are unremarkable.

The lower extremities are normally developed with inguinal scars, which are linear and measure approximately 6" to 7" in length. A vertically oriented, well healed surgical scar is present on the anterior right thigh and measures 10" in length. Horizontally oriented, linear scars are present just above the left knee and measure up to 3". There is a vertically oriented surgical scar present on the medial left calf just above the medial malleolus of the ankle, measuring 4" in length. The toenails are short and natural. The soles of the feet are unremarkable.

The posterior aspect of the body is unremarkable.

CRABWOOD ALIEN, AUGUST 2002

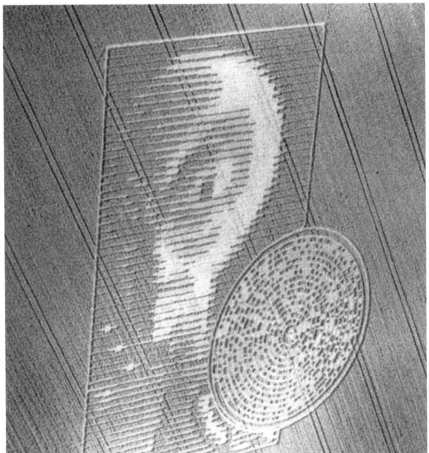

IMAGE FROM ULTRA-TECH WEBSITE, 1996

THE CHILBOLTON FACE, HAMPSHIRE, 2000

CHILBOLTON FACE AND ARECIBO GLYPH

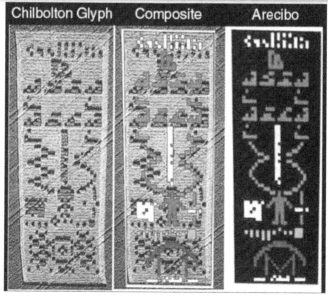

THE JULIA SET FORMATION, NR. STONEHENGE, 1996

JERZY SZPULECKI'S DRAWING OF UFO, CENTRAL POLAND, JULY

22,

ALIEN IMPLANTS FOUND IN ONE OF DR. ROGER LEIR'S PATIENTS

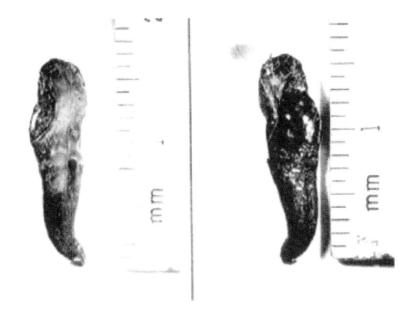

SEMJASE IN BEAMSHIP, TAKEN BY BILLY MEIER, SWITZERLAND,
JUNE 1975

'WEDDING CAKE' BEAMSHIP, TAKEN OUTSIDE MEIER'S HOUSE

BILLY MEIER BEAMSHIP PHOTOS, JULY 1975

Nr.66: 9. Juli, 1975; Fuchsbüel-Hofhalden   ©FIGU

Sfath

Ptaah

Quetzal

Semjase

The Statesman

Incorporating and directly descended from THE FRIEND OF INDIA—Founded 1818
PUBLISHED SIMULTANEOUSLY FROM DELHI AND CALCUTTA

DELHI, WEDNESDAY, SEPTEMBER 30, 1964

"THE FLYING SAUCER MAN" LEAVES DELHI

Swiss Claims He Has Visited Three Planets

BY A STAFF REPORTER

Is the "flying saucer" a myth? Far from it, according to Mr Edward Albert, a 28-year-old Swiss national, who left Delhi for Pakistan en route to Switzerland on Monday. "I have not only seen the objects from outer space, but have taken photographs and even travelled in them thrice", he says.

He has about 80 photographs of the space objects — all taken with an old folding camera. The objects in the photographs vary in size and shape. One is a globular object with a round disc in the centre; another is funnel-shaped; a third is like a neon lamp, a fourth is a big, bright cross and others bright zigzag lines. Some of these have been taken on the ground and some , flying in the sky. The sizes (one has to take Mr Albert's word for it) vary from two centimetres ("space scouts", he calls them) to 1,500 yards. Some of the photographs were taken in the day and some at night.

The photographs — taken in Greece, Jordan and India — are neatly kept in an album. Mr Albert politely declines a request for a copy of the photographs with the remark: "I can't spare them." He says he had

VISIT TO 3 PLANETS

The first "flying saucer" he saw, according to him, was in Switzerland in 1958. Since then he has been seeing and often photographing them. They come almost once a month, he says. In the last five years he claims to have met and spoken to men from outer space ("they come from different planets"). "I have travelled on three occasions with the space men, and have visited three planets — Satar, Kapar and Paranos, he says. In one, there was habitation ("all the objects were white", the other was shaped like a church and too hot to stay on and the third "was like a shimmering diamond" with no people. He says he was not allowed to stay in any planet for more than 10 to 15 minutes. Mr Albert nonchalantly says that he has collected some stones from the planets which he has kept at home (in Switzerland). "I won't be able to single out the planets now," he adds.

As for the space men, Mr Albert says that they look like human beings — "only they are much taller, have a certain glow about them and are spiritually much more advanced than human beings". They don't utter any words but understand any language and express themselves through telepathy, he says.

A MISSION

"I have a mission to fulfil," says Mr Albert, but refuses to explain what it is. "I will disclose it when the time comes — positively before a year."

Besides his none too impressive clothes, his space album, camera and a couple of bags, Mr Albert has a pet monkey which he has named "Emperor". Soon after he landed at Mehrauli his money — $350 — was stolen. Since then he had been trying to get work or money but in vain. A few days ago he met a German youth,

MR EDWARD ALBERT

taken about 400 photographs of the space objects but most of them have been stolen — some in Jordan, some in India.

Sitting bare-bodied in one of the cave-like monuments in Mehrauli in Delhi near the Buddha Vihara — where he had been staying since his arrival in India about five months ago — Mr Albert sounds rather weird. But then he clearly is not eager to talk about his experiences which, to say the least, are remarkable. Indeed, the little that he has to say has to be pried out of him. He doesn't want publicity, he doesn't care if anyone believes him or not. To the unbeliever he simply refuses to talk.

a hitch-hiker on his way back to Europe. The German (also with a pet monkey, "Empress") was glad to help the Swiss out. The Swiss, the German and the monkeys left on Monday evening by train for Lahore; from there they plan to hitch-hike their way to Europe — each to his native country.

The story of Mr Albert is as incredible as it is startling. He proposes to relate to German scientists his experiences, show his photographs and the objects that he says he has collected from the planets he visited. Has Mr Albert created history or is he a mystic who has let his imagination run wild? Time alone will tell.

FAX

Date _____ OCTOBER 12, 2005 _____   No. of pages including this one ____ 1 ____

To ____ J ____   From ____ BINAH H.S. MAJ ____

Fax ____   Phone ____ ROSWELL ____

Message

TOP SECRET: MAJIC EYES ONLY

To: The Most Honorable Dr. Danny B Catselas Burisch, Majestic ID# H-6196-E

From: The Most Honorable MJ#1, for the Consistory of the Majestic 12, Washington, D.C.

Within and for the Consistory of this Majority assembled; by order of the Majestic 12, in Formal High Session, Thursday, October 12, 2005 A.D., you are hereby instructed, ordered, and enjoined to the best of your abilities and talents to present the truth of the extraterrestrial reality, as you have personally known it, on dates yet to be established, to the population of the world. You will conduct this disclosure with the application of your sacred honor, without regard for personal security, and in an unwavering manner rely upon the Truth and the countenance of Almighty God as your personal defense. Know now that you have the personal assurance of the Majestic 12 that none shall prevail against you, that your message shall be for the unity of humanity during the time of the cycle's cross. Such supremacy of word, but subordinate to God, is established by Treaty with the future extraterrestrial intelligences. You are hereby held to all ethical and moral boundaries, as in keeping with the standards set forth for Senior Agents of the Majestic 12. May God be with you, O' Son of the Majestic! We will stand, unanimous and adjourned to your purpose.

Your acceptance of this order is hereby requested forthwith.

AFFIXED INITIALS OF THE OPERATIVE DECLARE ASSENT TO THE MOTION

BEFORE ALMIGHTY GOD I PROMISE TO DO MY VERY BEST.

GOD, HELP ME.

SOURCES

GENERAL AFFIDAVIT

State of **Nevada**

County of **Clark**

Before the undersigned, an officer duly commissioned by the laws of Nevada, on this 24th day of September, 2005, personally appeared Deborah Kay Burisch who, under penalty of perjury hereby states the following facts:

I, Deborah Kay Burisch became an agent for the Committee of the Majority (closed in 2002) and for the Majestic 12 in 1977 and remained an active agent until 2005, when I retired.

My husband, Dr. Danny B Catselas Burisch (formerly Dr. Danny B Crain) was an agent for the same groups from 1986-2005.

Both he and myself, as senior agents, are retired with Emeritus Status, which offers us many "perks."

In 1991 I removed my husband's "Doctor of Philosophy" degree (in "Cellular and Developmental Biology"), from the State University of New York at Stony Brook (SUNY SB), off his bedroom wall, where it was displayed inside of John and Doreen Crain's residence. I told everyone that I was just going to make a photocopy of it, but I had no intention to give it back, as I wanted to keep it "safe" for my husband.

In 1992, at our residence, I gave my husband a photocopy of his SUNY SB degree, and he displayed it on the livingroom's wall.

In 1998 my husband was censured by the Committee of the Majority for violating their rules and one of his punishments was to have his SUNY SB degree removed. I took the photocopy of his degree off the wall and sent it to be stored with his original degree, in the United Kingdom. That's where it remains to this date.

My husband can't have his degree back because those are the rules and he doesn't need it anyway because he's retired.

Signed under penalty of perjury by:

Deborah Kay Burisch: _____
[signature]

Sworn and subscribed before me this 24th day of September, 2005 A.D.

Notary Public: _____
[signature]

My Commission expires. [Date]

JULY 22, 2009

GENERAL AFFIDAVIT

State of **Nevada**

County of **Clark**

Before the undersigned, an officer duly commissioned by the laws of Nevada, on this 13th day of April, 2005 personally appeared the affiant **Danny B Catselas Burisch Ph.D.**, having first been duly sworn, does under penalty of perjury depose, say and admit to the truth of the following facts:

    Items 1-9 (inclusive), and

    Item 10: the transcript of an online chat believed dated on or about November 13th, 2003, between himself and Don Deppeller.

Affiant Signature _____

Affiant Printed Name _DANNY B CATSELAS BURISCH_

County _____CLARK_____ State ___NEVADA___

Sworn on Month _APRIL_ Day _13_ Year _2005_

NOTARY PUBLIC: [Notary Seal:]

> Notary Public - State of Nevada
> COUNTY OF CLARK
> SANDY GUDAITIS
> My Appointment Expires November 18, 2006

Notary Public Signature _____

My commission expires: __11-18-06__

           Month / Day / Year

1

1. I have been made aware by Mr. Deppeller that he and his family were placed under surveillance, by persons unknown in early 2002, and that such surveillance continued until the Deppeller family moved to Canada in early 2003. I have personally heard allusions by individuals with which you have associated, that the allegations in the aforementioned statement are a fact.

2. I have been allowed online (over the internet, using text and webcam) conversations with Don Deppeller, known by his public internet moniker "DonDep", and other apparently similarly-interested individuals, representing that they were from various locations from around the globe. Said internet personalities represented themselves as separate individuals, giving the public internet monikers: "Human Subject", "Boomerang", "Crackajack", "PageMarker", "Seion9", "Harrdrawk", "WhiteRabbit", (and others), at various times during 2003 and 2004.

3. The facts relevant to the subjects in this document, as stated by me during the conversations recalled at the time of signing this document were then true and correct to the best of my knowledge, and were not conveyed with the intention to deceive. This includes the handwritten statement "For the sake of humanity, tell the world".

4. I have been formally associated with the group known as Majestic 12, since 1986, were formally dissociated from the public on June 8, 2004 (then at the instruction of Majestic 12), and were professionally dissociated from Majestic 12, albeit under emeritus status, on March 21, 2005, at 05:00 hours (Greenwich Mean Time).

5. Some of the projects I have worked on have been named "Preserve Destiny", "Aquarius", "Lotus", and "Preserve Mother".

Affiant Signature

Date 4/13/05

Notary Signature
Notary Seal

2

427

6. To the best of my belief some implications of these projects (listed above as "5.") are of such a grave nature that, were the general world human population to know the entirety of the information contained within them, the resultant reactions of portions of the present human population may vary from "no reaction" to potential "panic."

7. I have also been a party during the negotiations of a treaty known as the "Tau-9 Conference for the Preservation of Humanity", between present human authorities and certain individuals representing themselves as extraterrestrial peoples, with their origin alleged to be the star constellations "Reticulum" and "Orion." I have had physical interaction with at least one such extraterrestrial.

8. The normally required secrecy for these issues, as a consequence of the gravity contained within the aforementioned statement ("7."), stipulated that individuals entrusted with such relevant information – including myself – must swear a secrecy oath upon pain of death. I am not currently under such an oath, the previous one having been discharged by the issuing authority.

9. Individuals that receive such information, from sworn agents of Majestic 12, but who have not been sworn to secrecy – including the principal Applicant of case IMM-7622-04 (Federal Court of Canada) – could possibly be subjected to many forms of harassment, by non-Majestic agencies that have been requested or otherwise authorized by that group

10.
DonDep: Hi Dan...so good to finally see you.
Dan Burisch: Who?
DonDep: This is dondep, who has practically memorized every word of your interview with Bill Hamilton
Dan Burisch: standby ....[Dan picks up a phone, I'm watching him on a webcam...]

_____
Affiant Signature

Date 4/13/05

_____
Notary Signature
Notary Seal

3

Notary Public - State of Nevada
COUNTY OF CLARK
SANDY GUDAITIS
My Appointment Expires November 18, 2006

428

DOCUMENT NUMBER

Q-94-109A

STATUS

THIS DOCUMENT IS CLASSIFIED COSMIC-MAGIC UNDER AUTHORITY OF TOP SECRET
EXECUTIVE DECISION 91-1612-4A

CLEARANCE

MAGIC

AUTHORITY

Written under authorization from the Government of the UNITED STATES OF AMERICA
DEPARTMENT OF DEFENSE, DEPARTMENT OF THE NAVY, Naval Intelligence
Command/Naval Space Command

RELEVANT SCOPE

This document is routed to the appropriate MAGIC-level directorate authorities of the Naval
Space Command, pursuant to UNOST (adopted 19 December 1966, enforced 10 October 1967)
The final routing has been approved to Razor Back, by direction of 92-NSC-117. The contents
of this document are to be regarded as a final report (spec. K-24) of the Principal Investigator,
Working Group Leader (R-4800, Occupant Papoose Site 4), as determined by his Commanding
Officer, Cmd. John Anthony McGuinness M.D. (U.S.N., N.S.A.) under final routing to R. Adm. J.
McConnell (U.S.N., N.S.A., MJ-Cosmic) for disbursement

ORDER

Directed by the N.R.L. "Determine, to scientific certainty, the reasons for in vivo neuronal repair
failure, at dendritic terminal ends, from a set of cellular samples. in vitro. Classify such reasons
functionally, to ascertain the mechanisms of such failure, then isolate the most probable pre-
existing cellular conditions giving allowance to proper regeneration."

SPECIFIC SCOPE

This results of in vitro experimentation under NSA/NSC directed Project Aquarius
(Subintegument Neuronal Aspirative Avulsion Sampling Subsection King-24 (K-24),
Extraterrestrial Biological Entity (EBE) A.K. "AO-J-Rod" (JR)) are herein related

COURSE OF ACTION

GENERAL. As cellular reclassification was necessary, dated by previous testing of culture
material from an " unknown origin ", the following methodology was employed. From Tuesday,
19 July 1994 (22 00 hrs. U.T.) to Wednesday, 25 September 1996 (00 00 hrs. U.T.) 275
individual aspirative (16mm x 4mm, 0.042 psPsc pressurized stick) samples were removed (at
C/Sphere S.T.P.) from the right upper-appendage of JR. 6.500 cm to 6.850 cm dorsocentral to
the medial supinator longus-analog musculature. located 1.610mm into (adducted) the sinuous
musculo-spiral-to-posterior interosseous-analog neuronal supraflexure. and 1.500cm (abducted)
along the median supinator brevis-analog. Such methodology required the introduction of the
Principal Investigator into the Pressurized Clean Sphere, which constituted an I.G.A.-declared
"Extraterrestrial Close Encounter (E.C.E.), Class IV c." Protocols for the debriefing of the
Principal Investigator were followed (Document Number unknown to the writer). Resultant
samples were imaged, labeled, and transferred to C/Sphere S.T.P. elation tubes for analysis

efficiency of receptor tyrosine kinases (Q-94-109C/D). From that line of evidence, repair processes were found altered, via translational control inhibition at pp90exp(rsk)-analog. Simply put, repair was faulted, via increasing age, by insufficient specific protein kinase levels.

Attempts to rectify the problem, via allogenic recombination, resulted in an allomeric response. The neuropathy continued. Human Subject #58-001 (refer to autopsy Document Q-96-029) supplied bone marrow for sequential plasmid recombinations via electroporation. Sequential addition of expression loci for pp44superscript(mapk/erk2) yielded a theorized alternate pathway, via pp70superscript(S6K) kinase, to translational control through S6 phosphorylation. Transplantation of such cell matrix inocula resulted in attenuation of the neuropathy, not localized, but over a considerably wide area (2 cu. mm inoculum to 100 sq. mm resolution). Under order from the investigator's Commanding Officer, transgenic inocula, resulting from liposomal fusions, were attempted using secondary spermatocyte stock, with the same degree of success, however, the mechanisms of that result remain unknown. Such lines of investigation, with a clear "cross breeding" intent, should be followed with the greatest concern and suggested "hesitation", as the leakage of such success could promote a 'wild' contaminant species to further the experimentation in an unabated fashion. The ultimate results of such a possible genetic introduction into the human population could be catastrophic.

This report is respectfully presented for consideration.

Danny Benjamin Crain, Ph.D. (Captain, United States Navy, N.R.L.)
Working Goup Leader, Project Aquarius, R-4800, Papoose Site 4

Dictated to

BIBLIOGRAPHY

Andrews, George C. – *Extra-Terrestrials Among Us*
Bramley, William – *Gods Of Eden*
Brown, Courtney - *Cosmic Explorers: Scientific Remote Viewing, Extraterrestrials, and a Message for Mankind*
- *Cosmic Voyage: A Scientific Discovery of Extraterrestrials Visiting Earth*
Cooper, William Milton – *Behold A Pale Horse*
Coppens, Philip – *The Ancient Alien Question*
Corso, Philip – *The Day After Roswell*
Farrell, Joseph P. – *Reich of the Black Sun*
Franz, Eric – *Space Faring Civilizations*
Friedman, Stanton T. and Marden, Kathleen – *Captured! The Betty and Barney Hill UFO Experience: The True Story of the World's First Documented Alien Abduction*
Greer, Dr. Stephen M. – *Disclosure*
Hancock, Graham, Bauval, Robert and Grigsby, John – *The Mars Mystery: A Tale of the End of Two Worlds*
Hamilton, William – *Project Aquarius: The Story of an Aquarian Scientist*
Hoagland, Richard – *Dark Mission: The Secret History of NASA*
Horn, Dr. Arthur David – *Humanity's Extraterrestrial Origins*
Hunt, Linda - *Secret Agenda: The United States Government, Nazi Scientists, and Project Paperclip, 1945–1990*
Jacobsen, Annie – *Area 51: An Uncensored History of America's Top Secret Military Base*
Kenyon, J. Douglas – *Forbidden History: Extraterrestrial Intervention, Prehistoric Technologies and the Suppressed Origins of Civilization*
Kerner, Nigel – *Grey Aliens and the Harvesting of Souls*
Kinder, Gary – *Light Years: An Investigation into the Extraterrestrial Experiences of Billy Meier*
Knight, Christopher and Butler, Alan – *Who Built The Moon*
Kolosimo, Peter – *Timeless Earth*
Leonard, George H. – *Somebody Else Is On The Moon*
Marrs, Jim – *Alien Agenda*
Piszkiewicz, Dennis - *Wernher von Braun: The Man Who Sold the Moon*
Swann, Ingo – *Penetration: The Question of Extraterrestrial and Human Telepathy*

Targ, Russell and Puthoff, Harold E. – *Mind-Reach: Scientific look at Psychic Abilities*
Tellinger, Michael – *Slave Species of god*
Turner, Dr. Karla – *Into The Fringe: A True Story of Alien Abduction*
- *Taken: Inside The Alien-Human Abduction Agenda*
Valerian, Valdamar – *Matrix (Series 1-5)*
Von Daniken, Erich – *Chariots of the Gods*
- *Return To The Stars*
Walton, Travis – *Fire In The Sky: The Walton Experience*
Wilson, Don – *Our Mysterious Spaceship Moon*

ABOUT THE AUTHOR

JP Robinson was born in Beverley on the East Yorkshire coast of England in 1975. He first became fascinated by the possibility of UFOs and extraterrestrial beings in his late teens during the early 90's; the last decade before the explosion of the internet. Influenced at that time by the extraordinary claims of ex-NASA employee and whistleblower Robert Oechsler, information regarding the complex alien situation began to surface the deeper he dug.

He began honing his writing skills as a keen singer-songwriter for the best part of two decades and following five years of study in Contemporary Photography right through to degree level at Northumbria University, he developed his ability to research extensively and applied this to his dissertation where he received a first with honours. Back in 1998, his work was recommended for a commissioned piece in The Guardian.

During a period as a self-employed freelance photographer he decided it was time to accumulate all of his knowledge of the alien hypothesis into one place and The Alien Enigma was born. He is currently living in Hull with his fiancé Frowynke and his daughters Amelie and Aiyana, where he is working on his second book.

Please feel free to contact the author with any questions at:
jp_robinson@hotmail.com

Made in the USA
Monee, IL
09 July 2023

38911022R00243